KAMA SUTRA

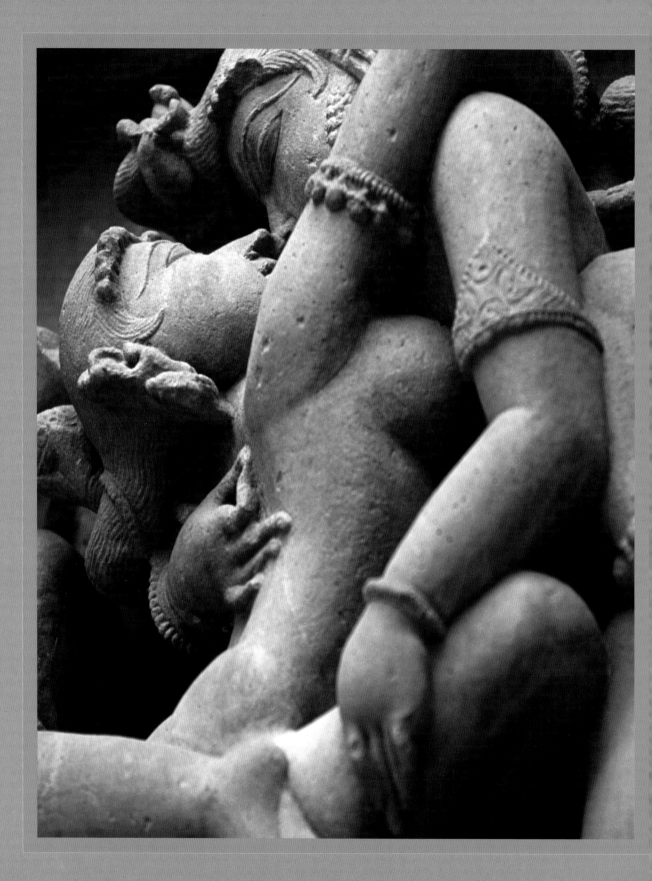

KAMA SUTRA

TRANSLATED BY
Sir Richard Burton

hamlyn

CONTENTS

A Note on the Text 10

Sir Richard Burton's Introduction 12

PART I
THE VATSYAYANA SUTRA

CHAPTER I *Preface: Salutation to Dharma, Artha & Kama* 18

CHAPTER II *On the Acquisition of Dharma, Artha & Kama* 20

CHAPTER III *On the Arts & Sciences to Be Studied* 26

CHAPTER IV *The Life of a Citizen* 34

CHAPTER V *About the Kinds of Women Resorted to by the Citizens,
& of Friends & Messengers* 42

PART II
ON SEXUAL UNION

CHAPTER I *Kinds of Sexual Union According to Dimensions,
Force of Desire or Passion, Time* 52

CHAPTER II *Of the Embrace* 60

CHAPTER III *On Kissing* 66

CHAPTER IV *On Pressing, or Marking, or Scratching with the Nails* 72

CHAPTER V *On Biting, & the Means to Be Employed
with Regard to Women of Different Countries* 76

CHAPTER VI *Of the Different Ways of Lying Down,
& Various Kinds of Congress* 82

CHAPTER VII *Of the Various Modes of Striking,
& of the Sounds Appropriate to Them* 88

CHAPTER VIII *About Women Acting the Part of a Man;
& of the Work of a Man* 94

CHAPTER IX *Of the Auparishtaka or Mouth Congress* 100

CHAPTER X *Of the Way How to Begin & How to End the Congress.
Different Kinds of Congress & Love Quarrels* 106

PART III
ABOUT THE ACQUISITION OF A WIFE

CHAPTER I *On Marriage* 112

CHAPTER II *Of Creating Confidence in the Girl* 116

CHAPTER III *On Courtship, & the Manifestation of the Feelings
by Outward Signs & Deeds* 120

CHAPTER IV *About Things to Be Done Only by the Man,
& the Acquisition of the Girl Thereby. Also What Is to Be Done by a Girl
to Gain Over a Man, & Subject Him to Her* 124

CHAPTER V *On Certain Forms of Marriage* 130

PART IV
ABOUT A WIFE

CHAPTER I *On the Manner of Living of a Virtuous Woman,*
& of Her Behaviour During the Absence of Her Husband 138

CHAPTER II *On the Conduct of the Elder Wife towards the Other Wives*
of Her Husband, & on That of a Younger Wife towards the Elder Ones.
Also on the Conduct of a Virgin Widow Re-Married;
Of a Wife Disliked by Her Husband; Of the Women in the King's Harem;
& Lastly on the Conduct of a Husband towards Many Wives 144

PART V
ABOUT THE WIVES OF OTHER MEN

CHAPTER I *Of the Characteristics of Men & Women. The Reasons Why Women Reject*
the Addresses of Men. About Men Who Have Success with Women,
& About Women Who Are Easily Gained Over 152

CHAPTER II *About Making Acquaintance with the Woman,*
& of the Efforts to Gain Her Over 160

CHAPTER III *Examination of the State of a Woman's Mind* 166

CHAPTER IV *About the Business of a Go-Between* 170

CHAPTER V *About the Love of Persons in Authority for the Wives of Other Men* 178

CHAPTER VI *About the Women of the Royal Harem;*
& of the Keeping of One's Own Wife 184

PART VI
ABOUT COURTESANS

Introductory Remarks 192

CHAPTER I *Of the Causes of a Courtesan Resorting to Men;*
Of the Means of Attaching to Herself the Man Desired;
& of the Kind of Man That It Is Desirable to Be Acquainted with 194

CHAPTER II *Of Living Like a Wife* 200

CHAPTER III *Of the Means of Getting Money, of the Signs of the Change*
of a Lover's Feelings, & of the Way to Get Rid of Him 206

CHAPTER IV *About Re-Union with a Former Lover* 214

CHAPTER V *Of Different Kinds of Gain* 220

CHAPTER VI *Of Gains & Losses; Attendant Gains & Losses; & Doubts;*
As Also of the Different Kinds of Courtesans 226

PART VII
ABOUT THE MEANS TO ATTRACT OTHERS TO YOURSELF

CHAPTER I *On Personal Adornment; On Subjugating the Hearts of Others;*
& on Tonic Medicines 236

CHAPTER II *Of the Ways of Exciting Desire,*
& Miscellaneous Experiments, & Recipes 244

Concluding Remarks 250

A Note on the Text

§ The *Kama Sutra*, compiled in the 3rd century CE by the celibate Brahmin and scholar Mallanaga Vatsyayana, is without doubt the most celebrated and renowned text ever to be written on the art of lovemaking.

Here we present the complete and unabridged English translation of this classic Sanskrit text, originally produced by the British explorer, ethnologist, linguist and diplomat, Sir Richard Burton, and published in 1883, along with his original introduction.

Considered the seminal guide to human sexuality, the *Kama Sutra* contains a wealth of advice and instruction on behaviour, etiquette and relationships, and remains – even in the 21st century – profoundly topical and relevant to our lives.

However, when reading this 2,000-year-old love treatise, it is important to keep in mind the cultural, social and religious context in which it was created, and the vaste differences between the world that it portrays and that which we inhabit today.

Today's reader may judge certain aspects of this age-old text challenging – even offensive. The domestic and social life of ancient India that is depicted within was one of deeply entrenched hierarchies, where social norms were based on the caste system, and the interaction of different social groups was strongly prohibited. Polygamy was practised freely, ritualized violence played an important part in lovemaking, women's freedom was restricted and their opportunities limited, and courtesans would routinely ply their trade from the threshold of the house. Even set against this backdrop, however, sections of the text may surprise and astonish the reader.

Two further warnings on the text are necessary. Firstly, many of the lovemaking positions described in the book will only be possible for accomplished yogis or very flexible athletes – the uninitiated should approach them with caution.

Secondly, great caution should be exercised by anyone who is tempted to experiment with the ancient recipes for 'love potions' given towards the end of the book, especially as the identification of particular botanicals mentioned in the original text of the *Kama Sutra* cannot be reliably certified.

णाकुंवरराचरतदेषनकरुढारुपा
यकारे विणाधागैगलन्दारकेतकां
होयाइद्याानेणन्त्रधीतंबोतमुषनहु
यारुणीघालौकाजल्तरिषकंदीस्रंश्र
रुतलपरहारैजीघाइ अेश्रुत्त्कु
णुवशला कक

Sir Richard Burton's Introduction

§ It may be interesting to some persons to learn how it came about that Vatsyayana was first brought to light and translated into the English language. It happened thus. While translating with the pundits the *Anunga Runga*, or *The Stage of Love*, reference was frequently found to be made to one Vatsya. The sage Vatsya was of this opinion, or of that opinion. The sage Vatsya said this, and so on. Naturally questions were asked who the sage was, and the pundits replied that Vatsya was the author of the standard work on love in Sanscrit literature, that no Sanscrit library was complete without his work, and that it was most difficult now to obtain in its entire state. The copy of the manuscript obtained in Bombay was defective, and so the pundits wrote to Benares, Calcutta and Jeypoor for copies of the manuscript from Sanscrit libraries in those places. Copies having been obtained, they were then compared with each other, and with the aid of a Commentary called 'Jayamangla' a revised copy of the entire manuscript was prepared, and from this copy the English translation was made. The following is the certificate of the chief pundit:

'The accompanying manuscript is corrected by me after comparing four different copies of the work. I had the assistance of a Commentary called 'Jayamangla" for correcting the portion in the first five parts, but found great difficulty in correcting the remaining portion, because, with the exception of one copy thereof which was tolerably correct, all the other copies I had were far too incorrect. However, I took that portion as correct in which the majority of the copies agreed with each other.'

The *Aphorisms on Love* by Vatsyayana contain about one thousand two hundred and fifty slokas or verses, and are divided into parts, parts into chapters, and chapters into paragraphs. The whole consists of seven parts, thirty-six chapters, and sixty-four paragraphs. Hardly anything is known about the author. His real name is supposed to be Mallinaga or Mrillana, Vatsyayana being his family name. At the close of the work this is what he writes about himself:

'After reading and considering the works of Babhravya and other ancient authors, and thinking over the meaning of the rules given by them, this treatise was composed, according to the precepts of the Holy Writ, for the benefit of the world, by Vatsyayana, while leading the life of a religious student at Benares, and wholly engaged in the contemplation of the Deity. This work is not to be used merely as an instrument for satisfying our desires. A person acquainted with the true principles of this science, who preserves his Dharma (virtue or religious merit), his Artha (worldly wealth) and his Kama (pleasure or sensual gratification), and who has regard to the customs of the people, is sure to obtain the mastery over his senses. In short, an intelligent and knowing person attending to Dharma and Artha and also to Kama, without becoming the slave of his passions, will obtain success in everything that he may do.'

> AN INTELLIGENT AND KNOWING PERSON ATTENDING TO DHARMA AND ARTHA AND ALSO TO KAMA, WITHOUT BECOMING THE SLAVE OF HIS PASSIONS, WILL OBTAIN SUCCESS IN EVERYTHING THAT HE MAY DO.

It is impossible to fix the exact date either of the life of Vatsyayana or of his work. It is supposed that he must have lived between the first and sixth century of the Christian era, on the following grounds. He mentions that Satakarni Satavahana, a king of Kuntal, killed Malayevati his wife with an instrument called kartari by striking her in the passion of love, and Vatsya quotes this case to warn people of the danger arising from some old customs of striking women when under the influence of this passion. Now this king of Kuntal is believed to have lived and reigned during the first century AD, and consequently Vatsya must have lived after him. On the other hand, Virahamihira, in the eighteenth chapter of his *Brihatsanhita*, treats of the science of love, and appears to have borrowed largely from Vatsyayana on the subject. Now Virahamihira is said to have lived during the sixth century AD, and as Vatsya must have written his works previously, therefore not earlier than the first century AD, and not later than the sixth century AD, must be considered as the approximate date of his existence.

On the text of the *Aphorisms on Love*, by Vatsyayana, only two commentaries have been found. One called 'Jayamangla' or 'Sutrabashya', and the other 'Sutra vritti'. The date of the 'Jayamangla' is fixed between the tenth and thirteenth century AD, because while treating of the sixty-four arts an example is taken from the *Kavyaprakasha* which was written about the tenth century AD. Again, the copy of the commentary procured was evidently a transcript of a manuscript which once had a place in the library of a Chaulukyan king named Vishaladeva, a fact elicited from the following sentence at the end of it.

'Here ends the part relating to the art of love in the commentary on the *Vatsyayana Kama Sutra*, a copy from the library of the king of kings, Vishaladeva, who was a powerful hero, as it were a second Arjuna, and head jewel of the Chaulukya family.'

Now it is well known that this king ruled in Guzerat from 1244 to 1262 AD, and founded a city called Visalnagur. The date, therefore, of the commentary is taken to be not earlier than the tenth and not later than the thirteenth century. The author of it is supposed to be one Yashodhara, the name given him by his preceptor being Indrapada. He seems to have written it during the time of affliction caused by his separation from a clever and shrewd woman, at least that is what he himself says at the end of each chapter. It is presumed that he called his work after the name of his absent mistress, or the word may have some connection with the meaning of her name.

This commentary was most useful in explaining the true meaning of Vatsyayana, for the commentator appears to have had a considerable knowledge of the times of the older author, and gives in some places very minute information. This cannot be said of the other commentary, called 'Sutra vritti', which was written about AD 1789, by Narsing Shastri, a pupil of a Sarveshwar Shastri; the latter was a descendant of Bhaskur, and so also was our author, for at the conclusion of every part he calls himself Bhaskur Narsing Shastri. He was induced to write the work by order of the learned Raja Vrijalala, while he was residing in Benares, but as to the merits of this commentary it does not deserve much commendation. In many cases the writer does not appear to have understood the meaning of the original author, and has changed the text in many places to fit in with his own explanations.

A complete translation of the original work now follows. It has been prepared in complete accordance with the text of the manuscript, and is given, without further comments, as made from it.

Sir Richard Burton
1883

PART I

THE VATSYAYANA SUTRA

CHAPTER I

Preface: Salutation to Dharma, Artha & Kama

§ In the beginning, the Lord of Beings created men and women, and in the form of commandments in one hundred thousand chapters laid down rules for regulating their existence with regard to Dharma [*1], Artha [*2], and Kama [*3]. Some of these commandments, namely those which treated of Dharma, were separately written by Swayambhu Manu; those that related to Artha were compiled by Brihaspati; and those that referred to Kama were expounded by Nandi, the follower of Mahadeva, in one thousand chapters.

Now these *Kama Sutra (Aphorisms on Love)*, written by Nandi in one thousand chapters, were reproduced by Shvetaketu, the son of Uddvalaka, in an abbreviated form in five hundred chapters, and this work was again similarly reproduced in an abridged form, in one hundred and fifty chapters, by Babhravya, an inheritant of the Punchala (South of Delhi) country. These one hundred and fifty chapters were then put together under seven heads or parts named severally

Sadharana § *(general topics)*
Samprayogika § *(embraces, etc.)*
Kanya Samprayuktaka § *(union of males and females)*
Bharyadhikarika § *(on one's own wife)*
Paradika § *(on the wives of other people)*
Vaisika § *(on courtesans)*
Aupamishadika § *(on the arts of seduction, tonic medicines, etc.)*

The sixth part of this last work was separately expounded by Dattaka at the request of the public women of Pataliputra (Patna), and in the same way Charayana explained the first part of it. The remaining parts, viz. the second, third, fourth, fifth, and seventh, were each separately expounded by

Suvarnanabha § (second part)
Ghotakamukha § (third part)
Gonardiya § (fourth part)
Gonikaputra § (fifth part)
Kuchumara § (seventh part), respectively.

Thus the work being written in parts by different authors was almost unobtainable and, as the parts which were expounded by Dattaka and the others treated only of the particular branches of the subject to which each part related, and moreover as the original work of Babhravya was difficult to be mastered on account of its length, Vatsyayana, therefore, composed his work in a small volume as an abstract of the whole of the works of the above named authors.

footnotes

---

1   Dharma is acquisition of religious merit, and is fully described in Chapter 5, volume III, of Talboys Wheeler's *History of India*, and in the edicts of Asoka.

2   Artha is acquisition of wealth and property, etc.

3   Kama is love, pleasure and sensual gratification. These three words are retained throughout in their original, as technical terms. They may also be defined as virtue, wealth and pleasure, the three things repeatedly spoken of in the *Laws of Manu*.

CHAPTER II

On the Acquisition of Dharma, Artha & Kama

§ Man, the period of whose life is one hundred years, should practise Dharma, Artha and Kama at different times and in such a manner that they may harmonize together and not clash in any way. He should acquire learning in his childhood, in his youth and middle age he should attend to Artha and Kama, and in his old age he should perform Dharma, and thus seek to gain Moksha, i.e. release from further transmigration. Or, on account of the uncertainty of life, he may practise them at times when they are enjoined to be practised. But one thing is to be noted, he should lead the life of a religious student until he finishes his education.

Dharma is obedience to the command of the Shastra or Holy Writ of the Hindoos to do certain things, such as the performance of sacrifices, which are not generally done, because they do not belong to this world, and produce no visible effect; and not to do other things, such as eating meat, which is often done because it belongs to this world, and has visible effects.

Dharma should be learnt from the Shruti (Holy Writ), and from those conversant with it.

Artha is the acquisition of arts, land, gold, cattle, wealth, equipages and friends. It is, further, the protection of what is acquired, and the increase of what is protected.

Artha should be learnt from the king's officers, and from merchants who may be versed in the ways of commerce.

Kama is the enjoyment of appropriate objects by the five senses of hearing, feeling, seeing, tasting and smelling, assisted by the mind together with the soul. The ingredient in this is a peculiar contact between the organ of sense and its object, and the consciousness of pleasure which arises from that contact is called Kama.

Kama is to be learnt from the *Kama Sutra (Aphorisms on Love)* and from the practice of citizens.

When all the three, viz. Dharma, Artha and Kama, come together, the former is better than the one which follows it, i.e. Dharma is better than Artha, and Artha is better than Kama. But Artha should always be first practised by the king for the livelihood of men is to be obtained from it only. Again, Kama being the occupation of public women, they should prefer it to the other two, and these are exceptions to the general rule.

OBJECTION 1

SOME LEARNED MEN SAY THAT AS DHARMA IS CONNECTED WITH THINGS NOT BELONGING TO THIS WORLD, IT IS APPROPRIATELY TREATED OF IN A BOOK; AND SO ALSO IS ARTHA, BECAUSE IT IS PRACTISED ONLY BY THE APPLICATION OF PROPER MEANS, AND A KNOWLEDGE OF THOSE MEANS CAN ONLY BE OBTAINED BY STUDY AND FROM BOOKS. BUT KAMA BEING A THING WHICH IS PRACTISED EVEN BY THE BRUTE CREATION, AND WHICH IS TO BE FOUND EVERYWHERE, DOES NOT WANT ANY WORK ON THE SUBJECT.

ANSWER

This is not so. Sexual intercourse being a thing dependent on man and woman requires the application of proper means by them, and those means are to be learnt from the *Kama Shastra*. The non-application of proper means, which we see in the brute creation, is caused by their being unrestrained, and by the females among them only being fit for sexual intercourse at certain seasons and no more, and by their intercourse not being preceded by thought of any kind.

OBJECTION 2

THE LOKAYATIKAS [*1] SAY: RELIGIOUS ORDINANCES SHOULD NOT BE OBSERVED, FOR THEY BEAR A FUTURE FRUIT, AND AT THE SAME TIME IT IS ALSO DOUBTFUL WHETHER THEY WILL BEAR ANY FRUIT AT ALL. WHAT FOOLISH PERSON WILL GIVE AWAY THAT WHICH IS IN HIS OWN HANDS INTO THE HANDS OF ANOTHER? MOREOVER, IT IS BETTER TO HAVE A PIGEON TODAY THAN A PEACOCK TOMORROW; AND A COPPER COIN WHICH WE HAVE THE CERTAINTY OF OBTAINING, IS BETTER THAN A GOLD COIN, THE POSSESSION OF WHICH IS DOUBTFUL.

ANSWER

It is not so.

1st. Holy Writ, which ordains the practice of Dharma, does not admit of a doubt.

2nd. Sacrifices such as those made for the destruction of enemies, or for the fall of rain, are seen to bear fruit.

3rd. The sun, moon, stars, planets and other heavenly bodies appear to work intentionally for the good of the world.

4th. The existence of this world is effected by the observance of the rules respecting the four classes of men and their four stages of life. [*2]

5th. We see that seed is thrown into the ground with the hope of future crops. Vatsyayana is therefore of opinion that the ordinances of religion must be obeyed.

OBJECTION 3

THOSE WHO BELIEVE THAT DESTINY IS THE PRIME MOVER OF ALL THINGS SAY: WE SHOULD NOT EXERT OURSELVES TO ACQUIRE WEALTH, FOR SOMETIMES IT IS NOT ACQUIRED ALTHOUGH WE STRIVE TO GET IT, WHILE AT OTHER TIMES IT COMES TO US OF ITSELF WITHOUT ANY EXERTION ON OUR PART. EVERYTHING IS THEREFORE IN THE POWER OF DESTINY, WHO IS THE LORD OF GAIN AND LOSS, OF SUCCESS AND DEFEAT, OF PLEASURE AND PAIN. THUS WE SEE THAT BALI [*3] WAS RAISED TO THE THRONE OF INDRA BY DESTINY, AND WAS ALSO PUT DOWN BY THE SAME POWER, AND IT IS DESTINY ONLY THAT CALL REINSTATE HIM.

ANSWER

It is not right to say so. As the acquisition of every object presupposes at all events some exertion on the part of man, the application of proper means may be said to be the cause of gaining all our ends, and this application of proper means being thus necessary (even where a thing is destined to happen), it follows that a person who does nothing will enjoy no happiness.

OBJECTION 4

THOSE WHO ARE INCLINED TO THINK THAT ARTHA IS THE CHIEF OBJECT TO BE OBTAINED ARGUE THUS. PLEASURES SHOULD NOT BE SOUGHT FOR, BECAUSE THEY ARE OBSTACLES TO THE PRACTICE OF DHARMA AND ARTHA, WHICH ARE BOTH SUPERIOR TO THEM, AND ARE ALSO DISLIKED BY MERITORIOUS PERSONS. PLEASURES ALSO BRING A MAN INTO DISTRESS, AND INTO CONTACT WITH LOW PERSONS; THEY CAUSE HIM TO COMMIT UNRIGHTEOUS DEEDS, AND PRODUCE IMPURITY IN HIM; THEY MAKE HIM REGARDLESS OF THE FUTURE, AND ENCOURAGE CARELESSNESS AND LEVITY. AND LASTLY, THEY CAUSE HIM TO BE DISBELIEVED BY ALL, RECEIVED BY NONE, AND DESPISED BY EVERYBODY, INCLUDING HIMSELF. IT IS NOTORIOUS, MOREOVER, THAT MANY MEN WHO HAVE GIVEN THEMSELVES UP TO PLEASURE ALONE, HAVE BEEN RUINED ALONG WITH THEIR FAMILIES AND RELATIONS. THUS, KING DANDAKYA, OF THE BHOJA DYNASTY, CARRIED OFF A BRAHMAN'S DAUGHTER WITH EVIL INTENT, AND WAS EVENTUALLY RUINED AND LOST HIS KINGDOM. INDRA, TOO, HAVING VIOLATED THE CHASTITY OF AHALYA, WAS MADE TO SUFFER FOR IT. IN A LIKE MANNER THE MIGHTY KICHAKA, WHO TRIED TO SEDUCE DRAUPADI, AND RAVANA, WHO ATTEMPTED TO GAIN OVER SITA, WERE PUNISHED FOR THEIR CRIMES. THESE AND MANY OTHERS FELL BY REASON OF THEIR PLEASURES. [*4]

ANSWER

This objection cannot be sustained, for pleasures, being as necessary for the existence and well being of the body as food, are consequently equally required. They are, moreover, the results of Dharma and Artha. Pleasures are, therefore, to be followed with moderation and caution. No one refrains from cooking food because there are beggars to ask for it, or from sowing seed because there are deer to destroy the corn when it is grown up.

Thus a man practising Dharma, Artha and Kama enjoys happiness both in this world and in the world to come. The good perform those actions in which there is no fear as to what is to result from them in the next world, and in which there is no danger to their welfare. Any action which conduces to the practice of Dharma, Artha and Kama together, or of any two, or even one of them, should be performed, but an action which conduces to the practice of one of them at the expense of the remaining two should not be performed.

footnotes

1   These were certainly materialists who seemed to think that a bird in the hand was worth two in the bush.

2   Among the Hindoos the four classes of men are the Brahmans or priestly class, the Kshutrya or warlike class, the Vaishya or agricultural and mercantile class, and the Shoodra or menial class. The four stages of life are, the life of a religious student, the life of a householder, the life of a hermit, and the life of a Sunyasi or devotee.

3   Bali was a demon who had conquered Indra and gained his throne, but was afterwards overcome by Vishnu at the time of his fifth incarnation.

4   Dandakya is said to have abducted from the forest the daughter of a Brahman, named Bhargava, and, being cursed by the Brahman, was buried with his kingdom under a shower of dust. The place was called after his name the Dandaka forest, celebrated in the Bamayana, but now unknown.

Ahalya was the wife of the sage Gautama. Indra caused her to believe that he was Gautama, and thus enjoyed her. He was cursed by Gautama and subsequently afflicted with a thousand ulcers on his body.

Kichaka was the brother-in-law of King Virata, with whom the Pandavas had taken refuge for one year. Kichaka was killed by Bhima, who assumed the disguise of Draupadi. For this story the *Mahabarata* should be referred to.

The story of Ravana is told in the *Ramayana*, which with the *Mahabarata* form the two great epic poems of the Hindoos; the latter was written by Vyasa, and the former by Valmiki.

CHAPTER III

On the Arts & Sciences to Be Studied

§ Man should study the *Kama Sutra* and the arts and sciences subordinate thereto, in addition to the study of the arts and sciences contained in Dharma and Artha. Even young maids should study this *Kama Sutra* along with its arts and sciences before marriage, and after it they should continue to do so with the consent of their husbands.

Here some learned men object, and say that females, not being allowed to study any science, should not study the *Kama Sutra*. But Vatsyayana is of opinion that this objection does not hold good, for women already know the practice of *Kama Sutra*, and that practice is derived from the *Kama Shastra*, or the science of Kama itself. Moreover, it is not only in this but in many other cases that, though the practice of a science is known to all, only a few persons are acquainted with the rules and laws on which the science is based. Thus the Yadnikas or sacrificers, though ignorant of grammar, make use of appropriate words when addressing the different Deities, and do not know how these words are framed. Again, persons do the duties required of them on auspicious days, which are fixed by astrology, though they are not acquainted with the science of astrology. In a like manner riders of horses and elephants train these animals without knowing the science of training animals, but from practice only. And similarly the people of the most distant provinces obey the laws of the kingdom from practice, and because there is a king over them, and without further reason [*1]. And from experience we find that some women, such as daughters of princes and their ministers, and public women, are actually versed in the *Kama Shastra*.

A female, therefore, should learn the *Kama Shastra*, or at least a part of it, by studying its practice from some confidential friend. She should study alone in private the sixty-four practices that form a part of the *Kama Shastra*. Her teacher should be one of the following persons: the daughter of a nurse brought up with her and already married [*2], or a female friend who can be trusted in everything, or the sister of her mother (i.e. her aunt), or an old female servant, or a female beggar who may have formerly lived in the family, or her own sister who can always be trusted.

The following are the arts to be studied, together with the *Kama Sutra*:

* *Singing*

* *Playing on musical instruments*

* *Dancing*

* *Union of dancing, singing, and playing instrumental music*

* *Writing and drawing*

* *Tattooing*

* *Arraying and adorning an idol with rice and flowers*

* *Spreading and arranging beds or couches of flowers, or flowers upon the ground*

* *Colouring the teeth, garments, hair, nails and bodies, i.e. staining, dyeing, colouring and painting the same*

* *Fixing stained glass into a floor*

* *The art of making beds, and spreading out carpets and cushions for reclining*

* *Playing on musical glasses filled with water*

* *Storing and accumulating water in aqueducts, cisterns and reservoirs*

* *Picture making, trimming and decorating*

* *Stringing of rosaries, necklaces, garlands and wreaths*

* *Binding of turbans and chaplets, and making crests and top-knots of flowers*

* *Scenic representations, stage playing*

* *Art of making ear ornaments*

* *Art of preparing perfumes and odours*

* *Proper disposition of jewels and decorations, and adornment in dress*

* *Magic or sorcery*

* *Quickness of hand or manual skill*

* *Culinary art, i.e. cooking and cookery*

* *Making lemonades, sherbets, acidulated drinks, and spirituous extracts with proper flavour and colour*

* *Tailor's work and sewing*

* *Making parrots, flowers, tufts, tassels, bunches, bosses, knobs, etc., out of yarn or thread*

* *Solution of riddles, enigmas, covert speeches, verbal puzzles and enigmatical questions*

* *A game, which consisted in repeating verses, and as one person finished, another person had to commence at once, repeating another verse, beginning with the same letter with which the last speaker's verse ended, whoever failed to repeat was considered to have lost, and to be subject to pay a forfeit or stake of some kind*

* *The art of mimicry or imitation*

این های این آسمانی برجو دو جودا وآراستہ کشت کہ مرلخط فاید رحمانی بجاہ اوپیوہ
١٥
دار دتاجہد و توفیق ہم طویلہ او اینچنین موفق دار د جہر جمع کردن علم و حکمت و
جلوہ کردن اصحاب وحق وحقیقت بر تفخم و تعظیم ارباب طریقت امین و رب العالمین

والحمد للہ رب العالمین والصلوۃ والسلام

علی رسولہ محمد وآلہ واصحابہ جمعین

فقیر الحقیر عبد الرحیم الہروی
عنبرین قلم تحریری اینشہ

* Reading, including chanting and intoning

* Study of sentences difficult to pronounce. It is played as a game chiefly by women, and children and consists of a difficult sentence being given, and when repeated quickly, the words are often transposed or badly pronounced

* Practice with sword, single stick, quarter staff and bow and arrow

* Drawing inferences, reasoning or inferring

* Carpentry, or the work of a carpenter

* Architecture, or the art of building

* Knowledge about gold and silver coins, and jewels and gems

* Chemistry and mineralogy

* Colouring jewels, gems and beads

* Knowledge of mines and quarries

* Gardening; knowledge of treating the diseases of trees and plants, of nourishing them, and determining their ages

* Art of cock fighting, quail fighting and ram fighting

* Art of teaching parrots and starlings to speak

* Art of applying perfumed ointments to the body, and of dressing the hair with unguents and perfumes and braiding it

* The art of understanding writing in cypher, and the writing of words in a peculiar way

* The art of speaking by changing the forms of words. It is of various kinds. Some speak by changing the beginning and end of words, others by adding unnecessary letters between every syllable of a word, and so on

* Knowledge of language and of the vernacular dialects

* Art of making flower carriages

* Art of framing mystical diagrams, of addressing spells and charms, and binding armlets

* Mental exercises, such as completing stanzas or verses on receiving a part of them; or supplying one, two or three lines when the remaining lines are given indiscriminately from different verses, so as to make the whole an entire verse with regard to its meaning; or arranging the words of a verse written irregularly by separating the vowels from the consonants, or leaving them out altogether; or putting into verse or prose sentences represented by signs or symbols. There are many other such exercises

* Composing poems

* Knowledge of dictionaries and vocabularies

* Knowledge of ways of changing and disguising the appearance of persons

* Knowledge of the art of changing the appearance of things, such as making cotton to appear as silk, coarse and common things to appear as fine and good

* Various ways of gambling

- *Art of obtaining possession of the property of others by means of muntras or incantations*
- *Skill in youthful sports*
- *Knowledge of the rules of society, and of how to pay respect and compliments to others*
- *Knowledge of the art of war, of arms, of armies, etc.*
- *Knowledge of gymnastics*
- *Art of knowing the character of a man from his features*
- *Knowledge of scanning or constructing verses*
- *Arithmetical recreations*
- *Making artificial flowers*
- *Making figures and images in clay*

A public woman, endowed with a good disposition, beauty and other winning qualities, and also versed in the above arts, obtains the name of a Ganika, or public woman of high quality, and receives a seat of honour in an assemblage of men. She is, moreover, always respected by the king, and praised by learned men, and her favour being sought for by all, she becomes an object of universal regard. The daughter of a king too as well as the daughter of a minister, being learned in the above arts, can make their husbands favourable to them, even though these may have thousands of other wives besides themselves. And in the same manner, if a wife becomes separated from her husband, and falls into distress, she can support herself easily, even in a foreign country, by means of her knowledge of these arts. Even the bare knowledge of them gives attractiveness to a woman, though the practice of them may be only possible or otherwise according to the circumstances of each case. A man who is versed in these arts, who is loquacious and acquainted with the arts of gallantry, gains very soon the hearts of women, even though he is only acquainted with them for a short time.

footnotes

1   The author wishes to prove that a great many things are done by people from practice and custom, without their being acquainted with the reason of things, or the laws on which they are based, and this is perfectly true.

2   The proviso of being married applies to all the teachers.

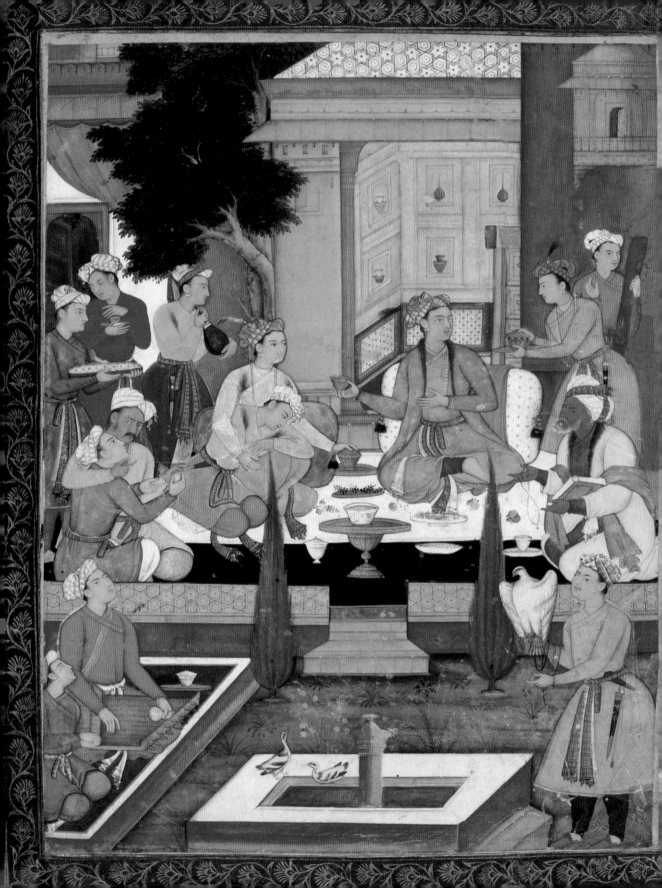

The Life of a Citizen

§ Having thus acquired learning, a man, with the wealth that he may have gained by gift, conquest, purchase, deposit [*1], or inheritance from his ancestors, should become a householder, and pass the life of a citizen [*2]. He should take a house in a city, or large village, or in the vicinity of good men, or in a place which is the resort of many persons. This abode should be situated near some water, and divided into different compartments for different purposes. It should be surrounded by a garden, and also contain two rooms, an outer and an inner one. The inner room should be occupied by the females, while the outer room, balmy with rich perfumes, should contain a bed, soft, agreeable to the sight, covered with a clean white cloth, low in the middle part, having garlands and bunches of flowers [*3] upon it, and a canopy above it, and two pillows, one at the top, another at the bottom. There should be also a sort of couch besides, and at the head of this a sort of stool, on which should be placed the fragrant ointments for the night, as well as flowers, pots containing collyrium and other fragrant substances, things used for perfuming the mouth, and the bark of the common citron tree. Near the couch, on the ground, there should be a pot for spitting, a box containing ornaments, and also a lute hanging from a peg made of the tooth of an elephant, a board for drawing, a pot containing perfume, some books, and some garlands of the yellow amaranth flowers. Not far from the couch, and on the ground, there should be a round seat, a toy cart, and a board for playing with dice; outside the outer room there should be cages of birds [*4], and a separate place for spinning, carving and such like diversions. In the garden there should be a whirling swing and a common swing, as also a bower of creepers covered with flowers, in which a raised parterre should be made for sitting.

Now the householder, having got up in the morning and performed his necessary duties [*5], should wash his teeth, apply a limited quantity of ointments and perfumes to his body, put some ornaments on his person and collyrium on his eyelids and below his eyes, colour his lips with alacktaka [*6], and look at himself in the glass. Having then eaten betel leaves, with other things that give fragrance to the mouth, he should perform his usual business. He should bathe daily, anoint his body with oil every other day, apply a lathering substance [*7] to his body every three days, get his head (including face) shaved every four days and the other parts of his body every five or ten days [*8]. All these things should be done without fail, and the sweat of the armpits should also be removed. Meals should be taken in the forenoon, in the afternoon, and again at night, according to Charayana. After breakfast, parrots and other birds should be taught to speak, and the fighting of cocks, quails, and rams should follow. A limited time should be devoted to diversions with Pithamardas, Vitas, and Vidushakas [*9], and then should be taken the midday sleep [*10]. After this the householder, having put on his clothes and ornaments, should, during the afternoon, converse with his friends. In the evening there should be singing, and after that the householder, along with his friend, should await in his room, previously decorated and perfumed, the arrival of the woman that may be attached to him, or he may send a female messenger for her, or go for her himself. After her arrival at his house, he and his friend should welcome her, and entertain her with a loving and agreeable conversation. Thus end the duties of the day.

The following are the things to be done occasionally as diversions or amusements:

Holding festivals [*11] *in honour of different Deities*

Social gatherings of both sexes

Drinking parties

Picnics

Other social diversions

Festivals

On some particular auspicious day, an assembly of citizens should be convened in the temple of Saraswati [*12]. There the skill of singers, and of others who may have come recently to the town, should be tested, and on the following day they should always be given some rewards. After that they may either be retained or dismissed, according as their performances are liked or not by the assembly. The members of the assembly should act in concert, both in times of distress as well as in times of prosperity, and it is also the duty of these citizens to show hospitality to strangers who may have come to the assembly. What is said above should be understood to apply to all the other festivals which may be held in honour of the different Deities, according to the present rules.

Social Gatherings

When men of the same age, disposition and talents, fond of the same diversions and with the same degree of education, sit together in company with public women [*13], or in an assembly of citizens, or at the abode of one among themselves, and engage in agreeable discourse with each other, such is called a Sitting in company or a social gathering. The subjects of discourse are to be the completion of verses half composed by others, and the testing the knowledge of one another in the various arts. The women who may be the most beautiful, who may like the same things that the men like, and who may have power to attract the minds of others, are here done homage to.

Drinking Parties

Men and women should drink in one another's houses. And here the men should cause the public women to drink, and should then drink themselves, liquors such as the Madhu, Aireya, Sara and Asawa, which are of bitter and sour taste; also drinks concocted from the barks of various trees, wild fruits and leaves.

Going to Gardens or Picnics

In the forenoon, men having dressed themselves should go to gardens on horseback, accompanied by public women and followed by servants. And having done there all the duties of the day, and passed the time in various agreeable diversions, such as the fighting of quails, cocks and rams, and other spectacles, they should return home in the afternoon in the same manner, bringing with them bunches of flowers, etc.

The same also applies to bathing in summer in water from which wicked or dangerous animals have previously been taken out, and which has been built in on all sides.

Other Social Diversions

Spending nights playing with dice

Going out on moonlight nights

Keeping the festive day in honour of spring

Plucking the sprouts and fruits of the mango trees

Eating the fibres of lotuses

Eating the tender ears of corn

Picnicing in the forests when the trees get their new foliage

The Udakakashvedika or sporting in the water

Decorating each other with the flowers of some trees

Pelting each other with the flowers of the Kadamba tree,
and many other sports which may either be known to the
whole country, or may be peculiar to particular parts of it

These and similar other amusements should always be carried on by citizens.

The above amusements should be followed by a person who diverts himself alone in company with a courtesan, as well as by a courtesan who can do the same in company with her maid servants or with citizens.

A Pithamarda [*14] is a man without wealth, alone in the world, whose only property consists of his Mallika [*15], some lathering substance and a red cloth, who comes from a good country, and who is skilled in all the arts; and by teaching these arts is received in the company of citizens, and in the abode of public women.

THUS A CITIZEN LIVING IN HIS TOWN OR VILLAGE, RESPECTED BY ALL, SHOULD CALL ON THE PERSONS OF HIS OWN CASTE WHO MAY BE WORTH KNOWING. HE SHOULD CONVERSE IN COMPANY AND GRATIFY HIS FRIENDS BY HIS SOCIETY...

A Vita [*16] is a man who has enjoyed the pleasures of fortune, who is a compatriot of the citizens with whom he associates, who is possessed of the qualities of a householder, who has his wife with him, and who is honoured in the assembly of citizens and in the abodes of public women, and lives on their means and on them. A Vidushaka [*17] (also called a Vaihasaka, i.e. one who provokes laughter) is a person only acquainted with some of the arts, who is a jester, and who is trusted by all.

These persons are employed in matters of quarrels and reconciliations between citizens and public women.

This remark applies also to female beggars, to women with their heads shaved, to adulterous women, and to public women skilled in all the various arts.

Thus a citizen living in his town or village, respected by all, should call on the persons of his own caste who may be worth knowing. He should converse in company and gratify his friends by his society, and obliging others by his assistance in various matters, he should cause them to assist one another in the same way.

There are some verses on this subject as follows:

*A citizen discoursing, not entirely in the Sanscrit language [*18],
nor wholly in the dialects of the country, on various topics in society,
obtains great respect. The wise should not resort to a society disliked
by the public, governed by no rules, and intent on the destruction
of others. But a learned man living in a society which acts according
to the wishes of the people, and which has pleasure for its only object
is highly respected in this world.*

footnotes

1   Gift is peculiar to a Brahman, conquest to a Kshatrya, while purchase, deposit, and other means of acquiring wealth belongs to the Vaishya.

2   This term would appear to apply generally to an inhabitant of Hindoostan. It is not meant only for a dweller in a city, like the Latin Urbanus as opposed to Rusticus.

3   Natural garden flowers.

4   Such as quails, partridges, parrots, starlings, etc.

5   The calls of nature are always performed by the Hindoos the first thing in the morning.

6   A colour made from lac.

7   This would act instead of soap, which was not introduced until the rule of the Mahomedans.

8   Ten days are allowed when the hair is taken out with a pair of pincers.

9   These are characters generally introduced in the Hindoo drama; their characteristics will be explained further on.

10   Noonday sleep is only allowed in summer, when the nights are short.

11   These are very common in all parts of India.

12   In the *Asiatic Miscellany*, and in Sir W. Jones's works, will be found a spirited hymn addressed to this goddess, who is adored as the patroness of the fine arts, especially of music and rhetoric, as the inventress of the Sanscrit language, etc. etc. She is the goddess of harmony, eloquence and language, and is somewhat analogous to Minerva. For farther information about her, see Edward Moor's *Hindoo Pantheon*.

13   The public women, or courtesans (Vesya), of the early Hindoos have often been compared with the Hetera of the Greeks. The subject is dealt with at some length in H. H. Wilson's *Select Specimens of the Theatre of the Hindoos*, in two volumes, Trubner and Co., 1871. It may be fairly considered that the courtesan was one of the elements, and an important element too, of early Hindoo society, and that her education and intellect were both superior to that of the women of the household. Wilson says, 'By the Vesya or courtesan, however, we are not to understand a female who has disregarded the obligation of law or the precepts of virtue, but a character reared by a state of manners unfriendly to the admission of wedded females into society, and opening it only at the expense of reputation to women who were trained for association with men by personal and mental acquirements to which the matron was a stranger.'

14 According to this description a Pithamarda would be a sort of professor of all the arts, and as such received as the friend and confidant of the citizen.

15 A seat in the form of the letter T.

16 The Vita is supposed to represent somewhat the character of the Parasite of the Greek comedy. It is possible that he was retained about the person of the wealthy and dissipated as a kind of private instructor, as well as an entertaining companion.

17 Vidushaka is evidently the buffoon and jester. Wilson says of him that he is the humble companion, not the servant, of a prince or man of rank, and it is a curious peculiarity that he is always a Brahman. He bears more affinity to Sancho Panza, perhaps than any other character in western fiction, imitating him in his combination of shrewdness and simplicity, his fondness of good living and his love of ease. In the dramas of intrigue he exhibits some of the talents of Mercury, but with less activity and ingenuity, and occasionally suffers by his interference. According to the technical definition of his attributes he is to excite mirth by being ridiculous in person, age, and attire.

18 This means, it is presumed, that the citizen should be acquainted with several languages. The middle part of this paragraph might apply to the Nihilists and Fenians of the day, or to secret societies. It was perhaps a reference to the Thugs.

About the Kinds of Women Resorted to by the Citizens, & of Friends & Messengers

§ When Kama is practised by men of the four castes according to the rules of the Holy Writ (i.e. by lawful marriage) with virgins of their own caste, it then becomes a means of acquiring lawful progeny and good fame, and it is not also opposed to the customs of the world. On the contrary the practice of Kama with women of the higher castes, and with those previously enjoyed by others, even though they be of the same caste, is prohibited. But the practice of Kama with women of the lower castes, with women excommunicated from their own caste, with public women, and with women twice married [*1], is neither enjoined nor prohibited. The object of practising Kama with such women is pleasure only.

Nayikas [*2], therefore, are of three kinds, viz. maids, women twice married, and public women. Gonikaputra has expressed an opinion that there is a fourth kind of Nayika, viz. a woman who is resorted to on some special occasion even though she be previously married to another. These special occasions are when a man thinks thus:

✷ *This woman is self-willed, and has been previously enjoyed by many others besides myself. I may, therefore, safely resort to her as to a public woman though she belongs to a higher caste than mine, and, in so doing, I shall not be violating the ordinances of Dharma. Or thus:*

✷ *This is a twice-married woman and has been enjoyed by others before me; there is,*

therefore, no objection to my resorting to her. Or thus:

✷ *This woman has gained the heart of her great and powerful husband, and exercises a mastery over him, who is a friend of my enemy; if, therefore, she becomes united with me she will cause her husband to abandon my enemy. Or thus:*

* *This woman will turn the mind of her husband, who is very powerful, in my favour, he being at present disaffected towards me, and intent on doing me some harm. Or thus:*

* *By making this woman my friend I shall gain the object of some friend of mine, or shall be able to effect the ruin of some enemy, or shall accomplish some other difficult purpose. Or thus:*

* *By being united with this woman, I shall kill her husband, and so obtain his vast riches which I covet. Or thus:*

* *The union of this woman with me is not attended with any danger, and will bring me wealth, of which, on account of my poverty and inability to support myself, I am very much in need. I shall therefore obtain her vast riches in this way without any difficulty. Or thus:*

* *This woman loves me ardently, and knows all my weak points; if therefore, I am unwilling to be united with her, she will make my faults public, and thus tarnish my character and reputation. Or she will bring some gross accusation against me, of which it may be hard to clear myself, and I shall be ruined. Or perhaps she will detach from me her husband who is powerful, and yet under her control, and will unite him to my enemy, or will herself join the latter. Or thus:*

* *The husband of this woman has violated the chastity of my wives, I shall therefore return that injury by seducing his wives. Or thus:*

* *By the help of this woman I shall kill an enemy of the king, who has taken shelter with her, and whom I am ordered by the king to destroy. Or thus:*

* *The woman whom I love is under the control of this woman. I shall, through the influence of the latter, be able to get at the former. Or thus:*

* *This woman will bring to me a maid, who possesses wealth and beauty, but who is hard to get at, and under the control of another. Or lastly thus:*

* *My enemy is a friend of this woman's husband, I shall therefore cause her to join him, and will thus create an enmity between her husband and him.*

For these and similar other reasons the wives of other men may be resorted to, but it must be distinctly understood that is only allowed for special reasons, and not for mere carnal desire.

Charayana thinks that under these circumstances there is also a fifth kind of Nayika, viz. a woman who is kept by a minister, or who repairs to him occasionally; or a widow who accomplishes the purpose of a man with the person to whom she resorts.

Suvarnanabha adds that a woman who passes the life of an ascetic and in the condition of a widow may be considered as a sixth kind of Nayika.

Ghotakamukha says that the daughter of a public woman, and a female servant, who are still virgins, form a seventh kind of Nayika.

Gonardiya puts forth his doctrine that any woman born of good family, after she has come of age, is an eighth kind of Nayika.

But these four latter kinds of Nayikas do not differ much from the first four kinds of them, as there is no separate object in resorting to them. Therefore, Vatsyayana is of opinion that there are only four kinds of Nayikas, i.e. the maid, the twice-married woman, the public woman, and the woman resorted to for a special purpose.

The following women are not to be enjoyed:

A leper

A lunatic

A woman turned out of caste

A woman who reveals secrets

A woman who publicly expresses desire for sexual intercourse

A woman who is extremely white

A woman who is extremely black

A bad-smelling woman

A woman who is a near relation

A woman who is a female friend

A woman who leads the life of an ascetic

And, lastly the wife of a relation, of a friend, of a learned Brahman, and of the king

The followers of Babhravya say that any woman who has been enjoyed by five men is a fit and proper person to be enjoyed. But Gonikaputra is of opinion that even when this is the case, the wives of a relation, of a learned Brahman and of a king should be excepted.

The following are of the kind of friends:

One who has played with you in the dust, i.e. in childhood

One who is bound by an obligation

One who is of the same disposition and fond of the same things

One who is a fellow student

One who is acquainted with your secrets and faults,
and whose faults and secrets are also known to you

One who is a child of your nurse

One who is brought up with you

One who is an hereditary friend

These friends should possess the following qualities:

They should tell the truth

They should not be changed by time

They should be favourable to your designs

They should be firm

They should be free from covetousness

They should not be capable of being gained over by others

They should not reveal your secrets

Charayana says that citizens form friendship with washermen, barbers, cowherds, florists, druggists, betel-leaf sellers, tavern keepers, beggars, Pithamardas, Vitas and Vidushekas, as also with the wives of all these people.

A messenger should possess the following qualities:

Skilfulness

Boldness

Knowledge of the intention of men by their outward signs

Absence of confusion, i.e. no shyness

Knowledge of the exact meaning of what others do or say

Good manners

Knowledge of appropriate times and places for doing different things

Ingenuity in business

Quick comprehension

Quick application of remedies, i.e. quick and ready resources

And this part ends with a verse:

The man who is ingenious and wise, who is accompanied
by a friend, and who knows the intentions of others,
as also the proper time and place for doing everything,
can gain over, very easily, even a woman
who is very hard to be obtained.

footnotes

1   This term does not apply to a widow, but to a woman who has probably left her husband, and is living with some other person as a married woman, *maritalement*, as they say in France.

2   Any woman fit to be enjoyed without sin. The object of the enjoyment of women is twofold, viz. pleasure and progeny. Any woman who can be enjoyed without sin for the purpose of accomplishing either the one or the other of these two objects is a Nayika. The fourth kind of Nayika which Vatsya admits further on is neither enjoyed for pleasure or for progeny, but merely for accomplishing some special purpose in hand. The word Nayika is retained as a technical term throughout.

PART II

ON SEXUAL UNION

Kinds of Sexual Union
According to Dimensions, Force of Desire
or Passion, Time

Kind of Union

§ Man is divided into three classes, viz. the hare man, the bull man, and the horse man, according to the size of his lingam.

Woman also, according to the depth of her yoni, is either a female deer, a mare, or a female elephant.

There are thus three equal unions between persons of corresponding dimensions, and there are six unequal unions, when the dimensions do not correspond, or nine in all, as the following table shows:

Equal		Unequal	
MEN	WOMEN	MEN	WOMEN
Hare	*Deer*	*Hare*	*Mare*
Bull	*Mare*	*Hare*	*Elephant*
Horse	*Elephant*	*Bull*	*Deer*
		Bull	*Elephant*
		Horse	*Deer*
		Horse	*Mare*

In these unequal unions, when the male exceeds the female in point of size, his union with a woman who is immediately next to him in size is called high union, and is of two kinds; while his union with the woman most remote from his size is called the highest union, and is of one kind only. On the other hand, when the female exceeds the male in point of size, her union with a man immediately next to her in size is called low union, and is of two kinds; while her union with a man most remote from her in size is called the lowest union, and is of one kind only.

In other words, the horse and mare, the bull and deer, form the high union, while the horse and deer form the highest union. On the female side, the elephant and bull, the mare and hare, form low unions, while the elephant and the hare make the lowest union. There are, then, nine kinds of union according to dimensions. Amongst all these, equal unions are the best, those of a superlative degree, i.e. the highest and the lowest, are the worst, and the rest are middling, and with them the high [*1] are better than the low.

There are also nine kinds of union according to the force of passion or carnal desire, as follows:

MEN	WOMEN		MEN	WOMEN
Small	Small		Small	Middling
Middling	Middling		Small	Intense
Intense	Intense		Middling	Small
			Middling	Intense
			Intense	Small
			Intense	Middling

A man is called a man of small passion whose desire at the time of sexual union is not great, whose semen is scanty, and who cannot bear the warm embraces of the female.

Those who differ from this temperament are called men of middling passion, while those of intense passion are full of desire.

In the same way, women are supposed to have the three degrees of feeling as specified above.

Lastly, according to time there are three kinds of men and women, the short-timed, the moderate-timed, and the long-timed; and of these, as in the previous statements, there are nine kinds of union.

But on this last head there is a difference of opinion about the female, which should be stated.

Auddalika says, 'Females do not emit as males do. The males simply remove their desire, while the females, from their consciousness of desire, feel a certain kind of pleasure, which gives them satisfaction, but it is impossible for them to tell you what kind of pleasure they feel. The fact from which this becomes evident is, that males, when engaged in coition, cease of themselves after emission, and are satisfied, but it is not so with females.'

This opinion is however objected to on the grounds that, if a male be a long-timed, the female loves him the more, but if he be short-timed, she is dissatisfied with him. And this circumstance, some say, would prove that the female emits also.

But this opinion does not hold good, for if it takes a long time to allay a woman's desire, and during this time she is enjoying great pleasure, it is quite natural then that she should wish for its continuation. And on this subject there is a verse as follows:

By union with men the lust, desire, or passion of women is satisfied, and the pleasure derived from the consciousness of it is called their satisfaction.

The followers of Babhravya, however, say that the semen of women continues to fall from the beginning of the sexual union to its end, and it is right that it should be so, for if they had no semen there would be no embryo.

To this there is an objection. In the beginning of coition the passion of the woman is middling, and she cannot bear the vigorous thrusts of her lover, but by degrees her passion increases until she ceases to think about her body, and then finally she wishes to stop from further coition.

This objection, however, does not hold good, for even in ordinary things that revolve with great force, such as a potter's wheel, or a top, we find that the motion at first is slow, but by degrees it becomes very rapid. In the same way the passion of the woman having gradually increased, she has a desire to discontinue coition, when all the semen has fallen away. And there is a verse with regard to this as follows:

The fall of the semen of the man takes place only at the end of coition, while the semen of the woman falls continually, and after the semen of both has all fallen away then they wish for the discontinuance of coition [*2].

— 55 —

Lastly, Vatsyayana is of opinion that the semen of the female falls in the same way as that of the male.

Now some may ask here: If men and women are beings of the same kind, and are engaged in bringing about the same results, why should they have different works to do?

Vatsya says that this is so, because the ways of working as well as the consciousness of pleasure in men and women are different. The difference in the ways of working, by which men are the actors, and women are the persons acted upon, is owing to the nature of the male and the female, otherwise the actor would be sometimes the person acted upon, and vice versa. And from this difference in the ways of working follows the difference in the consciousness of pleasure, for a man thinks, 'this woman is united with me', and a woman thinks, 'I am united with this man'.

It may be said that, if the ways of working in men and women are different, why should not there be a difference, even in the pleasure they feel, and which is the result of those ways.

But this objection is groundless, for, the person acting and the person acted upon being of different kinds, there is a reason for the difference in their ways of working; but there is no reason for any difference in the pleasure they feel, because they both naturally derive pleasure from the act they perform [*3] .

On this again some may say that when different persons are engaged in doing the same work, we find that they accomplish the same end or purpose; while, on the contrary, in the case of men and women we find that each of them accomplishes his or her own end separately, and this is inconsistent. But this is a mistake, for we find that sometimes two things are done at the same time, as for instance in the fighting of rams, both the rams receive the shock at the same time on their heads. Again, in throwing one wood apple against another, and also in a fight or struggle of wrestlers. If it be said that in these cases the things employed are of the same kind, it is answered that even in the case of men and women, the nature of the two persons is the same. And as the difference in their ways of working arises from the difference of their conformation only, it follows that men experience the same kind of pleasure as women do.

There is also a verse on this subject as follows:

Men and women, being of the same nature, feel the same kind of pleasure, and therefore a man should marry such a woman as will love him ever afterwards.

The pleasure of men and women being thus proved to be of the same kind, it follows that, in regard to time, there are nine kinds of sexual intercourse, in the same way as there are nine kinds, according to the force of passion.

There being thus nine kinds of union with regard to dimensions, force of passion, and time, respectively, by making combinations of them, innumerable kinds of union would be produced. Therefore in each particular kind of sexual union, men should use such means as they may think suitable for the occasion [*4].

At the first time of sexual union the passion of the male is intense, and his time is short, but in subsequent unions on the same day the reverse of this is the case. With the female, however, it is the contrary, for at the first time her passion is weak, and then her time long, but on subsequent occasions on the same day, her passion is intense and her time short, until her passion is satisfied.

On the Different Kind of Love

Men learned in the humanities are of opinion that love is of four kinds:

Love acquired by continual habit
Love resulting from the imagination
Love resulting from belief
Love resulting from the perception of external objects

– Love resulting from the constant and continual performance of some act is called love acquired by constant practice and habit, as for instance the love of sexual intercourse, the love of hunting, the love of drinking, the love of gambling, etc., etc.
– Love which is felt for things to which we are not habituated, and which proceeds entirely from ideas, is called love resulting from imagination, as for instance that love which some men and women and eunuchs feel for the Auparishtaka or mouth congress, and that which is felt by all for such things as embracing, kissing, etc., etc.
– The love which is mutual on both sides, and proved to be true, when each looks upon the other as his or her very own, such is called love resulting from belief by the learned.
– The love resulting from the perception of external objects is quite evident and well known to the world, because the pleasure which it affords is superior to the pleasure of the other kinds of love, which exists only for its sake.

What has been said in this chapter upon the subject of sexual union is sufficient for the learned; but for the edification of the ignorant, the same will now be treated of at length and in detail.

footnotes

1   High unions are said to be better than low ones, for in the former it is possible for the male to satisfy his own passion without injuring the female, while in the latter it is difficult for the female to be satisfied by any means.

2   The strength of passion with women varies a great deal, some being easily satisfied, and others eager and willing to go on for a long time. To satisfy these last thoroughly a man must have recourse to art. It is certain that a fluid flows from the woman in larger or smaller quantities, but her satisfaction is not complete until she has experienced the *spasme genetique*, as described in a French work recently published and called *Brevaire de l'Amour Experimental* by Dr Jules Guyot.

3   This is a long dissertation very common among Sanscrit authors, both when writing and talking socially. They start certain propositions, and then argue for and against them. What it is presumed the author means is that, though both men and women derive pleasure from the act of coition, the way it is produced is brought about by different means, each individual performing his own work in the matter, irrespective of the other, and each deriving individually their own consciousness of pleasure from the act they perform. There is a difference in the work that each does, and a difference in the consciousness of pleasure that each has, but no difference in the pleasure they feel, for each feels that pleasure to a greater or lesser degree.

4   This paragraph should be particularly noted, for it specially applies to married men and their wives. So many men utterly ignore the feelings of the women, and never pay the slightest attention to the passion of the latter. To understand the subject thoroughly, it is absolutely necessary to study it, and then a person will know that, as dough is prepared for baking, so must a woman be prepared for sexual intercourse, if she is to derive satisfaction from it.

CHAPTER II

Of the Embrace

§ This part of the *Kama Shastra*, which treats of sexual union, is also called 'Sixty-four' (Chatushshashti). Some old authors say that it is called so, because it contains sixty-four chapters. Others are of opinion that the author of this part being a person named Panchala, and the person who recited the part of the *Rig Veda* called Dashatapa, which contains sixty-four verses, being also called Panchala, the name 'sixty-four' has been given to the part of the work in honour of the *Rig Vedas*. The followers of Babhravya say on the other hand that this part contains eight subjects, viz. the embrace, kissing, scratching with the nails or fingers, biting, lying down, making various sounds, playing the part of a man, and the Auparishtaka, or mouth congress. Each of these subjects being of eight kinds, and eight multiplied by eight being sixty-four, this part is therefore named 'sixty-four'. But Vatsyayana affirms that as this part contains also the following subjects, viz. striking, crying, the acts of a man during congress, the various kinds of congress, and other subjects, the name 'sixty-four' is given to it only accidentally. As, for instance, we say this tree is 'Saptaparna', or seven-leaved, this offering of rice is 'Panchavarna', or five-coloured, but the tree has not seven leaves, neither has the rice five colours.

However the part sixty-four is now treated of, and the embrace, being the first subject, will now be considered.

Now the embrace which indicates the mutual love of a man and woman who have come together is of four kinds:

Touching

Rubbing

Piercing

Pressing

The action in each case is denoted by the meaning of the word which stands for it.

– When a man under some pretext or other goes in front or alongside of a woman and touches her body with his own, it is called the 'touching embrace'.

– When a woman in a lonely place bends down, as if to pick up something, and pierces, as it were, a man sitting or standing, with her breasts, and the man in return takes hold of them, it is called a 'piercing embrace'.

The above two kinds of embrace take place only between persons who do not, as yet, speak freely with each other.

– When two lovers are walking slowly together, either in the dark, or in a place of public resort, or in a lonely place, and rub their bodies against each other, it is called a 'rubbing embrace'.

– When on the above occasion one of them presses the other's body forcibly against a wall or pillar, it is called a 'pressing embrace'.

These two last embraces are peculiar to those who know the intentions of each other.

At the time of the meeting the four following kinds of embrace are used:

Jataveshtitaka, or the twining of a creeper

Vrikshadhirudhaka, or climbing a tree

Tila-Tandulaka, or the mixture of sesamum seed with rice

Kshaniraka, or milk and water embrace

– When a woman, clinging to a man as a creeper twines round a tree, bends his head down to hers with the desire of kissing him and slightly makes the sound of sut sut, embraces him, and looks lovingly towards him, it is called an embrace like the 'twining of a creeper'.

– When a woman, having placed one of her feet on the foot of her lover, and the other on one of his thighs, passes one of her arms round his back, and the other on his shoulders, makes slightly the sounds of singing and cooing, and wishes, as it were, to climb up him in order to have a kiss, it is called an embrace like the 'climbing of a tree'.

These two kinds of embrace take place when the lover is standing.

– When lovers lie on a bed, and embrace each other so closely that the arms and thighs of the one are encircled by the arms and thighs of the other, and are, as it were, rubbing up against them, this is called an embrace like 'the mixture of sesamum seed with rice'.

– When a man and a woman are very much in love with each other, and, not thinking of any pain or hurt, embrace each other as if they were entering into each other's bodies

either while the woman is sitting on the lap of the man, or in front of him, or on a bed, then it is called an embrace like a 'mixture of milk and water'.

※※※※※※※※※※※※※※※※※※※※※※※※※※※※※※※※※※※

WHEN A WOMAN, CLINGING TO A MAN AS A CREEPER TWINES ROUND A TREE, BENDS HIS HEAD DOWN TO HERS WITH THE DESIRE OF KISSING HIM... EMBRACES HIM, AND LOOKS LOVINGLY TOWARDS HIM, IT IS CALLED AN EMBRACE LIKE THE 'TWINING OF A CREEPER'.

※※※※※※※※※※※※※※※※※※※※※※※※※※※※※※※※※※※

These two kinds of embrace take place at the time of sexual union.

Babhravya has thus related to us the above eight kinds of embraces.

Suvarnanabha moreover gives us four ways of embracing simple members of the body, which are:

The embrace of the thighs

The embrace of the jaghana, i.e. the part of the body from the navel downwards to the thighs

The embrace of the breasts

The embrace of the forehead

– When one of two lovers presses forcibly one or both of the thighs of the other between his or her own, it is called the 'embrace of thighs'.

– When a man presses the jaghana or middle part of the woman's body against his own, and mounts upon her to practise, either scratching with the nail or finger, or biting, or striking, or kissing, the hair of the woman being loose and flowing, it is called the 'embrace of the jaghana'.

– When a man places his breast between the breasts of a of Vatsyayana woman and presses her with it, it is called the 'embrace of the breasts'.

– When either of the lovers touches the mouth, the eyes and the forehead of the other with his or her own, it is called the 'embrace of the forehead'.

Some say that even shampooing is a kind of embrace, because there is a touching of bodies in it. But Vatsyayana thinks that shampooing is performed at a different time, and for a different purpose, and it is also of a different character, it cannot be said to be included in the embrace.

There are also some verses on the subject as follows:

The whole subject of embracing is of such a nature that men who ask questions about it, or who hear about it, or who talk about it, acquire thereby a desire for enjoyment. Even those embraces that are not mentioned in the Kama Shastra should be practised at the time of sexual enjoyment, if they are in any way conducive to the increase of love or passion. The rules of the Shastra apply so long as the passion of man is middling; but when the wheel of love is once set in motion, there is then no Shastra and no order.

CHAPTER III

On Kissing

§ It is said by some that there is no fixed time or order between the embrace, the kiss, and the pressing or scratching with the nails or fingers, but that all these things should be done generally before sexual union takes place, while striking and making the various sounds generally takes place at the time of the union. Vatsyayana, however, thinks that anything may take place at any time, for love does not care for time or order.

On the occasion of the first congress, kissing and the other things mentioned above should be done moderately, they should not be continued for a long time, and should be done alternately. On subsequent occasions, however, the reverse of all this may take place, and moderation will not be necessary, they may continue for a long time, and, for the purpose of kindling love, they may be all done at the same time.

The following are the places for kissing: the forehead, the eyes, the cheeks, the throat, the bosom, the breasts, the lips, and the interior of the mouth. Moreover the people of the Lat country kiss also on the following places: the joints of the thighs, the arms and the navel. But Vatsyayana thinks that though kissing is practised by these people in the above places on account of the intensity of their love, and the customs of their country, it is not fit to be practised by all.

Now in a case of a young girl there are three sorts of kisses:

The nominal kiss

The throbbing kiss

The touching kiss

— When a girl only touches the mouth of her lover with her own, but does not herself do anything, it is called the 'nominal kiss'.

– When a girl, setting aside her bashfulness a little, wishes to touch the lip that is pressed into her mouth, and with that object moves her lower lip, but not the upper one, it is called the 'throbbing kiss'.

– When a girl touches her lover's lip with her tongue, and having shut her eyes, places her hands on those of her lover, it is called the 'touching kiss'.

Other authors describe four other kinds of kisses:

The straight kiss

The bent kiss

The turned kiss

The pressed kiss

– When the lips of two lovers are brought into direct contact with each other, it is called a 'straight kiss'.

– When the heads of two lovers are bent towards each other, and when so bent, kissing takes place, it is called a 'bent kiss'.

– When one of them turns up the face of the other by holding the head and chin, and then kissing, it is called a 'turned kiss'.

– Lastly when the lower lip is pressed with much force, it is called a 'pressed kiss'.

There is also a fifth kind of kiss called the 'greatly pressed kiss', which is effected by taking hold of the lower lip between two fingers, and then, after touching it with the tongue, pressing it with great force with the lip.

As regards kissing, a wager may be laid as to which will get hold of the lips of the other first. If the woman loses, she should pretend to cry, should keep her lover off by shaking her hands, and turn away from him and dispute with him saying, 'let another wager be laid'. If she loses this a second time, she should appear doubly distressed, and when her lover is off his guard or asleep, she should get hold of his lower lip, and hold it in her teeth, so that it should not slip away, and then she should laugh, make a loud noise, deride him, dance about, and say whatever she likes in a joking way, moving her eyebrows and rolling her eyes. Such are the wagers and quarrels as far as kissing is concerned, but the same may be applied with regard to the pressing or scratching with the nails and fingers, biting and striking. All these however are only peculiar to men and women of intense passion.

When a man kisses the upper lip of a woman, while she in return kisses his lower lip, it is called the 'kiss of the upper lip'.

When one of them takes both the lips of the other between his or her own, it is called 'a clasping kiss'. A woman, however, only takes this kind of kiss from a man who has no moustache. And on the occasion of this kiss, if one of them touches the teeth, the tongue, and the palate of the other, with his or her tongue, it is called the 'fighting of the tongue'. In the same way, the pressing of the teeth of the one against the mouth of the other is to be practised.

Kissing is of four kinds: moderate, contracted, pressed, and soft, according to the different parts of the body which are kissed, for different kinds of kisses are appropriate for different parts of the body.

* *When a woman looks at the face of her lover while he is asleep and kisses it to show her intention or desire, it is called a 'kiss that kindles love'.*

* *When a woman kisses her lover while he is engaged in business, or while he is quarrelling with her, or while he is looking at something else, so that his mind may be turned away, it is called a 'kiss that turns away'.*

* *When a lover coming home late at night kisses his beloved, who is asleep on her bed, in order to show her his desire, it is called a 'kiss that awakens'. On such an occasion the woman may pretend to be asleep at the time of her lover's arrival, so that she may know his intention and obtain respect from him.*

* *When a person kisses the reflection of the person he loves in a mirror, in water, or on a wall, it is called a 'kiss showing the intention'.*

* *When a person kisses a child sitting on his lap, or a picture, or an image, or figure, in the presence of the person beloved by him, it is called a 'transferred kiss'.*

* *When at night at a theatre, or in an assembly of caste men, a man coming up to a woman kisses a finger of her hand if she be standing, or a toe of her foot if she be sitting, or when a woman is shampooing her lover's body, places her face on his thigh (as if she was sleepy) so as to inflame his passion, and kisses his thigh or great toe, it is called a 'demonstrative kiss'.*

There is also a verse on this subject as follows:

*Whatever things may be done by one of the lovers
to the other, the same should be returned by the other,
i.e. if the woman kisses him he should kiss her in return,
if she strikes him he should also strike her in return.*

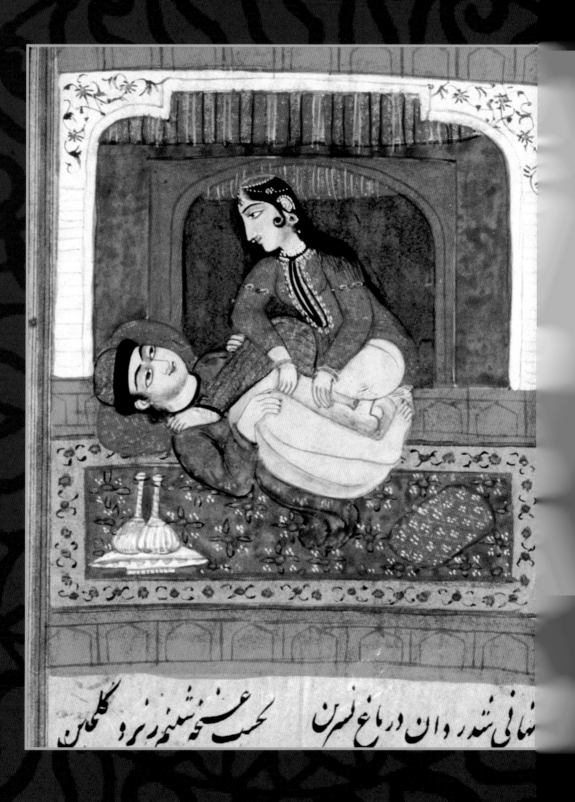

تنهایی شده روان در باغ نسرین   تحت خوشه نشینه و نره گلگلی

CHAPTER IV

On Pressing, or Marking, or Scratching with the Nails

§ When love becomes intense, pressing with the nails or scratching the body with them is practised, and it is done on the following occasions: on the first visit; at the time of setting out on a journey; on the return from a journey; at the time when an angry lover is reconciled; and lastly when the woman is intoxicated.

But pressing with the nails is not a usual thing except with those who are intensely passionate, i.e. full of passion. It is employed, together with biting, by those to whom the practice is agreeable.

Pressing with the nails is of the eight following kinds, according to the forms of the marks which are produced:

Sounding

Half moon

A circle

A line

A tiger's nail or claw

A peacock's foot

The jump of a hare

The leaf of a blue lotus

The places that are to be pressed with the nails are as follows: the arm pit, the throat, the breasts, the lips, the jaghana, or middle parts of the body, and the thighs.

But Suvarnanabha is of opinion that when the impetuosity of passion is excessive, the places need not be considered.

The qualities of good nails are that they should be bright, well set, clean, entire, convex, soft, and glossy in appearance. Nails are of three kinds according to their size:

Small

Middling

Large

– Large nails, which give grace to the hands, and attract the hearts of women from their appearance, are possessed by the Bengalees.
– Small nails, which can be used in various ways, and are to be applied only with the object of giving pleasure, are possessed by the people of the southern districts.
– Middling nails, which contain the properties of both the above kinds, belong to the people of the Maharashtra.
– When a person presses the chin, the breasts, the lower lip, or the jaghana of another so softly that no scratch or mark is left, but only the hair on the body becomes erect from the touch of the nails, and the nails themselves make a sound, it is called a 'sounding or pressing with the nails'. This pressing is used in the case of a young girl when her lover shampoos her, scratches her head, and wants to trouble or frighten her.
– The curved mark with the nails, which is impressed on the neck and the breasts, is called the 'half moon'.
– When the half moons are impressed opposite to each other, it is called a 'circle'. This mark with the nails is generally made on the navel, the small cavities about the buttocks, and on the joints of the thigh.
– A mark in the form of a small line, and which can be made on any part of the body, is called a 'line'.
– This same line, when it is curved, and made on the breast, is called a 'tiger's nail'.
– When a curved mark is made on the breast by means of the five nails, it is called a 'peacock's foot'. This mark is made with the object of being praised, for it requires a great deal of skill to make it properly.
– When five marks with the nails are made close to one another near the nipple of the breast, it is called 'the jump of a hare'.
– A mark made on the breast or on the hips in the form of a leaf of the blue lotus is called the 'leaf of a blue lotus'.

When a person is going on a journey, and makes a mark on the thighs, or on the breast, it is called a 'token of remembrance'. On such an occasion three or four lines are impressed close to one another with the nails.

Here ends the marking with the nails. Marks of other kinds than the above may also be made with the nails, for the ancient authors say that, as there are innumerable degrees of skill among men (the practice of this art being known to all), so there are innumerable ways of making these marks. And as pressing or marking with the nails is independent of love, no one can say with certainty how many different kinds of marks with the nails do actually exist. The reason of this is, Vatsyayana says, that as variety is necessary in love, so love is to be produced by means of variety. It is on this account that courtesans, who are well acquainted with various ways and means, become so desirable, for if variety is sought in all the arts and amusements, such as archery and others, how much more should it be sought after in the present case.

The marks of the nails should not be made on married women, but particular kinds of marks may be made on their private parts for the remembrance and increase of love.

There are also some verses on the subject, as follows:

The love of a woman who sees the marks of nails on the private parts of her body, even though they are old and almost worn out, becomes again fresh and new. If there be no marks of nails to remind a person of the passages of love, then love is lessened in the same way as when no union takes place for a long time.

Even when a stranger sees at a distance a young woman with the marks of nails on her breast, he is filled with love and respect for her [*1].

A man, also, who carries the marks of nails and teeth on some parts of his body, influences the mind of a woman, even though it be ever so firm. In short, nothing tends to increase love so much as the effects of marking with the nails, and biting.

footnote

1   From this it would appear that in ancient times the breasts of women were not covered, and this is seen in the paintings of the Ajunta and other caves, where we find that the breasts of even royal ladies and others are exposed.

On Biting, & the Means
to Be Employed with Regard to
Women of Different Countries

§ All the places that can be kissed are also the places that can be bitten, except the upper lip, the interior of the mouth, and the eyes.

The qualities of good teeth are as follows: They should be equal, possessed of a pleasing brightness, capable of being coloured, of proper proportions, unbroken, and with sharp ends.

The defects of teeth on the other hand are that they are blunt, protruding from the gums, rough, soft, large, and loosely set.

The following are the different kinds of biting:

The hidden bite

The swollen bite

The point

The line of points

The coral and the jewel

The line of jewels

The broken cloud

The biting of the boar

– The biting, which is shown only by the excessive redness of the skin that is bitten, is called the 'hidden bite'.
– When the skin is pressed down on both sides, it is called the 'swollen bite'.
– When a small portion of the skin is bitten with two teeth only, it is called the 'point'.
– When such small portions of the skin are bitten with all the teeth, it is called the 'line of points'.
– The biting, which is done by bringing together the teeth and the lips, is called the 'coral and the jewel'. The lip is the coral, and the teeth the jewel.
– When biting is done with all the teeth, it is called the 'line of jewels'.
– The biting, which consists of unequal risings in a circle, and which comes from the space between the teeth, is called the 'broken cloud'. This is impressed on the breasts.

THE BITING, WHICH IS DONE BY BRINGING TOGETHER THE TEETH AND THE LIPS, IS CALLED THE 'CORAL AND THE JEWEL'. THE LIP IS THE CORAL, AND THE TEETH THE JEWEL.

– The biting, which consists of many broad rows of marks near to one another, and with red intervals, is called the 'biting of a boar'. This is impressed on the breasts and the shoulders; and these two last modes of biting are peculiar to persons of intense passion.

The lower lip is the place on which the 'hidden bite', the 'swollen bite', and the 'point' are made; again the 'swollen bite' and the 'coral and the jewel' bite are done on the cheek. Kissing, pressing with the nails, and biting are the ornaments of the left cheek, and when the word cheek is used it is to be understood as the left cheek.

Both the 'line of points' and the 'line of jewels' are to be impressed on the throat, the arm pit, and the joints of the thighs; but the 'line of points' alone is to be impressed on the forehead and the thighs.

The marking with the nails, and the biting of the following things - an ornament of the forehead, an ear ornament, a bunch of flowers, a betel leaf, or a tamala leaf, which are worn by, or belong to the woman that is beloved - are signs of the desire of enjoyment.

Here end the different kinds of biting.

In the affairs of love a man should do such things as are agreeable to the women of different countries.

* The women of the central countries (i.e. between the Ganges and the Jumna) are noble in their character, not accustomed to disgraceful practices, and dislike pressing the nails and biting.

* The women of the Balhika country are gained over by striking.

* The women of Avantika are fond of foul pleasures, and have not good manners.

* The women of the Maharashtra are fond of practising the sixty-four arts, they utter low and harsh words, and like to be spoken to in the same way, and have an impetuous desire of enjoyment.

* The women of Pataliputra (i.e. the modern Patna) are of the same nature as the women of the Maharashtra, but show their likings only in secret.

* The women of the Dravida country, though they are rubbed and pressed about at the time of sexual enjoyment, have a slow fall of semen, that is they are very slow in the act of coition.

* The women of Vanavasi are moderately passionate, they go through every kind of enjoyment, cover their bodies, and abuse those who utter low, mean and harsh words.

* The women of Avanti hate kissing, marking with the nails, and biting, but they have a fondness for various kinds of sexual union.

* The women of Malwa like embracing and kissing, but not wounding, and they are gained over by striking.

* The women of Abhira, and those of the country about the Indus and five rivers (i.e. the Punjab), are gained over by the Auparishtaka or mouth congress.

* The women of Aparatika are full of passion, and make slowly the sound 'Sit'.

* The women of the Lat country have even more impetuous desire, and also make the sound 'Sit'.

* The women of the Stri Rajya, and of Koshola (Oude), are full of impetuous desire, their semen falls in large quantities and they are fond of taking medicine to make it do so.

* The women of the Andhra country have tender bodies, they are fond of enjoyment, and have a liking for voluptuous pleasures.

* The women of Ganda have tender bodies, and speak sweetly.

Now Suvarnanabha is of opinion that that which is agreeable to the nature of a particular person, is of more consequence than that which is agreeable to a whole nation, and that therefore the peculiarities of the country should not be observed in such cases. The various pleasures, the dress, and the sports of one country are in time borrowed by another, and in such a case these things must be considered as belonging originally to that country.

Among the things mentioned above, viz. embracing, kissing, etc., those which increase passion should be done first, and those which are only for amusement or variety should be done afterwards.

There are also some verses on this subject as follows:

When a man bites a woman forcibly, she should angrily do the same to him with double force. Thus a 'point' should be returned with a 'line of points', and a 'line of points' with a 'broken cloud', and if she be excessively chafed, she should at once begin a love quarrel with him. At such a time she should take hold of her lover by the hair, and bend his head down, and kiss his lower lip, and then, being intoxicated with love, she should shut her eyes and bite him in various places. Even by day, and in a place of public resort, when her lover shows her any mark that she may have inflicted on his body, she should smile at the sight of it, and turning her face as if she were going to chide him, she should show him with an angry look the marks on her own body that have been made by him. Thus if men and women act according to each other's liking, their love for each other will not be lessened even in one hundred years.

CHAPTER VI

Of the Different Ways of Lying Down, & Various Kinds of Congress

§ On the occasion of a 'high congress' the Mrigi (deer) woman should lie down in such a way as to widen her yoni, while in a 'low congress' the Hastini (elephant) woman should lie down so as to contract hers. But in an 'equal congress' they should lie down in the natural position (*see* page 53). What is said above concerning the Mrigi and the Hastini applies also to the Vadawa (mare) woman. In a 'low congress' the woman should particularly make use of medicine, to cause her desires to be satisfied quickly.

The deer woman has the following three ways of lying down:

The widely opened position

The yawning position

The position of the wife of Indra

– When she lowers her head and raises her middle parts, it is called the 'widely opened position'. At such a time the man should apply some unguent, so as to make the entrance easy.
– When she raises her thighs and keeps them wide apart and engages in congress, it is called the 'yawning position'.
– When she places her thighs with her legs doubled on them upon her sides, and thus engages in congress, it is called the position of Indrani and this is learnt only by practice. The position is also useful in the case of the 'highest congress'.

The 'clasping position' is used in 'low congress', and in the 'lowest congress', together with the 'pressing position', the 'twining position', and the 'mare's position'.

– When the legs of both the male and the female are stretched straight out over each other, it is called the 'clasping position'. It is of two kinds, the side position and the supine position, according to the way in which they lie down. In the side position the male should invariably lie on his left side, and cause the woman to lie on her right side, and this rule is to be observed in lying down with all kinds of women.

– When, after congress has begun in the clasping position, the woman presses her lover with her thighs, it is called the 'pressing position'.

– When the woman places one of her thighs across the thigh of her lover it is called the 'twining position'.

– When a woman forcibly holds in her yoni the lingam after it is in, it is called the 'mare's position'. This is learnt by practice only, and is chiefly found among the women of the Andhra country.

The above are the different ways of lying down, mentioned by Babhravya. Suvarnanabha, however, gives the following in addition:

* *When the female raises both of her thighs straight up, it is called the 'rising position'.*

* *When she raises both of her legs, and places them on her lover's shoulders, it is called the 'yawning position'.*

* *When the legs are contracted, and thus held by the lover before his bosom, it is called the 'pressed position'.*

* *When only one of her legs is stretched out, it is called the 'half pressed position'.*

* *When the woman places one of her legs on her lover's shoulder, and stretches the other out, and then places the latter on his shoulder, and stretches out the other, and continues to do so alternately, it is called the 'splitting of a bamboo'.*

* *When one of her legs is placed on the head, and the other is stretched out, it is called the 'fixing of a nail'. This is learnt by practice only.*

* *When both the legs of the woman are contracted, and placed on her stomach, it is called the 'crab's position'.*

* *When the thighs are raised and placed one upon the other, it is called the 'packed position'.*

* *When the shanks are placed one upon the other, it is called the 'lotus-like position'.*

* *When a man, during congress, turns round, and enjoys the woman without leaving her, while she embraces him round the back all the time, it is called the 'turning position', and is learnt only by practice.*

Thus, says Suvarnanabha, these different ways of lying down, sitting, and standing should be practised in water, because it is easy to do so therein. But Vatsyayana is of opinion that congress in water is improper, because it is prohibited by the religious law.

When a man and a woman support themselves on each other's bodies, or on a wall, or pillar, and thus while standing engage in congress, it is called the 'supported congress'.

When a man supports himself against a wall, and the woman, sitting on his hands joined together and held underneath her, throws her arms round his neck, and putting her thighs alongside his waist, moves herself by her feet, which are touching the wall against which the man is leaning, it is called the 'suspended congress'.

When a woman stands on her hands and feet like a quadruped, and her lover mounts her like a bull, it is called the 'congress of a cow'. At this time everything that is ordinarily done on the bosom should be done on the back.

ON THE OCCASION OF A 'HIGH CONGRESS' THE MRIGI (DEER) WOMAN SHOULD LIE DOWN IN SUCH A WAY AS TO WIDEN HER YONI, WHILE IN A 'LOW CONGRESS' THE HASTINI (ELEPHANT) WOMAN SHOULD LIE DOWN SO AS TO CONTRACT HERS. BUT IN AN 'EQUAL CONGRESS' THEY SHOULD LIE DOWN IN THE NATURAL POSITION.

In the same way can be carried on the congress of a dog, the congress of a goat, the congress of a deer, the forcible mounting of an ass, the congress of a cat, the jump of a tiger, the pressing of an elephant, the rubbing of a boar, and the mounting of a horse. And in all these cases the characteristics of these different animals should be manifested by acting like them.

When a man enjoys two women at the same time, both of whom love him equally, it is called the 'united congress'.

When a man enjoys many women altogether, it is called the 'congress of a herd of cows'.

The following kinds of congress-sporting in water, or the congress of an elephant with many female elephants which is said to take place only in the water, the congress of a collection of goats, the congress of a collection of deer take place in imitation of these animals.

In Gramaneri many young men enjoy a woman that may be married to one of them, either one after the other, or at the same time. Thus one of them holds her, another enjoys her, a third uses her mouth, a fourth holds her middle part, and in this way they go on enjoying her several parts alternately.

The same things can be done when several men are sitting in company with one courtesan, or when one courtesan is alone with many men. In the same way this can be done by the women of the king's harem when they accidentally get hold of a man.

The people in the Southern countries have also a congress in the anus, that is called the 'lower congress'.

Thus ends the various kinds of congress. There are also two verses on the subject as follows:

An ingenious person should multiply the kinds of congress after the fashion of the different kinds of beasts and of birds. For these different kinds of congress, performed according to the usage of each country, and the liking of each individual, generate love, friendship, and respect in the hearts of women.

Of the Various Modes of Striking, & of the Sounds Appropriate to Them

§ Sexual intercourse can be compared to a quarrel, on account of the contrarieties of love and its tendency to dispute. The place of striking with passion is the body, and on the body the special places are:

The shoulders

The head

The space between the breasts

The back

The jaghana, or middle part of the body

The sides

Striking is of four kinds:

Striking with the back of the hand

Striking with the fingers a little contracted

Striking with the fist

Striking with the open palm of the hand

On account of its causing pain, striking gives rise to the hissing sound, which is of various kinds, and to the eight kinds of crying:

The sound Hin

The thundering sound

The cooing sound

The weeping sound

The sound Phut

The sound Phat

The sound Sut

The sound Plat

Besides these, there are also words having a meaning, such as 'mother', and those that are expressive of prohibition, sufficiency, desire of liberation, pain or praise, and to which may be added sounds like those of the dove, the cuckoo, the green pigeon, the parrot, the bee, the sparrow, the flamingo, the duck, and the quail, which are all occasionally made use of.

Blows with the fist should be given on the back of the woman while she is sitting on the lap of the man, and she should give blows in return, abusing the man as if she were angry, and making the cooing and the weeping sounds. While the woman is engaged in congress the space between the breasts should be struck with the back of the hand, slowly at first, and then proportionately to the increasing excitement, until the end.

At this time the sounds Hin and others may be made, alternately or optionally, according to habit. When the man, making the sound Phat, strikes the woman on the head, with the fingers of his hand a little contracted, it is called Prasritaka, which means striking with the fingers of the hand a little contracted. In this case the appropriate sounds are the cooing sound, the sound Phat and the sound Phut in the interior of the mouth, and at the end of congress the sighing and weeping sounds. The sound Phat is an imitation of the sound of a bamboo being split, while the sound Phut is like the sound made by something falling into water. At all times when kissing and such like things are begun, the woman should give a reply with a hissing sound. During the excitement when the woman is not accustomed to striking, she continually utters words expressive of prohibition, sufficiently, or desire of liberation, as well as the words 'father', 'mother', intermingled with the sighing, weeping and thundering sounds [*1]. Towards the conclusion of the congress, the breasts, the jaghana, and the sides of the woman should be pressed with the open palms of the hand, with some force, until the end of it, and then sounds like those of the quail or the goose should be made.

There are two verses on the subject as follows:

The characteristics of manhood are said to consist of roughness and impetuosity, while weakness, tenderness, sensibility, and an inclination to turn away from unpleasant things are the distinguishing marks of womanhood. The excitement of passion, and peculiarities of habit may sometimes cause contrary results to appear, but these do not last long, and in the end the natural state is resumed.

The wedge on the bosom, the scissors on the head, the piercing instrument on the cheeks, and the pinchers on the breasts and sides, may also be taken into consideration with the other four modes of striking, and thus give eight ways altogether. But these four ways of striking with instruments are peculiar to the people of the southern countries, and the marks caused by them are seen on the breasts of their women. They are local peculiarities, but Vatsyayana is of opinion that the practice of them is painful, barbarous, and base, and quite unworthy of imitation.

In the same way anything that is a local peculiarity should not always be adopted elsewhere, and even in the place where the practice is prevalent, excess of it should always be avoided. Instances of the dangerous use of them may be given as follows. The king of the Panchalas killed the courtesan Madhavasena by means of the wedge during congress. King Satakarni Satavahana of the Kuntalas deprived his great Queen Malayavati of her life by a pair of scissors, and Naradeva, whose hand was deformed, blinded a dancing girl by directing a piercing instrument in a wrong way.

There are also two verses on the subject as follows:

About these things there cannot be either enumeration or any definite rule. Congress having once commenced, passion alone gives birth to all the acts of the parties.

Such passionate actions and amorous gesticulations or movements, which arise on the spur of the moment, and during sexual intercourse, cannot be defined, and are as irregular as dreams. A horse having once attained the fifth degree of motion goes on with blind speed, regardless of pits, ditches, and posts in his way; and in the same manner a loving pair become blind with passion in the heat of congress, and go on with great impetuosity, paying not the least regard to excess. For this reason one who is well acquainted with the science of love, and knowing his own strength, as also the tenderness, impetuosity, and strength of the young women, should act accordingly. The various modes of enjoyment are not for all times or for all persons, but they should only be used at the proper time, and in the proper countries and places.

footnote

1   Men who are well acquainted with the art of love are well aware how often one woman differs from another in her sighs and sounds during the time of congress. Some women like to be talked to in the most loving way, others in the most lustful way, others in the most abusive way, and so on. Some women enjoy themselves with closed eyes in silence, others make a great noise over it, and some almost faint away. The great art is to ascertain what gives them the greatest pleasure, and what specialities they like best.

CHAPTER VIII

About Women Acting the Part of a Man; & of the Work of a Man

§ When a woman sees that her lover is fatigued by constant congress, without having his desire satisfied, she should, with his permission, lay him down upon his back, and give him assistance by acting his part. She may also do this to satisfy the curiosity of her lover, or her own desire of novelty.

There are two ways of doing this, the first is when during congress she turns round, and gets on the top of her lover, in such a manner as to continue the congress, without obstructing the pleasure of it; and the other is when she acts the man's part from the beginning. At such a time, with flowers in her hair hanging loose, and her smiles broken by hard breathings, she should press upon her lover's bosom with her own breasts, and lowering her head frequently, should do in return the same actions which he used to do before, returning his blows and chaffing him, should say, 'I was laid down by you, and fatigued with hard congress, I shall now therefore lay you down in return.' She should then again manifest her own bashfulness, her fatigue, and her desire of stopping the congress. In this way she should do the work of a man, which we shall presently relate.

Whatever is done by a man for giving pleasure to a woman is called the work of a man, and is as follows:

While the woman is lying on his bed, and is as it were abstracted by his conversation, he should loosen the knot of her undergarments, and when she begins to dispute with him, he should overwhelm her with kisses. Then when his lingam is erect he should touch her with his hands in various places, and gently manipulate various parts of the body. If the woman is bashful, and if it is the first time that they have come together, the man should place his hands between her thighs, which she would probably keep close together, and if she is a very young girl, he should first get his hands upon her breasts, which she would probably cover with her own hands, and under her armpits and on her neck. If however she is a seasoned woman, he should do whatever is agreeable either to him or to her, and whatever is fitting for the occasion. After this he should take hold of her hair, and hold her chin in his fingers for the purpose of kissing her. On this, if she is a young girl, she will become bashful and close her eyes. Anyhow he should gather from the action of the woman what things would be pleasing to her during congress.

Here Suvarnanabha says that while a man is doing to the woman what he likes best during congress, he should always make a point of pressing those parts of her body on which she turns her eyes.

The signs of the enjoyment and satisfaction of the woman are as follows: her body relaxes, she closes her eyes, she puts aside all bashfulness, and shows increased willingness to unite the two organs as closely together as possible. On the other hand, the signs of her want of enjoyment and of failing to be satisfied are as follows: she shakes her hands, she does not let the man get up, feels dejected, bites the man, kicks him, and continues to go on moving after the man has finished. In such cases the man should rub the yoni of the woman with his hand and fingers (as the elephant rubs anything with his trunk) before engaging in congress, until it is softened, and after that is done he should proceed to put his lingam into her.

The acts to be done by the man are:

Moving forward

Friction or churning

Piercing

Rubbing

Pressing

Giving a blow

The blow of a boar

The blow of a bull

The sporting of a sparrow

- When the organs are brought together properly and directly it is called 'moving the organ forward'.
- When the lingam is held with the hand, and turned all round in the yoni, it is called 'churning'.

– When the yoni is lowered, and the upper part of it is struck with the lingam, it is called 'piercing'.

– When the same thing is done on the lower part of the yoni, it is called 'rubbing'.

– When the yoni is pressed by the lingam for a long time, it is called 'pressing'.

– When the lingam is removed to some distance from the yoni, and then forcibly strikes it, it is called 'giving a blow'.

– When only one part of the yoni is rubbed with the lingam, it is called the 'blow of a boar'.

– When both sides of the yoni are rubbed in this way, it is called the 'blow of a bull'.

– When the lingam is in the yoni, and moved up and down frequently, and without being taken out, it is called the 'sporting of a sparrow'. This takes place at the end of congress.

When a woman acts the part of a man, she has the following things to do in addition to the nine given above:

The pair of tongs

The top

The swing

– When the woman holds the lingam in her yoni, draws it in, presses it, and keeps it thus in her for a long time, it is called the 'pair of tongs'.

– When, while engaged in congress, she turns round like a wheel, it is called the 'top'. This is learnt by practice only.

– When, on such an occasion, the man lifts up the middle part of his body, and the woman turns round her middle part, it is called the 'swing'.

THE SIGNS OF THE ENJOYMENT AND SATISFACTION OF THE WOMAN ARE AS FOLLOWS: HER BODY RELAXES, SHE CLOSES HER EYES, SHE PUTS ASIDE ALL BASHFULNESS, AND SHOWS INCREASED WILLINGNESS TO UNITE THE TWO ORGANS AS CLOSELY TOGETHER AS POSSIBLE.

When the woman is tired, she should place her forehead on that of her lover, and should thus take rest without disturbing the union of the organs, and when the woman has rested herself the man should turn round and begin the congress again.

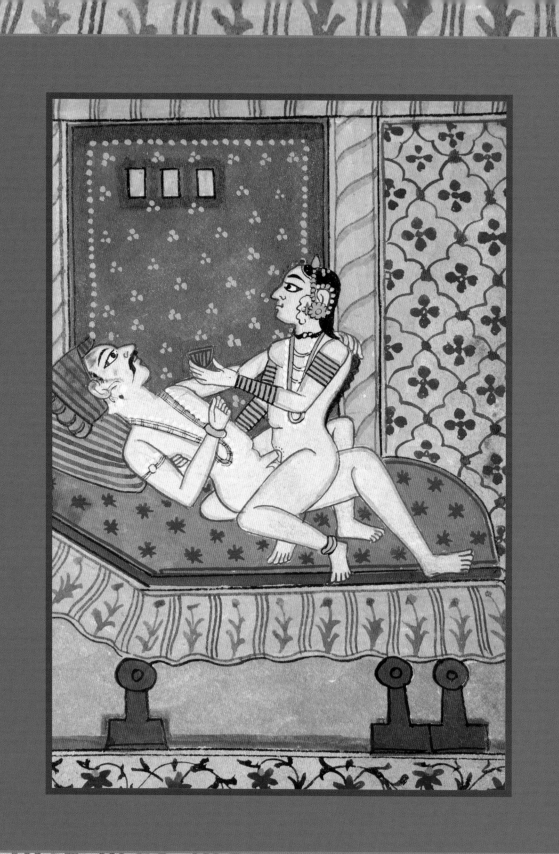

There are also some verses on the subject as follows:

*Though a woman is reserved, and keeps her feelings
concealed; yet when she gets on the top of a man,
she then shows all her love and desire. A man should
gather from the actions of the woman of what disposition
she is, and in what way she likes to be enjoyed.
A woman during her monthly courses, a woman who has
been lately confined, and a fat woman should not be made
to act the part of a man.*

Of the Auparishtaka or Mouth Congress

§ There are two kinds of eunuchs, those that are disguised as males, and those that are disguised as females. Eunuchs disguised as females imitate their dress, speech, gestures, tenderness, timidity, simplicity, softness and bashfulness. The acts that are done on the jaghana or middle parts of women, are done in the mouths of these eunuchs, and this is called Auparishtaka [*1]. These eunuchs derive their imaginable pleasure, and their livelihood from this kind of congress, and they lead the life of courtesans. So much concerning eunuchs disguised as females.

Eunuchs disguised as males keep their desires secret, and when they wish to do anything they lead the life of shampooers. Under the pretence of shampooing, a eunuch of this kind embraces and draws towards himself the thighs of the man whom he is shampooing, and after this he touches the joints of his thighs and his jaghana, or central portions of his body. Then, if he finds the lingam of the man erect, he presses it with his hands and chaffs him for getting into that state. If after this, and after knowing his intention, the man does not tell the eunuch to proceed, then the latter does it of his own accord and begins the congress. If however he is ordered by the man to do it, then he disputes with him, and only consents at last with difficulty.

The following eight things are then done by the eunuch one after the other:

The nominal congress

Biting the sides

Pressing outside

Pressing inside

Kissing

Rubbing
....

Sucking a mango fruit
....

Swallowing up
....

At the end of each of these, the eunuch expresses his wish to stop, but when one of them is finished, the man desires him to do another, and after that is done, then the one that follows it, and so on.

– When, holding the man's lingam with his hand, and placing it between his lips, the eunuch moves about his mouth, it is called the 'nominal congress'.

– When, covering the end of the lingam with his fingers collected together like the bud of a plant or flower, the eunuch presses the sides of it with his lips, using his teeth also, it is called 'biting the sides'.

– When, being desired to proceed, the eunuch presses the end of the lingam with his lips closed together, and kisses it as if he were drawing it out, it is called the 'outside pressing'.

– When, being asked to go on, he puts the lingam further into his mouth, and presses it with his lips and then takes it out, it is called the 'inside pressing'.

– When, holding the lingam in his hand, the eunuch kisses it as if he were kissing the lower lip, it is called 'kissing'.

– When, after kissing it, he touches it with his tongue everywhere, and passes the tongue over the end of it, it is called 'rubbing'.

– When, in the same way, he puts the half of it into his mouth, and forcibly kisses and sucks it, this is called 'sucking a mango fruit'.

– And lastly, when, with the consent of the man, the eunuch puts the whole lingam into his mouth, and presses it to the very end, as if he were going to swallow it up, it is called 'swallowing up'.

Striking, scratching, and other things may also be done during this kind of congress.

The Auparishtaka is practised also by unchaste and wanton women, female attendants and serving maids, i.e. those who are not married to anybody, but who live by shampooing.

The Acharyas (i.e. ancient and venerable authors) are of opinion that this Auparishtaka is the work of a dog and not of a man, because it is a low practice, and opposed to the orders of the Holy Writ, and because the man himself suffers by bringing his lingam into contact with the mouths of eunuchs and women. But Vatsyayana says that the orders of the Holy Writ do not affect those who resort to courtesans, and the law prohibits the practice of the Auparishtaka with married women only. As regards the injury to the male, that can be easily remedied.

The people of Eastern India do not resort to women who practise the Auparishtaka.

The people of Ahichhatra resort to such women, but do nothing with them, so far as the mouth is concerned.

The people of Saketa do with these women every kind of mouth congress, while the people of Nagara do not practise this, but do every other thing.

The people of the Shurasena country, on the southern bank of the Jumna, do everything without any hesitation, for they say that women being naturally unclean, no one can be certain about their character, their purity, their conduct, their practices, their confidences, or their speech. They are not however on this account to be abandoned, because religious law, on the authority of which they are reckoned pure, lays down that the udder of a cow is clean at the time of milking, though the mouth of a cow, and also the mouth of her calf, are considered unclean by the Hindoos. Again a dog is clean when he seizes a deer in hunting, though food touched by a dog is otherwise considered very unclean. A bird is clean when it causes a fruit to fall from a tree by pecking at it, though things eaten by crows and other birds are considered unclean. And the mouth of a woman is clean for kissing and such like things at the time of sexual intercourse. Vatsyayana moreover thinks that in all these things connected with love, everybody should act according to the custom of his country, and his own inclination.

There are also the following verses on the subject:

The male servants of some men carry on the mouth congress with their masters. It is also practised by some citizens, who know each other well, among themselves. Some women of the harem, when they are amorous, do the acts of the mouth on the yonis of one another, and some men do the same thing with women. The way of doing this (i.e. of kissing the yoni) should be known from kissing the mouth. When a man and woman lie down in an inverted order, i.e. with the head of the one towards the feet of the other and carry on this congress, it is called the 'congress of a crow'.

For the sake of such things courtesans abandon men possessed of good qualities, liberal and clever, and become attached to low persons, such as slaves and elephant drivers. The Auparishtaka, or mouth congress, should never be done by a learned Brahman, by a minister that carries on the business of a state, or by a man of good reputation, because though the practice is allowed by the Shastras, there is no reason why it should be carried on, and need only be practised in particular cases. As for instance, the taste, and the strength, and the digestive qualities of the flesh of dogs are mentioned in works on medicine, but it does not therefore follow that it should be eaten by the wise. In the same way there are some men, some places and some times, with respect to which these practices can be made use of. A man should therefore pay regard to the place, to the time, and to the practice which is to be carried out, as also as to whether it is agreeable to his nature and to himself, and then he may or may not practise these things according to circumstances. But after all, these things being done secretly, and the mind of the man being fickle, how can it be known what any person will do at any particular time and for any particular purpose?

footnote

1   This practice appears to have been prevalent in some parts of India from a very ancient time. *The Shustruta*, a work on medicine some two thousand years old, describes the wounding of the lingam with the teeth as one of the causes of a disease treated upon in that work. Traces of the practice are found as far back as the eighth century, for various kinds of the Auparishtaka are represented in the sculptures of many Shaiva temples at Bhuvaneshwara, near Cuttack, in Orissa, and which were built about that period. From these sculptures being found in such places, it would seem that this practice was popular in that part of the country at that time. It does not seem to be so prevalent now in Hindustan, its place perhaps is filled up by the practice of sodomy, introduced since the Mahomedan period.

Of the Way How to Begin & How to End the Congress. Different Kinds of Congress & Love Quarrels

§ In the pleasure-room, decorated with flowers, and fragrant with perfumes, attended by his friends and servants, the citizen should receive the woman, who will come bathed and dressed, and will invite her to take refreshment and to drink freely. He should then seat her on his left side, and holding her hair, and touching also the end and knot of her garment, he should gently embrace her with his right arm. They should then carry on an amusing conversation on various subjects, and may also talk suggestively of things which would be considered as coarse, or not to be mentioned generally in society. They may then sing, either with or without gesticulations, and play on musical instruments, talk about the arts, and persuade each other to drink. At last when the woman is overcome with love and desire, the citizen should dismiss the people that may be with him, giving them flowers, ointments, and betel leaves, and then when the two are left alone, they should proceed as has been already described in the previous chapters.

Such is the beginning of sexual union. At the end of the congress, the lovers with modesty, and not looking at each other, should go separately to the washing-room. After this, sitting in their own places, they should eat some betel leaves, and the citizen should apply with his own hand to the body of the woman some pure sandal wood ointment, or ointment of some other kind. He should then embrace her with his left arm, and with agreeable words should cause her to drink from a cup held in his own hand, or he may give her water to drink. They can then eat sweetmeats, or anything else, according to their likings and may drink fresh juice, soup[*1], gruel, extracts of meat, sherbet, the juice of mango fruits, the extract of the juice of the citron tree mixed with sugar, or anything that may be liked in different countries, and known to be sweet, soft, and pure. The lovers may also sit on the terrace of the palace or house, and enjoy the moonlight, and carry on an agreeable conversation. At this time, too, while the woman lies in his lap, with her face towards the moon, the citizen should show her the different planets, the morning star, the polar star, and the seven Rishis, or Great Bear.

This is the end of sexual union.

Congress is of the following kinds:

Loving congress

Congress of subsequent love

Congress of artificial love

Congress of transferred love

Congress like that of eunuchs

Deceitful congress

Congress of spontaneous love

– When a man and a woman, who have been in love with each other for some time, come together with great difficulty, or when one of the two returns from a journey, or is reconciled after having been separated on account of a quarrel, then congress is called the 'loving congress'. It is carried on according to the liking of the lovers, and as long as they choose.

– When two persons come together, while their love for each other is still in its infancy, their congress is called the 'congress of subsequent love'.

– When a man carries on the congress by exciting himself by means of the sixty-four ways, such as kissing, etc., etc., or when a man and a woman come together, though in reality they are both attached to different persons, their congress is then called 'congress of artificial love'. At this time all the ways and means mentioned in the *Kama Shastra* should be used.

– When a man, from the beginning to the end of the congress, though having connection with the woman, thinks all the time that he is enjoying another one whom he loves, it is called the 'congress of transferred love'.

– Congress between a man and a female water carrier, or a female servant of a caste lower than his own, lasting only until the desire is satisfied, is called 'congress like that of eunuchs'. Here external touches, kisses, and manipulation are not to be employed.

– The congress between a courtesan and a rustic, and that between citizens and the women of villages, and bordering countries, is called 'deceitful congress'.

– The congress that takes place between two persons who are attached to one another, and which is done according to their own liking is called 'spontaneous congress'.

Thus end the kinds of congress.

We shall now speak of love quarrels.

A woman who is very much in love with a man cannot bear to hear the name of her rival mentioned, or to have any conversation regarding her, or to be addressed by her name through mistake. If such takes place, a great quarrel arises, and the woman cries, becomes angry, tosses her hair about, strikes her lover, falls from her bed or seat, and, casting aside her garlands and ornaments, throws herself down on the ground.

At this time, the lover should attempt to reconcile her with conciliatory words, and should take her up carefully and place her on her bed. But she, not replying to his questions, and with increased anger, should bend down his head by pulling his hair, and having kicked him once, twice, or thrice on his arms, head, bosom or back, should then proceed to the door of the room. Dattaka says that she should then sit angrily near the door and shed tears, but should not go out, because she would be found fault with for going away. After a time, when she thinks that the conciliatory words and actions of her lover have reached their utmost, she should then embrace him, talking to him with harsh and reproachful words, but at the same time showing a loving desire for congress.

When the woman is in her own house, and has quarrelled with her lover, she should go to him and show how angry she is, and leave him. Afterwards the citizen having sent the Vita, the Vidushaka or the Pithamarda [*2] to pacify her, she should accompany them back to the house, and spend the night with her lover.

Thus end the love quarrels.

In conclusion:

A man, employing the sixty-four means mentioned by Babhravya, obtains his object, and enjoys the woman of the first quality. Though he may speak well on other subjects, if he does not know the sixty-four divisions, no great respect is paid to him in the assembly of the learned. A man, devoid of other knowledge, but well acquainted with the sixty-four divisions, becomes a leader in any society of men and women. What man will not respect the sixty-four arts [*3], considering they are respected by the learned, by the cunning, and by the courtesans. As the sixty-four arts are respected, are charming, and add to the talent of women, they are called by the Acharyas dear to women. A man skilled in the sixty-four arts is looked upon with love by his own wife, by the wives of others, and by courtesans.

footnotes

1   The fresh juice of the cocoa nut tree, the date tree, and other kinds of palm trees are drunk in India. It will keep fresh very long, but ferments rapidly, and is then distilled into liquor.

2   The characteristics of these three individuals have been given in Part I, Chapter IV, page 36.

3   A definition of the sixty-four arts is given in Part I, Chapter III, pages 27–32.

PART III

ABOUT THE ACQUISITION OF A WIFE

CHAPTER I

On Marriage

§ When a girl of the same caste, and a virgin, is married in accordance with the precepts of Holy Writ, the results of such a union are the acquisition of Dharma and Artha, offspring, affinity, increase of friends, and untarnished love. For this reason a man should fix his affections upon a girl who is of good family, whose parents are alive, and who is three years or more younger than himself. She should be born of a highly respectable family, possessed of wealth, well connected, and with many relations and friends. She should also be beautiful, of a good disposition, with lucky marks on her body, and with good hair, nails, teeth, ears, eyes and breasts, neither more nor less than they ought to be, and no one of them entirely wanting, and not troubled with a sickly body. The man should, of course, also possess these qualities himself. But at all events, says Ghotakamukha, a girl who has been already joined with others (i.e. no longer a maiden) should never be loved, for it would be reprochable to do such a thing.

Now in order to bring about a marriage with such a girl as described above, the parents and relations of the man should exert themselves, as also such friends on both sides as may be desired to assist in the matter. These friends should bring to the notice of the girl's parents, the faults, both present and future, of all the other men that may wish to marry her, and should at the same time extol even to exaggeration all the excellencies, ancestral, and paternal, of their friend, so as to endear him to them, and particularly to those that may be liked by the girl's mother. One of the friends should also disguise himself as an astrologer, and declare the future good fortune and wealth of his friend by showing the existence of all the lucky omens [*1] and signs [*2], the good influence of planets, the auspicious entrance of the sun into a sign of the Zodiac, propitious stars and fortunate marks on his body. Others again should rouse the jealousy of the girl's mother by telling her that their friend has a chance of getting from some other quarter even a better girl than hers.

A girl should be taken as a wife, as also given in marriage, when fortune, signs, omens, and the words [*3] of others are favourable, for, says Ghotakamukha, a man should not marry at any time he likes. A girl who is asleep, crying, or gone out of the house when sought in marriage, or who is betrothed to another, should not be married.

The following also should be avoided:

* One who is kept concealed
* One who has an ill-sounding name
* One who has her nose depressed
* One who has her nostril turned up
* One who is formed like a male
* One who is bent down
* One who has crooked thighs
* One who has a projecting forehead
* One who has a bald head

* One who does not like purity
* One who has been polluted by another
* One who is affected with the Gulma [*4]
* One who is disfigured in any way
* One who has fully arrived at puberty
* One who is a friend
* One who is a younger sister
* One who is a Varshakari [*5]

In the same way a girl who is called by the name of one of the twenty-seven stars, or by the name of a tree, or of a river, is considered worthless, as also a girl whose name ends in 'r' or 'l'. But some authors say that prosperity is gained only by marrying that girl to whom one becomes attached, and that therefore no other girl but the one who is loved should be married by anyone.

When a girl becomes marriageable her parents should dress her smartly, and should place her where she can be easily seen by all. Every afternoon, having dressed her and decorated her in a becoming manner, they should send her with her female companions to sports, sacrifices, and marriage ceremonies, and thus show her to advantage in society, because she is a kind of merchandise. They should also receive with kind words and signs of friendliness those of an auspicious appearance who may come accompanied by their friends and relations for the purpose of marrying their daughter, and under some pretext or other having first dressed her becomingly, should then present her to them. After this they should await the pleasure of fortune, and with this object should appoint a future day on which a determination could be come to with regard to their daughter's marriage. On this occasion when the persons have come, the parents of the girl should ask them to bathe and dine, and should say, 'Everything will take place at the proper time', and should not then comply with the request, but should settle the matter later.

When a girl is thus acquired, either according to the custom of the country, or according to his own desire, the man should marry her in accordance with the precepts of the Holy Writ, according to one of the four kinds of marriage.

Thus ends marriage.

There are also some verses on the subject as follows:

Amusement in society, such as completing verses begun by others, marriages, and auspicious ceremonies should be carried on neither with superiors, nor inferiors, but with our equals. That should be known as a high connection when a man, after marrying a girl, has to serve her and her relations afterwards like a servant, and such a connection is censured by the good. On the other hand, that reproachable connection, where a man, together with his relations, lords it over his wife, is called a low connection by the wise. But when both the man and the woman afford mutual pleasure to each other, and when the relatives on both sides pay respect to one another, such is called a connection in the proper sense of the word. Therefore a man should contract neither a high connection by which he is obliged to bow down afterwards to his kinsmen, nor a low connection, which is universally reprehended by all.

footnotes

1   The flight of a blue jay on a person's left side is considered a lucky omen when one starts on any business; the appearance of a cat before anyone at such a time is looked on as a bad omen. There are many omens of the same kind.

2   Such as the throbbing of the right eye of men and the left eye of women, etc.

3   Before anything is begun it is a custom to go early in the morning to a neighbour's house, and overhear the first words that may be spoken in his family, and according as the words heard are of good or bad import, to draw an inference as to the success or failure of the undertaking.

4   A disease consisting of any glandular enlargement in any part of the body.

5   A woman, the palms of whose hands and the soles of whose feet are always perspiring.

CHAPTER II

Of Creating Confidence in the Girl

§ For the first three days after marriage, the girl and her husband should sleep on the floor, abstain from sexual pleasures, and eat their food without seasoning it either with alkali or salt. For the next seven days they should bathe amidst tire sounds of auspicious musical instruments, should decorate themselves, dine together, and pay attention to their relations as well as to those who may have come to witness their marriage. This is applicable to persons of all castes. On the night of the tenth day the man should begin in a lonely place with soft words, and thus create confidence in the girl.

Some authors say that for the purpose of winning her over he should not speak to her for three days, but the followers of Babhravya are of opinion that if the man does not speak with her for three days, the girl may be discouraged by seeing him spiritless like a pillar, and, becoming dejected, she may begin to despise him as a eunuch. Vatsyayana says that the man should begin to win her over, and to create confidence in her, but should abstain at first from sexual pleasures. Women, being of a tender nature, want tender beginnings, and when they are forcibly approached by men with whom they are but slightly acquainted, they sometimes suddenly become haters of sexual connection, and sometimes even haters of the male sex. The man should therefore approach the girl according to her liking, and should make use of those devices by which he may be able to establish himself more and more into her confidence.

These devices are as follows:

He should embrace her first of all in a way she likes most, because it does not last for a long time.

He should embrace her with the upper part of his body because that is easier and simpler. If the girl is grown up, or if the man has known her for some time, he may embrace her by the light of a lamp, but if he is not well acquainted with her, or if she is a young girl, he should then embrace her in darkness.

— 117 —

When the girl accepts the embrace, the man should put a tambula or screw of betel nut and betel leaves in her mouth, and if she will not take it, he should induce her to do so by conciliatory words, entreaties, oaths, and kneeling at her feet, for it is a universal rule that however bashful or angry a woman may be she never disregards a man's kneeling at her feet. At the time of giving this tambula he should kiss her mouth softly and gracefully without making any sound. When she is gained over in this respect he should then make her talk, and so that she may be induced to talk he should ask her questions about things of which he knows or pretends to know nothing, and which can be answered in a few words. If she does not speak to him, he should not frighten her, but should ask her the same thing again and again in a conciliatory manner. If she does not then speak he should urge her to give a reply because, as Ghotakamukha says, 'all girls hear everything said to them by men, but do not themselves sometimes say a single word'. When she is thus importuned, the girl should give replies by shakes of the head, but if she has quarrelled with the man she should not even do that. When she is asked by the man whether she wishes for him, and whether she likes him, she should remain silent for a long time, and when at last importuned to reply, should give him a favourable answer by a nod of her head. If the man is previously acquainted with the girl he should converse with her by means of a female friend, who may be favourable to him, and in the confidence of both, and carry on the conversation on both sides. On such an occasion the girl should smile with her head bent down, and if the female friend say more on her part than she was desired to do, she should chide her and dispute with her. The female friend should say in jest even what she is not desired to say by the girl, and add, 'she says so', on which the girl should say indistinctly and prettily, 'O no! I did not say so', and she should then smile and throw an occasional glance towards the man.

If the girl is familiar with the man, she should place near him, without saying anything, the tambula, the ointment, or the garland that he may have asked for, or she may tie them up in his upper garment. While she is engaged in this, the man should touch her young breasts in the sounding way of pressing with the nails, and if she prevents him doing this he should say to her, 'I will not do it again if you will embrace me', and should in this way cause her to embrace him. While he is being embraced by her he should pass his hand repeatedly over and about her body. By and by he should place her in his lap, and try more and more to gain her consent, and if she will not yield to him he should frighten her by saying 'I shall impress marks of my teeth and nails on your lips and breasts, and then make similar marks on my own body, and shall tell my friends that you did them. What will you say then?' In this and other ways, as fear and confidence are created in the minds of children, so should the man gain her over to his wishes.

On the second and third nights, after her confidence has increased still more, he should feel the whole of her body with his hands, and kiss her all over; he should also place his hands upon her thighs and shampoo them, and if he succeed in this he should then shampoo the joints of her thighs. If she tries to prevent him doing this he should say to her, 'What harm is there in doing it?' and should persuade her to let him do it. After gaining this point he should touch her private parts, should loosen her girdle and the knot of her dress, and turning up her lower garment should shampoo the joints of her naked thighs. Under various pretences he should do all these things, but he should not at that time begin actual congress. After this he should teach her the sixty-four arts, should tell her how much he loves her, and describe to her the hopes which he formerly entertained regarding her. He should also promise to be faithful to her in future, and should dispel all her fears with respect to rival women, and, at last, after having overcome her bashfulness, he should begin to enjoy her in a way so as not to frighten her. So much about creating confidence in the girl; and there are, moreover, some verses on the subject as follows:

A man acting according to the inclinations of a girl should try to gain her over so that she may love him and place her confidence in him. A man does not succeed either by implicitly following the inclination of a girl, or by wholly opposing her, and he should therefore adopt a middle course. He who knows how to make himself beloved by women, as well as to increase their honour and create confidence in them, this man becomes an object of their love. But he who neglects a girl, thinking she is too bashful, is despised by her as a beast ignorant of the working of the female mind. Moreover, a girl forcibly enjoyed by one who does not understand the hearts of girls becomes nervous, uneasy, and dejected, and suddenly begins to hate the man who has taken advantage of her; and then, when her love is not understood or returned, she sinks into despondency, and becomes either a hater of mankind altogether, or, hating her own man, she has recourse to other men [*1].

footnote

1   These last few lines were exemplified in many ways in many novels of the nineteenth century.

CHAPTER III

On Courtship, & the Manifestation of the Feelings by Outward Signs & Deeds

§ A poor man possessed of good qualities, a man born of a low family possessed of mediocre qualities, a neighbour possessed of wealth, and one under the control of his father, mother or brothers, should not marry without endeavouring to gain over the girl from her childhood to love and esteem him. Thus a boy separated from his parents, and living in the house of his uncle, should try to gain over the daughter of his uncle, or some other girl, even though she be previously betrothed to another. And this way of gaining over a girl, says Ghotakamukha, is unexceptional, because Dharma can be accomplished by means of it as well as by any other way of marriage.

When a boy has thus begun to woo the girl he loves, he should spend his time with her and amuse her with various games and diversions fitted for their age and acquaintanceship, such as picking and collecting flowers, making garlands of flowers, playing the parts of members of a fictitious family, cooking food, playing with dice, playing with cards, the game of odd and even, the game of finding out the middle finger, the game of six pebbles, and such other games as may be prevalent in the country, and agreeable to the disposition of the girl. In addition to this, he should carry on various amusing games played by several persons together, such as hide and seek, playing with seeds, hiding things in several small heaps of wheat and looking for them, blindman's buff, gymnastic exercises, and other games of the same sort, in company with the girl, her friends and female attendants. The man should also show great kindness to any woman whom the girl thinks fit to be trusted, and should also make new acquaintances, but above all he should attach to himself by kindness and little services the daughter of the girl's nurse, for if she be gained over, even though she comes to know of his design, she does not cause any obstruction, but is sometimes even able to effect a union between him and the girl. And though she knows the true character of the man, she always talks of his many excellent qualities to the parents and relations of the girl, even though she may not be desired to do so by him.

In this way the man should do whatever the girl takes most delight in, and he should get for her whatever she may have a desire to possess. Thus he should procure for her such playthings as may be hardly known to other girls. He may also show her a ball dyed with various colours, and other curiosities of the same sort; and should give her dolls made of cloth, wood, buffalo-horn, wax, flour, or earth; also utensils for cooking food, and figures in wood, such as a man and woman standing, a pair of rams, or goats, or sheep; also temples made of earth, bamboo, or wood, dedicated to various goddesses; and cages for parrots, cuckoos, starlings, quails, cocks, and partridges; water-vessels of different sorts and of elegant forms, machines for throwing water about, guitars, stands for putting images upon, stools, lac, red arsenic, yellow ointment, vermilion and collyrium, as well as sandalwood, saffron, betel nut and betel leaves. Such things should be given at different times whenever he gets a good opportunity of meeting her, and some of them should be given in private, and some in public, according to circumstances. In short, he should try in every way to make her look upon him as one who would do for her everything that she wanted to be done.

In the next place he should get her to meet him in some place privately, and should then tell her that the reason of his giving presents to her in secret was the fear that the parents of both of them might be displeased, and then he may add that the things which he had given her had been much desired by other people. When her love begins to show signs of increasing he should relate to her agreeable stories if she expresses a wish to hear such narratives. Or if she takes delight in legerdemain, he should amaze her by performing various tricks of jugglery; or if she feels a great curiosity to see a performance of the various arts, he should show his own skill in them. When she is delighted with singing he should entertain her with music, and on certain days, and at the time of going together to moonlight fairs and festivals, and at the time of her return after being absent from home, he should present her with bouquets of flowers, and with chaplets for the head, and with ear ornaments and rings, for these are the proper occasions on which such things should be presented.

He should also teach the daughter of the girl's nurse all the sixty-four means of pleasure practised by men, and under this pretext should also inform her of his great skill in the art of sexual enjoyment. All this time he should wear a fine dress, and make as good an appearance as possible, for young women love men who live with them, and who are handsome, good looking and well dressed. As for the sayings that though women may fall in love, they still make no effort themselves to gain over the object of their affections, that is only a matter of idle talk.

Now a girl always shows her love by outward signs and actions, such as the following:

She never looks the man in the face, and becomes abashed when she is looked at by him; under some pretext or other she shows her limbs to him; she looks secretly at him though he has gone away from her side, hangs down her head when she is asked some question by him, and answers in indistinct words and unfinished sentences, delights to be in his company for a long time, speaks to her attendants in a peculiar tone with the hope of attracting his attention towards her when she is at a distance from him, does not wish to go from the place where he is, under some pretext or other she makes him look at different things, narrates to him tales and stories very slowly so that she may continue conversing with him for a long time, kisses and embraces before him a child sitting in her lap, draws ornamental marks on the foreheads of her female servants, performs sportive and graceful movements when her attendants speak jestingly to her in the presence of her lover, confides in her lover's friends, and respects and obeys them, shows kindness to his servants, converses with them, and engages them to do her work as if she were their mistress, and listens attentively to them when they tell stories about her lover to somebody else, enters his house when induced to do so by the daughter of her nurse, and by her assistance manages to converse and play with him, avoids being seen by her lover when she is not dressed and decorated, gives him by the hand of her female friend her ear ornament, ring, or garland of flowers that he may have asked to see, always wears anything that he may have presented to her, becomes dejected when any other bridegroom is mentioned by her parents, and does not mix with, those who may be of his party, or who may support his claims.

There are also some verses on the subject as follows:

A man, who has seen and perceived the feelings of the girl towards him, and who has noticed the outward signs and movements by which those feelings are expressed, should do everything in his power to effect a union with her. He should gain over a young girl by childlike sports, a damsel come of age by his skill in the arts, and a girl that loves him by having recourse to persons in whom she confides.

About Things to Be Done Only by the Man, & the Acquisition of the Girl Thereby. Also What Is to Be Done by a Girl to Gain Over a Man, & Subject Him to Her

§ Now when the girl begins to show her love by outward signs and motions, as described in the last chapter, the lover should try to gain her over entirely by various ways and means, such as the following:

When engaged with her in any game or sport he should intentionally hold her hand. He should practise upon her the various kinds of embraces, such as the touching embrace, and others already described in a preceding chapter (Part II, Chapter II). He should show her a pair of human beings cut out of the leaf of a tree, and such like things, at intervals. When engaged in water sports, he should dive at a distance from her, and come tip close to her. He should show an increased liking for the new foliage of trees and such like things. He should describe to her the pangs he suffers on her account. He should relate to her the beautiful dream that he has had with reference to other women. At parties and assemblies of his caste he should sit near her, and touch her under some pretence or other, and having placed his foot upon hers, he should slowly touch each of her toes, and press the ends of the nails; if successful in this, he should get hold of her foot with his hand and repeat the same thing. He should also press a finger of her hand between his toes when she happens to be washing his feet; and whenever he gives anything to her or takes anything from her, he should show her by his manner and look how much he loves her.

He should sprinkle upon her the water brought for rinsing his mouth; and when alone with her in a lonely place, or in darkness, he should make love to her, and tell her the true state of his mind without distressing her in any way.

Whenever he sits with her on the same seat or bed he should say to her, 'I have something to tell you in private', and then, when she comes to hear it in a quiet place, he should express his love to her more by manner and signs than by words. When he comes to know the state of her feelings towards him he should pretend to be ill, and should make her come to his house to speak to him. There he should intentionally hold her hand and place it on his eyes and forehead, and under the pretence of preparing some medicine for him he should ask her to do the work for his sake in the following words: 'This work must be done by you, and by nobody else.' When she wants to go away he should let her go, with an earnest request to come and see him again. This device of illness should be continued for three days and three nights. After this, when she begins coming to see him frequently, he should carry on long conversations with her, for, says Ghotakamukha, 'though a man loves a girl ever so much, he never succeeds in winning her without a great deal of talking'. At last, when the man finds the girl completely gained over, he may then begin to enjoy her. As for the saying that women grow less timid than usual during the evening, and in darkness, and are desirous of congress at those times, and do not oppose men then, and should only be enjoyed at these hours, it is a matter of talk only.

When it is impossible for the man to carry on his endeavours alone, he should, by means of the daughter of her nurse, or of a female friend in whom she confides, cause the girl to be brought to him without making known to her his design, and he should then proceed with her in the manner above described. Or he should in the beginning send his own female servant to live with the girl as her friend, and should then gain her over by her means.

At last, when he knows the state of her feelings by her outward manner and conduct towards him at religious ceremonies, marriage ceremonies, fairs, festivals, theatres, public assemblies, and such like occasions, he should begin to enjoy her when she is alone, for Vatsyayana lays it down, that women, when resorted to at proper times and in proper places, do not turn away from their lovers.

When a girl, possessed of good qualities and well-bred, though born in a humble family, or destitute of wealth, and not therefore desired by her equals, or an orphan girl, or one deprived of her parents, but observing the rules of her family and caste, should wish to bring about her own marriage when she comes of age, such a girl should endeavour to gain over a strong and good looking young man, or a person whom she thinks would marry her on account of the weakness of his mind, and even without the consent of his parents. She should do this by such means as would endear her to the said person, as well as by

frequently seeing and meeting him. Her mother also should constantly cause them to meet by means of her female friends, and the daughter of her nurse. The girl herself should try to get alone with her beloved in some quiet place, and at odd times should give him flowers, betel nut, betel leaves and perfumes. She should also show her skill in the practice of the arts, in shampooing, in scratching and in pressing with the nails. She should also talk to him on the subjects he likes best, and discuss with him the ways and means of gaining over and winning the affections of a girl.

But old authors say that although the girl loves the man ever so much, she should not offer herself, or make the first overtures, for a girl who does this loses her dignity, and is liable to be scorned and rejected. But when the man shows his wish to enjoy her, she should be favourable to him and should show no change in her demeanour when he embraces her, and should receive all the manifestations of his love as if she were ignorant of the state of his mind. But when he tries to kiss her she should oppose him; when he begs to be allowed to have sexual intercourse with her she should let him touch her private parts only and with considerable difficulty; and though importuned by him, she should not yield herself up to him as if of her own accord, but should resist his attempts to have her. It is only, moreover, when she is certain that she is truly loved, and that her lover is indeed devoted to her, and will not change his mind, that she should then give herself up to him, and persuade him to marry her quickly. After losing her virginity she should tell her confidential friends about it.

Here end the efforts of a girl to gain over a man.

There are also some verses on the subject as follows:

A girl who is much sought after should marry the man that she likes, and whom she thinks would be obedient to her, and capable of giving her pleasure. But when from the desire of wealth a girl is married by her parents to a rich man without taking into consideration the character or looks of the bridegroom, or when given to a man who has several wives, she never becomes attached to the man, even though he be endowed with good qualities, obedient to her will, active, strong, and healthy, and anxious to please her in every way [*1].
A husband who is obedient but yet master of himself, though he be poor and not good looking, is better than one who is common to many women, even though he be handsome and attractive.

The wives of rich men, where there are many wives, are not generally attached to their husbands, and are not confidential with them, and even though they possess all the external enjoyments of life, still have recourse to other men. A man who is of a low mind, who has fallen from his social position, and who is much given to travelling, does not deserve to be married; neither does one who has many wives and children, or one who is devoted to sport and gambling, and who comes to his wife only when he likes. Of all the lovers of a girl he only is her true husband who possesses the qualities that are liked by her, and such a husband only enjoys real superiority over her, because he is the husband of love.

footnote

1   There is a good deal of truth in the last few observations. Woman is a monogamous animal, and loves but one, and likes to feel herself alone in the affections of one man, and cannot bear rivals. It may also be taken as a general rule that women either married to, or kept by, rich men love them for their wealth but not for themselves.

CHAPTER V

On Certain Forms of Marriage [*1]

§ When a girl cannot meet her lover frequently in private, she should send the daughter of her nurse to him, it being understood that she has confidence in her, and had previously gained her over to her interests. On seeing the man, the daughter of the nurse should, in the course of conversation, describe to him the noble birth, the good disposition, the beauty, talent, skill, knowledge of human nature and affection of the girl in such a way as not to let him suppose that she had been sent by the girl, and should thus create affection for the girl in the heart of the man. To the girl also she should speak about the excellent qualities of the man, especially of those qualities which she knows are pleasing to the girl. She should, moreover, speak with disparagement of the other lovers of the girl, and talk about the avarice and indiscretion of their parents, and the fickleness of their relations. She should also quote samples of many girls of ancient times, such as Sakoontala and others, who, having united themselves with lovers of their own caste and their own choice, were ever happy afterwards in their society. And she should also tell of other girls who married into great families, and being troubled by rival wives, became wretched and miserable, and were finally abandoned. She should further speak of the good fortune, the continual happiness, the chastity, obedience, and affection of the man, and if the girl gets amorous about him, she should endeavour to allay her shame [*2] and her fear as well as her suspicions about any disaster that might result from her marriage. In a word, she should act the whole part of a female messenger by telling the girl all about the man's affection for her, the places he frequented, and the endeavours he made to meet her, and by frequently repeating, 'It will be all right if the man will take you away forcibly and unexpectedly.'

The Forms of Marriage

When the girl is gained over, and acts openly with the man as his wife, he should cause fire to be brought from the house of a Brahman, and having spread the Kusha grass upon the ground, and offered an oblation to the fire, he should marry her according to the precepts of the religious law. After this he should inform his parents of the fact, because it is the opinion of ancient authors that a marriage solemnly contracted in the presence of fire cannot afterwards be set aside.

After the consummation of the marriage, the relations of the man should gradually be made acquainted with the affair, and the relations of the girl should also be apprised of it in such a way that they may consent to the marriage, and overlook the manner in which it was brought about, and when this is done they should afterwards be reconciled by affectionate presents and favourable conduct. In this manner the man should marry the girl according to the Gandharva form of marriage.

When the girl cannot make up her mind, or will not express her readiness to marry, the man should obtain her in any one of the following ways:

✳ *On a fitting occasion, and under some excuse, he should, by means of a female friend with whom he is well acquainted, and whom he can trust, and who also is well known to the girl's family, get the girl brought unexpectedly to his house, and he should then bring fire from the house of a Brahman, and proceed as before described.*

✳ *When the marriage of the girl with some other person draws near, the man should disparage the future husband to the utmost in the mind of the mother of the girl, and then having got the girl to come with her mother's consent to a neighbouring house, he should bring fire from the house of a Brahman, and proceed as above.*

✳ *The man should become a great friend of the brother of the girl, the said brother being of the same age as himself, and addicted to courtesans, and to intrigues with the wives of other people, and should give him assistance in such matters, and also give him occasional presents.*

He should then tell him about his great love for his sister, as young men will sacrifice even their lives for the sake of those who may be of the same age, habits, and dispositions as themselves. After this the man should get the girl brought by means of her brother to some secure place, and having brought fire from the house of a Brahman should proceed as before.

✳ *The man should on the occasion of festivals get the daughter of the nurse to give the girl some intoxicating substance, and then cause her to be brought to some secure place under the pretence of some business, and there having enjoyed her before she recovers from her intoxication, should bring fire from the house of a Brahman, and proceed as before.*

✳ *The man should, with the connivance of the daughter of the nurse, carry off the girl from her house while she is asleep, and then, having enjoyed her before she recovers from her sleep, should bring fire from the house of a Brahman, and proceed as before.*

✳ *When the girl goes to a garden, or to some village in the neighbourhood, the man should, with his friends, fall on her guards, and having killed them, or frightened them away, forcibly carry her off, and proceed as before.*

There are verses on this subject as follows:

In all the forms of marriage given in this chapter of this work, the one that precedes is better than the one that follows it on account of its being more in accordance with the commands of religion, and therefore it is only when it is impossible to carry the former into practice that the latter should be resorted to, As the fruit of all good marriages is love, the Gandharva [*3] form of marriage is respected, even though it is formed under unfavourable circumstances, because it fulfils the object sought for. Another cause of the respect accorded to the Gandharva form of marriage is that it brings forth happiness, causes less trouble in its performance than the other forms of marriage, and is above all the result of previous love.

footnotes

1   These forms of marriage differ from the four kinds of marriage mentioned in Chapter I, and are only to be made use of when the girl is gained over in the way mentioned in Chapters III and IV.

2   About this, see a story on the fatal effects of love in *Early Ideas: a Group of Hindoo Stories*, collected and collated by Anaryan, W. H. Allen and Co., London, 1881.

3   About the Gandharvavivaha form of marriage, see note to page 28 of Captain R. F. Burton's *Vickram and the Vampire or Tales of Hindu Devilry*, Longmans, Green and Co., London 1870. This form of matrimony was recognised by the ancient Hindoos, and is frequent in books. It is a kind of Scotch wedding – ultra-Caledonian – taking place by mutual consent without any form or Ceremony. The Gandharvas are heavenly minstrels of Indra's court, who are opposed to be witnesses.

PART IV

ABOUT A WIFE

On the Manner of Living of a Virtuous Woman, & of Her Behaviour During the Absence of Her Husband

§ A virtuous woman, who has affection for her husband, should act in conformity with his wishes as if he were a divine being, and with his consent should take upon herself the whole care of his family. She should keep the whole house well cleaned, and arrange flowers of various kinds in different parts of it, and make the floor smooth and polished so as to give the whole a neat and becoming appearance. She should surround the house with a garden, and place ready in it all the materials required for the morning, noon and evening sacrifices. Moreover she should herself revere the sanctuary of the Household Gods, for, says Gonardiya, 'nothing so much attracts the heart of a householder to his wife as a careful observance of the things mentioned above'.

Towards the parents, relations, friends, sisters, and servants of her husband she should behave as they deserve. In the garden she should plant beds of green vegetables, bunches of the sugar cane, and clumps of the fig tree, the mustard plant, the parsley plant, the fennel plant, and the *Xanthochymus pictorius.* Clusters of various flowers such as the *Trapa bispinosa*, the jasmine, the *Jasminum grandiflorum,* the yellow amaranth, the wild jasmine, the *Tabernamontana coronaria*, the nadyaworta, the china rose and others, should likewise be planted, together with the fragrant grass *Andropogon schaenanthus,* and the fragrant root of the plant *Andropogon miricatus.* She should also have seats and arbours made in the garden, in the middle of which a well, tank, or pool should be dug.

The wife should always avoid the company of female beggars, female Buddhist mendicants, unchaste and roguish women, female fortune tellers and witches. As regards meals she should always consider what her husband likes and dislikes and what things are good for him, and what are injurious to him. When she hears the sounds of his footsteps coming home she should at once get up and be ready to do whatever he may command her, and either order her female servant to wash his feet, or wash them herself. When going anywhere with her husband, she should put on her ornaments, and without his consent she should not either give or accept invitations, or attend marriages and sacrifices, or sit in the company of female friends, or visit the temples of the Gods. And if she wants to engage in any kind of games or sports, she should not do it against his will. In the same way she should always sit down after him, and get up before him, and should never awaken him when he is asleep. The kitchen should be situated in a quiet and retired place, so as not to be accessible to strangers, and should always look clean.

A VIRTUOUS WOMAN, WHO HAS AFFECTION FOR HER HUSBAND, SHOULD ACT IN CONFORMITY WITH HIS WISHES AS IF HE WERE A DIVINE BEING, AND WITH HIS CONSENT SHOULD TAKE UPON HERSELF THE WHOLE CARE OF HIS FAMILY.

In the event of any misconduct on the part of her husband, she should not blame him excessively, though she be a little displeased. She should not use abusive language towards him, but rebuke him with conciliatory words, whether he be in the company of friends or alone. Moreover, she should not be a scold, for, says Gonardiya, 'there is no cause of dislike on the part of a husband so great as this characteristic in a wife'. Lastly she should avoid bad expressions, sulky looks, speaking aside, standing in the doorway, and looking at passers-by, conversing in the pleasure groves, and remaining in a lonely place for a long time; and finally she should always keep her body, her teeth, her hair and everything belonging to her tidy, sweet, and clean.

When the wife wants to approach her husband in private her dress should consist of many ornaments, various kinds of flowers, and a cloth decorated with different colours, and some sweet-smelling ointments or unguents. But her everyday dress should be composed of a thin, close-textured cloth, a few ornaments and flowers, and a little scent, not too much. She should also observe the fasts and vows of her husband, and when he tries to prevent her doing this, she should persuade him to let her do it.

At appropriate times of the year, and when they happen to be cheap, she should buy earth, bamboos, firewood, skins, and iron pots, as also salt and oil. Fragrant substances, vessels made of the fruit of the plant *Wrightea antidysenterica*, or oval leaved wrightea, medicines, and other things which are always wanted, should be obtained when required and kept in a secret place of the house. The seeds of the radish, the potato, the common beet, the Indian wormwood, the mango, the cucumber, the egg plant, the kushmanda, the pumpkin gourd, the surana, the *Bignonia indica*, the sandal wood, the *Premna spinosa*, the garlic plant, the onion, and other vegetables, should be bought and sown at the proper seasons. The wife, moreover, should not tell to strangers the amount of her wealth, nor the secrets which her husband has confided to her. She should surpass all the women of her own rank in life in her cleverness, her appearance, her knowledge of cookery, her pride, and her manner of serving her husband. The expenditure of the year should be regulated by the profits. The milk that remains after the meals should be turned into ghee or clarified butter. Oil and sugar should be prepared at home; spinning and weaving should also be done there; and a store of ropes and cords, and barks of trees for twisting into ropes should be kept. She should also attend to the pounding and cleaning of rice, using its small grain and chaff in some way or other. She should pay the salaries of the servants, look after the tilling of the fields, and keeping of the flocks and herds, superintend the making of vehicles, and take care of the rams, cocks, quails, parrots, starlings, cuckoos, peacocks, monkeys, and deer; and finally adjust the income and expenditure of the day. The worn-out clothes should be given to those servants who have done good work, in order to show them that their services have been appreciated, or they may be applied to some other use. The vessels in which wine is prepared, as well as those in which it is kept, should be carefully looked after, and put away at the proper time. All sales and purchases should also be well attended to. The friends of her husband she should welcome by presenting them with flowers, ointment, incense, betel leaves, and betel nut. Her father-in-law and mother-in-law she should treat as they deserve, always remaining dependent on their will, never contradicting them, speaking to them in few and not harsh words, not laughing loudly in their presence, and acting with their friends and enemies as with her own. In addition to the above she should not be vain, or too much taken up with her enjoyments. She should be liberal towards her servants, and reward them on holidays and festivals; and not give away anything without first making it known to her husband.

Thus ends the manner of living of a virtuous woman.

During the absence of her husband on a journey the virtuous woman should wear only her auspicious ornaments, and observe the fasts in honour of the Gods. While anxious to hear the news of her husband, she should still look after her household affairs. She should sleep near the elder women of the house, and make herself agreeable to them. She should look after and keep in repair the things that are liked by her husband, and continue the works that have been begun by him. To the abode of her relations she should not go except on occasions of joy and sorrow, and then she should go in her usual travelling dress, accompanied by her husband's servants, and not remain there for a long time. The fasts and feasts should be observed with the consent of the elders of the house. The resources should be increased by making purchases and sales according to the practice of the merchants and by means of honest servants, superintended by herself. The income should be increased, and the expenditure diminished as much possible. And when her husband returns from his journey, she should receive him at first in her ordinary clothes, so that he may know in what way she has lived during his absence, and should bring to him some presents, as also materials for the worship of the Deity.

Thus ends the part relating to the behaviour of a wife during the absence of her husband on a journey.

There are also some verses on the subject as follows:

The wife, whether she be a woman of noble family, or a virgin widow [*1] remarried, or a concubine, should lead a chaste life, devoted to her husband, and doing everything for his welfare. Women acting thus acquire Dharma, Artha, and Kama, obtain a high position, and generally keep their husbands devoted to them.

footnote

1   This probably refers to a girl married in her infancy, or when very young and whose husband had died before she arrived at the age of puberty. Infant marriages were still the common custom of the Hindoos in the nineteenth century.

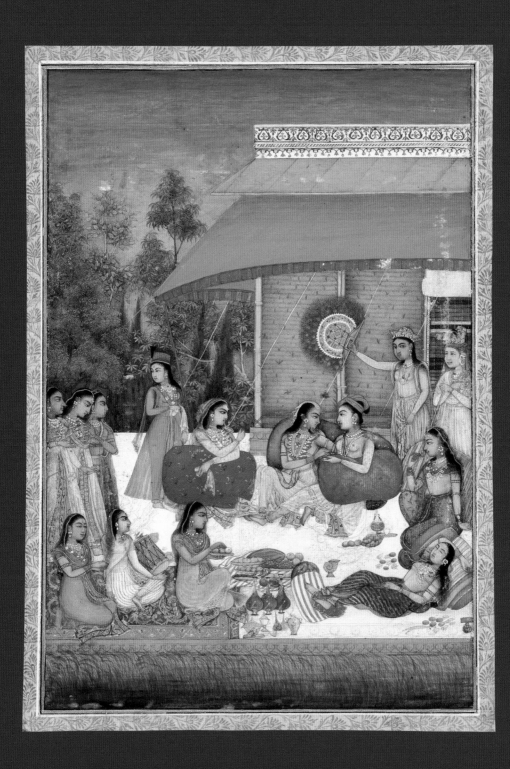

On the Conduct of the Elder Wife towards the Other Wives of Her Husband, & on That of a Younger Wife towards the Elder Ones. Also on the Conduct of a Virgin Widow Re-Married; Of a Wife Disliked by Her Husband; Of the Women in the King's Harem; & Lastly on the Conduct of a Husband towards Many Wives

§ The causes of re-marrying during the lifetime of the wife are as follows:

The folly or ill-temper of the wife

Her husband's dislike to her

The want of offspring

The continual birth of daughters

The incontinence of the husband

From the very beginning, a wife should endeavour to attract the heart of her husband, by showing to him continually her devotion, her good temper, and her wisdom. If however she bears him no children, she should herself toilette her husband to marry another woman. And when the second wife is married, and brought to the house, the first wife should give her a position superior to her own, and look upon her as a sister. In the morning the elder wife should forcibly make the younger one decorate herself in the presence of their husband, and should not mind all the husband's favour being given to her. If the younger wife does anything to displease her husband the elder one should not neglect her, but should always be ready to give her most careful advice, and should teach her to do various things in the presence of her husband. Her children she should treat as her own, her attendants she should look upon with more regard, even than on her own servants, her friends she should cherish with love and kindness, and her relations with great honour.

When there are many other wives besides herself, the elder wife should associate with the one who is immediately next to her in rank and age, and should instigate the wife who has recently enjoyed her husband's favour to quarrel with the present favourite. After this she should sympathize with the former, and having collected all the other wives together, should get them to denounce the favourite as a scheming and wicked woman, without however committing herself in any way. If the favourite wife happens to quarrel with the husband, then the elder wife should take her part and give her false encouragement, and thus cause the quarrel to be increased. If there be only a little quarrel between the two, the elder wife should do all she can to work it up into a large quarrel. But if after all this she finds the husband still continues to love his favourite wife she should then change her tactics, and endeavour to bring about a conciliation between them, so as to avoid her husband's displeasure.

Thus ends the conduct of the elder wife.

The younger wife should regard the elder wife of her husband as her mother, and should not give anything away, even to her own relations, without her knowledge. She should tell her everything about herself, and not approach her husband without her permission. Whatever is told to her by the elder wife she should not reveal to others, and she should take care of the children of the senior even more than of her own. When alone with her husband she should serve him well, but should not tell him of the pain she suffers from the existence of a rival wife. She may also obtain secretly from her husband some marks of his particular regard for her, and may tell him that she lives only for him, and for the regard that he has for her. She should never reveal her love for her husband, nor her husband's love for her to any person, either in pride or in anger, for a wife that reveals the secrets of her husband is despised by him. As for seeking to obtain the regard of her husband, Gonardiya says, that it should always be done in private, for fear of the elder wife.

If the elder wife be disliked by her husband, or be childless, she should sympathize with her, and should ask her husband to do the same, but should surpass her in leading the life of a chaste woman.

Thus ends the conduct of the younger wife towards the elder.

A widow in poor circumstances, or of a weak nature, and who allies herself again to a man, is called a widow remarried.

The followers of Babhravya say that a virgin widow should not marry a person whom she may be obliged to leave on account of his bad character, or of his being destitute of the excellent qualities of a man, she thus being obliged to have recourse to another person. Gonardiya is of opinion that as the cause of a widow's marrying again is her desire for happiness, and as happiness is secured by the possession of excellent qualities in her husband, joined to love of enjoyment, it is better therefore to secure a person endowed with such qualities in the first instance. Vatsyayana however thinks that a widow may marry any person that she likes, and that she thinks will suit her.

WHEN ALONE WITH HER HUSBAND SHE SHOULD SERVE HIM WELL, BUT SHOULD NOT TELL HIM OF THE PAIN SHE SUFFERS FROM THE EXISTENCE OF A RIVAL WIFE.

At the time of her marriage the widow should obtain from her husband the money to pay the cost of drinking parties, and picnics with her relations, and of giving them and her friends kindly gifts and presents; or she may do these things at her own cost if she likes. In the same way she may wear either her husband's ornaments or her own. As to the presents of affection mutually exchanged between the husband and herself there is no fixed rule about them. If she leaves her husband after marriage of her own accord, she should restore to him whatever he may have given her, with the exception of the mutual presents. If however she is driven out of the house by her husband she should not return anything to him.

After her marriage she should live in the house of her husband like one of the chief members of the family, but should treat the other ladies of the family with kindness, the servants with generosity, and all the friends of the house with familiarity and good temper. She should show that she is better acquainted with the sixty-four arts than the other ladies of the house, and in any quarrels with her husband she should not rebuke him severely but in private do everything that he wishes, and make use of the sixty-four ways of enjoyment. She should be obliging to the other wives of her husband, and to their children she should give presents, behave as their mistress, and make ornaments and playthings for their use. In the friends and servants of her husband she should confide more than in his other wives, and finally she should have a liking for drinking parties, going to picnics, attending fairs and festivals, and for carrying out all kinds of games and amusements.

Thus ends the conduct of a virgin widow remarried.

A woman who is disliked by her husband, and annoyed and distressed by his other wives, should associate with the wife who is liked most by her husband, and who serves him more than the others, and should teach her all the arts with which she is acquainted. She should act as the nurse to her husband's children, and having gained over his friends to her side, should through them make him acquainted of her devotion to him. In religious ceremonies she should be a leader, as also in vows and fasts, and should not hold too good an opinion of herself. When her husband is lying on his bed she should only go near him when it is agreeable to him, and should never rebuke him, or show obstinacy in any way. If her husband happens to quarrel with any of his other wives, she should reconcile them to each other, and if he desires to see any woman secretly, she should manage to bring about the meeting between them. She should moreover make herself acquainted with the weak points of her husband's character, but always keep them secret, and on the whole behave herself in such a way as may lead him to look upon her as a good and devoted wife.

Here ends the conduct of a wife disliked by her husband.

The above sections will show how all the women of the king's seraglio are to behave, and therefore we shall now speak separately only about the king.

The female attendants in the harem (called severally Kanchukiyas[*1], Mahallarikas[*2], and Mahallikas[*3]) should bring flowers, ointments and clothes from the king's wives to the king, and he having received these things should give them as presents to the servants, along with the things worn by him the previous day. In the afternoon the king, having dressed and put on his ornaments, should interview the women of the harem, who should also be dressed and decorated with jewels. Then having given to each of them such a place and such respect as may suit the occasion and as they may deserve, he should carry on with them a cheerful conversation. After that he should see such of his wives as may be virgin widows remarried, and after them the concubines and dancing girls. All of these should be visited in their own private rooms.

When the king rises from his noonday sleep, the woman whose duty it is to inform the king regarding the wife who is to spend the night with him should come to him accompanied by the female attendants of that wife whose turn may have arrived in the regular course, and of her who may have been accidentally passed over as her turn arrived, and of her who may have been unwell at the time of her turn. These attendants should place before the king the ointments and unguents sent by each of these wives, marked with the seal of her ring, and their names and their reasons for sending the ointments should be told to the king. After this the king accepts the ointment of one of them, who then is informed that her ointment has been accepted, and that her day has been settled [*4].

At festivals, singing parties and exhibitions, all the wives of the king should be treated with respect and served with drinks.

But the women of the harem should not be allowed to go out alone, neither should any women outside the harem be allowed to enter it except those whose character is well known. And lastly the work which the king's wives have to do should not be too fatiguing.

Thus ends the conduct of the king towards the women of the harem, and of their own conduct.

A man marrying many wives should act fairly towards them all. He should neither disregard nor pass over their faults, and should not reveal to one wife the love, passion, bodily blemishes and confidential reproaches of the other. No opportunity should be given to any one of them of speaking to him about their rivals, and if one of them should begin to speak ill of another, he should chide her and tell her that she has exactly the same blemishes in her character. One of them he should please by secret confidence, another by secret respect, and another by secret flattery, and he should please them all by going to gardens, by amusements, by presents, by honouring their relations, by telling them secrets, and lastly by loving unions. A young woman who is of a good temper, and who conducts herself according to the precepts of the Holy Writ, wins her husband's attachments, and obtains a superiority over her rivals.

Thus ends the conduct of a husband towards many wives.

footnotes

1   A name given to the maid servants of the zenana of the kings in ancient times, on account of their always keeping their breasts covered with a cloth called Kanchuki. It was customary in the olden time for the maid servants to cover their breasts with a cloth, while the queens kept their breasts uncovered. This custom is distinctly to be seen in the Ajunta cave paintings.

2   The meaning of this word is a superior woman, so it would seem that a Mahallarika must be a person in authority over the maid servants of the house.

3   This was also appertaining to the rank of women employed in the harem. In latter times this place was given to eunuchs.

4   As kings generally had many wives, it was usual for them to enjoy their wives by turns. But as it happened sometimes that some of them lost their turns owing to the king's absence, or to their being unwell, then in such cases the women whose turns had been passed over, and those whose turns had come, used to have a sort of lottery, and the ointments of all the claimants were sent to the king, who accepted the ointment of one of them, and thus settled the question.

PART V

ABOUT THE WIVES OF OTHER MEN

Of the Characteristics of Men & Women. The Reasons Why Women Reject the Addresses of Men. About Men Who Have Success with Women, & About Women Who Are Easily Gained Over

§ The wives of other people may be resorted to on the occasions already described in Part I, Chapter V, of this work, but the possibility of their acquisition, their fitness for cohabitation, the danger to oneself in uniting with them, and the future effect of these unions, should first of all be examined. A man may resort to the wife of another, for the purpose of saving his own life, when he perceives that his love for her proceeds from one degree of intensity to another. These degrees are ten in number, and are distinguished by the following marks:

Love of the eye

Attachment of the mind

Constant reflection

Destruction of sleep

Emaciation of the body

Turning away from objects of enjoyment

Removal of shame

Madness
....
Fainting
....
Death
....

Ancient authors say that a man should know the disposition, truthfulness, purity, and will of a young woman, as also the intensity, or weakness of her passions, from the form of her body, and from her characteristic marks and signs. But Vatsyayana is of opinion that the forms of bodies, and the characteristic marks or signs are but erring tests of character, and that women should be judged by their conduct, by the outward expression of their thoughts, and by the movements of their bodies.

Now as a general rule Gonikaputra says that a woman falls in love with every handsome man she sees, and so does every man at the sight of a beautiful woman, but frequently they do not take any further steps, owing to various considerations. In love the following circumstances are peculiar to the woman. She loves without regard to right or wrong[*1], and does not try to gain over a man simply for the attainment of some particular purpose. Moreover, when a man first makes up to her she naturally shrinks from him, even though she may be willing to unite herself with him. But when the attempts to gain her are repeated and renewed, she at last consents. But with a man, even though he may have begun to love, he conquers his feelings from a regard for morality and wisdom, and although his thoughts are often on the woman, he does not yield, even though an attempt be made to gain him over. He sometimes makes an attempt or effort to win the object of his affections, and having failed, he leaves her alone for the future. In the same way, when a woman is once gained, he often becomes indifferent about her. As for the saying that a man does not care for what is easily gained, and only desires a thing which cannot be obtained without difficulty, it is only a matter of talk.

The causes of a woman rejecting the addresses of a man are as follows:

* *Affection for her husband*

* *Desire of lawful progeny*

* *Want of opportunity*

* *Anger at being addressed by the man too familiarly*

* *Difference in rank of life*

* *Want of certainty on account of the man being devoted travelling*

* *Thinking that the man may be attached to some other person*

* *Fear of the man's not keeping his intentions secret*

- *Thinking that the man is too devoted to his friends, and has too great a regard for them*

- *The apprehension that he is not in earnest*

- *Bashfulness on account of his being an illustrious man*

- *Fear on account of his being powerful, or possessed of too impetuous passion, in the case of the deer woman*

- *Bashfulness on account of his being too clever*

- *The thought of having once lived with him on friendly terms only*

- *Contempt of his want of knowledge of the world*

- *Distrust of his low character*

- *Disgust at his want of perception of her love for him*

- *In the case of an elephant woman, the thought that he is a hare man, or a man of weak passion*

- *Compassion lest anything should befall him on account of his passion*

- *Despair at her own imperfections*

- *Fear of discovery*

- *Disillusion at seeing his grey hair or shabby appearance*

- *Fear that he may be employed by her husband to test her chastity*

- *The thought that he has too much regard for morality*

Whichever of the above causes a man may detect, he should endeavour to remove it from the very beginning. Thus, the bashfulness that may arise from his greatness or his ability, he should remove by showing his great love and affection for her. The difficulty of the want of opportunity, or of his inaccessibility, he should remove by showing her some easy way of access. The excessive respect entertained by the woman for him should be removed by making himself very familiar. The difficulties that arise from his being thought a low character he should remove by showing his valour and his wisdom; those that come from neglect by extra attention; and those that arise from fear by giving her proper encouragement.

The following are the men who generally obtain success with women:

- *Men well versed in the science of love*

- *Men skilled in telling stories*

- *Men acquainted with women from their childhood*

- *Men who have secured their confidence*

- *Men who send presents to them*

- *Men who talk well*

- *Men who do things that they like*

- *Men who have not loved other women previously*

- Men who act as messengers

- Men who know their weak points

- Men who are desired by good women

- Men who are united with their female friends

- Men who are good looking

- Men who have been brought up with them

- Men who are their neighbours

- Men who are devoted to sexual pleasures, even though these be with their own servants

- The lovers of the daughters of their nurse

- Men who have been lately married

- Men who like picnics and pleasure parties

- Men who are liberal

- Men who are celebrated for being very strong (bull men)

- Enterprising and brave men

- Men who surpass their husbands in learning and good looks, in good qualities, and in liberality

- Men whose dress and manner of living are magnificent

The following are the women who are easily gained over:

- Women who stand at the doors of their houses

- Women who are always looking out on the street

- Women who sit conversing in their neighbour's house

- A woman who is always staring at you

- A female messenger

- A woman who looks sideways at you

- A woman whose husband has taken another wife without any just cause

- A woman who hates her husband, or who is hated by him

- A woman who has nobody to look after her, or keep her in check

- A woman who has not had any children

- A woman whose family or caste is not well known

- A woman whose children are dead

- A woman who is very fond of society

- A woman who is apparently very affectionate with her husband

- The wife of an actor

- A widow

- A poor woman

- A woman fond of enjoyments

- The wife of a man with many younger brothers

- A vain woman

- A woman whose husband is inferior to her in rank or abilities
- A woman who is proud of her skill in the arts
- A woman disturbed in mind by the folly of her husband
- A woman who has been married in her infancy to a rich man, and not liking him when she grows up, desires a man possessing a disposition, talents, and wisdom suitable to her own tastes
- A woman who is slighted by her husband without any cause
- A woman who is not respected by other women of the same rank or beauty as herself
- A woman whose husband is devoted to travelling
- The wife of a jeweller
- A jealous woman
- A covetous woman
- An immoral woman
- A barren woman
- A lazy woman
- A cowardly woman
- A humpbacked woman
- A dwarfish woman
- A deformed woman
- A vulgar woman
- An ill-smelling woman
- A sick woman
- An old woman

There are also two verses on the subject as follows:

*Desire, which springs from nature,
and which is increased by art, and from which all danger is
taken away by wisdom, becomes firm and secure.*

*A clever man, depending on his own ability, and observing carefully
the ideas and thoughts of women, and removing the causes of their
turning away from men, is generally successful with them.*

footnote

1   *On peut tout attendre et tout supposer d'une femme amoureuse* – Balzac

CHAPTER II

About Making Acquaintance with the Woman, & of the Efforts to Gain Her Over

§ Ancient authors are of opinion that girls are not so easily seduced by employing female messengers as by the efforts of the man himself, but that the wives of others are more easily got at by the aid of female messengers than by the personal efforts of the man. But Vatsyayana lays it down that whenever it is possible a man should always act himself in these matters, and it is only when such is impracticable, or impossible, that female messengers should be employed. As for the saying that women who act and talk boldly and freely are to be won by the personal efforts of the man, and that women who do not possess those qualities are to be got at by female messengers, it is only a matter of talk.

Now when a man acts himself in the matter he should first of all make the acquaintance of the woman he loves in the following manner:

He should arrange to be seen by the woman either on a natural or special opportunity. A natural opportunity is when one of them goes to the house of the other, and a special opportunity is when they meet either at the house of a friend, or a caste-fellow, or a minister, or a physician, as also on the occasion of marriage ceremonies, sacrifices, festivals, funerals, and garden parties.

When they do meet, the man should be careful to look at her in such a way as to cause the state of his mind to be made known to her; he should pull about his moustache, make a sound with his nails, cause his own ornaments to tinkle, bite his lower lip, and make various other signs of that description. When she is looking at him he should speak to his friends about her and other women, and should show to her his liberality and his appreciation of enjoyments. When sitting by the side of a female friend he should yawn and twist his body, contract his eyebrows, speak very slowly as if he was weary, and listen to her indifferently.

A conversation having two meanings should also be carried on with a child or some other person, apparently having regard to a third person, but really having reference to the woman he loves, and in this way his love should be made manifest under the pretext of referring to others rather than to herself. He should make marks that have reference to her, on the earth with his nails, or with a stick, and should embrace and kiss a child in her presence, and give it the mixture of betel nut and betel leaves with his tongue, and press its chin with his fingers in a caressing way. All these things should be done at the proper time and in proper places.

The man should fondle a child that may be sitting on her lap, and give it something to play with, and also take the same back again. Conversation with respect to the child may also be held with her, and in this manner he should gradually become well acquainted with her, and he should also make himself agreeable to her relations. Afterwards, this acquaintance should be made a pretext for visiting her house frequently, and on such occasions he should converse on the subject of love in her absence but within her hearing. As his intimacy with her increases he should place in her charge some kind of deposit or trust, and take away from it a small portion at a time; or he may give her some fragrant substances, or betel nuts to be kept for him by her. After this he should endeavour to make her well acquainted with his own wife, and get them to carry on confidential conversations, and to sit together in lonely places. In order to see her frequently he should arrange so that the same goldsmith, the same jeweller, the same basket maker, the same dyer, and the same washerman should be employed by the two families. And he should also pay her long visits openly under the pretence of being engaged with her on business, and one business should lead to another, so as to keep up the intercourse between them. Whenever she wants anything, or is in need of money, or wishes to acquire skill in one of the arts, he should cause her to understand that he is willing and able to do anything that she wants, to give her money, or teach her one of the arts, all these things being quite within his ability and power. In the same way he should hold discussions with her in company with other people, and they should talk of the doings and sayings of other persons, and examine different things, like jewellery, precious stones, etc. On such occasions he should show her certain things with the values of which she may be unacquainted, and if she begins to dispute with him about the things or their value, he should not contradict her, but point out that he agrees with her in every way.

Thus end the ways of making the acquaintance of woman desired.

Now after a girl has become acquainted with the man as above described, and has manifested her love to him by the various outward signs and by the motions of her body, the man should make every effort to gain her over. But as girls are not acquainted with sexual union, they should be treated with the greatest delicacy, and the man should proceed with

considerable caution, though in the case of other women, accustomed to sexual intercourse, this is not necessary. When the intentions of the girl are known, and her bashfulness put aside, the man should begin to make use of her money, and an interchange of clothes, flowers should be made. In this the man should take particular care that the things given by him are handsome and valuable. He should moreover receive from her a mixture of betel nut and betel leaves, and when he is going to a party he should ask for the flower in her hair, or for the flower in her hand. If he himself gives her a flower it should be a sweet smelling one, and marked with marks made by his nails or teeth. With increasing assiduity he should dispel her fears, and by degrees get her to go with him to some lonely place, and there he should embrace and kiss her. And finally at the time of giving her some betel nut, or of receiving the same from her, or at the time of making an exchange of flowers, he should touch and press her private parts, thus bringing his efforts to a satisfactory conclusion.

When a man is endeavouring to seduce one woman, he should not attempt to seduce any other at the same time. But after he has succeeded with the first, and enjoyed her for a considerable time, he can keep her affections by giving her presents that she likes, and then commence making up to another woman. When a man sees the husband of a woman going to some place near his house, he should not enjoy the woman then, even though she may be easily gained over at that time. A wise man having a regard for his reputation should not think of seducing a woman who is apprehensive, timid, not to be trusted, well guarded, or possessed of a father-in-law, or mother-in-law.

CHAPTER III

Examination of
the State of a Woman's Mind

§ When a man is trying to gain over a woman he should examine the state of her mind, and act as follows:

✳ *If she listens to him, but does not manifest to him in any way her own intentions, he should then try to gain her over by means of a go-between.*

✳ *If she meets him once, and again comes to meet him better dressed than before, or comes to him in some lonely place, he should be certain that she is capable of being enjoyed by the use of a little force. A woman who lets a man make up to her, but does not give herself up, even after a long time, should be considered as a trifler in love, but owing to the fickleness of the human mind, even such a woman can be conquered by always keeping up a close acquaintance with her.*

✳ *When a woman avoids the attentions of a man, and on account of respect for him, and pride in herself, will not meet him or approach him, she can be gained over with difficulty, either by endeavouring to keep on familiar terms with her, or else by an exceedingly clever go-between.*

✳ *When a man makes up to a woman, and she reproaches him with harsh words, she should be abandoned at once.*

✳ *When a woman reproaches a man, but at the same time acts affectionately towards him, she should be made love to in every way.*

A woman, who meets a man in lonely places, and puts up with the touch of his foot, but pretends, on account of the indecision of her mind, not to be aware of it, should be conquered by patience, and by continued efforts as follows:

If she happens to go to sleep in his vicinity he should put his left arm round her, and see when she awakes whether she repulses him in reality, or only repulses him in such a way as if she was desirous of the same thing being done to her again. And what is done by the arm can also be done by the foot. If the man succeeds in this point he should embrace her more closely, and if she will not stand the embrace and gets up, but behaves with him as usual the next day, he should consider then that she is not unwilling to be enjoyed by him. If however she does not appear again, the man should try to get over her by means of a go-between; and if, after having disappeared for some time, she again appears, and behaves with him as usual, the man should then consider that she would not object to be united with him.

When a woman gives a man an opportunity, and makes her own love manifest to him, he should proceed to enjoy her. And the signs of a woman manifesting her love are these:

✳ *She calls out to a man without being addressed by him in the first instance.*

✳ *She shows herself to him in secret places.*

✳ *She speaks to him tremblingly and inarticulately.*

✳ *She has the fingers of her hand, and the toes of her feet moistened with perspiration, and her face blooming with delight.*

✳ *She occupies herself with shampooing his body and pressing his head.*

✳ *When shampooing him she works with one hand only, and with the other she touches and embraces parts of his body.*

✳ *She remains with both hands placed on his body motionless as if she had been surprised by something, or was overcome by fatigue.*

✳ *She sometimes bends down her face upon his thighs and, when asked to shampoo them does not manifest any unwillingness to do so.*

✳ *She places one of her hands quite motionless on his body, and even though the man should press it between two members of his body, she does not remove it for a long time.*

✳ *Lastly, when she has resisted all the efforts of the man to gain her over, she returns to him next day to shampoo his body as before.*

When a woman neither gives encouragement to a man, nor avoids him, but hides herself and remains in some lonely place, she must be got at by means of the female servant who may be near her. If when called by the man she acts in the same way, then she should be gained over by means of a skilful go-between. But if she will have nothing to say to the man, he should consider well about her before he begins any further attempts to gain her over.

Thus ends the examination of the state of a woman's mind.

A man should first get himself introduced to a woman, and then carry on a conversation with her. He should give her hints of his love for her, and if he finds from her replies that she receives these hints favourably, he should then set to work to gain her over without any fear. A woman who shows her love by outward signs to the man at his first interview should be gained over very easily. In the same way a lascivious woman, who when addressed in loving words replies openly in words expressive of her love, should be considered to have been gained over at that very moment. With regard to all women, whether they be wise, simple, or confiding, this rule is laid down that those who make an open manifestation of their love are easily gained over.

CHAPTER IV

About the Business of a Go-Between

§ If a woman has manifested her love or desire, either by signs or by motions of the body, and is afterwards rarely or never seen anywhere, or if a woman is met for the first time, the man should get a go-between to approach her.

Now the go-between, having wheedled herself into the confidence of the woman by acting according to her disposition, should try to make her hate or despise her husband by holding artful conversations with her, by telling her about medicines for getting children, by talking to her about other people, by tales of various kinds, by stories about the wives of other men, and by praising her beauty, wisdom, generosity and good nature, and then saying to her: 'It is indeed a pity that you, who are so excellent a woman in every way, should be possessed of a husband of this kind. Beautiful lady, he is not fit even to serve you.' The go-between should further talk to the woman about the weakness of the passion of her husband, his jealousy, his roguery, his ingratitude, his aversion to enjoyments, his dullness, his meanness, and all the other faults that he may have, and with which she may be acquainted. She should particularly harp upon that fault or that failing by which the wife may appear to be the most affected. If the wife be a deer woman, and the husband a hare man, then there would be no fault in that direction, but in the event of his being a hare man, and she a mare woman or elephant woman, then this fault should be pointed out to her.

IF A WOMAN HAS MANIFESTED HER LOVE OR DESIRE, EITHER BY SIGNS OR BY MOTIONS OF THE BODY, AND IS AFTERWARDS RARELY OR NEVER SEEN ANYWHERE, OR IF A WOMAN IS MET FOR THE FIRST TIME, THE MAN SHOULD GET A GO-BETWEEN TO APPROACH HER.

Gonikaputra is of opinion that when it is the first affair of the woman, or when her love has only been very secretly shown, the man should then secure and send to her a go-between, with whom she may be already acquainted, and in whom she confides.

But to return to our subject. The go-between should tell the woman about the obedience and love of the man, and as her confidence and affection increase, she should then explain to her the thing to be accomplished in the following way. 'Hear this, Oh beautiful lady, that this man, born of a good family, having seen you, has gone mad on your account. The poor young man, who is tender by nature, has never been distressed in such a way before, and it is highly probable that he will succumb under his present affliction, and experience the pains of death.' If the woman listens with a favourable ear, then on the following day the go-between, having observed marks of good spirits in her face, in her eyes, and in her manner of conversation, should again converse with her on the subject of the man, and should tell her the stories of Ahalya [*1] and Indra, of Sakoontala [*2] and Dushyanti, and such others as may be fitted for the occasion. She should also describe to her the strength of the man, his talents, his skill in the sixty-four sorts of enjoyments mentioned by Babhravya, his good looks, and his liaison with some praiseworthy woman, no matter whether this last ever took place or not.

In addition to this, the go-between should carefully note the behaviour of the woman, which if favourable would be as follows: She would address her with a smiling look, would seat herself close beside her, and ask her, 'Where have you been? What have you been doing? Where did you dine? Where did you sleep? Where have you been sitting?' Moreover, the woman would meet the go-between in lonely places and tell her stories there, would yawn contemplatively, draw long sighs, give her presents, remember her on occasions of festivals, dismiss her with a wish to see her again, and say to her jestingly, 'Oh, well-speaking woman, why do you speak these bad words to me?', would discourse on the sin of her union with the man, would not tell her about any previous visits or conversations that she may have had with him, but wish to be asked about these, and lastly would laugh at the man's desire, but would not reproach him in any way.

Thus ends the behaviour of the woman with the go-between.

When the woman manifests her love in the manner above described, the go-between should increase it by bringing to her love tokens from the man. But if the woman be not acquainted with the man personally, the go-between should win her over by extolling and praising his good qualities, and by telling stories about his love for her. Here Auddalaka says that when a man or woman are not personally acquainted with each other, and have not shown each other any signs of affection, the employment of a go-between is useless.

The followers of Babhravya on the other hand affirm that even though they be personally unacquainted, but have shown each other signs of affection there is an occasion for the employment of a go-between. Gonikaputra asserts that a go-between should be employed, provided they are acquainted with each other, even though no signs of affection may have passed between them. Vatsyayana however lays it down that even though they may not be personally acquainted with each other, and may not have shown each other any signs of affection, still they are both capable of placing confidence in a go-between.

Now the go-between should show the woman the presents, such as the betel nut and betel leaves, the perfumes, the flowers, and the rings which the man may have given to her for the sake of the woman, and on these presents should be impressed the marks of the man's teeth, and nails, and other signs. On the cloth that he may send he should draw with saffron both his hands joined together as if in earnest entreaty.

The go-between should also show to the woman ornamental figures of various kinds cut in leaves, together with ear ornaments, and chaplets made of flowers containing love letters expressive of the desire of the man[*3], and she should cause her to send affectionate presents to the man in return. After they have mutually accepted each other's presents, then a meeting should be arranged between them on the faith of the go-between.

The followers of Babhravya say that this meeting should take place at the time of going to the temple of a Deity, or on occasions of fairs, garden parties, theatrical performances, marriages, sacrifices, festivals and funerals, as also at the time of going to the river to bathe, or at times of natural calamities[*4], fear of robbers or hostile invasions of the country.

Gonikaputra is of opinion however that these meetings had better be brought about in the abodes of female friends, mendicants, astrologers, and ascetics. But Vatsyayana decides that that place is only well suited for the purpose which has proper means of ingress and egress, and where arrangements have been made to prevent any accidental occurrence, and when a man who has once entered the house can also leave it at the proper time without any disagreeable encounter.

Now go-betweens or female messengers are of the following different kinds:

A go-between who takes upon herself the whole burden of the business

A go-between who does only a limited part of the business

A go-between who is the bearer of a letter only

A go-between acting on her own account

The go-between of an innocent young woman

A wife serving as a go-between

A mute go-between

A go-between who acts the part of the wind

– A woman who, having observed the mutual passion of a man and woman, brings them together and arranges it by the power of her own intellect, such a one is called a go-between who takes upon herself the whole burden of the business. This kind of go-between is chiefly employed when the man and the woman are already acquainted with each other, and have conversed together, and in such cases she is sent not only by the man (as is always done in all other cases) but by the woman also. The above name is also given to a go-between who, perceiving that the man and the woman are suited to each other, tries to bring about a union between them, even though they be not-acquainted with each other.

– A go-between who, perceiving that some part of the affair is already done, or that the advances on the part of the man are already made, completes the rest of the business, is called a go-between who performs only a limited part of the business.

– A go-between who simply carries messages between a man and a woman, who love each other, but who cannot frequently meet, is called the bearer of a letter or message. This name is also given to one who is sent by either of the lovers to acquaint either the one or the other with the time and place of their meeting.

– A woman who goes herself to a man, and tells him of her having enjoyed sexual union with him in a dream, and expresses her anger at his wife having rebuked him for calling her by the name of her rival instead of by her own name, and gives him something bearing the marks of her teeth and nails and informs him that she knew she was formerly desired by him, and asks him privately whether she or his wife is the best looking, such a person is called a woman who is a go-between for herself. Now such a woman should be met and interviewed by the man in private and secretly. The above name is also given to a woman who having made an agreement with some other woman to act as her go-between, gains over the man to herself, by the means of making him personally acquainted with herself, and thus causes the other woman to fail. The same applies to a man who, acting as a go-between for another, and having no previous connection with the woman, gains her over for himself, and thus causes the failure of the other man.

– A woman who has gained the confidence of the innocent young wife of any man, and who has learned her secrets without exercising any pressure on her mind, and found out from her how her husband behaves to her, if this woman then teaches her the art of securing his favour, and decorates her so as to show her love, and instructs her how and when to be angry, or to pretend to be so, and then, having herself made marks of the nails and teeth on the body of the wife, gets the latter to send for her husband to show these marks to him, and thus excite him for enjoyment, such is called the go-between of an innocent young woman. In such cases the man should send replies to his wife through the same woman.

– When a man gets his wife to gain the confidence of a woman whom he wants to enjoy, and to call on her and talk to her about the wisdom and ability of her husband, that wife is called a wife serving as a go-between. In this case the feelings of the woman with regard to the man should also be made known through the wife.

– When any man sends a girl or a female servant to any woman under some pretext or other, and places a letter in her bouquet of flowers, or in her ear ornaments, or marks something about her with his teeth or nails, that girl or female servant is called a mute go-between. In this case the man should expect an answer from the woman through the same person.

– A person, who carries a message to a woman, which has a double meaning, or which relates to some past transactions, or which is unintelligible to other people, is called a go-between who acts the part of the wind. In this case the reply should be asked for through the same woman.

Thus end the different kinds of go-betweens.

A GO-BETWEEN CAN, BY THE ARTFULNESS OF HER CONVERSATION, UNITE A WOMAN WITH A MAN EVEN THOUGH HE MAY NOT HAVE BEEN THOUGHT OF BY HER, OR MAY HAVE BEEN CONSIDERED BEYOND HER ASPIRATIONS. SHE CAN ALSO BRING BACK A MAN TO A WOMAN, WHO, OWING TO SOME CAUSE OR OTHER, HAS SEPARATED HIMSELF FROM HER.

A female astrologer, a female servant, a female beggar, or a female artist are well acquainted with the business of a go-between, and very soon gain the confidence of other women. Any one of them can raise enmity between any two persons if she wishes to do so, or extol the loveliness of any woman that she wishes to praise, or describe the arts practised by other women in sexual union. They can also speak highly of the love of a man, of his skill in sexual enjoyment, and of the desire of other women, more beautiful even than the woman they are addressing, for him, and explain the restraint under which he may be at home.

Lastly a go-between can, by the artfulness of her conversation, unite a woman with a man even though he may not have been thought of by her, or may have been considered beyond her aspirations. She can also bring back a man to a woman, who, owing to some cause or other, has separated himself from her.

footnotes

1   The wife of the sage Gautama, she was seduced by Indra the king of the Gods.

2   The heroine of one of the best, if not the best, of Hindoo plays, and the best known in Sanscrit dramatic literature. It was first brought to notice by Sir William Jones, and has been well and poetically translated by Dr Monier Williams under the title of *Sakoontala*, or the lost ring, an Indian drama, translated into English prose and verse from the Sanscrit of Kalidasa.

3   It is presumed that something like the following French verses are intended:

Quand on a jure le plus profond hommage,

Voulez vous qu'infidele on change de langage;

Vous seul captivez mon esprit et mon coeur

Que je puisse dans vos bras seuls gouter le bonheur;

Je voudrais, mais en vain, que mon coeur en delire

Couche ou ce papier n'oserait vous dire.

Avec soin, de ces vers lisez leurs premiers mots,

Vous verrez quel remede il faut a tous mes maux

Or these:

Quand on vous voit, on vous aime;

Quand on vous aime, ou vous voit on?

4   It is supposed that storms, earthquakes, famines and pestilent diseases are here alluded to.

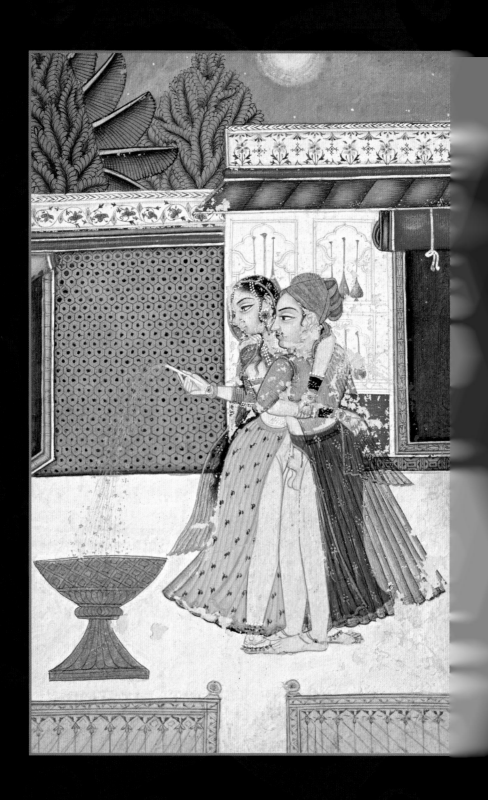

CHAPTER V

About the Love of Persons in Authority for the Wives of Other Men

§ Kings and their ministers have no access to the abodes of others, and moreover their mode of living is constantly watched and observed and imitated by the people at large, just as the animal world, seeing the sun rise, get up after him, and when he sits in the evening, lie down again in the same way. Persons in authority should not therefore do any improper act in public, as such are impossible from their position, and would be deserving of censure. But if they find that such an act is necessary to be done, they should make use of the proper means as described in the following paragraphs.

The head man of the village, the king's officer employed there, and the man whose business it is to glean corn [*1], can gain over female villagers simply by asking them. It is on this account that this class of woman are called unchaste women by voluptuaries.

The union of the above mentioned men with this class of woman takes place on the occasions of unpaid labour, of filling the granaries in their houses, of taking things in and out of the house, of cleaning the houses, of working in the fields, and of purchasing cotton, wool, flax, hemp, and thread, and at the season of the purchase, sale, and exchange of various other articles, as well as at the time of doing various other works. In the same way the superintendents of cow pens enjoy the women in the cow pens; and the officers, who crave the superintendence of widows, of the women who are without supporters, and of women who have left their husbands, have sexual intercourse with these women. The intelligent accomplish their object by wandering at night in the village, and while villagers also unite with the wives of their sons, being much alone with them. Lastly the superintendents of markets have a great deal to do with the female villagers at the time of their making purchases in the market.

During the festival of the eighth moon, i.e. during the bright half of the month of Nargashirsha, as also during the moonlight festival of the month of Kartika, and the spring festival of Chaitra, the women of cities and towns generally visit the women of the king's harem in the royal palace. These visitors go to the several apartments of the women of the harem, as they are acquainted with them, and pass the night in conversation, and in proper sports, and amusement, and go away in the morning. On such occasions a female attendant of the king (previously acquainted with the woman whom the king desires) should loiter about, and accost this woman when she sets out to go home, and induce her to come and see the amusing things in the palace. Previous to these festivals even, she should have caused it to be intimated to this woman that on the occasion of this festival she would show her all the interesting things in the royal palace. Accordingly she should show her the bower of the coral creeper, the garden house with its floor inlaid with precious stones, the bower of grapes, the building on the water, the secret passages in the walls of the palace, the pictures, the sporting animals, the machines, the birds, and the cages of the lions and the tigers. After this, when alone with her, she should tell her about the love of the king for her, and should describe to her the good fortune which would attend upon her union with the king, giving her at the time a strict promise of secrecy. If the woman does not accept the offer, she should conciliate and please her with handsome presents befitting the position of the king, and having accompanied her for some distance should dismiss her with great affection.

Or, having made the acquaintance of the husband of the woman whom the king desires, the wives of the king should get the wife to pay them a visit in the harem, and on this occasion a female attendant of the king, having been sent thither, should act as above described.

Or, one of the king's wives should get acquainted with the woman that the king desires, by sending one of the female attendants to her, who should, on their becoming more intimate, induce her to come and see the royal abode. Afterwards when she has visited the harem, and acquired confidence, a female confidante of the king, sent thither, should act as before described.

Or, the king's wife should invite the woman, whom the king desires, to come to the royal palace, so that she might see the practice of the art in which the king's wife may be skilled, and after she has come to the harem, a female attendant of the king, sent thither, should act as before described.

Or, a female beggar, in league with the king's wife, should say to the woman desired by the king, and whose husband may have lost his wealth, or may have some cause of fear from the king: 'This wife of the king has influence over him, and she is, moreover, naturally kind-hearted, we must therefore go to her in this matter. I shall arrange for your entrance into the harem, and she will do away with all cause of danger and fear from the king.' If the woman accepts this offer, the female beggar should take her two or three times to the harem, and the king's wife there should give her a promise of protection. After this, when

the woman, delighted with her reception and promise of protection, again goes to the harem, then a female attendant of the king, sent thither, should act as directed.

What has been said above regarding the wife of one who has some cause of fear from the king applies also to the wives of those who seek service under the king, or who are oppressed by the king's ministers, or who are poor, or who are not satisfied with their position, or who are desirous of gaining the king's favour, or who wish to become famous among the people, or who are oppressed by the members of their own caste, or who want to injure their caste fellows, or who are spies of the king, or who have any other object to attain.

Lastly, if the woman desired by the king be living with some person who is not her husband, then the king should cause her to be arrested, and having made her a slave, on account of her crime, should place her in the harem. Or the king should cause his ambassador to quarrel with the husband of the woman desired by him, and should then imprison her as the wife of an enemy of the king, and by this means should place her in the harem.

Thus end the means of gaining over the wives of others secretly.

PERSONS IN AUTHORITY SHOULD NOT DO ANY IMPROPER ACT IN PUBLIC, AS SUCH ARE IMPOSSIBLE FROM THEIR POSITION, AND WOULD BE DESERVING OF CENSURE.

The above mentioned ways of gaining over the wives of other men are chiefly practised in the palaces of kings. But a king should never enter the abode of another person, for Abhira [*2], the king of the Kottas, was killed by a washerman while in the house of another, and in the same way Jayasana, the king of the Kashis, was slain by the commandant of his cavalry.

But according to the customs of some countries there are facilities for kings to make love to the wives of other men. Thus in the country of the Andhras [*3] the newly married daughters of the people thereof enter the king's harem with some presents on the tenth day of their marriage, and having been enjoyed by the king are then dismissed. In the country of the Vatsagulmas [*4] the wives of the chief ministers approach the king at night to serve him. In the country of the Vaidarbhas [*5] the beautiful wives of the inhabitants pass a month in the king's harem under the pretence of affection for the king. In the country of the Aparatakas [*6] the people gave their beautiful wives as presents to the ministers and the kings. And lastly in the country of the Saurashtras [*7] the women of the city and the country enter the royal harem for the king's pleasure either together or separately.

There are also two verses on the subject as follows:

*The above and other ways are the means employed
in different countries by kings with regard to the wives of other
persons. But a king, who has the welfare of his people at heart,
should not on any account put them into practice.*

*A king, who has conquered the six enemies of mankind [*8],
becomes the master of the whole earth.*

CHAPTER VI

About the Women of the Royal Harem; & of the Keeping of One's Own Wife

§ The women of the royal harem cannot see or meet any men on account of their being strictly guarded, neither do they have their desires satisfied, because their only husband is common to many wives. For this reason among themselves they give pleasure to each other in various ways as now described.

Having dressed the daughters of their nurses, or their female friends, or their female attendants, like men, they accomplish their object by means of bulbs, roots, and fruits having the form of the lingam, or they lie down upon the statue of a male figure, in which the lingam is visible and erect.

Some kings, who are compassionate, take or apply certain medicines to enable them to enjoy many wives in one night, simply for the purpose of satisfying the desire of their women, though they perhaps have no desire of their own. Others enjoy with great affection only those wives that they particularly like, while others only take them, according as the turn of each wife arrives in due course. Such are the ways of enjoyment prevalent in Eastern countries, and what is said about the means of enjoyment of the female is also applicable to the male.

By means of their female attendants the ladies of the royal harem generally get men into their apartments in the disguise or dress of women. Their female attendants, and the daughters of their nurses, who are acquainted with their secrets, should exert themselves to get men to come to the harem in this way by telling them of the good fortune attending it, and by describing the facilities of entering and leaving the palace, the large size of the premises, the carelessness of the sentinels, and the irregularities of the attendants about the persons of the royal wives. But these women should never induce a man to enter the harem by telling him falsehoods, for that would probably lead to his destruction.

As for the man himself he had better not enter a royal harem, even though it may be easily accessible, on account of the numerous disasters to which he may be exposed there. If however he wants to enter it, he should first ascertain whether there is an easy way to get out, whether it is closely surrounded by the pleasure garden, whether it has separate enclosures belonging to it, whether the sentinels are careless, whether the king has gone abroad, and then, when he is called by the women of the harem, he should carefully observe the localities, and enter by the way pointed out by them. If he is able to manage it, he should hang about the harem every day, and under some pretext or other, make friends with the sentinels, and show himself attached to the female attendants of the harem, who may have become acquainted with his design, and to whom he should express his regret at not being able to obtain the object of his desire. Lastly he should cause the whole business of a go-between to be done by the woman who may have access to the harem, and he should be careful to be able to recognize the emissaries of the king.

When a go-between has no access to the harem, then the man should stand in some place where the lady, whom he loves and whom he is anxious to enjoy, can be seen.

If that place is occupied by the king's sentinels, he should then disguise himself as a female attendant of the lady who comes to the place, or passes by it. When she looks at him he should let her know his feelings by outward signs and gestures, and should show her pictures, things with double meanings, chaplets of flowers, and rings. He should carefully mark the answer she gives, whether by word or by sign, or by gesture, and should then try and get into the harem. If he is certain of her coming to some particular place he should conceal himself there, and at the appointed time should enter along with her as one of the guards. He may also go in and out, concealed in a folded bed, or bed covering, or with his body made invisible [*1], by means of external applications, a receipt for one of which is as follows:

The heart of an ichneumon, the fruit of the long gourd (tumbi), and the eyes of a serpent should all be burnt without letting out the smoke. The ashes should then be ground and mixed in equal quantities with water. By putting this mixture upon the eyes a man can go about unseen.

Other means of invisibility are prescribed by Duyana Brahmans and Jogashiras.

Again the man may enter the harem during the festival of the eighth moon in the month of Nargashirsha, and during the moonlight festivals when the female attendants of the harem are all busily occupied, or in confusion.

The following principles are laid down on this subject.

The entrance of young men into harems, and their exit from them, generally take place when things are being brought into the palace, or when things are being taken out of it, or when drinking festivals are going on, or when the female attendants are in a hurry, or when the residence of some of the royal ladies is being changed, or when the king's wives go to gardens, or to fairs, or when they enter the palace on their return from them, or lastly, when the king is absent on a long pilgrimage. The women of the royal harem know each other's secrets, and having but one object to attain, they give assistance to each other. A young man, who enjoys all of them, and who is common to them all, can continue enjoying his union with them so long as it is kept quiet, and is not known abroad.

Now in the country of the Aparatakas the royal ladies are not well protected, and consequently many young men are passed into the harem by the women who have access to the royal palace. The wives of the king of the Ahira country accomplish their objects with those sentinels in the harem who bear the name of Kashtriyas. The royal ladies in the country of the Vatsagulmas cause such men as are suitable to enter into the harem along with their female messengers. In the country of the Vaidarbhas the sons of the royal ladies enter the royal harem when they please and enjoy the women, with the exception of their own mothers. In the Stri-rajya the wives of the king are enjoyed by his caste fellows and relations. In the Ganda country the royal wives are enjoyed by Brahmans, friends, servants and slaves. In the Samdhava country servants, foster children, and other persons like them enjoy the women of the harem. In the country of the Haimavatas adventurous citizens bribe the sentinels and enter the harem. In the country of the Vanyas and the Kalmyas, Brahmans, with the knowledge of the king, enter the harem under the pretence of giving flowers to the ladies, and speak with them from behind a curtain, and from such conversation union afterwards takes place. Lastly the women in the harem of the king of the Prachyas conceal one young man in the harem for every batch of nine or ten of the women.

Thus act the wives of others.

For these reasons a man should guard his own wife. Old authors say that a king should select for sentinels in his harem such men as have their freedom from carnal desires well tested. But such men, though free themselves from carnal desire, by reason of their fear or avarice, may cause other persons to enter the harem, and therefore Gonikaputra says that kings should place such men in the harem as may have had their freedom from carnal desires, their fears, and their avarice well tested. Lastly Vatsyayana says that under the influence of Dharma [*2] people might be admitted, and therefore men should be selected who are free from carnal desires, fear, avarice, and Dharma [*3].

The followers of Babhravya say that a man should cause his wife to associate with a young woman who would tell him the secrets of other people, and thus find out from her about his wife's chastity. But Vatsyayana says that, as wicked persons are always successful with women, a man should not cause his innocent wife to be corrupted by bringing her into the company of a deceitful woman.

The following are the causes of the destruction of a woman's chastity:

Always going into society, and sitting in company

Absence of restraint

The loose habits of her husband

Want of caution in her relations with other men

Continued and long absence of her husband

Living in a foreign country

Destruction of her love and feelings by her husband

The company of loose women

The jealousy of her husband

There are also the following verses on the subject:

A clever man, learning from the Shastras the ways of winning over the wives of other people, is never deceived in the case of his own wives. No one, however, should make use of these ways for seducing the wives of others, because they do not always succeed, and, moreover, often cause disasters, and the destruction of Dharma and Artha. This book, which is intended for the good of the people, and to teach them the ways of guarding their own wives, should not be made use of merely for gaining over the wives of others.

footnotes

1   The way to make oneself invisible, the knowledge of the art of transmigration, or changing ourselves or others into any shape or form by the use of charms and spells, the power of being in two places at once, and other occult sciences are frequently referred to in all Oriental literature.

2   This may be considered as meaning religious influence, and alludes to persons who may be gained over by that means.

3   It will be noted from the above remarks that eunuchs do not appear to have been employed in the king's harem in those days, though they seem to have been employed for other purposes. See Part II, Chapter II.

PART VI

ABOUT COURTESANS

Introductory Remarks

§ This Part VI, about courtesans, was prepared by Vatsyayana from a treatise on the subject that was written by Dattaka, for the women of Pataliputra (the modern Patna), some two thousand years ago. Dattaka's work does not appear to be extant now, but this abridgement of it is very clever, and quite equal to any of the productions of Emile Zola, and other writers of the realistic school.

Although a great deal has been written on the subject of the courtesan, nowhere will be found a better description of her, of her belongings, of her ideas, and of the working of her mind, than is contained in the following pages.

The details of the domestic and social life of the early Hindoos would not be complete without mention of the courtesan, and Part VI is entirely devoted to this subject. The Hindoos have ever had the good sense to recognise courtesans as a part and portion of human society, and so long as they behaved themselves with decency and propriety they were regarded with a certain respect. Anyhow, they have never been treated in the East with that brutality and contempt so common in the West, while their education has always been of a superior kind to that bestowed upon the rest of womankind in Oriental countries.

In the earlier days the well-educated Hindoo dancing girl and courtesan doubtless resembled the Hetera of the Greeks, and, being educated and amusing, were far more acceptable as companions than the generality of the married or unmarried women of that period. At all times and in all countries, there has ever been a little rivalry between the chaste and the unchaste. But while some women are born courtesans, and follow the instincts of their nature in every class of society, it has been truly said by some authors that every woman has got an inkling of the profession in her nature, and does her best, as a general rule, to make herself agreeable to the male sex.

The subtlety of women, their wonderful perceptive powers, their knowledge, and their intuitive appreciation of men and things are all shown in the following pages, which may be looked upon as a concentrated essence that has been since worked up into detail by many writers in every quarter of the globe.

Of the Causes of a Courtesan Resorting to Men; Of the Means of Attaching to Herself the Man Desired; & of the Kind of Man That It Is Desirable to Be Acquainted with

§ By having intercourse with men courtesans obtain sexual pleasure, as well as their own maintenance. Now when a courtesan takes up with a man from love, the action is natural; but when she resorts to him for the purpose of getting money, her action is artificial or forced. Even in the latter case, however, she should conduct herself as if her love were indeed natural, because men repose their confidence on those women who apparently love them. In making known her love to the man, she should show an entire freedom from avarice, and for the sake of her future credit she should abstain from acquiring money from him by unlawful means.

SHE SHOULD TAKE DELIGHT IN SEXUAL UNIONS, RESULTING FROM LOVE, AND SHOULD BE OF A FIRM MIND, AND OF THE SAME CLASS AS THE MAN WITH REGARD TO SEXUAL ENJOYMENT.

A courtesan, well dressed and wearing her ornaments, should sit or stand at the door of her house, and, without exposing herself too much, should look on the public road so as to be seen by the passers by, she being like an object on view for sale [*1]. She should form friendships with such persons as would enable her to separate men from other women, and attach them to herself, to repair her own misfortunes, to acquire wealth, and to protect her from being bullied, or set upon by persons with whom she may have dealings of some kind or another.

These persons are:

The guards of the town, or the police

The officers of the courts of justice

Astrologers

Powerful men, or men with interest

Learned men

Teachers of the sixty-four arts

Pithamardas or confidants

Vitas or parasites

Vidushakas or jesters

Flower sellers

Perfumers

Vendors of spirits

Washermen

Barbers

Beggars

And such other persons as may be found necessary for the particular object to be acquired.

The following kinds of men may be taken up with, simply for the purpose of getting their money:

Men of independent income

Young men

Men who are free from any ties

Men who hold places of authority under the king

Men who have secured their means of livelihood without difficulty

Men possessed of unfailing sources of income

Men who consider themselves handsome

Men who are always praising themselves

One who is a eunuch, but wishes to be thought a man

One who hates his equals

One who is naturally liberal

One who has influence with the king or his ministers

One who is always fortunate

One who is proud of his wealth

One who disobeys the orders of his elders

One upon whom the members of his caste keep an eye

An only son whose father is wealthy

An ascetic who is internally troubled with desire

A brave man

A physician of the king

Previous acquaintances

On the other hand, those who are possessed of excellent qualities are to be resorted to for the sake of love, and fame. Such men are as follows:

Men of high birth, learned, with a good knowledge of the world, and doing the proper things at the proper times, poets, good story tellers, eloquent men, energetic men, skilled in various arts, far-seeing into the future, possessed of great minds, full of perseverance, of a firm devotion, free from anger, liberal, affectionate to their parents, and with a liking for all social gatherings, skilled in completing verses begun by others and in various other sports, free from all disease, possessed of a perfect body, strong, and not addicted to drinking, powerful in sexual enjoyment, sociable, showing love towards women and attracting their hearts to himself, but not entirely devoted to them, possessed of independent means of livelihood, free from envy, and last of all, free from suspicion.

Such are the good qualities of a man.

The woman also should have the following characteristics:

She should be possessed of beauty, and amiability, with auspicious body marks. She should have a liking for good qualifies in other people, as also a liking for wealth. She should take delight in sexual unions, resulting from love, and should be of a firm mind, and of the same class as the man with regard to sexual enjoyment.

She should always be anxious to acquire and obtain experience and knowledge, be free from avarice, and always have a liking for social gatherings, and for the arts.

The following are the ordinary qualities of all women:

To be possessed of intelligence, good disposition, and good manners; to be straightforward in behaviour, and to be grateful; to consider well the future before doing anything; to possess activity, to be of consistent behaviour, and to have a knowledge of the proper times and places for doing things; to speak always without meanness, loud laughter, malignity, anger, avarice, dullness, or stupidity; to have a knowledge of the *Kama Sutra*, and to be skilled in all the arts connected with it.

The faults of women are to be known by the absence of any of the above mentioned good qualities.

The following kinds of men are not fit to be resorted to by courtesans:

One who is consumptive; one who is sickly; one whose mouth contains worms; one whose breath smells like human excrement; one whose wife is dear to him; one who speaks harshly; one who is always suspicious; one who is avaricious; one who is pitiless; one who is a thief; one who is self-conceited; one who has a liking for sorcery; one who does not care for respect or disrespect; one who can be gained over even by his enemies by means of money; and lastly, one who is extremely bashful.

Ancient authors are of opinion that the causes of a courtesan resorting to men are love, fear, money, pleasure, returning some act of enmity, curiosity, sorrow, constant intercourse, Dharma, celebrity, compassion, the desire of having a friend, shame, the likeness of the man to some beloved person, the search after good fortune, the getting rid of the love of somebody else, the being of the same class as the man with respect to sexual union, living in the same place, constancy, and poverty. But Vatsyayana decides that desire of wealth, freedom from misfortune, and love are the only causes that affect the union of courtesans with men.

Now a courtesan should not sacrifice money to her love, because money is the chief thing to be attended to. But in cases of fear, etc., she should pay regard to strength and other qualities. Moreover, even though she be invited by any man to join him, she shoUld not at once consent to a union, because men are apt to despise things which are easily acquired. On such occasions she should first send the shampooers, and the singers, and the jesters, who may be in her service, or, in their absence the Pithamardas, or confidants, and others, to find out the state of his feelings, and the condition of his mind. By means of these persons she should ascertain whether the man is pure or impure, affected, or the reverse, capable of attachment, or indifferent, liberal or niggardly; and if she finds him to her liking, she should then employ the Vita and others to attach his mind to her.

Accordingly, the Pithamarda should bring the man to her house, under the pretence of seeing the fights of quails, cocks, and rams, of hearing the mania (a kind of starling) talk, or of seeing some other spectacle, or the practice of some art; or he may take the woman to the abode of the man. After this, when the man comes to her house the woman should give him something capable of producing curiosity, and love in his heart, such as an affectionate present, telling him that it was specially designed for his use. She should also amuse him for a long time by telling him such stories, and doing such things as he may take most delight in. When he goes away she should frequently send to him a female attendant, skilled in carrying on a jesting conversation, and also a small present at the same time. She should also sometimes go to him herself under the pretence of some business, and accompanied by the Pithamarda.

Thus end the means of attaching to herself the man desired.

There are also some verses on the subject as follows:

When a lover comes to her abode, a courtesan should give him a mixture of betel leaves and betel nut, garlands of flowers, and perfumed ointments, and, showing her skill in arts, should entertain him with a long conversation. She should also give him some loving presents, and make an exchange of her own things with his, and at the same time should show him her skill in sexual enjoyment. When a courtesan is thus united with her lover she should always delight him by affectionate gifts, by conversation, and by the application of tender means of enjoyment.

footnote

1   In England the lower classes of courtesans walk the streets: in India and other places in the East, they sit at the windows, or at the doors of their houses.

CHAPTER II

Of Living Like a Wife

§ When a courtesan is living as a wife with her lover, she should behave like a chaste woman, and do everything to his satisfaction. Her duty in this respect, in short, is, that she should give him pleasure, but should not become attached to him, though behaving as if she were really attached.

Now the following is the manner in which she is to conduct herself, so as to accomplish the above mentioned purpose. She should have a mother dependent on her, one who should be represented as very harsh, and who looked upon money as her chief object in life. In the event of there being no mother, then an old and confidential nurse should play the same role. The mother or nurse, on their part, should appear to be displeased with the lover, and forcibly take her away from him. The woman herself should always show pretended anger, dejection, fear, and shame on this account, but should not disobey the mother or nurse at any time.

She should make out to the mother or nurse that the man is suffering from bad health, and making this a pretext for going to see him, she should go on that account. She is, moreover, to do the following things for the purpose of gaining the man's favour:

* *Sending her female attendant to bring the flowers used by him on the previous day, in order that she may use them herself as a mark of affection*

* *Also asking for the mixture of betel nut and leaves that have remained uneaten by him*

* *Expressing wonder at his knowledge of sexual intercourse, and the several means of enjoyment used by him*

* *Learning from him the sixty-four kinds of pleasure mentioned by Babhravya*

* *Continually practising the ways of enjoyment as taught by him, and according to his liking*

* *Keeping his secrets*

* *Telling him her own desires and secrets*

* *Concealing her anger*

* Never neglecting him on the bed when he turns his face towards her

* Touching any parts of his body according to his wish

* Kissing and embracing him when he is asleep

* Looking at him with apparent anxiety when he is wrapt in thought, or thinking of some other subject than herself

* Showing neither complete shamelessness, nor excessive bashfulness when he meets her, or sees her standing on the terrace of her house from the public road

* Hating his enemies

* Loving those who are dear to him

* Showing a liking for that which he likes

* Being in high or low spirits according to the state that he is in himself

* Expressing a curiosity to see his wives

* Not continuing her anger for a long time

* Suspecting even the marks and wounds made by herself with her nails and teeth on his body to have been made by some other woman

* Keeping her love for him unexpressed by words, but showing it by deeds, and signs, and hints

* Remaining silent when he is asleep, intoxicated, or sick

* Being very attentive when he describes his good actions, and reciting them afterwards to his praise and benefit

* Giving witty replies to him if he be sufficiently attached to her

* Listening to all his stories, except those that relate to her rivals

* Expressing feelings of dejection and sorrow if he sighs, yawns, or falls down

* Pronouncing the words 'live long' when he sneezes

* Pretending to be ill, or to have the desire of pregnancy, when she feels dejected

* Abstaining from praising the good qualities of anybody else, and from censuring those who possess the same faults as her own man

* Wearing anything that may have been given to her by him

* Abstaining from putting on her ornaments, and from taking food when he is in pain, sick, low-spirited, or suffering from misfortune, and condoling and lamenting with him over the same

* Wishing to accompany him if he happens to leave the country himself or if he be banished from it by the king

* Expressing a desire not to live after him

* Telling him that the whole object and desire of her life was to be united with him

* Offering previously promised sacrifices to the Deity when he acquires wealth, or has some desire fulfilled, or when he has recovered from some illness or disease

* Putting on ornaments every day

- ✳ Not acting too freely with him

- ✳ Reciting his name and the name of his family in her songs

- ✳ Placing his hand on her loins, bosom and forehead, and falling asleep after feeling the pleasure of his touch

- ✳ Sitting on his lap and falling asleep there

- ✳ Wishing to have a child by him

- ✳ Desiring not to live longer than he does

- ✳ Abstaining from revealing his secrets to others

- ✳ Dissuading him from vows and fasts by saying 'let the sin fall upon me'

- ✳ Keeping vows and fasts along with him when it is impossible to change his mind on the subject

- ✳ Telling him that vows and fasts are difficult to be observed, even by herself, when she has any dispute with him about them

- ✳ Looking on her own wealth and his without any distinction

- ✳ Abstaining from going to public assemblies without him, and accompanying him when he desires her to do so

- ✳ Taking delight in using things previously used by him, and in eating food that he has left uneaten

- ✳ Venerating his family, his disposition, his skill in the arts, his learning, his caste, his complexion, his native country, his friends, his good qualities, his age, and his sweet temper

- ✳ Asking him to sing, and to do other such like things, if able to do them

- ✳ Going to him without paying any regard to fear, to cold, to heat, or to rain

- ✳ Saying with regard to the next world that he should be her lover even there

- ✳ Adapting her tastes, disposition and actions to his liking

- ✳ Abstaining from sorcery

- ✳ Disputing continually with her mother on the subject of going to him, and, when forcibly taken by her mother to some other place, expressing her desire to die by taking poison, by starving herself to death, by stabbing herself with some weapon, or by hanging herself

- ✳ And lastly assuring the man of her constancy and love by means of her agents, and receiving money herself, but abstaining from any dispute with her mother with regard to pecuniary matters.

When the man sets out on a journey, she should make him swear that he will return quickly, and in his absence should put aside her vows of worshipping the Deity, and should wear no ornaments except those that are lucky. If the time fixed for his return has passed, she should endeavour to ascertain the real time of his return from omens, from the reports of the people, and from the positions of the planets, the moon and the stars. On occasions of amusement, and of auspicious dreams, she should say 'Let me be soon united to him.' If, moreover, she feels melancholy, or sees any inauspicious omen, she should perform some rite to appease the Deity [*1].

When the man does return home she should worship the God Kama, and offer oblations to other Deities, and having caused a pot filled with water to be brought by her friends, she should perform the worship in honour of the crow who eats the offerings which we make to the manes of deceased relations. After the first visit is over she should ask her lover also to perform certain rites, and this he will do if he is sufficiently attached to her.

Now a man is said to be sufficiently attached to a woman when his love is disinterested; when he has the same object in view as his beloved one; when he is quite free from any suspicions on her account; and when he is indifferent to money with regard to her.

Such is the manner of a courtesan living with a man like a wife, and set forth here for the sake of guidance from the rules of Dattaka. What is not laid down here should be practised according to the custom of the people, and the nature of each individual man.

There are also two verses on the subject as follows:

The extent of the love of women is not known, even to those who are the objects of their affection, on account of its subtlety, and on account of the avarice, and natural intelligence of womankind.

Women are hardly ever known in their true light, though they may love men, or become indifferent towards them, may give them delight, or abandon them, or may extract from them all the wealth that they may possess.

footnote

1   Kama, i.e. the Indian Cupid.

Of the Means of Getting Money, of the Signs of the Change of a Lover's Feelings, & of the Way to Get Rid of Him

§ Money is got out of a lover in two ways:

By natural or lawful means, and by artifices. Old authors are of opinion that when a courtesan can get as much money as she wants from her lover, she should not make use of artifice. But Vatsyayana lays down that though she may get some money from him by natural means, yet when she makes use of artifice he gives her doubly more, and therefore artifice should be resorted to for the purpose of extorting money from him at all events.

Now the artifices to be used for getting money from her lover are as follows:

🌟 Taking money from him on different occasions, for the purpose of purchasing various articles, such as ornaments, food, drink, flowers, perfumes and clothes, and either not buying them, or getting from him more than their cost.

🌟 Praising his intelligence to his face.

🌟 Pretending to be obliged to make gifts on occasion of festivals connected with vows, trees, gardens, temples, or tanks [*1].

🌟 Pretending that at the time of going to his house, her jewels have been stolen either by the king's guards, or by robbers.

🌟 Alleging that her property has been destroyed by fire, by the falling of her house, or by the carelessness of her servants.

🌟 Pretending to have lost the ornaments of her lover along with her own.

🌟 Causing him to hear through other people of the expenses incurred by her in coming to see him.

* Contracting debts for the sake of her lover.

* Disputing with her mother on account of some expense incurred by her for her lover, and which was not approved of by her mother.

* Not going to parties and festivities in the houses of her friends for the want of presents to make to them, she having previously informed her lover of the valuable presents given to her by these very friends.

* Not performing certain festive rites under the pretence that she has no money to perform them with.

* Engaging artists to do something for her lover.

* Entertaining physicians and ministers for the purpose of attaining some object.

* Assisting friends and benefactors both on festive occasions, and in misfortune.

* Performing household rites.

* Having to pay the expenses of the ceremony of marriage of the son of a female friend.

* Having to satisfy curious wishes including her state of pregnancy.

* Pretending to be ill, and charging her cost of treatment.

* Having to remove the troubles of a friend.

* Selling some of her ornaments, so as to give her lover a present.

* Pretending to sell some of her ornaments, furniture, or cooking utensils to a trader, who has been already tutored how to behave in the matter.

* Having to buy cooking utensils of greater value than those of other people, so that they might be more easily distinguished, and not changed for others of an inferior description.

* Remembering the former favours of her lover, and causing them always to be spoken of by her friends and followers.

* Informing her lover of the great gains of other courtesans.

* Describing before them, and in the presence of her lover, her own great gains, and making them out to be greater even than theirs, though such may not have been really the case.

* Openly opposing her mother when she endeavours to persuade her to take up with men with whom she has been formerly acquainted, on account of the great gains to be got from them.

* Lastly, pointing out to her lover the liberality of his rivals.

Thus end the ways and means of getting money.

A woman should always know the state of the mind, of the feelings, and of the disposition of her lover towards her from the changes of his temper, his manner, and the colour of his face.

The behaviour of a waning lover is as follows:

* He gives the woman either less than is wanted, or something else than that which is asked for.

* He keeps her in hopes by promises.

* He pretends to do one thing, and does something else.

* He does not fulfil her desires.

* He forgets his promises, or does something else than that which he has promised.

* He speaks with his own servants in a mysterious way.

* He sleeps in some other house under the pretence of having to do something for a friend.

* Lastly, he speaks in private with the attendants of a woman with whom he was formerly acquainted.

Now when a courtesan finds that her lover's disposition towards her is changing, she should get possession of all his best things before he becomes aware of her intentions, and allow a supposed creditor to take them away forcibly from her in satisfaction of some pretended debt. After this, if the lover is rich, and has always behaved well towards her, she should ever treat him with respect; but if he is poor and destitute, she should get rid of him as if she had never been acquainted with him in any way before.

The means of getting rid of a lover are as follows:

* Describing the habits and vices of the lover as disagreeable and censurable, with the sneer of the lip, and the stamp of the foot.

* Speaking on a subject with which he is not acquainted.

* Showing no admiration for his learning, and passing a censure upon it.

* Putting down his pride.

* Seeking the company of men who are superior to him in learning and wisdom.

* Showing a disregard for him on all occasions.

* Censuring men possessed of the same faults as her lover.

* Expressing dissatisfaction at the ways and means of enjoyment used by him.

* Not giving him her mouth to kiss.

* Refusing access to her jaghana, i.e. the part of the body between the navel and the thighs.

* Showing a dislike for the wounds made by his nails and teeth.

* Not pressing close up against him at the time when he embraces her.

- Keeping her limbs without movement at the time of congress.

- Desiring him to enjoy her when he is fatigued.

- Laughing at his attachment to her.

- Not responding to his embraces.

- Turning away from him when he begins to embrace her.

- Pretending to be sleepy.

- Going out visiting, or into company, when she perceives his desire to enjoy her during the daytime.

- Mis-constructing his words.

- Laughing without any joke, or, at the time of any joke made by him, laughing under some pretence.

- Looking with side glances at her own attendants, and clapping her hands when he says anything.

- Interrupting him in the middle of his stories, and beginning to tell other stories herself.

- Reciting his faults and his vices, and declaring them to be incurable.

- Saying words to her female attendants calculated to cut the heart of her lover to the quick.

- Taking care not to look at him when he comes to her.

- Asking him what cannot be granted.

- And, after all, finally dismissing him.

There are also two verses on this subject as follows:

> The duty of a courtesan consists in forming connections with suitable men after due and full consideration, and attaching the person with whom she is united to herself; in obtaining wealth from the person who is attached to her, and then dismissing him after she has taken away all his possessions.

> A courtesan leading in this manner the life of a wife is not troubled with too many lovers, and yet obtains abundance of wealth.

footnote

1   On the completion of a vow a festival takes place. Some trees, such as the Peepul and Banyan trees, are invested with sacred threads like the Brahman's, and on the occasion of this ceremony a festival is given. In the same way when gardens are made, and tanks or temples built, then also festivals are observed.

CHAPTER IV

About Re-Union with a Former Lover

§ When a courtesan abandons her present lover after all his wealth is exhausted, she may then consider about her reunion with a former lover. But she should return to him only if he has acquired fresh wealth, or is still wealthy, and if he is still attached to her. And if this man be living at the time with some other woman she should consider well before she acts.

Now such a man can only be in one of the six following conditions:

> *He may have left the first woman of his own accord,*
> *and may even have left another woman since then.*
>
> *He may have been driven away from both women.*
>
> *He may have left the one woman of her own accord,*
> *and been driven away by the other.*
>
> *He may have left the one woman of his own accord,*
> *and be living with another woman.*
>
> *He may have been driven away from the one woman,*
> *and left the other of his own accord.*
>
> *He may have been driven away by the one woman,*
> *and may be living with another.*

— Now if the man has left both women of his own accord, he should not be resorted to, on account of the fickleness of his mind, and his indifference to the excellences of both of them.

— As regards the man who may have been driven away from both women, if he has been driven away from the last one because the woman could get more money from some other man, then he should be resorted to, for if attached to the first woman he would give her more money, through vanity and emulation to spite the other woman. But if he has been driven away by the woman on account of his poverty, or stinginess, he should not then be resorted to.

– In the case of the man who may have left the one woman of his own accord, and been driven away by the other, if he agrees to return to the former and give her plenty of money beforehand, then he should be resorted to.

– In the case of the man who may have left the one woman of his own accord, and be living with another woman, the former (wishing to take up with him again) should first ascertain if he left her in the first instance in the hope of finding some particular excellence in the other woman, and that not having found any such excellence, he was willing to come back to her, and to give her much money on account of his conduct, and on account of his affection still existing for her.

Or, whether, having discovered many faults in the other woman, he would now see even more excellences in herself than actually exist, and would be prepared to give her much money for these qualities.

Or, lastly, to consider whether he was a weak man, or a man fond of enjoying many women, or one who liked a poor woman, or one who never did anything for the woman that he was with. After maturely considering all these things, she should resort to him or not, according to circumstances.

– As regards the man who may have been driven away from the one woman, and left the other of his own accord, the former woman (wishing to reunite with him) should first ascertain whether he still has any affection for her, and would consequently spend much money upon her; or whether, being attached to her excellent qualities, he did not take delight in any other woman; or whether, being driven away from her formerly before completely satisfying his sexual desires, he wished to get back to her, so as to be revenged for the injury done to him; or whether he wished to create confidence in her mind, and then take back from her the wealth which she formerly took from him, and finally destroy her; or, lastly, whether he wished first to separate her from her present lover, and then to break away from her himself. If, after considering all these things, she is of opinion that his intentions are really pure and honest, she can reunite herself with him. But if his mind be at all tainted with evil intentions, he should be avoided.

– In the case of the man who may have been driven away by one woman, and be living with another, if the man makes overtures to return to the first one, the courtesan should consider well before she acts, and while the other woman is engaged in attracting him to herself, she should try in her turn (though keeping herself behind the scenes) to gain him over, on the grounds of any of the following considerations:

* *That he was driven away unjustly and for no proper reason, and now that he has gone to another woman, every effort must be used to bring him back to myself.*

* *That if he were once to converse with me again, he would break away from the other woman.*

* *That the pride of my present lover would be put down by means of the former one.*

* *That he has become wealthy, has secured a higher position, and holds a place of authority under the king.*

* *That he is separate from his wife.*

* *That he is now independent.*

* *That he lives apart from his father, or brother.*

* *That by making peace with him, I shall be able to get hold of a very rich man, who is now prevented from coming to me by my present lover.*

* *That as he is not respected by his wife, I shall now be able to separate him from her.*

* *That the friend of this man loves my rival, who hates me cordially, I shall therefore by this means separate the friend from his mistress.*

* *And lastly, I shall bring discredit upon him by bringing him back to me, thus showing the fickleness of his mind.*

When a courtesan is resolved to take up again with a former lover, her Pithamarda and other servants should tell him that his former expulsion from the woman's house was caused by the wickedness of her mother; that the woman loved him just as much as ever at that time, but could not help the occurrence on account of her deference to her mother's will; that she hated the union of her present lover, and disliked him excessively. In addition to this, they should create confidence in his mind by speaking to him of her former love for him, and should allude to the mark of that love that she has ever remembered. This mark of her love should be connected with some kind of pleasure that may have been practised by him, such as his way of kissing her, or manner of having connection with her.

Thus end the ways of bringing about a reunion with a former lover.

When a woman has to choose between two lovers, one of whom was formerly united with her, while the other is a stranger, the Acharyas (sages) are of opinion that the first one is preferable, because his disposition and character being already known by previous careful observation, he can be easily pleased and satisfied; but Vatsyayana thinks that a former lover, having already spent a great deal of his wealth, is not able or willing to give much money again, and is not therefore to be relied upon so much as a stranger. Particular cases may however arise differing from this general rule on account of the different natures of men.

There are also verses on the subject as follows:

Reunion with a former lover may be desirable
so as to separate some particular woman from some particular man,
or some particular man from some particular woman,
or to have a certain effect upon the present lover.

When a man is excessively attached to a woman,
he is afraid of her coming into contact with other men;
he does not then regard or notice her faults and he gives her
much wealth through fear of her leaving him.

A courtesan should be agreeable to the man who is attached to her,
and despise the man who does not care for her. If while she is living
with one man, a messenger comes to her from some other man, she
may either refuse to listen to any negotiations on his part, or appoint
a fixed time for him to visit her, but she should not leave the man
who may be living with her and who may be attached to her.

A wise woman should only renew her connection with
a former lover, if she is satisfied that good fortune, gain, love,
and friendship, are likely to be the result of such a reunion.

CHAPTER V

Of Different Kinds of Gain

§ When a courtesan is able to realize much money every day, by reason of many customers, she should not confine herself to a single lover; under such circumstances, she should fix her rate for one night, after considering the place, the season, and the condition of the people, and having regard to her own good qualities and good looks, and after comparing her rates with those of other courtesans. She can inform her lovers, and friends, and acquaintances about these charges. If, however, she can obtain a great gain from a single lover, she may resort to him alone, and live with him like a wife.

Now the sages are of opinion that, when a courtesan has the chance of an equal gain from two lovers at the same time, a preference should be given to the one who would give her the kind of thing which she wants. But Vatsyayana says that the preference should be given to the one who gives her gold, because it cannot be taken back like some other things, it can be easily received, and is also the means of procuring anything that may be wished for. Of such things as gold, silver, copper, bell metal, iron, pots, furniture, beds, upper garments, under vestments, fragrant substances, vessels made of gourds, ghee, oil, corn, cattle, and other things of a like nature, the first — gold — is superior to all the others.

> WHEN A COURTESAN IS ABLE TO REALIZE MUCH MONEY EVERY
> DAY... SHE SHOUD NOT CONFINE HERSELF TO A SINGLE LOVER.

When the same labour is required to gain any two lovers, or when the same kind of thing is to be got from each of them, the choice should be made by the advice of a friend, or it may be made from their personal qualities, or from the signs of good or bad fortune that may be connected with them.

When there are two lovers, one of whom is attached to the courtesan, and the other is simply very generous, the sages say that the preference should be given to the generous lover, but Vatsyayana is of opinion that the one who is really attached to the courtesan should be preferred, because he can be made to be generous, even as a miser gives money if he becomes fond of a woman, but a man who is simply generous cannot be made to love with real attachment. But among those who are attached to her, if there is one who is poor, and one who is rich, the preference is of course to be given to the latter.

When there are two lovers, one of whom is generous, and the other ready to do any service for the courtesan, some sages say that the one who is ready to do the service should be preferred, but Vatsyayana is of opinion that a man who does a service thinks that he has gained his object when he has done something once, but a generous man does not care for what he has given before. Even here the choice should be guided by the likelihood of the future good to be derived from her union with either of them.

WHEN AN OCCASION FOR COMPLYING WITH THE REQUEST OF A FRIEND, AND A CHANCE OF GETTING MONEY COME TOGETHER, THE SAGES SAY THAT THE CHANCE OF GETTING MONEY SHOULD BE PREFERRED.

When one of the two lovers is grateful, and the other liberal, some sages say that the liberal one should be preferred, but Vatsyayana is of opinion that the former should be chosen, because liberal men are generally haughty, plain spoken, and wanting in consideration towards others. Even though these liberal men have been on friendly terms for a long time, yet if they see any fault in the courtesan, or are told lies about her by some other woman, they do not care for past services, but leave abruptly. On the other hand the grateful man does not at once break off from her, on account of a regard for the pains she may have taken to please him. In this case also the choice is to be guided with respect to what may happen in future.

When an occasion for complying with the request of a friend, and a chance of getting money come together, the sages say that the chance of getting money should be preferred. But Vatsyayana thinks that the money can be obtained tomorrow as well as today, but if the request of a friend be riot at once complied with, he may become disaffected. Even here, in making the choice, regard must be paid to future good fortune.

On such an occasion, however, the courtesan might pacify her friend by pretending to have some work to do, and telling him that his request will be complied with next day, and in this way secure the chance of getting the money that has been offered her.

When the chance of getting money and the chance of avoiding some disaster come at the same time, the sages are of opinion that the chance of getting money should be preferred, but Vatsyayana says that money has only a limited importance, while a disaster that is once averted may never occur again. Here, however, the choice should be guided by the greatness or smallness of the disaster.

The gains of the wealthiest and best kind of courtesans are to be spent as follows:

Building temples, tanks, and gardens; giving a thousand cows to different Brahmans; carrying on the worship of the Gods, and celebrating festivals in their honour; and lastly, performing such vows as may be within their means.

The gains of other courtesans are to be spent as follows:

Having a white dress to wear every day; getting sufficient food and drink to satisfy hunger and thirst; eating daily a perfumed tambula, i.e. a mixture of betel nut and betel leaves; and wearing ornaments gilt with gold. The sages say that these represent the gains of all the middle and lower classes of courtesans, but Vatsyayana is of opinion that their gains cannot be calculated, or fixed in any way, as these depend on the influence of the place, the customs of the people, their own appearance, and many other things.

When a courtesan wants to keep some particular man from some other woman; or wishes to get him away from some woman to whom he may be attached or to deprive some woman of the gains realized by her from him; or if she thinks that she would raise her position or enjoy some great good fortune or become desirable to all men by uniting herself with this man; or if she wishes to get his assistance in averting some misfortune; or is really attached to him and loves him; or wishes to injure some body through his means; or has regard to some former favour conferred upon her by him; or wishes to be united with him merely from desire; for any of the above reasons, she should agree to take from him only a small sum of money in a friendly way.

When a courtesan intends to abandon a particular lover, and take up with another one; or when she has reason to believe that her lover will shortly leave her, and return to his wives; or that having squandered all his money, and become penniless, his guardian, or master, or father would come and take him away; or that her lover is about to lose his position or, lastly, that he is of a very fickle mind, she should, under any of these circumstances, endeavour to get as much money as she can from him as soon as possible.

On the other hand, when the courtesan thinks that her lover is about to receive valuable presents; or get a place of authority from the king; or be near the time of inheriting a fortune; or that his ship would soon arrive laden with merchandise; or that he has large stocks of corn and other commodities; or that if anything was done for him it would not be done in vain; or that he is always true to his word; then should she have regard to her future welfare, and live with the man like a wife.

There are also verses on the subject as follows:

In considering her present gains, and her future welfare,
a courtesan should avoid such persons as have gained their means
of subsistence with very great difficulty, as also those who have
become selfish and hard-hearted by becoming the favourites of kings.

She should make every endeavour to unite herself with
prosperous and well-to-do people, and with those whom it is
dangerous to avoid, or to slight in any way. Even at some cost to
herself she should become acquainted with energetic and liberal-
minded men, who when pleased would give her a large sum of
money, even for very little service, or for some small thing.

Of Gains & Losses; Attendant Gains & Losses; & Doubts; As Also of the Different Kinds of Courtesans

§ It sometimes happens that while gains are being sought for, or expected to be realized, losses only are the result of our efforts. The causes of these losses are:

Weakness of intellect

Excessive love

Excessive pride

Excessive self conceit

Excessive simplicity

Excessive confidence

Excessive anger

Carelessness

Recklessness

Influence of evil genius

Accidental circumstances

The results of these losses are:

Expense incurred without any result

Destruction of future good fortune

Stoppage of gains about to be realized

Loss of what is already obtained

Acquisition of a sour temper

Becoming unamiable to every body

Injury to health

Loss of hair and other accidents

Now gain is of three kinds: gain of wealth, gain of religious merit, and gain of pleasure; and similarly loss is of three kinds: loss of wealth, loss of religious merit, and loss of pleasure.

At the time when gains are sought for, if other gains come along with them, these are called attendant gains. When gain is uncertain, the doubt of its being a gain is called a simple doubt. When there is a doubt whether either of two things will happen or not, it is called a mixed doubt. If while one thing is being done two results take place, it is called a combination of two results, and if several results follow from the same action, it is called a combination of results on every side.

We shall now give examples of the above.

As already stated, gain is of three kinds, and loss, which is opposed to gain, is also of three kinds.

When by living with a great man a courtesan acquires present wealth, and in addition to this becomes acquainted with other people, and thus obtains a chance of future fortune, and an accession of wealth, and becomes desirable to all, this is called a gain of wealth attended by other gain.

When by living with a man a courtesan simply gets money, this is called a gain of wealth not attended by any other gain.

When a courtesan receives money from other people besides her lover, the results are the chance of the loss of future good from her present lover; the chance of disaffection of a man securely attached to her; the hatred of all; and the chance of a union with some low person, tending to destroy her future good. This gain is called a gain of wealth attended by losses.

When a courtesan, at her own expense, and without any results in the shape of gain, has connection with a great man, or an avaricious minister, for the sake of diverting some misfortune, or removing some cause that may be threatening the destruction of a great gain, this loss is said to be a loss of wealth attended by gains of the future good which it may bring about.

When a courtesan is kind, even at her own expense, to a man who is very stingy, or to a man proud of his looks, or to an ungrateful man skilled in gaining the hearts of others, without any good resulting from these connections to her in the end, this loss is called a loss of wealth not attended by any gain.

When a courtesan is kind to any such man as described above, but who in addition is a favourite of the king, and moreover cruel and powerful, without any good result in the end, and with a chance of her being turned away at any moment, this loss is called a loss of wealth attended by other losses.

In this way gains and losses, and attendant gains and losses in religious merit and pleasures may become known to the reader, and combinations of all of them may also be made.

Thus end the remarks on gains and losses, and attendant gains and losses.

IT SOMETIMES HAPPENS THAT WHILE GAINS ARE BEING SOUGHT FOR, OR EXPECTED TO BE REALIZED, LOSSES ONLY ARE THE RESULT OF OUR EFFORTS.

In the next place we come to doubts, which are again of three kinds: doubts about wealth, doubts about religious merit, and doubts about pleasures.

The following are examples:

When a courtesan is not certain how much a man may give her, or spend upon her, this is called a doubt about wealth.

When a courtesan feels doubtful whether she is right in entirely abandoning a lover from whom she is unable to get money, she having taken all his wealth from him in the first instance, this doubt is called a doubt about religious merit.

When a courtesan is unable to get hold of a lover to her liking, and is uncertain whether she will derive any pleasure from a person surrounded by his family, or from a low person, this is called a doubt about pleasure.

When a courtesan is uncertain whether some powerful but low principled fellow would cause loss to her on account of her not being civil to him this is called a doubt about the loss of wealth.

When a courtesan feels doubtful whether she would lose religious merit by abandoning a man who is attached to her without giving him the slightest favour, and thereby causing him unhappiness in this world and the next [*1], this doubt is called a doubt about the loss of a religious merit.

When a courtesan is uncertain as to whether she might create disaffection by speaking out, and revealing her love and thus not get her desire satisfied, this is called a doubt about the loss of pleasure.

Thus end the remarks on doubts.

Mixed Doubts

The intercourse or connection with a stranger, whose disposition is unknown, and who may have been introduced by a lover, or by one who possessed authority, may be productive either of gain or loss, and therefore this is called a mixed doubt about the gain and loss of wealth.

When a courtesan is requested by a friend, or is impelled by pity to have intercourse with a learned Brahman, a religious student, a sacrificer, a devotee, or an ascetic who may have all fallen in love with her, and who may be consequently at the point of death, by doing this she might either gain or lose religious merit, and therefore this is called a mixed doubt about the gain and loss of religious merit.

If a courtesan relies solely upon the report of other people (i.e. hearsay) about a man, and goes to him without ascertaining herself whether he possesses good qualities or not, she may either gain or lose pleasure in proportion as he may be good or bad, and therefore this is called a mixed doubt about the gain and loss of pleasure.

Uddalika has described the gains and losses on both sides as follows:

If, when living with a lover, a courtesan gets both wealth and pleasure from him, it is called a gain on both sides.

When a courtesan lives with a lover at her own expense without getting any profit out of it, and the lover even takes back from her what he may have formerly given her, it is called a loss on both sides.

When a courtesan is uncertain whether a new acquaintance would become attached to her, and, moreover, if he became attached to her, whether he would give her anything, it is then called a doubt on both sides about gains.

When a courtesan is uncertain whether a former enemy, if made up by her at her own expense, would do her some injury on account of his grudge against her; or, if becoming attached to her, would take away angrily from her anything that he may have given to her, this is called a doubt on both sides about loss.

Babhravya has described the gains and losses on both sides as follows:

When a courtesan can get money from a man whom she may go to see, and also money from a man whom she may not go to see, this is called a gain on both sides.

When a courtesan has to incur further expense if she goes to see a man, and yet runs the risk of incurring an irremediable loss if she does not go to see him, this is called a loss on both sides.

When a courtesan is uncertain whether a particular man would give her anything on her going to see him, without incurring expense on her part or whether on her neglecting him another man would give her something, this is called a doubt on both sides about gain.

When a courtesan is uncertain whether, on going at her own expense to see an old enemy, he would take back from her what he may have given her, or whether by her not going to see him he would cause some disaster to fall upon her, this is called a doubt on both sides about loss.

By combining the above, the following six kinds of mixed results are produced:

Gain on one side, and loss on the other

Gain on one side, and doubt of gain on the other

Gain on one side, and doubt of loss on the other

Loss on one side, and doubt of gain on the other

Doubt of gain on one side, and doubt of loss on the other

Doubt of loss on one side, and loss on the other

A courtesan, having considered all the above things and taken counsel with her friends, should act so as to acquire gain, the chances of great gain, and the warding off of any great disaster. Religious merit and pleasure should also be formed into separate combinations like those of wealth, and then all should be combined with each other, so as to form new combinations.

When a courtesan consorts with men she should cause each of them to give her money as well as pleasure. At particular times, such as the Spring Festivals, etc., she should make her mother announce to the various men, that on a certain day her daughter would remain with the man who would gratify such and such a desire of hers.

When young men approach her with delight, she should think of what she may accomplish through them.

The combination of gains and losses on all sides are gain on one side, and loss on all others; loss on one side and gain on all others; gain on all sides, loss on all sides.

A courtesan should also consider doubts about gain and doubts about loss with reference both to wealth, religious merit, and pleasure.

Thus ends the consideration of gain, loss, attendant gains, attendant losses, and doubts.

The different kinds of courtesans are:

A bawd

A female attendant

An unchaste woman

A dancing girl

A female artisan

A woman who has left her family

A woman living on her beauty

And, finally, a regular courtesan

All the above kinds of courtesans are acquainted with various kinds of men, and should consider the ways of getting money from them of pleasing them, of separating themselves from them, and of reuniting with them. They should also take into consideration particular gains and losses, attendant gains and losses, and doubts in accordance with their several conditions.

Thus end the considerations of courtesans.

There are also two verses on the subject as follows:

Men want pleasure, while women want money, and therefore this part, which treats of the means of gaining wealth, should be studied.

There are some women who seek for love, and there are others who seek for money; for the former the ways of love are told in previous portions of this work, while the ways of getting money, as practised by courtesans, are described in this part.

footnote

1   The souls of men who die with their desires unfulfilled are said to go to the world of the Manes, and not direct to the Supreme Spirit.

PART VII

ABOUT THE MEANS TO ATTRACT
OTHERS TO YOURSELF

CHAPTER I

On Personal Adornment;
On Subjugating the Hearts of Others;
& on Tonic Medicines

§ When a person fails to obtain the object of his desires by any of the ways previously related, he should then have recourse to other ways of attracting others to himself.

Now good looks, good qualities, youth, and liberality are the chief and most natural means of making a person agreeable in the eyes of others. But in the absence of these a man or a woman must have resort to artificial means, or to art, and the following are some recipes that may be found useful.

* *An ointment made of the* Tabernamontana coronaria, *the* Costus speciosus *or* arabicus, *and the* Flacourtia cataphracta, *can be used as an unguent of adornment.*

* *If a fine powder is made of the above plants, and applied to the wick of a lamp, which is made to burn with the oil of blue vitrol, the black pigment or lamp black produced therefrom, when applied to the eyelashes, has the effect of making a person look lovely.*

* *The oil of the hogweed, the* Echites putescens, *the sarina plant, the yellow amaranth, and the leaf of the nymphae, if applied to the body, has the same effect.*

* *A black pigment from the same plants produces a similar effect.*

* *By eating the powder of the* Nelumbrium speciosum, *the blue lotus, and the* Mesna roxburghii, *with ghee and honey, a man becomes lovely in the eyes of others.*

* *The above things, together with the* Tabernamontana coronaria, *and the* Xanthochymus pictorius, *if used as an ointment, produce the same results.*

* *If the bone of a peacock or of a hyena be covered with gold, and tied on the right hand, it makes a man lovely in the eyes of other people.*

✳ In the same way, if a bead, made of the seed of the jujube, or of the conch shell, be enchanted by the incantations mentioned in the Atharvana Veda, or by the incantations of those well skilled in the science of magic, and tied on the hand, it produces the same result as described above.

✳ When a female attendant arrives at the age of puberty, her master should keep her secluded, and when men ardently desire her on account of her seclusion, and on account of the difficulty of approaching her, he should then bestow her hand on such a person as may endow her with wealth and happiness.

This is a means of increasing the loveliness of a person in the eyes of others.

In the same way, when the daughter of a courtesan arrives at the age of puberty, the mother should get together a lot of young men of the same age, disposition, and knowledge as her daughter, and tell them that she would give her in marriage to the person who would give her presents of a particular kind.

After this the daughter should be kept in seclusion as far as possible, and the mother should give her in marriage to the man who may be ready to give her the presents agreed upon. If the mother is unable to get so much out of the man, she should show some of her own things as having been given to the daughter by the bridegroom.

Or the mother may allow her daughter to be married to the man privately, as if she was ignorant of the whole affair, and then pretending that it has come to her knowledge, she may give her consent to the union.

The daughter, too, should make herself attractive to the sons of wealthy citizens, unknown to her mother, and make them attached to her, and for this purpose should meet them at the time of learning to sing, and in places where music is played, and at the houses of other people, and then request her mother, through a female friend, or servant, to be allowed to unite herself to the man who is most agreeable to her [*1].

When the daughter of a courtesan is thus given to a man, the ties of marriage should be observed for one year, and after that she may do what she likes. But even after the end of the year, when otherwise engaged, if she should be now and then invited by her first husband to come and see him, she should put aside her present gain, and go to him for the night.

Such is the mode of temporary marriage among courtesans, and of increasing their loveliness, and their value in the eyes of others. What has been said about them should also be understood to apply to the daughters of dancing women, whose mothers should give them only to such persons as are likely to become useful to them in various ways.

Thus end the ways of making oneself lovely in the eyes of others.

– If a man, after anointing his lingam with a mixture of the powders of the white thorn apple, the long pepper and, the black pepper, and honey, engages in sexual union with a woman, he makes her subject to his will.

- The application of a mixture of the leaf of the plant vatodbhranta, of the flowers thrown on a human corpse when carried out to be burnt, and the powder of the bones of the peacock, and of the jiwanjiva bird produces the same effect.
- The remains of a kite who has died a natural death, ground into powder, and mixed with cowach and honey, has also the same effect.
- Anointing oneself with an ointment made of the plant *Emblica myrabolans* has the power of subjecting women to one's will.
- If a man cuts into small pieces the sprouts of the vajnasunhi plant, and dips them into a mixture of red arsenic and sulphur, and then dries them seven times, and applies this powder mixed with honey to his lingam, he can subjugate a woman to his will directly that he has had sexual union with her, or if, by burning these very sprouts at night and looking at the smoke, he sees a golden moon behind, he will then be successful with any woman; or if he throws some of the powder of these same sprouts mixed with the excrement of a monkey upon a maiden, she will not be given in marriage to anybody else.
- If pieces of the arris root are dressed with the oil of the mango, and placed for six months in a hole made in the trunk of the sisu tree, and are then taken out and made up into an ointment, and applied to the lingam, this is said to serve as the means of subjugating women.
- If the bone of a camel is dipped into the juice of the plant *Eclipta prostata*, and then burnt, and the black pigment produced from its ashes is placed in a box also made of the bone of a camel, and applied together with antimony to the eye lashes with a pencil also made of the bone of a camel, then that pigment is said to be very pure, and wholesome for the eyes, and serves as a means of subjugating others to the person who uses it. The same effect can be produced by black pigment made of the bones of hawks, vultures, and peacocks.

Thus end the ways of subjugating others to one's own will.

Now the means of increasing sexual vigour are as follows:

☀ *A man obtains sexual vigour by drinking milk mixed with sugar, the root of the uchchata plant, the* Piper chaba, *and liquorice.*

☀ *Drinking milk, mixed with sugar, and having the testicle of a ram or a goat boiled in it, is also productive of vigour.*

☀ *The drinking of the juice of the* Hedysarum gangeticum, *the kuili, and the kshirika plant mixed with milk, produces the same effect.*

☀ *The seed of the long pepper along with the seeds of the* Sanseviera roxburghiana, *and the* Hedysarum gangeticum *plant, all pounded together, and mixed with milk, is productive of a similar result.*

☀ *According to ancient authors, if a man pounds the seeds or roots of the* Trapa bispinosa, *the kasurika, the tuscan jasmine, and liquorice, together with the kshirakapoli (a kind of onion), and puts the powder into milk mixed with sugar and ghee, and having boiled the whole* mixture on a moderate fire, drinks the paste so formed, he will be able to enjoy innumerable women.

✳ In the same way, if a man mixes rice with the eggs of the sparrow, and having boiled this in milk, adds to it ghee and honey, and drinks as much of it as necessary, this will produce the same effect.

✳ If a man takes the outer covering of sesamum seeds, and soaks them with the eggs of sparrows, and then, having boiled them in milk, mixed with sugar and ghee, along with the fruits of the Trapa bispinosa and the kasurika plant, and adding to it the flour of wheat and beans, and then drinks this composition, he is said to be able to enjoy many women.

✳ If ghee, honey, sugar and liquorice in equal quantities, the juice of the fennel plant, and milk are mixed together, this nectar-like composition is said to be holy, and provocative of sexual vigour, a preservative of life, and sweet to the taste.

✳ The drinking of a paste composed of the Asparagus racemosus, the shvadaushtra plant, the guduchi plant, the long pepper, and liquorice, boiled in milk, honey, and ghee, in the spring, is said to have the same effect as the above.

✳ Boiling the Asparagus racemosus, and the shvadaushtra plant, along with the pounded fruits of the Premna spinosa in water, and drinking the same, is said to act in the same way.

✳ Drinking boiled ghee, or clarified butter, in the morning during the spring season, is said to be beneficial to health and strength and agreeable to the taste.

✳ If the powder of the seed of the shvadaushtra plant and the flower of barley are mixed together in equal parts, and a portion of it, i.e. two palas in weight, is eaten every morning on getting up, it has the same effect as the preceding recipe.

There are also verses on the subject as follows:

The means [*2] of producing love and sexual vigour should be learnt
from the science of medicine, from the Vedas, from those who are
learned in the arts of magic, and from confidential relatives.
No means should be tried which are doubtful in their effects,
which are likely to cause injury to the body, which involve the death
of animals, and which bring us in contact with impure things.
Such means should only be used as are holy, acknowledged to be
good, and approved of by Brahmans, and friends.

footnotes

1 It is a custom of the courtesans of Oriental countries to give their daughters temporarily in marriage when they come of age, and after they have received a education in the *Kama Sutra* and other arts. Full details are given of this in *Early Ideas*, a group of Hindoo stories, collected and collated by Anarya, W. H. Allen and Co., London, 1881.

2 From the earliest times Oriental authors have occupied themselves about aphrodisiacs. The following note on the subject is taken from a translation of *The Hindoo Art of Love*, otherwise the *Anunga Runga*, Part I, pages 87 and 88. "Most Eastern treatises divide aphrodisiacs into two different kinds; 1. the mechanical or natural, such as scarification, flagellation, etc; and 2. the medicinal or artificial. To the former belong the application of insects, as is practised by some savage races; and all orientalists will remember the tale of the old Brahman, whose young wife insisted upon his being again stung by a wasp."

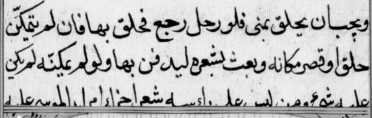

CHAPTER II

Of the Ways of Exciting Desire, & Miscellaneous Experiments, & Recipes

§ If a man is unable to satisfy a Hastini, or elephant woman, he should have recourse to various means to excite her passion. At the commencement he should rub her yoni with his hand or fingers, and not begin to have intercourse with her until she becomes excited, or experiences pleasure. This is one way of exciting a woman.

Or, he may make use of certain Apadravyas, or things which are put on or around the lingam to supplement its length or its thickness, so as to fit it to the yoni. In the opinion of Babhravya, these Apadravyas should be made of gold, silver, copper, iron, ivory, buffalo's horn, various kinds of wood, tin or lead, and should be soft, cool, provocative of sexual vigour, and well fitted to serve the intended purpose. Vatsyayana, however, says that they may be made according to the natural liking of each individual.

The following are the different kinds of Apadravyas:

* *'The armlet' (Valaya) should be of the same size as the lingam, and should have its outer surface made rough with globules.*

* *'The couple' (Sanghati) is formed of two armlets.*

* *'The bracelet' (Chudaka) is made by joining three or more armlets, until they come up to the required length of the lingam.*

* *'The single bracelet' is formed by wrapping a single wire around the lingam, according to its dimensions.*

* *The Kantuka or Jalaka is a tube open at both ends, with a hole through it, outwardly rough and studded with soft globules, and made to fit the side of the yoni, and tied to the waist.*

When such a thing cannot be obtained, then a tube made of the wood apple, or tubular stalk of the bottle gourd, or a reed made soft with oil and extracts of plants, and tied to the waist with strings, may be made use of, as also a row of soft pieces of wood tied together.

The above are the things that can be used in connection with or in the place of the lingam.

The people of the southern countries think that true sexual pleasure cannot be obtained without perforating the lingam, and they therefore cause it to be pierced like the lobes of the ears of an infant pierced for earrings.

Now, when a young man perforates his lingam he should pierce it with a sharp instrument, and then stand in water so long as the blood continues to flow. At night, he should engage in sexual intercourse, even with vigour, so as to clean the hole. After this he should continue to wash the hole with decoctions, and increase the size by putting into it small pieces of cane, and the *Wrightia antidysenterica*, and thus gradually enlarging the orifice. It may also be washed with liquorice mixed with honey, and the size of the hole increased by the fruit stalks of the simapatra plant. The hole should also be anointed with a small quantity of oil.

In the hole made in the lingam a man may put Apadravyas of various forms, such as the 'round', the 'round on one side', the 'wooden mortar', the 'flower', the 'armlet', the 'bone of the heron', the 'goad of the elephant', the 'collection of eight balls', the 'lock of hair', the 'place where four roads meet', and other things named according to their forms and means of using them. All these Apadravyas should be rough on the outside according to their requirements.

The ways of enlarging the lingam must be now related.

When a man wishes to enlarge his lingam, he should rub it with the bristles of certain insects that live in trees, and then, after rubbing it for ten nights with oils, he should again rub it with the bristles as before. By continuing to do this a swelling will be gradually produced in the lingam, and he should then lie on a cot, and cause his lingam to hang down through a hole in the cot. After this he should take away all the pain from the swelling by using cool concoctions. The swelling, which is called 'Suka', and is often brought about among the people of the Dravida country, lasts for life.

If the lingam is rubbed with the following things, the plant *Physalis flexuosa*, the shavara-kandaka plant, the jalasuka plant, the fruit of the egg plant, the butter of a she-buffalo, the hastri-charma plant, and the juice of the vajrarasa plant, a swelling lasting for one month will be produced.

By rubbing it with oil boiled in the concoctions of the above things, the same effect will be produced, but lasting for six months.

The enlargement of the lingam is also effected by rubbing it or moistening it with oil boiled on a moderate fire along with the seeds of the pomegranate, and the cucumber, the juices of the valuka plant, the hastri-charma plant, and the egg plant.

In addition to the above, other means may be learnt from experienced and confidential persons.

The miscellaneous experiments and recipes are as follows:

* If a man mixes the powder of the milk hedge plant, and the kantaka plant with the excrement of a monkey and the powdered root of the lanjalika plant, and throws this mixture on a woman, she will not love anybody else afterwards.

* If a man thickens the juice of the fruits of the cassia fistula, and the eugenia jambolana by mixing them with the powder of the soma plant, the Vernonia anthelmintica, the Eclipta prostata, and the lohopa-jihirka, and applies this composition to the yoni of a woman, and then has sexual intercourse with her, his love for her will be destroyed.

* The same effect is produced if a man has connection with a woman who has bathed in the buttermilk of a she-buffalo mixed with the powders of the gopalika plant, the banu-padika plant and the yellow amaranth.

* An ointment made of the flowers of the Nauclea cadamba, the hog plum, and the Eugenia jambolana, and used by a woman, causes her to be disliked by her husband.

* Garlands made of the above flowers, when worn by the woman, produce the same effect.

* An ointment made of the fruit of the Asteracantha longifolia (kokilaksha) will contract the yoni of a Hastini or Elephant woman, and this contraction lasts for one night.

* An ointment made by pounding the roots of the Nelumbrium speciosum, and of the blue lotus, and the powder of the plant Physalis flexuosa mixed with ghee and honey, will enlarge the yoni of the Mrigi or deer woman.

* An ointment made of the fruit of the Emblica myrabolans soaked in the milky juice of the milk hedge plant, of the soma plant, the Calotropis gigantean, and the juice of the fruit of the Vernonia anthelmintica, will make the hair white.

* The juice of the roots of the madayantaka plant, the yellow amaranth, the anjanika plant, the Clitoria ternateea, and the shlakshnaparin plant, used as a lotion, will make the hair grow.

* An ointment made by boiling the above roots in oil, and rubbed in, will make the hair black, and will also gradually restore hair that has fallen off.

* If lac is saturated seven times in the sweat of the testicle of a white horse, and applied to a red lip, the lip will become white.

* The colour of the lips can be regained by means of the madayantika and other plants mentioned above.

* A woman who hears a man playing on a reed pipe which has been dressed

with the juices of the bahupadika plant, *the* Tabernamontana coronaria, *the* Costus speciosus *or* arabicus, *the* Pinus deodora, *the* Euphorbia antiquorum, *the vajra and the kantaka plant, becomes his slave.*

✹ *If food be mixed with the fruit of the thorn apple (dathura) it causes intoxication.*

✹ *If water be mixed with oil and the ashes of any kind of grass except the kusha grass, it becomes the colour of milk.*

✹ *If yellow myrabolans, the hog plum, the shrawana plant, and the priyangu plant be* all pounded together, and applied to iron pots, these pots become red.

✹ *If a lamp, trimmed with oil extracted from the shrawana and priyangu plants, its wick being made of cloth and the slough of the skins of snakes, is lighted, and long pieces of wood placed near it, those pieces of wood will resemble so many snakes.*

✹ *Drinking the milk of a white cow who has a white calf at her foot is auspicious, produces fame, and preserves life.*

✹ *The blessings of venerable Brahmans, well propitiated, have the same effect.*

There are also some verses in conclusion:

Thus have I written in a few words the Science of love, after reading the texts of ancient authors, and following the ways of enjoyment mentioned in them.

He who is acquainted with the true principles of this science pays regard to Dharma, Artha, Kama, and to his own experiences, as well as to the teachings of others, and does not act simply on the dictates of his own desire. As for the errors in the science of love which I have mentioned in this work, on my own authority as an author, I have, immediately after mentioning them, carefully censured and prohibited them.

An act is never looked upon with indulgence for the simple reason that it is authorised by the science, because it ought to be remembered that it is the intention of the science, that the rules which it contains should only be acted upon in particular cases.

*After reading and considering the works of Babhravya
and other ancient authors, and thinking over the meaning
of the rules given by them, the Kama Sutra was composed,
according to the precepts of Holy Writ, for the benefit of the world,
by Vatsyayana, while leading the life of a religious student, and
wholly engaged in the contemplation of the Deity.*

*This work is not intended to be used merely as an instrument
for satisfying our desires. A person, acquainted with the true
principles of this science, and who preserves his Dharma,
Artha, and Kama, and has regard for the practices of the people,
is sure to obtain the mastery over his senses.*

*In short, an intelligent and prudent person, attending to Dharma
and Artha, and attending to Kama also, without becoming the slave
of his passions, obtains success in everything that he may undertake.*

Concluding Remarks

§ Thus ends, in seven parts, the *Kama Sutra* of Vatsyayana, which might otherwise be called a treatise on men and women, their mutual relationship, and connection with each other.

It is a work that should be studied by all, both old and young; the former will find in it real truths, gathered by experience, and already tested by themselves, while the latter will derive the great advantage of learning things, which some perhaps may otherwise never learn at all, or which they may only learn when it is too late ('too late' those immortal words of Mirabeau) to profit by the learning.

It can also be fairly commended to the student of social science and of humanity, and above all to the student of those early ideas, which have gradually filtered down through the sands of time, and which seem to prove that the human nature of today is much the same as the human nature of the long ago.

It has been said of Balzac the great, if not the greatest of French novelists, that he seemed to have inherited a natural and intuitive perception of the feelings of men and women, and has described them with an analysis worthy of a man of science. The author of the present work must also have had a considerable knowledge of the humanities. Many of his remarks are so full of simplicity and truth that they have stood the test of time, and stand out still as clear and true as when they were first written, some eighteen hundred years ago.

As a collection of facts, told in plain and simple language, it must be remembered that in those early days there was apparently no idea of embellishing the work, either with a literary style, a flow of language, or a quantity of superfluous padding. The author tells the world what he knows in very concise language, without any attempt to produce an interesting story. From his facts how many novels could be written! Indeed much of the matter contained in Parts III, IV, V and VI has formed the basis of many of the stories and the tales of past centuries.

There will be found in Part VII some curious recipes. Many of them appear to be as primitive as the book itself, but in later works of the same nature these recipes and prescriptions appear to have increased, both as regards quality and quantity. In the *Anunga Runga* or *The Stage of Love*, there are found no less than thirty-three different subjects for which one hundred and thirty recipes and prescriptions are given.

As the details may be interesting, these subjects are described as follows:

- For hastening the paroxysm of the woman
- For delaying the orgasm of the man
- Aphrodisiacs
- For thickening and enlarging the lingam, rendering it sound and strong, hard and lusty
- For narrowing and contracting the yoni
- For perfuming the yoni
- For removing and destroying the hair of the body
- For removing the sudden stopping of the monthly ailment
- For abating the immoderate appearance of the monthly ailment
- For purifying the womb
- For causing pregnancy
- For preventing miscarriage and other accidents
- For ensuring easy labour and ready deliverance
- For limiting the number of children
- For thickening and beautifying the hair
- For obtaining a good black colour to it
- For whitening and bleaching it
- For renewing it

- For clearing the skin of the face from eruptions that break out and leave black spots upon it
- For removing the black colour of the epidermis
- For enlarging the breasts of women
- For raising and hardening pendulous breasts
- For giving a fragrance to the skin
- For removing the evil savour of perspiration
- For anointing the body after bathing
- For causing a pleasant smell to the breath
- Drugs and charms for the purposes of fascinating, overcoming, and subduing either men or women
- Recipes for enabling a woman to attract and preserve her husband's love
- Magical collyriums for winning love and friendship
- Prescriptions for reducing other persons to submission
- Philtre pills, and other charms
- Fascinating incense, or fumigation
- Magical verses which have the power of fascination

Of the one hundred and thirty recipes given, many of them are absurd, but not more perhaps than many of the recipes and prescriptions in use in Europe not so very long ago. Love-philtres, charms, and herbal remedies have been, in early days, as freely used in Europe as in Asia, and doubtless some people believe in them still in many places.

And now, one word about the author of the work, the good old sage Vatsyayana. It is much to be regretted that nothing can be discovered about his life, his belongings, and his surroundings. At the end of Part VII, he states that he wrote the work while leading the life of a religious student [probably at Benares] and while wholly engaged in the contemplation of the Deity. He must have arrived at a certain age at that time, for throughout he gives us the benefit of his experience, and of his opinions, and these bear the stamp of age rather than of youth; indeed the work could hardly have been written by a young man.

In a beautiful verse of the *Vedas* of the Christians it has been said of the peaceful dead, that they rest from their labours, and that their works do follow them. Yes indeed, the works of men of genius do follow them, and remain as a lasting treasure. And though there may be disputes and discussions about the immortality of the body or the soul, nobody can deny the immortality of genius, which ever remains as a bright and guiding star to the struggling humanities of succeeding ages. This work, then, which has stood the test of centuries, has placed Vatsyayana among the immortals, and on This, and on Him no better elegy or eulogy can be written than the following lines:

So long as lips shall kiss, and eyes shall see,
So long lives This, and This gives life to Thee.

An Hachette UK Company
www.hachette.co.uk

First published in Great Britain in 2012 by Hamlyn,
a division of Octopus Publishing Group Ltd
Endeavour House, 189 Shaftesbury Avenue
London WC2H 8JY

www.octopusbooks.co.uk
www.octopusbooksusa.com

Distributed in the US by Hachette Book Group USA,
237 Park Avenue, New York, NY 10017, USA

Distributed in Canada by Canadian Manda Group,
165 Dufferin Street, Toronto, Ontario, Canada M6K 3H6

ISBN 978-0-600-62321-2

A CIP catalogue record for this book is available from the British Library.

Printed and bound in China.

1 3 5 7 9 10 8 6 4 2

All reasonable care has been taken in the preparation of this book,
but the publishers cannot accept any liability for any consequence arising
from the use thereof, or the information contained therein.

Transformations in Classical Architecture

New Directions in Research and Practice

OSCAR RIERA OJEDA
PUBLISHERS

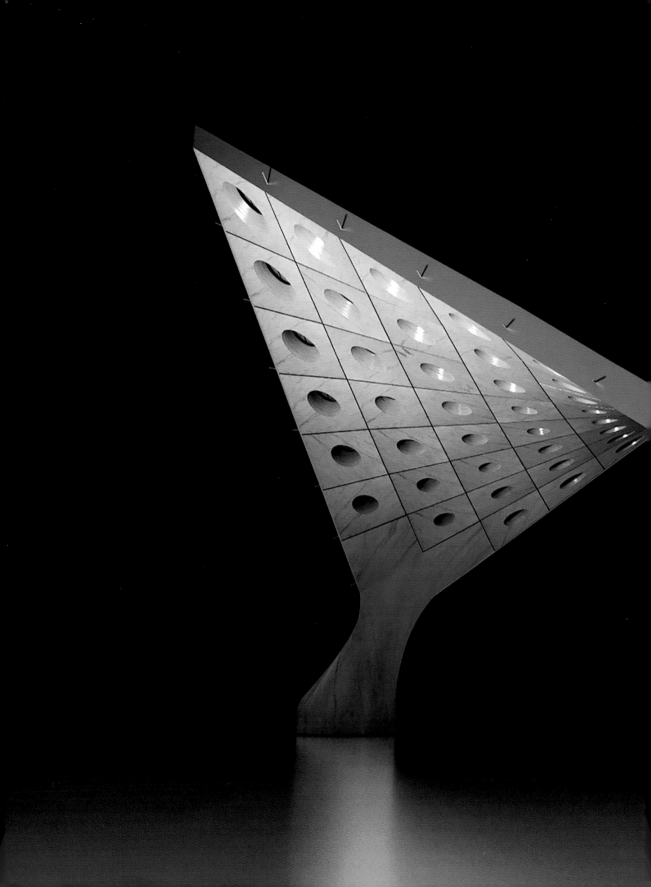

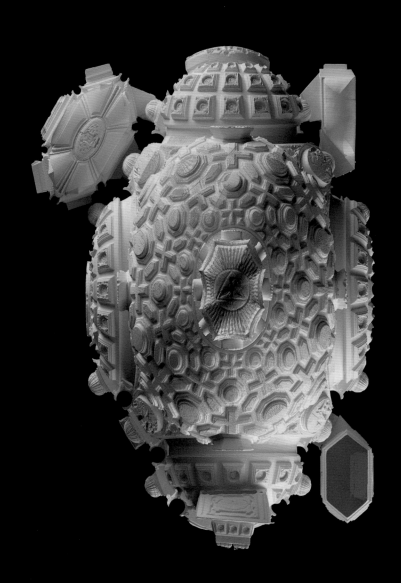

Transformations in Classical Architecture

New Directions in Research and Practice

Preface by
Rodolphe el-Khoury

Essays by
Jean- François Lejeune,
Rocco Ceo, Victor Deupi & Eric Firley,
Nathaniel Robert Walker,
Juan Manuel Yactayo, Andres Duany,
Javier Cenicacelaya, Richard John.

**Edited with
an Introduction by**
Victor Deupi

Contributions by
Pier Carlo Bontempi, Melissa and Jacob Brillhart, Steven Brooke,
Pablo Cano, Josemaría de Churtichaga & Cayetana de la Quadra- Salcedo, Andrea Collesano,
Jaime Correa, Adib Cúre & Carie Penabad, Benjamin Dillenburger & Michael Hansmeyer,
Duany Plater-Zyberk, Giuseppi Fallacara, Steven Fett, Giuseppi Greci, Harrison Design,
Michael G. Imber Architects, Gary Justiss, Khoury & Vogt Architects, Leon Krier, Robert
Levit, Frank Martinez & Ana Alvarez, Merrill, Pastor & Colgan Architects, Peter Pennoyer
Architects, Elizabeth Plater- Zyberk, James Prosek, R & R Studios / Roberto Behar & Rosario
Marquardt, Andrew Saunders, Lucien Steil, Nader Tehrani, Trelles Cabarrocas Architects,
Urban Design Associates, Teofilo Victoria, and Thomas Woltz of Nelson Byrd Woltz.

With special thanks to Sydney Maubert and Wenting Lan
for their remarkable research assistance.

School of Architecture **University of Miami**

OSCAR RIERA OJEDA
PUBLISHERS

Table of contents

This book is made possible with the
generous support of William H. Harrison

Preface
Rodolphe el-Khoury
10

Introduction
The New Discourse in Classical Architecture,
Victor Deupi
12

Chapter 1
The Lessons of Loos,
Jean- François Lejeune
20

Chapter 2
On Representation,
Rocco Ceo
84

Chapter 3
Resilience, Technology and Sustainability,
Victor Deupi & Eric Firley
134

Chapter 4
Geography and Culture,
Nathaniel Robert Walker
178

Chapter 5
Digital Technologies,
Juan Manuel Yactayo
218

Chapter 6
Towards a Populist Classical Language,
Andres Duany et al.
282

Chapter 7
Towards a Utilitarian Classicism,
Javier Cenicacelaya
316

Chapter 8
The Scientific Method,
Richard John
354

Preface

The University of Miami School of Architecture is among a handful of institutions in North America that offers courses in Classical and Traditional architecture. The investment dates back to efforts in the seventies and eighties that sought to loosen the positivist grip of the the social sciences and functionalism with claims of architectural autonomy and a concomitant interest in semiotics. They revived a pre-modernist preoccupation with architectural styles and presented classicism as a versatile idiom for contemporary practice. The rediscovery and repurposing of Classicism initially had a polemical and strategic edge. It was polemical in its challenge of modernist orthodoxy and its disavowal of style as a legitimate pursuit; strategic when complementing the New Urbanist project of recovering the scale, morphology, and social ecology of the traditional city. It is especially because of a predisposition for city-making that classical/traditional architecture has sustained its influence at the University of Miami School of Architecture. The typological makeup, the articulation of human scale in the classical orders, the differentiation between front and back, the transition from the public to the private realm embedded in urban typologies, among other features encoded in the DNA of classical buildings, proved to be effective proponents of viable streets and public squares when building walkable and livable small towns.

Given the intensification of suburban sprawl and the corollary environmental challenges we now face with climate change, the sustainability and resilience sedimented in traditional forms are particularly relevant and remain valued assets among the diverse resources and tools we make available to our students—from South Florida's modern vernacular and its copious experiments in tropical architecture, to parametric modeling and landscape urbanism. The William H. Harrison Studio for Classical and Traditional Architecture has enabled us to sustain and cultivate such assets with explorations that test and flesh out the potential of classical architecture in the practice of architecture and urbanism today.

In an area of research and practice that is primarily dedicated to upholding tradition this studio called for change and innovation, challenging the authority of the canons and embracing disrupters such parametric design and 3D printing. The aim is

Rodolphe El-Khoury

not only to test the enduring relevance of classicism but also to probe its capacity to thrive in and contribute to the rapidly changing professional landscape, from capitalizing on new technology for building economically with better quality and with greater intricacy, to testing new typologies that accommodate and empower emerging economies.

The themes addressing change and innovation are picked up and developed in Transformations in Classical Architecture: New Directions in Research and Practice, in essays by contributing authors including Andres Duany, Jean-François Lejeune, and Juan Manuel Yactayo, along with salient projects from current practice and especially by my colleagues at the university of Miami who have long exemplified the productive alignment of tradition with invention: Elizabeth Plater-Zyberk, Teofilo Victoria, and R & R Studios (Roberto Behar & Rosario Marquardt).

The book also features samples form the three first editions of the William H. Harrison Studio: 1. "Transect Studies," led by Andres Duany and Victor Deupi, explored the idea of a "lean urbanism" and challenged the stability of the canon with diverse and heterodox orders; 2. "The Territory between Ornament and Structure," led by Robert Levit and Victor Deupi with Juan Manuel Yactayo, explored digital parametric techniques and physics engines for modeling complex forms derived from gothic and renaissance vaults; 3. "Classicism in Civic Architecture," lead by Peter Pennoyer Architects, Richard John and Tim Kelley, explored the flexibility of the canon in culturally diverse regions and climates. These examples point to promising directions for the co-creation of knowledge in classical architecture.

I would like to thank all who have contributed to this publication—students, professors, practitioner—for asking how classical/traditional architecture could leap from its prodigious roots to fertile new ground, when unburdened of dogma. Gratitude is especially due to William H. Harrison for compelling us to ask such questions, for his faith in the project, and for investing in this publication and its dedicated studio.

Rodolphe El-Khoury, Dean University of Miami School of Architecture, Miami, Florida, May 29th, 2018.

Introduction

The New Discourse
in
Classical Architecture

"Classicism is something alive",
  Javier Cenicacelaya.[1]

We are still unable to agree on what classicism in architecture means today, despite several millennia of building practice. A clear, singular, and firm definition of classicism has always been elusive. We use the words *classical*, and *classicism*, as frequently as we use the words *modern*, and *modernism*, often in tandem as when we say classic modernism, or modern classicism. Yet despite the broad familiarity that their common usage implies, arguments on the origins, meanings, and uses of the terms "classical" and "modern" continue to proliferate in debates on architecture and visual culture, and indeed these debates became concerned with one another at least since the post-war period when Le Corbusier's *Modulor* (ca. 1945), Colin Rowe's *Mathematics of the Ideal Villa* (1947), and Rudolf Wittkower's *Architectural Principles in the Age of Humanism* (1949), all sought to imbue modern architecture with something more ineffable, humane, or simply tried and trusted - which is to say, something more *classical* (figs. 1-2).[2]

For many people, classicism is defined as being fundamentally concerned with the canonical orders of architecture - the Doric, Ionic, and Corinthian column and beam unit derived from Ancient Greece and Rome, codified stylistically in the Renaissance, and continually employed in Western architecture, and in places where Western traditions have spread and blended with other traditions, to the present.[3] By the early modern period - at least in the eighteenth century - the words *classic* and *classical* suggested authority and excellence, even if in the ancient world they had been associated with notions of superior class distinction. The various classes of Roman society were graded according to income, and *classicus* (highest rank) was distinguished from *proletarius* (lowest).[4] Today we recognize that class distinction has always been a problem, even if it was not always perceived as problematic by the elite class, and so we find that association with upper crust Romans has been a persistent desire of many classicists from Alberti to Jefferson. Despite the associative meanings, the canonical language of classicism has been prevalent in Renaissance treatises, Enlightenment and Early-Modern academies, and finally in pattern books and building manu-

Victor Deupi

als virtually everywhere. Moreover, it has been an extremely effective approach to building that focuses essentially on the syntactic relations of the stylistic elements of classical design and composition, and its results can be seen today in many high-end residential projects, institutional buildings, and preservation projects throughout the world. In an increasingly pluralist world, there is certainly a place for canonical classicism.

Unfortunately, for the last fifty years many classicists have argued that canonical classicism is the antithesis of modernism, and a wholesale rejection of everything that the modern movement in architecture represents - a reverse engineering of the claim that modernism did away with classicism. This kind of anti-modernist rhetoric usually takes the form of a reductive argument, emphasizing endurance and beauty as the natural guarantors of authority and timelessness in building, a truth easily confirmed through a selective case study of the classical tradition's continuity over centuries, or its restoration in pivotal moments of history. Modernism is conceived as a monolithic orthodoxy that is unnatural and degrading and therefore needs to be dismissed, with a renewal of classicism

as the perfect tonic for a new era of artistic flourishing. Never mind the many pressing issues of the day, including matters of fabrication, technology, sustainability, climate change, or resilience. Never mind that contemporary classicism represents a small fraction of what is built today. All that matters is that the current revival of classicism takes shape and proves once again to be the bearer of truth and immutability in building. Clearly, the anti-modernist rhetoric espoused by many classicists has done little to make contemporary classicism seem anything other than reactionary or egregious. It hasn't even solved the stylistic problem of imitation classicism and ersatz construction that can be seen in virtually every suburban development throughout North America and in many other countries - a sprawling phenomenon that only cheapens the value of classicism worldwide. Regrettably, canonical classicism remains at best an elite academic discipline.

A more critical interpretation of the classical orders of architecture has been advanced by those who draw a close relationship between vernacular construction and classicism. Here the orders are not seen stylistically but rather as tectonic elab-

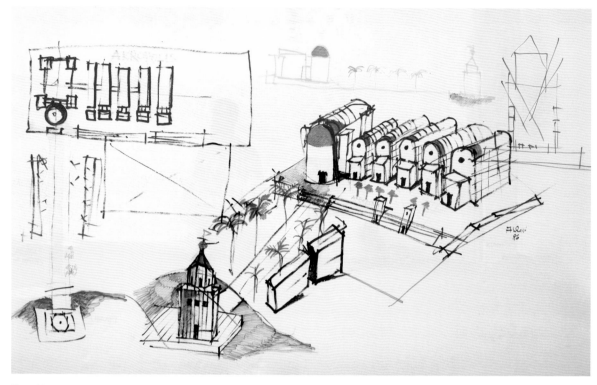

Fig. 1 Aldo Rossi, Proposal for a New School of Architecture at the University of Miami, 1986

orations on trabeated construction.[5] The intimate reciprocity between the vernacular and the classical is parallel to that of the larger context of building and architecture. The classical canon remains untouched, but the larger body of grammar and syntax is increased to include all kinds of arcuated forms, wall systems, decorative punctuations (primarily eaves and

window and door surrounds), and other basic building practices. Here we find great expanses of wall, simple punctured openings, and covered terraces and loggias all of which contribute to the kind of character many people associate with idyllic travel destinations (figs. 3-4). The critical element here is that tectonic classicism is seen as a way of craft building that responds to the natural contingencies of making and dwelling. In this sense it is posited as an organic response to mass production and industrial waste. While this approach may seem more intellectually satisfying as it is not primarily focused on stylistic matters, it does not address the simple truth that building materials and methods of construction today have a carbon footprint that far exceeds the standards of pre-industrial eras. Moreover, tectonic classicism is largely limited to the Mediterranean and Caribbean contexts where masonry building and simple wood construction are prevalent. Unfortunately, this tectonic approach does not translate readily – at least not classically – to other regions and cultures where weather and climate are not as arid or tropical. In more temperate zones like northern Europe, America, and significant parts of the southern hemisphere, such explicit tectonic practices require increasingly different forms of articulation. There is a reason that the more one moves away from Rome, the less Roman things become.

Fig. 2 Aldo Rossi, Proposal for a New School of Architecture at the University of Miami, 1986

For many others, classicism is more concerned with the inherent principles of proportion and composition and other essentials of architecture, a common language more than a style, and in that sense it is far more open-ended endeavor than an exclusive one. Here human scale, symmetry, and decorative ornament prevail whether it be Chinese, Indian, Ancient American, or Western European. This approach welcomes hybrid languages and heterodox decorative vocabularies, and has done so since antiquity. Yet, while all of this is intellectually stimulating and culturally tolerant, we should not be fooled in thinking that these analogous building traditions follow the same set of principles, or that principles alone make up a classical building. As noted by John Summerson, a well-proportioned Gothic portal is not the same as a classical pediment.[6] At a very basic level - if only skin-deep - we know when we are confronted with a classical building as opposed to something else. Nevertheless, this understanding of classicism as an abstract system of relations has the widest appeal today as it is global in reach and much more accepting of invention and adaptation than canonical classicism.

In a related sense, classicism is also associated with a great deal of twentieth-century modern architecture, and the so-called pioneers who sought out an unprecedented and universally recognized way of building, an international style.[7] Adolf Loos, Peter Behrens, Mies van der Rohe and Walter Gropius were, after all, mostly educated in the Beaux-Arts, Polytechnic, or Arts and Crafts traditions that at the very least covered the rudiments of classical design. In view of this continuity, it has been argued that the procession from Antiquity to the Romanesque and Gothic, followed by the Renaissance and Baroque of Europe and the New World, concludes triumphantly with the new international spirit of the Modern Movement - a lovely, albeit misleading, idea that continues to seduce new students of architecture and beginning professionals today (partially because their knowledge of the past is usually limited to what can be quickly parsed from rudimentary architectural history surveys). But we know too well that the twentieth century was a far more complex and contradictory period of architecture where no single individual or approach achieved such universal recognition[8] (figs. 7-11). Moreover, we know that a great deal of twentieth-century modern architecture was a hybrid of classical principles with abstract, reductive tendencies, and technological advances – both at the beginning of the century and by the end (fig. 5). This modern/classical hybrid can still be seen in architecture throughout the world today and it is an effective meth-

Figs. 3-4 Brendan McNee, Beach Hut, Isla Holbox, Yucatan Peninsula, Mexico, Dec. 2015, 9" x 12," graphite on paper

odology for discussing what the lasting influence of the twentieth century may truly be. We will have to accept that those pioneers of modern design did in fact inherit some of classicism's genes, and/or their techniques, and conversely that ideas can be cut from the modernist vine and then grafted on to classicism.

Finally, classicism is seen by many contemporary critics of architecture as a tradition that belongs to an increasingly distant past, a series of bygone eras that are no longer recognizable or relevant, and it is therefore incapable of addressing the multifaceted contingencies of the present in any meaningful or significant way. Peter Eisenman's influential essay "The End of the Classical: The End of the Beginning, the End of the End," takes this argument further by suggesting that the modern architecture of the early twentieth century - however stylistically different from previous centuries - falls into the same continuum as it aspired to the same set of timeless values as the classical, and therefore it too must be seen as a distant phenomenon.[9] Eisenman argues that the inability of representation, reason, or history to confer legitimacy on architecture makes it impossible to convey any kind of meaning, truth, or timelessness. His plea for a "not-classical" architecture that re-sists notions of origins (beginnings) or timelessness (ends) assumes that nothing is true because everything is relative. Such pessimism is ultimately a surrender to chaos, as few people would ever cast as relative the need for humanist values, such as community and caring, or the reverence and respect for nature (and/or the divine). Moreover, as he is not principally concerned with the past he overlooks the fact that we are still confronted with a vast collection of historical artifacts (cities, buildings, landscapes, and ruins) whose mere presence continues to shape our lives, habits, and patterns of thinking. It is simply impossible to dismiss the presence of the past, and its continuous influence on our lives, however appealing it may seem theoretically.

So, what is one to make of such a problem - whether old or new, western or international, arbitrary or positive, there seems to be as many arguments in favor of classicism to-day as there are in its rejection. Yet, however one defines the problem, one thing is undeniably clear: the environ-mental, technological, economic, and cultural demands of contemporary practice require levels of complexity and nuance that were never previously anticipated, and if clas-sicism is to be a part of contemporary debates on building it will have to address these demands. For instance, Miami is a diverse and vibrant city situated in a hurricane prone region, and the threat of sea level rise and erosion poses an immediate and long-term risk to its stability and sur-roundings. Large sections of Miami-Dade County could be inundated within 30 years, resulting in a severely disrupted transportation system, lost or damaged property, and an in-determinate and contaminated water supply. The city and the scientific community have been studying the phenom-enon for some time now, proposing solutions to the man-agement of such threatening uncertainty, yet classicists for the most part remain uninterested in such problems.

Instead, the discourse of classical architecture has been largely focused on issues of style and anti-modernist rhet-oric, and the limitations of such an approach have proven to be generally unproductive. The style debate is a dead-end as people have preferences be they ancient or mod-ern. Similarly, reactionary classicism has become a very minor voice in contemporary architectural education and practice, as its devoted corps of extremely vocal propo-nents tend to heap all the ills of the contemporary world on the shoulders of modern architecture and planning. If classicism is to have any continuity and relevance in the modern world, then a new classical discourse will have to

seek a progressive architecture that is rooted in modern-ism as well as the western tradition of Greco-Roman clas-sicism. Pre-Vitruvian and post-Venturian practice and the-ory will also influence the discourse as will non-Western traditions. If classicism is to remain relevant going forward, it will have to seek new paradigms of research and prac-tice, and develop upstream solutions to solving the many crises in architecture and the built environment. Classicism will have to position itself within the mainstream of con-temporary architecture and not define itself in opposition to it, learning from the last century rather than turning the clock back to a time when it was still the dominant trend in architecture. It will have to become an open system that addresses the pressing issues of the here and now, as well as the far and wide.

We really don't know what the future of classical architec-ture will be. It could very well end up remaining an elite ac-ademic discipline that primarily informs high-end architec-tural projects and preservation efforts around the world. Alternatively, it may take on new forms and meanings that are largely unrecognizable or unpredictable. After all, un-predictability is a reasonably reliable indicator that some-thing is alive. But it could also fall victim to the belief that it is irrelevant to the future fabric of our cities and towns, and therefore not something with which architects should be concerned. The truth of the matter is that there is a great dissonance in the classical heritage, marked by a lack of consistency and agreement as to what the meaning of classical architecture is – not just as a historical phenome-non but as a living tradition. There are conflicting claims to the ownership of the classical past, and also with respect to who is capable of reconciling such ownership. Can the classical past even be owned or only shepherded into the future, making our relationship with it a matter of careful stewardship? The present book does not try to solve such intractable problems, but rather shows that over the last 30 years many faculty, students, alumni, and friends of the University of Miami School of Architecture have sincerely sought to address these issues in an environment of in-tellectual freedom and creative license. The essays, proj-ects, and drawings in this book stand as a testament to the belief that classicism is something alive, and that we can project it far and wide into the future however difficult it may be to define it in the present. It is a work that defines classicism in favor of things or ideas, rather than against them – always in favor as that is the surest way to avoid egregious arguments and alliances. And maybe, just may-be, classical architecture has always worked this way, and

Figs. 5-6 Michael G. Imber Architects, Proposal for a House in Aspen Colorado (ongoing)

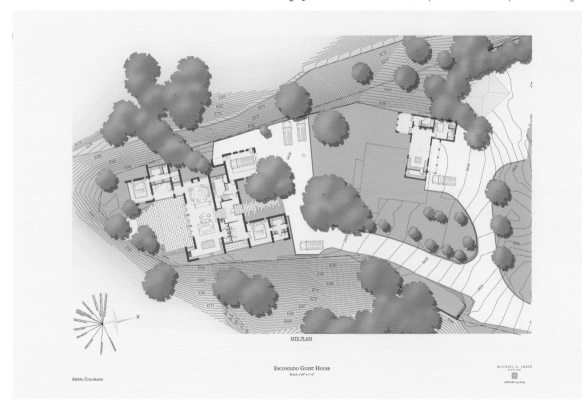

SITE PLAN

ESCONDIDO GUEST HOUSE
Scale: 1/16" = 1'-0"

ASPEN, COLORADO

MICHAEL G. IMBER
architect

JANUARY 14, 2014

Fig. 11 Museo di Civiltà Romana, EUR. Photograph by (c) Steven Brooke Studios

Fig. 7 Casa Madre dei Mutilati. Photograph by (c) Steven Brooke Studios

Fig. 8 Roro Italico. Photograph by (c) Steven Brooke Studios

Fig. 9 University of Rome, entrance. Photograph by (c) Steven Brooke Studios

Fig. 10 Museo di Civiltà Romana, EUR. Photograph by (c) Steven Brooke Studios

that this view of an open and forward-looking classicism is not a particularly new or modern phenomenon, but an obvious one.

Since the mid 1980's when Aldo Rossi produced his proposal for a "New Acropolis" for the School of Architecture at the University of Miami, many faculty, students, alumni and friends of the school have tirelessly explored the potentially enriching results of a modernism that reaches toward some aspects of the classical or a classical that is open to the potential gifts of the modern. The result has been a new wave of progressive classicism that has persistently sought to address the pressing issues of our cities, towns and landscapes. The aim of *Transformations in Classical Architecture* is to bring to light some of this work and examine how classical - and traditional - architecture can evolve in relation to new paradigms of research and practice (digital media and fabrication, sustainability, ecology, and emerging economies). The book will not concern itself with canonical classicism, or any historically inspired trends. Rather it will consider selected examples of con-

temporary work, some of which may not even be called classical by conventional standards, that seek to propel classicism forward. Based on recent work by leading figures associated with the University of Miami School of Architecture, and a series of design studios (the William H. Harrison Visiting Critics in Classical Architecture), the book redefines the new classical discourse in terms of popular, professional, and academic appeal.

[1] Andres Duany et al., *Heterodoxia Architectonica* (unpublished manuscript), Bk I, p. 1.
[2] Le Corbusier, *Modulor I and II*. Cambridge, Mass: Harvard University Press, 1980; Colin Rowe, *The Mathematics of the Ideal Villa, and Other Essays*, Cambridge, Mass: MIT Press, 1976, pp. 1-27; and Rudolf Wittkower, *Architectural Principles in the Age of Humanism*. New York: W.W. Norton, 1971.
[3] See in particular John Summerson, *The Classical Language of Architecture*, Cambridge Mass: MIT Press, 1963.
[4] Joseph Rykwert, *The First Moderns*, Cambridge, Mass: MIT Press, 1980, pp. 1-22.
[5] See in particular Demetri Porphyrios, *Classicism is not a Style*. London: AD, 1982.
[6] *The Classical Language of Architecture*, p. 8.
[7] Nikolaus Pevsner, *Pioneers of Modern Design: From William Morris to Walter Gropius*. Harmondsworth: Penguin Books, 1960.
[8] See for instance Dennis P. Doordan, Twentieth-century Architecture. New York: H.N. Abrams, 2002; and Alan Colquhoun, *Modern Architecture*. Oxford: Oxford University Press, 2002.
[9] Op.cit, *Perspecta*, Vol. 21 (1984), pp. 154-173.

Chapter 1

The Lessons of Loos

"The architect is a bricklayer who has studied Latin."
Adolf Loos, *Ornament and Education*, 1924.

"Instead of the style of construction learned in our schools, which is divided between, on the one hand, the adaptation of past construction styles to our current way of life and, on the other hand, the search for a new style, I want to promote my own teaching: tradition [...] Our culture is built on the recognition of the extreme greatness of the classical age. The technique of our thinking and feeling has been inherited from the Romans. From the Romans we mold our social sense and the cultivation of the soul."
Adolf Loos, *My Construction School*, 1913.

From Rome
The scene is in black and white, on a roof terrace in Noto, the scenographic Baroque city rebuilt in southern Sicily after the earthquake of 1693. "I have been twenty-three years old too, and I was in so many fights you can't even imagine," responds Sandro, half-defensively, half-aggressively to the angry student whose inkpot he has just spilled over a beautiful sketch of a cathedral window. In Michelangelo Antonioni's *L'avventura* (1960),

Sandro is the successful architect-businessman who has relinquished all hope to build "beautiful things." His macho words of self-denial cannot conceal the very reason of his deliberate act of destruction. The sketch excites his frustration, perhaps his jealousy; the extraverted freedom of the young draughtsman reminds him of the naïve optimism of his own youth during which everything is possible, including creating beauty and an architecture that can last more than "ten or twenty years."[1] The sketch is a provocation; it must be destroyed.

In a world dominated by ugliness, violence, and crass commercialism, beauty and the image of beauty have become increasingly anachronistic, if not outright dangerous or revolutionary. Even when the image of beauty is used to "sell"—from Prada stores to blockbusters exhibitions of Cézanne's works—it is often contested as "elitist," not in tune with our chaotic times. After all, isn't beauty a perilous relief from the reality of war and the stock market? "Who needs beautiful things nowadays?" asks Sandro to Claudia/Monica Vitti? Who needs *L'avventura*, Wim Wenders' *Wings of Desire*, Mozart's *Don Giovanni* or Mahler's *Fifth Symphony*? Architects

Jean-François Lejeune

are, in that sense, luckier than artists. They continue to be trained to do beautiful drawings, a lasting privilege of education that many disciplines have lost. To draw remains a goal and a virtue, not yet a pathetic and old-fashioned habit of the past. Sketching remains not only the purest expression of the physical presence of an object (it is not a virtual image, it is a real building or body), but it is also a tolerated and encouraged instant of retreat from the reality of the contemporary world.

"The lesson of Rome is for the wise—Le Corbusier wrote in *Towards an Architecture*—for those who know and can appreciate, for those who can resist, who can verify. Rome is the perdition of those who don't know much. To put architecture students in Rome is to wound them for life."[2] This provocative statement was first and foremost an attack on the system of the École des Beaux-Arts and the Grand Prix de Rome. Nowadays, the "academies" that he so despised have dramatically changed; hundreds of architecture students study in Rome every year, and, the first lesson—the invaluable one—is to live and work in the city. Rome is not for the faint-hearted; it is exciting, but can also be inhibiting, overwhelming; it can humble the best and estrange the weakest.[3]

University of Miami students have been coming to Rome since 1989. Working within the walls of the city, these young architects have sharpened their design and thinking skills, and particularly— for the great majority of them born and raised in suburbia—their emerging understanding of the city, its urban fabric, its public spaces, and its very life. They have tried to create new public spaces, improve some that have been neglected, or rescue ill-guided interventions by Mussolini's architects and planners. They have designed a "fantastic" *columbarium* bridge across the Tiber and imagined new itineraries along the walls. Most of the times, it is through urban design, more specifically through the relation between the house and the city, that they have understood Rome. And, not unlike Goethe, Schinkel, Hoffmann, and others, it is the vernacular of the city—its streets and houses—that has revealed the value of a design process founded on tradition and modernity. Thanks to the contacts with the School of Architecture at La Sapienza Università, and particularly with

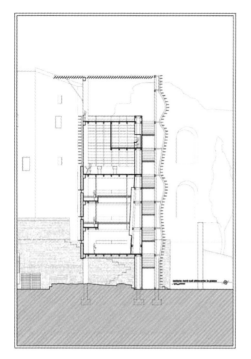

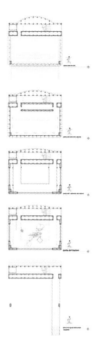

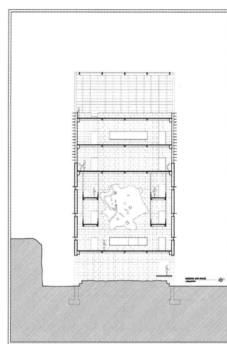

n-s section through Piazza of Colosseum   plans   e-w section cut through exhibit

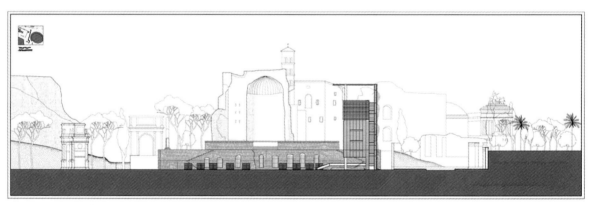

east elevation through piazza del colosseo

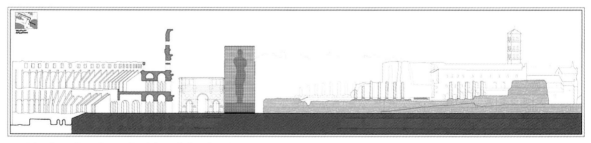

north elevation through piazza del colosseo

Giuseppe Strappa, they have learnt—or started to learn—how to "read" the city and follow its laws of formation, using the typological studies and maps of Saverio Muratori. Over the years, understanding how a city was built house by house has become as significant, if not more significant, than interpreting Bramante and the proportions of the Tempietto.

They have made proposals for never developed areas of the Trastevere and reimagined the current Ghetto district, going back to Giovannoni's and Muratori's ideas. Likewise, they have expanded the concept of tradition to the Third Rome, or rather to the Other Rome, the Rome built since the late 1800s around the walls, the Rome of the Splendid Ordinary, i.e., the social districts of Trionfale, Mazzini, San Saba, Garbatella, Tuscolano, but also the Foro Italico and the new town of Sabaudia. Here and there they have discovered how 20th century architects have reimagined the concept of "urban continuity" while providing for modern and hygienic dwellings for the disfavored classes.

In all these efforts and teaching opportunities, the intellectual relationship of the School to the figure, the writings, and the works of Aldo Rossi is immense and remains to be studied. But, I would argue here as well that, in relation to a contemporary project for the classical, the contribution of Adolf Loos has been central to the philosophy of the School, even though it is rarely mentioned. Many of us concur with Loos's aphorism:

> "Today is built on yesterday, just as yesterday was built on the day before yesterday. It was never otherwise - it will never be otherwise. It is the truth that I teach."[4]

To be sure, the conjunction of these influences is striking as the young Italian architect played a critical role in the return and, to a great extent, the rehabilitation of the Viennese on the international scene.[5] For Loos, tradition was the essence of modernity and Roman antiquity its most important expression. Antiquity was thus, for him, both reference and stimulation.[6] As Rossi wrote:

> "Loos is perhaps the first who spoke about tradition in a modern sense... and he spoke about it as a man of the city, who knows places and houses like family photographs...."[7]

If all of us, the faculty, see Letarouilly's *Edifices de la Rome moderne* as the indispensable teaching tool, the return to Antique Rome with the help of Rodolfo Lanciani's *Forma Urbis Romae*, Piranesi's *Campo marzio,* and the *Atlante di Roma antica* has become again increasingly relevant to a contem-

Above Columbarium bridge, Rome, McKenzie O'Neil, Josh Upshaw, Geoff Yanovich, with Rocco Ceo, 2012

porary approach to classical project. Loos himself made this position clear in many of his writings.[8] In his essay about his school, he wrote:

> "Since mankind has experienced the greatness of the classical age, the great master builders have been united by an idea. They thought: just as I built, the ancient Romans would have solved this task as well. I want to instill these ideas into my students."[9]

And in his notorious essay *Architektur* (1910):

> "But every time that architecture moves away from its model with minor actors and decorators, the great architect reappears who will lead it back to antiquity. Fisher von Erlach in the south and Schlüter in the north, were rightly the great masters of the eighteenth century. And on the threshold of the nineteenth century there was Schinkel. We forgot him. May the light of this extraordinary figure enlighten our future generation of architects."[10]

Thanks to Romolo Martemucci and Pier Fedrico Caliari, founders of the Accademia Adrianae and their work on museography and archeology, there is no more taboo in approaching the archeological areas of the city and its surroundings as a new frontier for teaching.[11] University of Miami projects like the reinterpretation of the Colossus of Nero next to the Coliseum, the installation of the *Forma Urbis Romae* within its original confines at the Tempio della Pace, the transfer of the great model of Rome now at EUR within the Velia hill facing the Basilica di Massenzio, or the projects for the Premio Piranesi, *Architettura e Acqua* at Villa Adriana, are self-assured experiments. They certainly raise the question posted by Nelson Mota and his advisors in the introduction of his dissertation *The Archeology of Housing*, "Archaeological techniques should be included in the curriculum of architectural schools to develop architects' expertise in activating collective memory."[12]

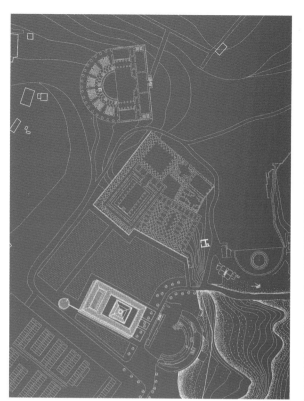

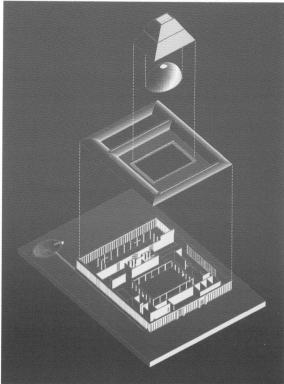

This spread Andrew Schneider, Anna Zaat, et al., Piranesi Pirix de Rome, Villa Adriana, Designing Archaeology with Frank Martinez, 2017

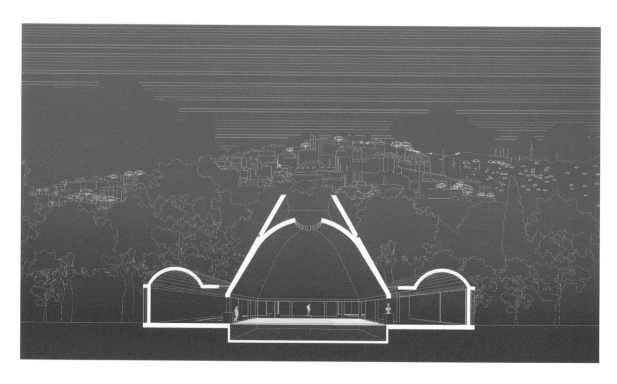

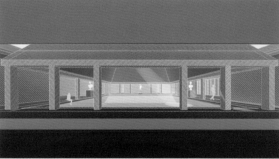

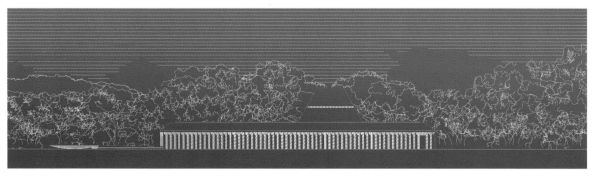

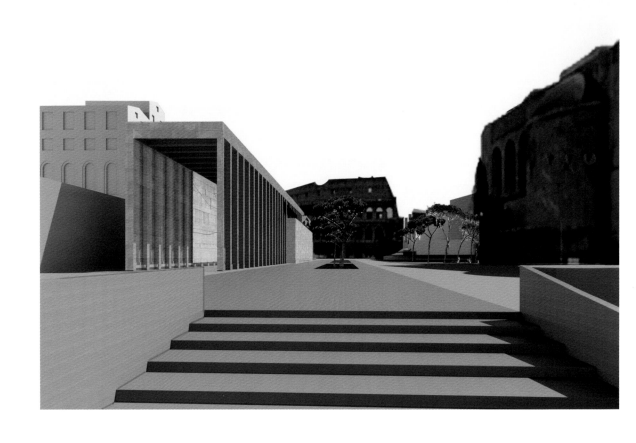

MUSEO
FORMA URBIS ROMAE

Forma Urbis Romae - Re-installation in the Central Archeo-logical Forum Area

The Forma Urbis Romae was a 60 feet x 45 feet marble map of ancient Rome. Dating to the reign of Septimius Severus (between 203 and 211), it was the single most important document on ancient Roman topography and urban form. Located on a wall in the Forum Pacis, it was carved out of 150 slabs of marble mounted on an interior wall of the Temple of Peace. The 1186 fragments that survived the vicissitudes of centuries are not visible to the public. Using Rodolfo Lanciani's topography of ancient Rome (Forma urbis Romae) and further excavation results, Italo Gismondi was commissioned by Mussolini to build a large scale 3-d model that was first shown at the Mostra Augustea in 1930. It is currently at the Museo della Civiltà Roma at EUR. The studio proposed to re-install the surviving fragments of the Forma Urbis Romae and to move the existing model to a new museum to be built along the Via dei Fori Imperiali on the site of the Tempio della Pace and the Velia Hill.

This spread Museum for the Re-Installation of the Forma Urbis Romae (Severan Marble Plan) on the Via dei Fori Imperiali, Rome, Katja Kuznik, with Jean-Fran-cois Lejeune, 2016

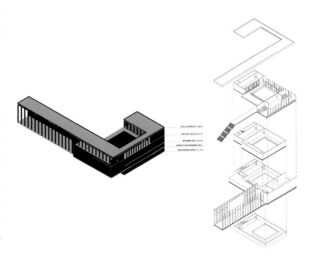

This spread Museum for the Re-Installation of the Forma Urbis Romae (Severan Marble Plan) on the Via dei Fori Imperiali, Rome, Jessica Flores and Frank Noska, with Jean-Francois Lejeune, 2016

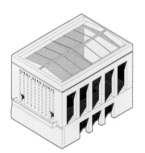

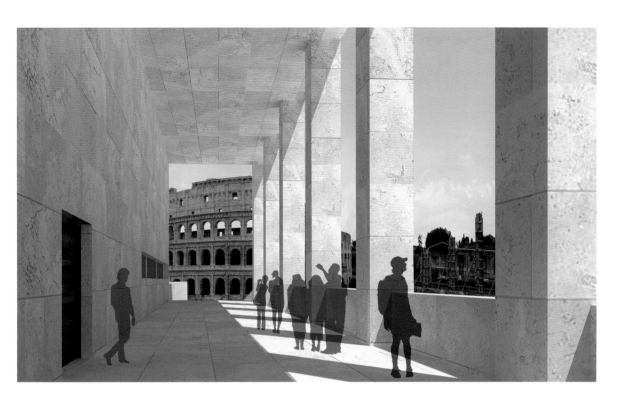

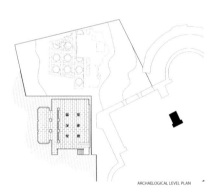

ARCHAELOGICAL LEVEL PLAN

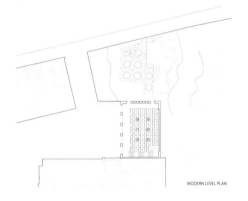

MODERN LEVEL PLAN

This and following spread Rome Contemporary Chapel "Impluvium". Students: Arnost Wallach, Nicholas J Meury. Rome Fall 2017. Professor: Veruska Vasconez

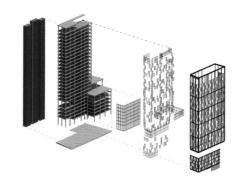

This spread John Degirolamo & Giancarlo Belledonne. Soho Youth Hostel 2015. New York City Studio. Professor: Roberto Behar

To New York

Like Rome, New York is a universe of solid matter. Its geographic location is like in Rome, a primary reason of its being—one of defense and community, the other of exchange and business—but, to some extent, its natural context disappears within the world of the man-made. Like Rome, it is a womb that keeps you inside. If, as Christian Norberg-Schulz has argued, the streets of Rome are like the ravines that define the Etruscan country, then the streets of New York are like the cliffs that define the Hudson River, a couple of miles up the river.[13] Like Rome, its walls are thick, solid, and seemingly made to resist time and action of men and women. Like Rome, New York has been for University of Miami students a privileged terrain to analyze and understand, as the projects realized under the direction of Roberto Behar demonstrate, the complexity, the challenge, and the exhilaration of an architecture and urbanism anchored in tradition and modernity.

Interestingly, Adolf Loos can help us to analyze the link between Rome and New York—certainly a critical one for the curriculum and the pedagogy of the School of Architecture. In my essay "Living *all'antica* in the New Bourgeois City," I have studied Schinkel's projects for urban and suburban houses in light of the conflict between the individual and the collective that characterized the emerging metropolis of Berlin.[14] Loos's approach to dwelling in the city can be framed within a parallel concern for reciprocity between the romantic and modern interest for self-expression and the necessary subordination of the individual to a collective vision. Schinkel's pioneering concept of anti-Palladian asymmetry through his discovery of the vernacular during his first *Italienische Reise* was not only implemented in Berlin, but also imagined, at a larger scale, in his vision of the emerging industrial city. In Vienna Fin-de-Siècle, Loos saw in the classical language of Antiquity and in the Mediterranean vernacular a solution to reduce the tensions between the individual and the collective. The

terraced apartment buildings, high-rise structures, and other public buildings and spaces he designed for Vienna, Paris and Southern France—unfortunately almost all unbuilt—were all expression of and research for a modern, and thus for him "American," understanding of the Antique.

It is indeed in America, between 1893 and 1896, that Loos developed his thesis on ornament. Not to reject it systematically and completely—as his modernist apologists have argued and a fact that he denounced himself in his essay "Ornament and Education" (1924)—but to use it parsimoniously and only when necessary to function.[15] In fact, classical ornament was, for Loos, part of the education of the architect and as such played in the teaching of drawing the same role than grammar in language. Likewise, architecture was not art because it had to be responsible to the collective and the community.[16] Uniformity was thus not a problem but an expression of culture, a statement that probably related closely to his interest in American architecture.[17]

For Rossi, what really distinguished Loos from the moderns was neither the question of ornament nor the classical references, but "the defense of the city of man against any utopia enslaved by power."[18] He recalls that, while the European modernists were enthused by Frank Lloyd Wright and its so-called "democratic" vision, Loos was walking the streets of Downtown New York, "falling in admiration in front of the enormous and somber buildings of Broadway, before discovering the perspectives of Wall Street."[19] In America, Loos realized "that in the leap in scale, in the unheard-of proportions, in the distortion and in the repetition, there is an observation of and a respect for the classical laws."[20]

These are, for University of Miami students, the lessons of walking, drawing, and designing in New York and Rome. These are the lessons of Loos.

SOHO HAUS
NEW YORK CITY

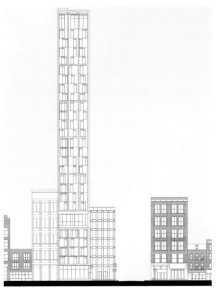

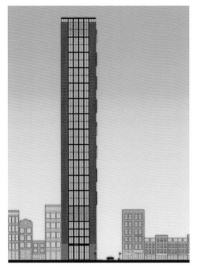
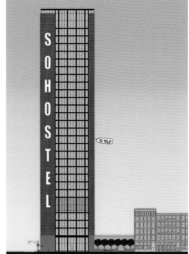

This spread Andrea Gamboa & Tehilah Weiss. Soho Youth Hostel 2015. New York City Studio. Professor: Roberto Behar

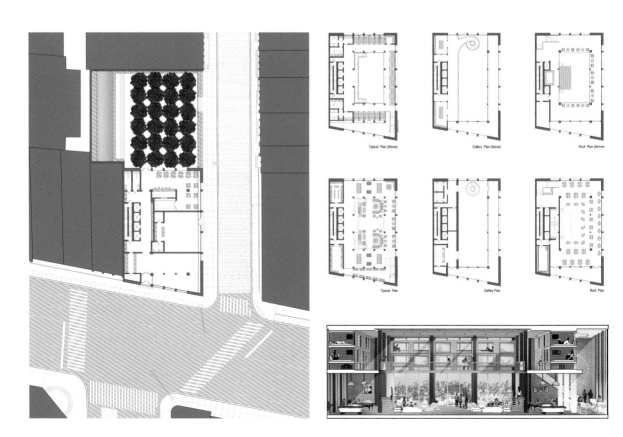

Typical Plan (Above)

Gallery Plan (Above)

Roof Plan (Above)

Typical Plan

Gallery Plan

Roof Plan

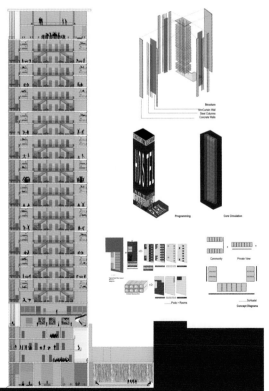

This spread Mohammed Alwadie & Wenxin Jiang. Mix Use Tower Lower Manhattan 2017. New York City Studio. Professor: Roberto Behar

1 See Jean-François Lejeune, "La EUR de Antonioni y el eclipse de la Arquitectura," *Teatro Maritimo*, n°5 June 2016, pp. 8-19. All quotes are from the English subtitles in the restored version of *L'avventura*, The Criteria Collection, DVD, 2001.

2 Le Corbusier, *Towards an Architecture* (Los Angeles: Getty Research Institute, 2007), p. 212 (translation John Goodman).

3 I have borrowed these first two paragraphs from my essay ""La EUR de Antonioni y el eclipse de la Arquitectura," op. cit., p. 8.

4 Adolf Loos, "Meine Bauschule" ("My Construction School") in *Der Architekt*, 10 October 1913, republished in Adolf Loos, *Trotzdem* (Innsbruck, 1931): 322. All translations by author unless otherwise noted.

5 See the special issue of *Casabella-continuità* 233, November 1959, on Adolf Loos and Rossi's essay, *Adolf Loos 1870-1933*, pp. 5-11.

6 For this section, see Roland L. Schachel, "Adolf Loos, l'Amérique et l'Antiquité," in *Adolf Loos 1870-1933* (Liège: Mardaga, 1985), pp. 33-38.

7 Aldo Rossi, "Introduction à Adolf Loos," *Adolf Loos 1870-1933*, p. 30.

8 Paul Letarouilly, Edifices de Rome moderne (Paris: A. Morel, 1868-1874); Rodolfo Lanciani, Forma Urbis Romae (Rome, 1893); [Andrea Carandini, *Atlante di Roma antica* (Milano: Electa, 2012).

9 Adolf Loos, "Meine Bauschule (My Construction School), p. 322-3.

10 Adolf Loos, "Architektur (Architecture) [1910]," in *Spoken in the Void* (Cambridge, MA: The MIT Press, 1987), p. °.

11 See Luca Basso Peressut and Pier Federico Caliari, *Architettura per l'archeologia: museografia e allestimento* (Roma: Prospettive edizioni, 2014).

12 See Nelson Mota, "Propositions," in *An Archeology of the Ordinary. Rethinking the Architecture of Dwelling from CIAM to Siza*, Dissertation, TU Delft, 2014, p. ix.

13 See Christian Norberg-Schulz, "The Genius Loci of Rome," in *Roma interrotta: twelve interventions on the Nolli's Plan of Rome* (Monza : Johan & Levi, 2014).

14 Jean-François Lejeune, "Schinkel's *Entwürfe Zu Städtischen Wohngebaüde*: Living *all'antica* in the New Bourgeois City" in *The Classicist*, n° 9, 2012, pp. 6-25.

15 See Adolf Loos, "Ornament und Erziehung (Ornament and Education) [1924], in *Adolf Loos: Ornament and Crime. Selected Essays* (Riverside, CA: Ariadne Press, 1998), p. 187.

16 See Schachel, p. 37 and Adolf Loos, "Architecture", 1910.

17 See Schachel, p. 37 and Adolf Loos, *Die Überflüssingen* [The Superfluous], 1908.

18 Aldo Rossi, "Introduction à Adolf Loos," p. 30.

19 Aldo Rossi, "Introduction à Adolf Loos," p. 29.

20 Aldo Rossi, "The Architecture of Adolf Loos," Preface to Benedetto Gravagnuolo, *Adolf Loos* (New York: Rizzoli, 1982), p. 13.

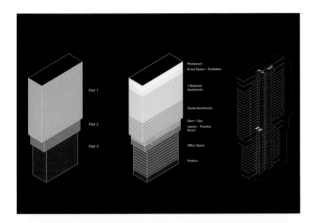

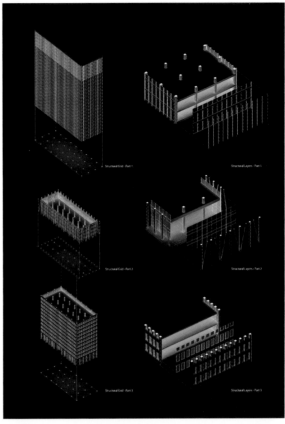

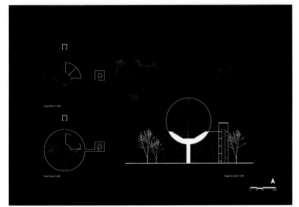

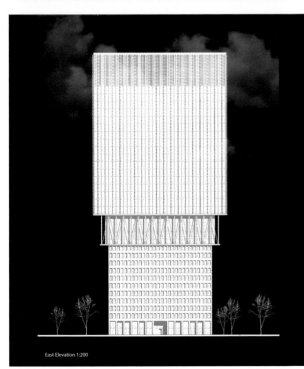

East Elevation 1:200

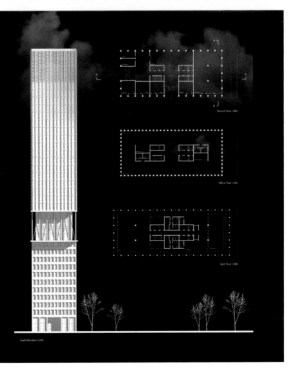

SELECTED WORKS

George M. Perez Architecture Center
University of Miami School of Architecture | 2004
Leon Krier & Merrill, Pastor & Colgan Architects
042

Ibis House
Miami, FL | 2012
Elizabeth Plater- Zyberk of DPZ
& Jorge L. Esteban of Accolade
052

Almeria Row
Coral Gables, FL | ongoing
de la Guardia Victoria Architects & Urbanists
060

Brillhart Residence
Miami, FL | 2014
Melissa and Jacob Brillhart
068

Youth Build Academy
Luly, Haiti | ongoing
Steven Fett Architecture
078

Valby Square & Town Center
Copenhagen, Denmark | 2008
R & R Studios / Roberto Behar & Rosario Marquardt
080

George M. Perez Architecture Center

University of Miami School of
Architecture, Miami, FL | 2004

Leon Krier & Merrill, Pastor & Colgan Architects

Text by Elizabeth Plater-Zyberk

The Stanley and Jewel Glasgow Lecture Hall, The Irvin
Korach Gallery, The Marshall and Vera Lea Rinker Class-
room, The Thomas F. Daly Loggia, The Leonard and Jayne
L. Abess Breezeway.

The School of Architecture was established in 1983, after
decades as a department at the University of Miami. Its new
status brought the program to its own campus of re-purposed
post-war buildings. Designed by Marion Manley, Miami's
first woman architect, they are representative of the most
appealing aspects of International Style modernism: honesty
of construction, rational minimalism, and transparency.

A central space among them was created by re-routing a
campus street, and a program for growth was formulated
to include a lecture hall, a large classroom and an exhibition
space. A team of architects, all meaningful in the history of
the School, was selected for the new building. Following
design sessions that included faculty and students, Leon
Krier finalized the design of the building, assisted by Merrill
Pastor and Colgan, with Nati Soto of FGSS implementing
the design in construction documents.

Below The Jorge M. Perez Architecture Center, Aerial site plan | **Opposite page**
Photograph by (c) Steven Brooke Studios

Above and opposite page Photography (c) Steven Brooke Studios | Below The Irvin Korach Gallery | Opposite page below left Sketch Elevation by Leon Krier | Opposite page below right Elevation by Leon Krier

Above Loggia. As originally intended by Leon Krier. The correct profile of the UM-SOA arcade is now realized faultlessly in the Eremita building designed in Cayala Guatemala in 2012 | **Opposite page** Photograph by (c) Steven Brooke Studios

Its site plan defines a series of outdoor spaces: the lakefront courtyard terminated by the lecture hall, a triangular lawn between the historic buildings and the arcade of the new wing, and a street crossing the assemblage.

The lecture hall is articulated as an octagon and stands out as the monumental civic space of the School. A reminder of Vincent Scully's 1996 book about the School, Between Two Towers, its tower and lantern are long distance markers of important axes: centered on and visible from the distant MetroRail station, terminating approach views along Dickinson Drive, and also the courtyard view from Lake Osceola.

The gallery and classroom wing presents a powerful gable end to the arrival from the south, its single story pediment matching the height of the flanking three-story buildings. The trident of buildings, all the same width, defines three pedestrian entrances to the School, including the arcaded pergola lining the gallery and classroom wing.

The relationship of the new building to its surroundings is a tour de force, equally emphasizing similarities and differences. In terms of building type, linear bars and a centering mass form an urban ensemble. The octagonal lecture hall and the gallery wing pivot the two grids of the historic buildings, creating a variety of spaces, terminating multiple vistas, in an ensemble of spaces and buildings. The old and new bar buildings, differing in transparency, share width and height. The lecture

hall, of unique girth in its setting, nevertheless acknowledges its delicately scaled historic surroundings, its horizontal reveals dividing its height in thirds, are reiterated in the arcade, the tower, the lantern, buttresses and high lunettes.

The morphology of the buildings emphasizes their differences. The studio buildings are characterized by modern horizontality, long and low in mass, with strip windows shaded by cantilevered eyebrows. The Perez Center's traditional vertical proportions are reiterated in the tower and lantern, in the arcade, in the weighty portico, in beak, ovolo and cavetto mouldings, in the pulvinated imposts of the arcade piers, and in the acroteria that accompany the pediments. At the parapet, a stepped recess recalls elements of Art Deco, that like the decorative shapes of the arcade, celebrate the daily trajectory of sun and shadow.

In its play of different and unifying elements the Perez Architecture Center is a rare contemporary example of coexistence: unified as structures of masonry and stucco, differentiated by solidity and transparency reflecting interior program; dimensions similar in new and old buildings, all focusing on the center hall and towers. It is a lesson in the capacity of urbanism for diversity and contrast - classical and modern, solid and transparent, type and scale, the monumental and vernacular urban fabric, materiality and decoration. In this way, the Perez Architecture Center and its surroundings reflect the educational program of the University of Miami School of Architecture, long unique among its peers.

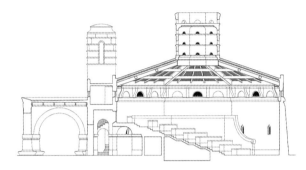

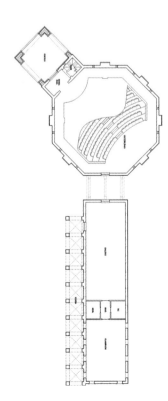

Ibis House
Miami, FL | 2012

Elizabeth Plater-Zyberk, FAIA, DPZ Partners with Jorge L. Esteban, AIA, Accolade Construction

The University of Miami's President's House is a two-story residence designed to serve the sometimes contradictory needs of institutional entertaining and family residence.

On a heavily-wooded property, the layout of the structures, pavements and pool preserves all existing trees. Inspired by early South Florida courtyard mansions, the floor plan is one room deep to foster cross-ventilation, with generous loggias for outdoor living, traditional proportions to manage scale and relate to surrounding houses, and white walls and roof to minimize heat gain and provide a backdrop to the beautiful trees.

Two wings splay to fit the house among the trees, focusing the axial view of the entrance on a particular specimen. A curved porte-cochere surrounds a group of front-yard trees, and serves as auto-arrival and porch with a terrace above. The arc of the entry foyer conceals symmetrical stairways, directing the arrival view to the courtyard and focal tree, and to the doorway of the music room with the living room beyond. These public rooms accommodate large groups while still intimate in scale. From the living room, one traverses the length of the first floor around the courtyard to reach the dining room.

A large kitchen-family room and two bedrooms on the ground floor, and four bedrooms on the second floor, including a master suite and a guest suite, complete the main house program. A two-car garage, with apartment above, a pool cabana and roofed cooking area, complete the site plan.

A strict budget guided the simple masonry and stucco construction, with standard doors, windows and loggia screening. The pavements and interior finishes and furnishings include materials made in South Florida. The President's House is LEED Certified.

Photography credits Miami In Focus, except aerial photography above

Top The aerial photo shows the distribution of structures, pavements and pool amidst the heavily wooded site | Above First and second floor plan | Opposite page from top to bottom, left to right Porte-cochère and entry setback in arc to preserve trees; dining room loggia with courtyard and living room beyond; living room wing, courtyard, and dining room wing viewed from rear garden; courtyard viewed from living room and foyer loggias; bridge between main house on the left and garage on the right | Following spread Courtyard with living room (left), foyer (center), and dining room (right). The second floor terrace serves the master bedroom (left), family room (center), and guest wing (right)

This page The foyer is axially focused on the courtyard and a special tree beyond, distributes entry to the music room and the living room to the right, and the hall to the dining room to the left. The foyer extends in a curve that conceals the symmetrical stairways from the front door | Opposite page The living room is a square room with exterior windows and doors on three sides, including a tall bay window. The living room and the adjacent music room allow a crowd to gather informally. The hall to the dining room is part of an intentional procession from living to dining that emulates floor plans of early South Florida mansions. The dining room, like the living room, has doors and windows on three sides with a tall bay window

This spread The house at night: The lighting of the house is intended to be low-key and reflective, and focused on its interior spaces, in the manner of traditional buildings, with landscape lighting of only a few special trees

Almeria Row
Coral Gables, FL | complete

De La Guardia Victoria Architects And Urbanists

Almeria Row is a multi family development project built in Coral Gables, Florida. The project consist of ten individual townhouses sited on ten fee simple parcels measuring on average 23' in width by 120' in depth The project is the first to be built in the City of Coral Gables in response to the in-corporation to the current zoning code of legislation which allows for the building of a traditional townhouse typology. The introduction of the townhouse as a new housing option for urban living addresses and advances the principles of the Charter of the New Urbanism.

At the scale of the block, street and building, the townhouse reiterates the usefulness of the mid-block alley, character-istic in several residential and commercial districts of Coral Gables, and yields a new and more urban street section. The revised setbacks dimensions and the reduction of the parcel to practically half the size of the present minimum size lot for a single family residence makes it possible to increase the number of units per block without relying exclusively on the condominium apartment building. The townhouse as a housing option is of particular pertinence in residential districts adjacent to downtowns, as is the case with Almeria Row, because they provide a gradual reduction of density from the town center to the periphery.

Almeria Row takes advantage of the proximity of the site to the amenities prevalent in the city center; shopping, places of work, entertainment and leisure. It promotes the best of urban living. Daily life activities occur within walking distance, providing independence to those who do not drive, specially the elderly and the young. In fact, the townhouse type is ideal for young professionals who desire to live in an urban setting as well as empty nesters whishing to downsize but retain the many advantages of the single family home. The formal character of the townhouse with stoop and porch and the pedestrian traffic generated by virtue of location promotes the idea of neighborhood and enhances the definition of a community in a distinct district of the city.

Photography credits Carlos Ignacio Morales

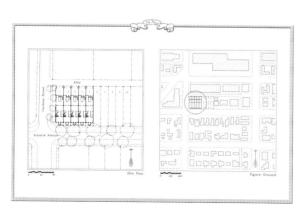

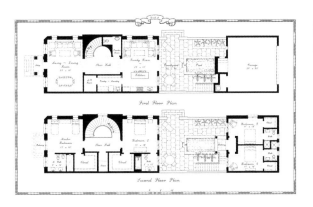

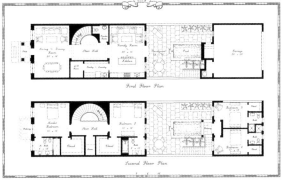

Brillhart Residence
Miami, FL | 2014

Melissa and Jacob Brillhart

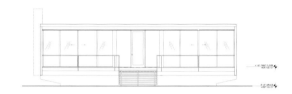

This 1,500 sf, steel and glass house is nestled within the Spring Garden Historic District, one of Miami's oldest neighborhoods, located along the Miami River in the heart of downtown. The goal was to create a new and sustainable architecture for the tropics, beginning with the idea of living in the landscape. Other design decisions challenged the culture for building big: what is necessary; how can we minimize our impact on the earth; and how do we respect the context of the neighborhood?

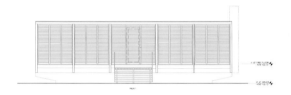

Some answers came from past building models – the Dog Trot, American Glass pavilion, and Tropical Modernism designs – all of which had embedded environmental considerations. Historically, the Dog Trot was comprised of two small wooden buildings – connected by a central breezeway – under one roof. The simple structure was modest and rich in cultural meaning; maximized efficiency, space, and energy; relied on vernacular materials; and celebrated the breezes. The plan of the house is a modern interpretation of the Dog Trot, with sleeping on the left, a central corridor (with kitchen), and living space on the right.

The American Glass pavilion and principles of Tropical Modernism also offered direction. In an era of optimism and experimentation, architects in South Florida's postwar period turned to local landscape, climate and materials to inform their designs, marrying building traditions with passive systems, new technologies, and innovative construction techniques. Emphasis on construction methodology was central to their work. Their simple, rational, efficient, buildings became models for sustainable design in the tropics.

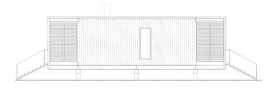

In that same spirit, we sought a more sustainable alternative to the use of concrete (today the dominant residential building material in South Florida), by constructing a steel and glass superstructure. With today's advances in the thermal qualities of glass and insulation, we were able to resurrect old models for a future building that could meet current Florida Building Code and energy requirements.

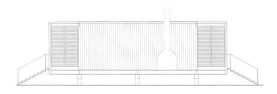

Opposite page Elevations | **Above** South elevation, front entry. Photograph by Claudia Uribe | **Below** Foor plan

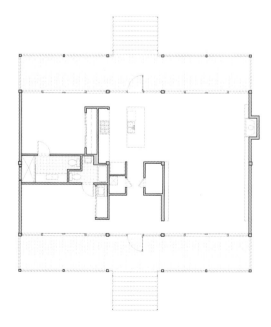

We used as many off-the-shelf materials as possible to minimize construction costs. Placing emphasis on materiality and construction logic, we were also able to create a structural order that carries an embedded composition that recalls the local vernacular.

Floating five feet above the ground, the house is raised as a response to our zchanging coastal environment as well as wanting to be "light on the land." Perched in the center of the 330-foot long lot, the house includes 100 feet of uninterrupted glass – 50 feet spanning the full length of the front and back sides of the house, with four sets of sliding glass doors to allow the house to be entirely open. As a result, the landscape functions like the walls of the house. Also included are two porches along the front and back, totaling 800 square feet. Shutters along the front façade create an outdoor room with ever-changing shadows and provide added privacy and protection. These elements allow the house to essentially act as a filter, creating varying levels of transparency.

Opposite page above Back yard elevation. Photograph by Claudia Uribe | **Opposite page below left and right** Under construction | **Above** South elevation with operable shutters | **Below** Axonometric | **Following spread** Front entry. Photograph by Claudia Uribe

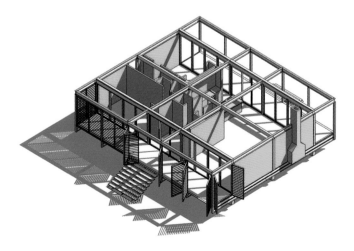

Above and opposite page above Living room. Photograph by Claudia Uribe | Below left Kitchen. Photograph by Claudia Uribe | Below right Kitchen. Photograph by Bruce Buck | Opposite page below left Bedroom. Photograph by Claudia Uribe | Opposite page below right Master bathroom. Photograph by Bruce Buck

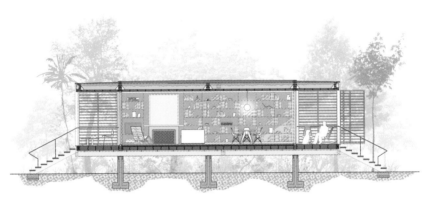

Above Back yard elevation. Photograph by Claudia Uribe.

Youth Build Academy
Luly, Haiti | ongoing

Steven Fett Architecture

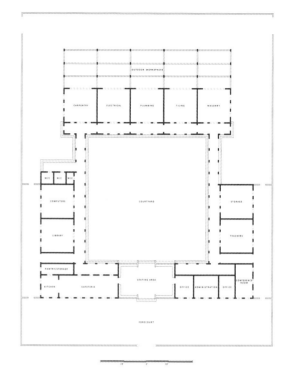

In Arachaie, Haiti, long distances to the closest Universities make advanced education unattainable for most. Those who can pursue higher education often leave Arachaie permanently in pursuit of better opportunities elsewhere. The limited access to vocational and university education starves the region of growth.

Youth Build, a non-profit organization that provides education, job skills and counseling to at risk youth partnered with the University of Miami's Center for Urban and Community Design with goals to build a new vocational school in Luly, a centrally located town in the Arachaie region.

The design of the building is centered around an open aired outdoor space. The courtyard has dimensions of approximately 85 feet by 85 feet. Surrounding the space are groupings of gable-ended structures containing one room each. The gable end is a primitive and memorable form. Ask anyone to draw their image of a school house and regardless of age, ethnicity, or education, most probably he/she will draw a square with a pointed roof. Here this ubiquitous form is repeated for every classroom. A colonnade connects the classrooms and support spaces of the school. This circulation device also provides shade for the students and relief from the rain. The side-wings use a post and beam configuration, while a "Serlian" motif is repeated on the rear classrooms. These rooms are designed to house classes with access to outdoor spaces beyond by means of large, operable doors.

In addition to the outdoor spaces and classroom facilities, the school also has a relatively large kitchen and cafeteria. We believe that these spaces could be used as training rooms and could include a small restaurant. The kitchen staff could cook meals for the students and the community. This engagement with the town would help to define the school as a building built by and for the community and could teach students methods of healthy cooking and business management.

Collaborators: Steven Fett, Tyler Nussbaum, Ana Luiza Leite, Jess Tsiris, Rhys Gilbertson and Katherine Flores.

Opposite page Plan of school. Three sequential public spaces are enclosed by classroom buildings | Above Folkloric image placing the building in a symbolic context | Below left Programatic diagram, showing the repetition of building form

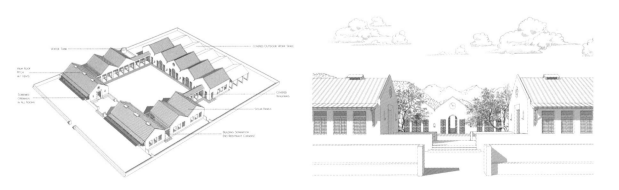

Valby Square & Town Center
Copenhagen, Denmark | 2008

R & R Studios / Roberto Behar
& Rosario Marquardt

Valby Square invents a new urban space for the people of Copenhagen. Located in the periphery of the city, the project resembles an open or unfinished castle and performs as an analogue of the historical center. Urban elements and architectural events are reconsidered to expand the historical memory of the city into contemporary Copenhagen.

The urban intervention is simultaneously landmark, square

and distinct urban ensemble. The Valby Towers are gateway to Copenhagen and landmark of Valby. The three towers create the appearance of a contemporary skyline and announce the presence of the square. Their size and materials relate to the architecture of Copenhagen towers.

Valby Square is a public hall open to the sky, a living room at the scale of the town. Stairs, terraces and openings connect bordering public and private buildings to the square and provide alternative points of view adding life and experiences to the public space. Valby Square is a unique contemporary addition to the exceptional collection of Plads of the City of Copenhagen.

Collaborators: Georgy John Project Manager, Abraham Aluicio & Michael Mahal
Client: City of Copenhagen & Architects Association of Denmark. International Competition. Purchase Award

Opposite page Valby Square. View from train station and park across the street | **Above** Night view | **Below left** Composite Drawing | **Below right** Urban ensemble. Axonometric | **Following Spread** Valby Square. View of the square and towers

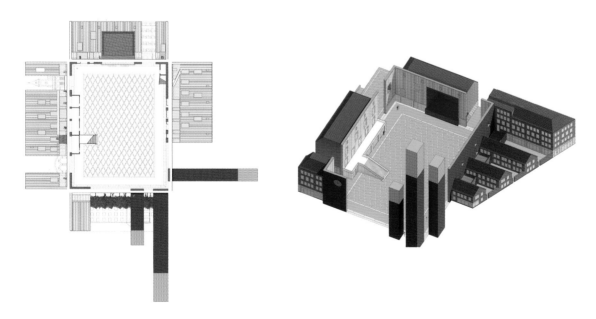

Chapter 2

On Representation

If one could write one would still need to draw, for unlike a good piece of writing, there is little that is more transformative than a drawing that transcends its subject. In a drawing of this type, the viewer is given something not easily conveyed in any other medium. In drawing, a subject is at the very least a point of departure, sometimes an inspiration, and at times a trap. It is the delineator's task to draw not only what appears in full view but more importantly what is not seen as well. The drawn work of the University of Miami School of Architecture is one that pursues this dialogue between the seen and unseen in architecture. Common subjects and events often have uncommon dispositions and show us something about the importance of a subjective gaze of reality. This gaze is the beginning of the training of the architect and through the language of drawing one finds more than a subject, one finds something to say. This 'act of drawing' rather than its finished product, is the beginning.

Nature

Without a doubt the natural world in Miami is more evident and present than its architecture and urbanism. Historically the best architecture here is often nature reconfigured and still evident in the making of the walls, ornament and completed buildings, reminding us of the importance of maintaining a bridge to the natural world. So nature is not just 'a' source it is 'the' source from where we must begin. Form, color, light, shadow, texture, line, and the ordering principles that create beauty and meaning are found in nature. Drawing nature is putting the observer in intimate contact with place and its elusiveness. Once one has looked at and drawn the flora and fauna of a place, as in the case of Miami and their inseparable context of tropical air, water, foliage and ground, one understands from where architecture is born and how it must coexist to have a meaningful connection to it. The act of wanting to understand nature through drawing is an ancient and time-honored tradition and we can look at the past and present to find a wealth of examples that are proof of this.

Nature in Miami is seen through the eyes of an architect and is at once inspiring and terrible – for nature does not sit still. Scale, dimension and the taking apart and putting back together again of nature in multi-view or even single

Rocco Ceo

view drawings is more than technique - it is arresting. To know nature in plan, section and elevation is to know more than its appearance. When nature as a subject is measured and studied through the act of drawing and composition it becomes intimate knowledge, foundational. It is these restrictive techniques that help us 'capture' nature for as Ruskin has observed "clouds will not wait" and "shadows will escape from us when we try to shape them."[1]

Nature is elusive and changing but it has given birth to the vernacular which in its unpretentious forms has shown it can be arrested and represented. From nature architecture is born and through nature's weathering it shall return. The study of nature is also to find its real presence not abstracted but in its iconic and timeless detail. To do this one must be in it.

In- situ drawing

The importance of being in nature while representing it is essential. In hot and humid Miami one leaves the oppressive shelter of buildings to escape the cold. Outside one experiences punishing sun, the succor of shade and for most months of the year an accommodating place to draw. Architecture is sensorial and *plien air* drawing is the reminder of how one needs to be in nature if one is going to understand nature's hold on architecture. After a few hours drawing outside one is reminded of how architecture controls temperature, sound, place and provides for the inhabitant all the comforts of rest and respite. On site, one understands the concept of permanence, weathering and change. One knows not to look into the sun, and that shade and shadow are more dramatic at the beginning or end of the day but also more elusive as shadows change more rapidly. Here the paper is wet and the pencils must be soft or they will not make a mark, watercolors and oil pastels are fluid but do not dry. This engagement is a reminder of the lack of control of nature and that hurricanes, torrential rain and wind make us more a part of the Caribbean than the rest of the United States. In Miami, *in-situ* drawings can be quick, private first impressions such as drawings made on travel trips, or long studied collaborative affairs, made by many hands and with many preparatory drawings becoming something like their subject itself, studied, reworked, constructed and compre-

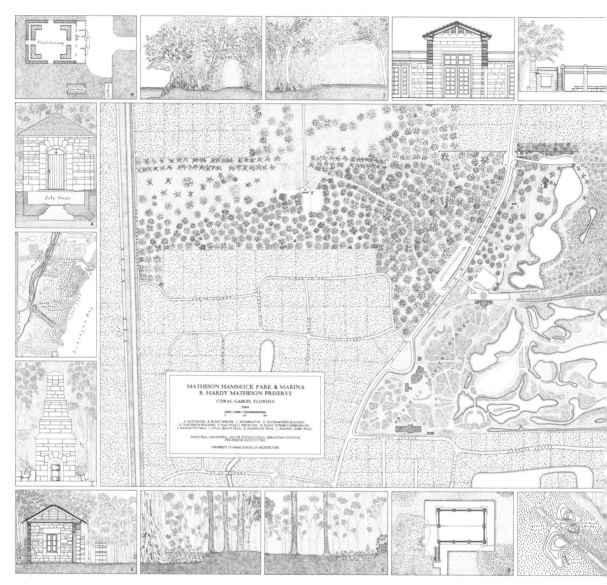

Matheson Hammock Park & Marina, R. Hardy Matheson Preserve, 2004, Students: Marcela Gamarra, Jacob Dunayczan, Sebastian Munoz, Ink on Mylar, 29" x 64"

hensive. These drawings begun outdoors are, because of their scale, finished indoors and become projects that attempt to test every compositional question and are elevated above the mere documental drawing. These drawings are thesis projects and when studied tell many things about and beyond their subject.

Many worlds in one

Once one has looked closely at a subject or subjects the idea of intensification sets in. The real in architecture is made of many things that all fight for a place in space as well as on the page. Call it what you will a *capriccio*, a collage, assemblage, or something yet to be named, but it is the possibility of fantasy, invention or the thoughtful juxtaposition of elements that models a new desired reality. This is a constructed process that can be made from many disciplines, from photography to architecture. In this process one is looking to order a world not as it is, but as it should or could be. Here the frame is present and the space inside it is made theatrical and for a moment we can see what could be. In this act of drawing, the subjective gaze is most present and most impressive and full of possibilities.

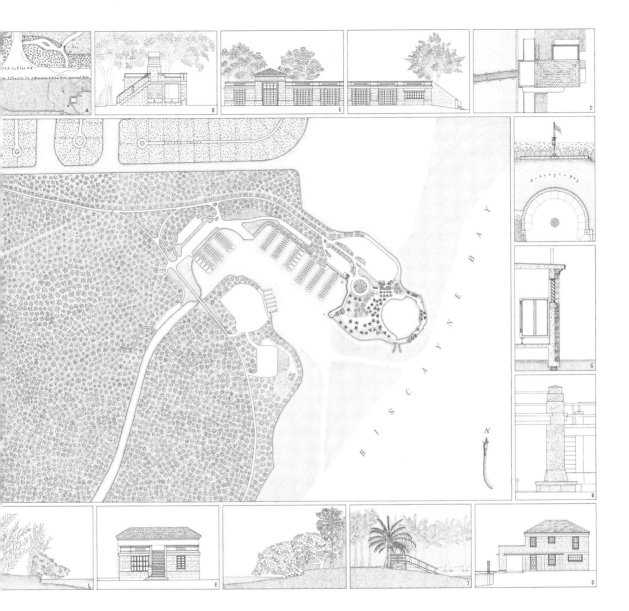

All that is left

Most often the drawing is the education, the will of the delineator, something one desires to know or build. What happens
when it is all that is left? We often think of representation as a
means to an end but what happens when the building made
from it, is no longer there. Drawings here (and elsewhere) are a
part of the building not in service of making it exclusively, they
persist. In the same way our eyes receive light that registers
an image in our brain. Drawings and buildings reflect light and
their images create memories and meaning equally. If either are
good they can be forever inhabited and memorable - the act
of drawing is the beginning of this lasting memory. A drawing is
a record of memory, engagement, will, the hand and the built
work. Architecture is about making. The drawing is the first act
of making and a reminder of the values and knowledge that
inspires imagination. I do not know of a place that puts more
value in the primacy of drawing than Miami, a place that is
paradoxically so naturally predisposed to its destruction. One
must be reminded to draw not write future ideas for that act
has the potential to be unambiguous, lasting and memorable.

[1] See the Letter II: Sketching from Nature in: The Elements of Drawing: In Three
Letters to Beginners. By John Ruskin, 1881.

SELECTED WORKS

Art, Architecture, and Nature
James Prosek, Andrea Collesano, Rocco Ceo
090

In situ Drawings and Watercolors
Jacob Brillhart, Victor Deupi
096

Caprice Sketches and Architecture
Jaime Correa, Lucien Steil, Giuseppe Greci,
R & R Studios / Roberto Behar & Rosario Marquardt
106

Constructed Process
Pablo Cano, Steven Brooke, Nader Tehrani
124

Art, Architecture, and Nature

JAMES PROSEK

These works belong to a series of watercolors and graphite drawings I began back in 2005 that attempted to address some thoughts I'd been having about how we discuss, classify, name and order the natural world.

Humans seem to want to impose order on a nature that is probably more messy multifarious, interconnected and constantly changing than we'd like it to be. One way we make sense of the world, and bring structure to it, is by fragmenting this continuum and labeling the pieces—by naming things. In order to name creatures (the first task given to man by God in the garden on Eden) we have to draw lines between things, fragment what is essentially a unified whole. Humans do this instinctually—we call things trees and birds and cats and stones. But by naming things we essentially give the impression that these things fit into the neat little boxes separated by walls.

I began to wonder, what do we miss by communicating the world through names? What is lost? What about the sinews we have severed to uphold this convenient fiction—this reduction of a beautifully tangled web into concepts and symbols that can easily be digested?

For years I had employed a traditional style in the natural history tradition where the drawing of a creature is accompanied by its common and scientific name, written beneath

(as you see in botanicals or paintings of birds, like Audubon's). But I didn't want people to be influenced by the name, to simply say—"Oh, I know what that is... that's a sunfish..." and walk away. A name is an entry point to making an observation but many people think that if they know the name of something they KNOW the thing. I had become a little disillusioned by this hubris.

So I started making works, paintings of creatures like birds or fish, but I left out the names. Instead I replaced them with curvilinear lines that to me expressed the position of the creature in space—acknowledged those spaces in between that were left behind in the process of naming. This method seemed to enhance the fact that the drawing itself was a way of communicating the creature without language, a quality that was partially eclipsed by adjacent written language.

Conceptual thinking aside, I was also just trying to make something visually interesting—works that had natural history elements, but also activated the spaces between them.

I had been inspired to make works that mixed animals with geometric shapes by looking at south Asian miniature paintings and also illuminated manuscripts. The abstract lines and the animal together both nodded at some supreme architect of life (whether it be a god or evolution or both). I asked myself what would God's blueprints for these creatures, if he had ever made any, look like?!

Below left Flying Fish, 2009, Watercolor, gouache, colored pencil and graphite on tea-stained paper, 18 1/2 x 21 inches | **Below** Double-pheasant, 2006, watercolor, gouache and graphite on tea-stained paper, 24 x 32 inches | **Opposite page above** Atlantic Cod, 2011, watercolor, gouache and graphite on tea-stained paper, 24 x 32 inches | **Opposite page below left** Permit, 2010, watercolor, gouache and graphite on tea-stained paper, 19 x 25 inches | **Opposite page below right** Brook Trout, 2007, watercolor, colored pencil, gouache and graphite on tea-stained paper, 19 x 24 in

Atlantic Cod (Gadus morhua) Chatham, Mass

Beach Rose (Rosa rugosa) with rose hips
Cape Cod

James Prosek 2011

Bluefish Agate & northern mussel
Cape Cod

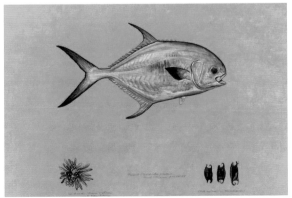

Andrea Collesano

Text by Enrico Mattei

Andrea Collesano brings to light a long and detailed process revealing an unreal world where the many species of the animal kingdom live in perfect harmony, an equilibrium with the universe realized through the union of differences. His work displays living creatures together, above ground and in the sky, with trees as the real protagonist. The trees serve as a stage where the animals play at different heights, a kind of theater where the actors are the same creatures in different roles, but in the end the true hero is the tree. Collesano imagines parallel universes where the undisputed ruling kingdom is the animal one, a timeless world. Animals float in the air and every species lives in perfect harmony with the others, sharing the same space.

Collesano's method is simple and clear, India black ink on stained paper. He does not produce any preliminary drawings and the work arises directly out of the prepared paper; after the surface has been dried, stains and darker areas appear on the sheets, and Collesano imagines the shapes and discovers where to place the sea, the rocks, the whale's stomach, a bug and consequently all of the rest.

His work invites us to sail into a world where boundaries have fallen, to discover the depth of the unconscious, to enlarge our scope of enquiry, to face our life and the magic of dreaming, and in particular to safeguard everything around us for our own existence.

Text by Andrea Collesano

Within the space of two days I was bitten by a wasp, a hornet and a bee. It was the sign I was waiting for - to finish the Tree of Beatitude. So I drew Wasps, Hornets and Bees, among the leaves of a fig. My work often arises in this manner. I pay attention to what is happening to me. I observe, I remember, I ponder over what I have seen and what I have experienced. The strange trees of Supra Terram are born in this way.

I would very much like that everyone could imagine themselves climbing onto their torso, and passing branch by branch realize how much we have without the need to possess, how much Fortune just grows around us, searching no further. Fortune is external, it is born from the seed flying in the wind, wrapped in the bud, it explodes in the fragrance of the flower and it feeds our soul and body with its generous fruit. Once you have arrived on the top of the trees, observe in silence what they safeguard, those nests so precious, without touching, without disturbing the animals that, in my mind, are immortal and superior to all. Don't be scared of them and they won't be scared of you. Animals lead us to the place where we dream, that we can all have if we just allow ourselves to learn, starting from the little things, to respect the gift given to us from birth, our inheritance, the earth and the life surrounding us.

Eco-sustainability, recycling and energy saving. "Do not put off till tomorrow what you can do today" my father told me many years ago. Let's start now.

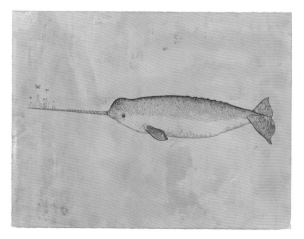

Left Perlucidum (transparent), Ink on paper, 67 x 47 cm., 2015 | **Opposite page above left** Ananasso, Paguri e Diamante (Pineapple, Hermit Crabs and Diamond), Ink on paper, 34 X 48 cm., 2015 | **Opposite page above center** Albero del Silenzio (Tree of Silence), Ink on paper, 100 X 140 cm., 2015 | **Opposite page above right** Pappagallo, Ciliegie e Formiche (Parrot, Cherries and Ants), Ink on paper, 34 X 48 cm, 2015 | **Opposite page center** Levitate (Right Whale, Lobster, and Seahorse), Ink on paper, 33 X 24.5 cm., 2015 | **Opposite page below left** Polpo e Frutti (Octopus and Fruits), Ink on paper, 35 X 45 cm., 2015 | **Opposite page below right** Capodoglio (Sperm Whale), Ink on paper, 35 X 45 cm., 2015

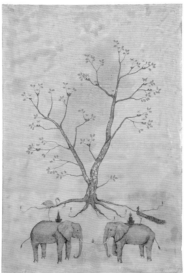

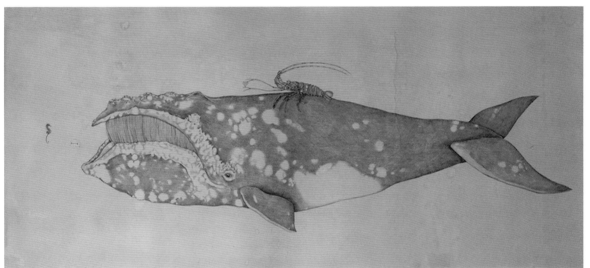

Rocco Ceo

Jungle Floor

Living in a sea of pavement and made surfaces one is apt to forget what was once ubiquitous here in the tropics. This long drawing is a full size drawing of a piece of the hammock floor of what was once the 'Orchid Jungle' a mostly untouched piece of land, once an attraction garden and now a nature preserve. Full of ankle twisting buttressing roots that bridge and dive into solution holes dissolving the oolitic rock floor, is a landscape that took thousands of years to make. Raw and uncompromising, this ground is a thesis of slow growth, degradation and renewal, complete with delicate ferns adjusting to changes in water and light. The drawing is a parallel story in its making formed from brushed charcoal dust to line drawing and eventually fully rendered leaves, roots, rock and moss. Like the landscape it is constructed. The drawing gets its organization and relief from the presence or lack of light just like in the hammock. Where light finds its way to the jungle floor things are in detail, and in focus, visible. Where little or no light exists the drawing begins to wither to line and deep heavy layers of black charcoal. Light and shadow are the enablers of form in landscape as they are in architecture. In resurrecting the importance of the ground again one can begin to think about how it is the beginning and end of all things. Architecture stands in it, on it and is of course of it. For these reasons we might look at it more considerately.

Above Jungle Floor, Size: 30' x 4', charcoal on Fabriano artistico hot press | **Opposite page below** Silver Palm, 22"x 30", colored pencil on Fabriano hot press, 1996 | **Below left** Gumbo Limbo Detail, 16" x 11 1/2", colored pencil on Fabriano hot press, 2001 | **Bottom left** Balsa Tree, 23 ½" x 16 1/8", colored pencil on bond, 1990 | **Below right** Live Oak, 24 1/2" x 28 3/4", colored pencil on bond paper, 1990 | **Bottom right** Maleluca Allegory, 36" x 18", colored pencil on bond, 2000

In Situ Drawings and Watercolors

Jacob Brillhart

Jacob Brillhart's research engages the creative search through drawing, painting and design. This ongoing curiosity focuses on the ever-changing relationship between design and methods of representation and visualization. His scholarly investigation of the creative search is based on Le Corbusier's travel drawings and into his architectural theories and built work.

Opposite page above Roma Termini, Rome, Italy, pencil and watercolor on hot press, 9 x 12 inches | Opposite page below Palazzo delle Poste in Ostia, Italy, pencil and watercolor on hot press, 8 x 11 inches | Above Versailles Hotel, Miami Beach, FL, pencil and watercolor on hot press, 10 x 12 inches | Below Parthenon, Athens, Greece, pencil and watercolor on hot press, 9 x 12 inches

Above Santa Maria Novella, Florence | **Below left** Hospital of the Innocents, Florence | **Below right** Old church street | **Opposite page above** Gate House Berlin, Karl Friedrich Schinkel | **Opposite page center** Winged Victory of Samothrace, Louvre, Paris | **Opposite page below** Santa Maria della Salute, Venice, Light Fixtures

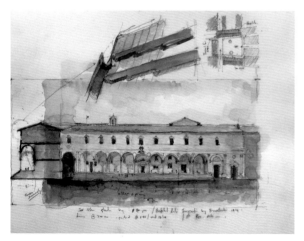

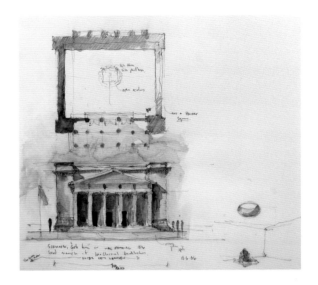

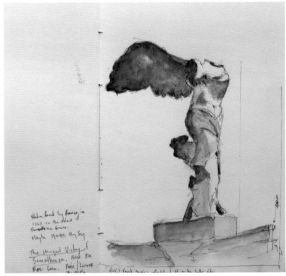

Victor Deupi

Victor Deupi is dedicated to promoting representational painting as a critical component of contemporary art and architecture. Inspired by architects and artists from Piranesi to Ruskin, as well as 20th-century Cuban realists such as Leopoldo Romañach and Emilio Sanchez, his sketches, watercolors, and paintings represent the timeless expression of architectural form and space. Painted largely in situ, Deupi's works capture the spirit of art, architecture, and landscape while providing compelling vistas onto classicism's enduring resonance in the modern age.

Opposite page Stone Barge, Villa Vizcaya, Miami, FL (26/02/15), pencil and watercolor, 31 x 41 cm. | **Above** Biltmore Hotel and Casino, Coral Gables, FL (24/02/15), pencil and watercolor, 31 x 41 cm. | **Below left** DeSoto Fountain, Coral Gables (23/01/17), pencil and watercolor, 31 x 41 cm. | **Below right** Esquina universal con dos puertas, South Miami (April 2017) pencil, watercolor and gouache, 15 x 22 inches

Above Biltmore Casino, Coral Gables (4/06/15), pencil and watercolor, 28 x 45 cm. | **Below** Tempio di Ercole, Rome (23/10/06), pencil and watercolor, 23 x 31 cm. | **Opposite page above** Vizcaya, Miami (17/02/09), pencil and watercolor, 33 x 38 cm. | **Opposite page below** *Edificios y sueños*, Havana, Cuba (18/08/17), pencil, watercolor, pen and brown ink, 22 x 30 inches

Caprice Sketches and Architecture

Jaime Correa

SALT LAKE CITY INTERROTTA: a concrete urban design intervention for Salt Lake City. The block proposal advocates the type of unitary urbanism in which modern planning techniques and art in public spaces are integrated. The meta-graphic writing is a rational comment on two conditions: the existing extra-large and the ideal block size. Typological diversity is illustrated with alphabetized building plans and landscape dispositions indicating the necessity for urban semantics. Technically, the new porosity of the block, the alignment and continuity of buildings on incremental lots, the presence of a new public space, the reconfiguration of streets and sidewalks, and the superabundance of design serve to settle the typical challenges suffered by the contemporary urban designer in the American everyday territories. The figure-ground plan is a reference to Giambattista Nolli's plan for the City of Rome.

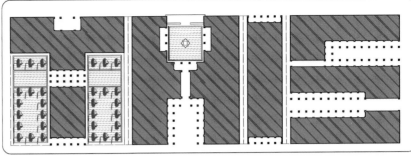

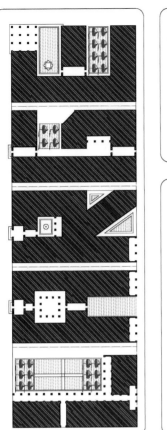

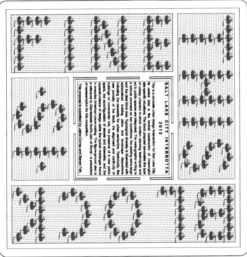

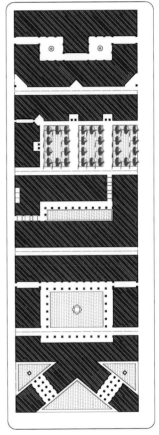

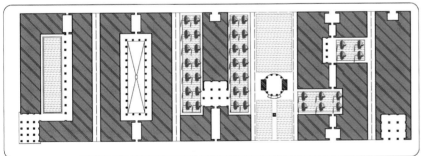

Above Salt Lake City Interrotta, 2015, Jaime Correa and Steve Fett

Lucien Steil

In the Mood for Architecture
"Emotion is the multisensory medium through which we engage the world, and human reason is but an evolutionary refinement of the emotional process...,"[1]

I stopped making a difference between my building and urban designs and my architectural 'capricci' realizing ultimately that they develop in the same realm of memory, intuition, emotion and desire. Whether they are built or not does not affect the intensity of their reality. They are imaginatively engaging and meditating on the poetics of inhabiting this world in happiness. I believe that they are born in a mythical desire for building, a desire imbedded in a collective memory of many generations. Even though they are built I like to re-envision and idealize in fresh renderings which enhance the real with refined suggestions of potentials of beauty and harmony. I do the same with unbuilt projects enjoying revisiting and re-inventing the same ideas and ideals in the same mood, and with unbound passion for the poetic necessity of architecture. I have come to accept and celebrate the imaginary, dreams and feelings, as well as spontaneity, intuition and empathy as the foundation of my design work which I consider reasonably rational, and passionately romantic.

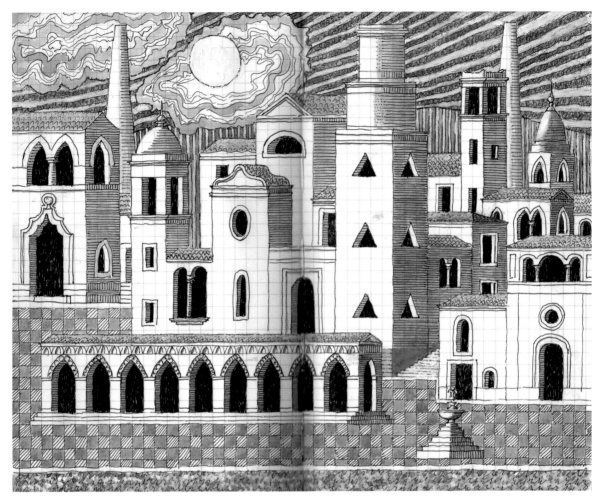

Opposite page "The Forgotten Island", Sketchbook, 2018 | **Above** "Retour de Seville", Summer Sketchbook, 2016 | **Below** "Citta Felice", from 'Adriatic Sketchbooks', 2014

I now understand much better what drew me to the work of De Chirico and 'romantic' rationalists like Aldo Rossi and Massimo Scolari, and finally what led me to what I consider a revelation and transformational experience with the designs and writings of Leon and Rob Krier. I would probably not have become an architect would there not have been this providential encounter with Leon Krier's drawings and polemics, and his correspondence with Maurice Culot published in the mythical "Archives d'Architecture Moderne" in Bruxelles.

[1] Harry Francis Malgrave in: "Know Thyself, or what designers can learn from the contemporary biological sciences" / in "Mind in Architecture" Sarah Robinson, Juhani Pallasma editors/ MIT Press (2015)

Opposite page above "Rue St. Vincent", Social Housing, Esch/ Alzette (Lucien Steil, 1986) | **Opposite page below** "Musee Brassicole National", Bivange (Mulhern & Steil 1993) | **Above** "Service Residence", Place des Bains, Esch/ Alzette (Mulhern & Steil, 1994)

Opposite page above "Waterfront Promenade", 2018 | **Opposite page center** "Evening Sky", 2018 | **Opposite page below** "Fountain and Square", 2018 |
Above Seaside Capriccio

Giuseppe Greci

Drawing is still the most effective way of representing architecture. Through this technique one can describe towns, villages, streets and squares, even if they are only imagined and not yet realized.

Like traditional buildings that are made to last, watercolors can also endure. Giuseppe Greci, who works at Studio Bontempi in Parma, produces watercolors using natural materials on cotton papers to preserve them from alterations; in fact, they are designed for future generations.

His watercolors are real portraits of projects, where architecture is the focus. They are extremely accurate representations, that can reveal the most elegant portal to the single tile of a roof.

Shadows alternating with bright areas provide three-dimensional effects to the buildings; the trees and the landscape in the background give a sense of depth to the drawing.

The balance between the built and natural landscape, together with a measured use of light, makes the spectator feel the atmosphere of these places, which are sometimes real and sometimes ideal, such as in the case of his "capricci". Historically speaking, a "capriccio" is a realistic representation of an imaginary place. As a painted theoretical manifesto, it offers the opportunity to show a perfect vision of a building, even as a ruin.

This kind of representation, inspired by the landscape painters of XVIII century such as Canaletto, Bernardo Bellotto or the incomparable Giambattista Lusieri, renders the visions of Studio Bontempi particularly convincing, recognizable and personal.

Above Capriccio with Spa Village, 2011 (designed by Studio Bontempi)

Above Piazzetta on the Sea in Seaside, 2005 (designed by Pier Carlo Bontempi & Victor Deupi) |
Left Ostrich Egg, 2008 | **Opposite page** Monumental Staircase of the Palazzo del Governatore in
Parma, 2009 | **Following spread** Capriccio with Piazza, 2011 (designed by Studio Bontempi)

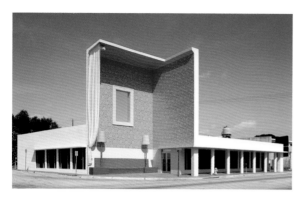

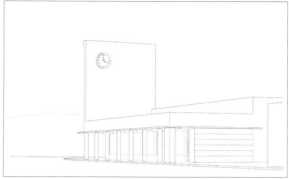

R & R Studios / Roberto Behar & Rosario Marquardt

The Living Room, Design District (Miami, FL, 2001)

The aim of our practice is to reclaim, enhance and develop the public dimension of the city. We resist the privatization of public space and seek to produce a public architecture that emphasizes the communal and civic dimension of the city. We understand our practice as experiments in public space that might imbue the construction of the city with new meaning and emotion.

The Living Room transforms one corner of an urban intersection in the Miami Design District into a domestic interior that simultaneously doubles as a small square for the District. The Living Room appears as a mirage where art and life meet, public and private spaces collide and the real and the fantastic coexist. The Living Room challenges the sameness of the city, an offers a moment of wonder where the home and monument become one.

We weave together diverse architectures, scales, parts and elements of the project to elicit an avalanche of meanings that enrich and unsettle the encounter with the building. The Living Room is a place of encounters open to multiple interpretations and everyday life.

Collaborators: Georgy John, Adolfo Albaisa, Christopher Musumano & Nikolai Nedev
Client: Craig Robbins / Dacra Development
Construction Company: MGM Builders

Opposite page above left View from across the street | **Opposite page above right** Gallery and street corner. Line drawing | **Opposite page below** Line drawing | **Above left** Entrance. Line drawing | **Above right** Close up view | **Below** Composite drawing | **Following spread** View from across the street. Photography by R & R Studios

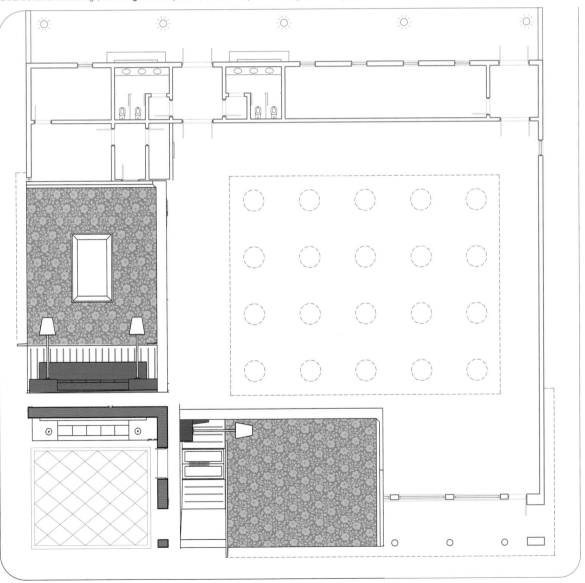

Constructed Process

Pablo Cano
La Santa Sebastiana, 1984

In 1980, 10,865 Cubans tried to gain asylum by taking refuge at the Peruvian Embassy in Havana Cuba. The Mariel boatlift freed 125,000 Cubans. My collage mural, ink on paper of LaSebastiana, was a political statement triggered by this mass emigration. The painting of St. Sebastian by Andrea Mantegna and Pablo Picasso's Guernica was a vital source of inspiration for me.

Miami's Cuban exiles wait for change to happen for the Cuban people. St. Theresa holds an arrow as she waits for Cuba to be freed from bondage. A constructivist knight on a white horse, a symbol of American freedom and technology is slowly coming to the rescue. Cuba is personified as Lady Liberty in bondage, her front and back is seen pierced with arrows. Cuba is slowly healing and untying herself from these oppressive ropes. Her legs are depicted untied. 33 years after I created La Sebastiana, America finally arrived on the Island. I pray Cuba will soon be freed.

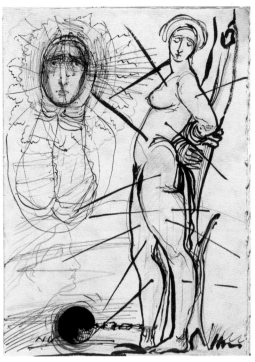

Opposite page La Santa Sebastiana, Collage and ink on paper, 1984, Paris, France, 6 X 12 feet. Collection of Mr. and Mrs. John and Lauren Oramas | **This page** Pablo Cano, La Santa Sebastiana Sketchbook, Collection of Linda Cheverton Wick

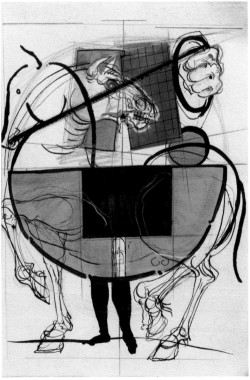

Pablo Cano
Puppetry Arts, 2014

My interest in Puppetry Arts began while studying for my
Masters in Fine Arts degree in Queens College New York.
As a painter and sculptor, I wanted to break through the
tableaux and experiment with movement. Puppetry Arts was
the most inspiring way to go about it for me. I discovered
DADA and Russian Constructivism and learned that the
history of modern art began with a marionette play called
UBU ROI by Alfred Jarry.

At a frenzied pace I started I building the Florabel Theater
with found wood and objects that were plentiful along the
streets of Queens New York. Discarded Marlboro cigarette
boxes with silver paper wrappers became my favorite collage material for the surface of my theater and puppets. My
friend, Florabel Webster loyally mailed me hundreds of silver
wrappers from Miami. I christened my puppet theater after
her. The first performance at the Florabel Theater was for
the opening of my Masters Thesis solo exhibition at Queens
College New York, Animated Altarpieces, now part of the
Rubell Family Collection, Miami, Fl.

Since then, my marionette productions became more and
more elaborate with the help and support of the Museum of
Contemporary Art, North Miami. For 10 years Choreographer
Katherine Kramer and I collaborated in creating original
marionette productions commissioned by MOCA. Queen
Marie Antoinette was one of the most elaborate life size rod
puppets I designed. Created with discarded materials and
my silver cigarette paper wrappers, she is now the grand
finale of my Cricket Theater, Musical Marionette Shows.

This spread NSU Museum of Art, The Miami Generation Revisited, Fort Lauderdale, FL, 2014. Photography by (c) Steven Brooke Studios

Steven Brooke

Luigi Rossini's Vedute di Roma (Views of Rome), produced in the late 1800s, was the last such complete view of the Eternal City. In 1991 and 1992 I was a Fellow of the American Academy in Rome. Inspired by the work of the 17th - and 18th -century Italian and Dutch view painters such as de Hooch, Vasi, Canaletto, and Piranesi, I produced my own 200-view Vedute di Roma.

My book, published in 1995 by Rizzoli, documented the iconic monuments of Ancient and Christian Rome. Further, I decided that no late-20th-century Vedute di Roma would be complete without the architecture of the Modern Era (1850–1950); therefore, I also included 44 buildings from this period. Many of these projects have never been and are still not appreciated by architectural critics, students, or the Roman citizenry. Criticism has focused on their stylistic excesses (Il Palazzo Giustizia, Il Vittoriano, Il Ministero della Pubblica Instruzione; on their austerity (Palazzo della Civiltà

Italica, Palazzo Postale di Via Marmorata); or on their original political patronage (Foro Italico and Esposizione Universale Roma - E. U. R.). By depicting these buildings with the same respect and rigor shown for architecture of the earlier eras, I sought to promote a renewed appreciation of their histor-ical significance if not of their architectural merit. Works by Adelberto Libera, Marcello Piacentini, Angiolo Mazzoni, and others are, in fact, among the finest examples of modernist architecture in the world. The early structures and urban planning of E. U. R., demonstrated that an assemblage of modernist buildings could effectively form a humanely scaled urban environment. I had hoped to include more examples of early Modern Era architecture, but unfortunately many of these neglected buildings had deteriorated into such disrepair and structural instability that they were isolated behind barbed wire and completely inaccessible. Restoration activities in Rome's Garbatella district and elsewhere promise that architecture of this era is finally gaining the attention it merits. Fortunately, many of the modernist buildings of the Fascist Era new towns near Rome — Pontinia, Pomezia, Aprilia, Latina, and Sabaudia — have fared far better.

Opposite page Palazzo della Civiltà Italica, EUR | Above SS. Pietro e Paolo | Below Stazione Termini | Following spread Palazzo dei Ricevimenti e Congressi, EUR | Photography by (c) Steven Brooke Studios

Nader Tehrani

St. Peter's Inverted Crucifixion: Down to Earth, Looking up to the Heavens. Nader Tehrani, 2018

The altar of the Tempietto, located on axis with the entry into the courtyard of San Pietro in Montorio, appears to be composed of monolithic pieces of marble. It is distinct from the conventional altar conceived as a free-standing piece of furniture. Encrypted into the logic of the building's architecture, the altar is set against the outer wall, further thickening the mass of the load-bearing structure. Consistent with Robin Evans's article "Perturbed Circles" in *The Projective Cast*, the position of the altar contributes to the effect of multiple centers achieved in this building, and its de-centering underlines the importance of this choice. Indeed, the altar is not only not monolithic, but the inverse. It is composed of a series of thin marble slabs, behind which a cavity allows for a clerestory window into the crypt. The altar serves as the window's frame, and thus the two are co-dependent.[1]

As partial as it may seem, the sectional detail of this altar reveals something about this building that not only subverts the conventions of its time, but also requires a form of representation beyond the normative techniques of drawing. Due to its curious spatial reciprocity, the figure-ground relationship between the space of the clerestory and the form of the altar is so tight that the building is exempted of the poché characteristic of the structures of this period. If the mass of a traditional wall is meant to provide structural support for a building, it is also the means by which ancillary spaces such as niches and other figural voids can be carved out. The Tempietto does away with this mass altogether, ingeniously conjoining the two functions by using one as the alibi for the other—the altar gives light, and the clerestory offers mass.

This telltale detail of the Tempietto also exposes the difficulty of drawing complex circumstances that require simultaneously looking up and down, if only to show two facets of something inextricably bound together. For this reason, this small structure offers the ideal opportunity with which to advance a form of representation whose purpose is not to illustrate what is already known but to expose the inner workings of something that can only be unearthed forensically. This drawing is the result of the "flip-flop" technique, coined by Daniel Castor in his 1996 book *Drawing Berlage's Exchange*, where he demonstrates how this drawing type produces a beguiling form of visual ambiguity that enables the eye to invert the perception of foreground and background.[2] Not dissimilar to El Lissitzky's *Abstract Cabinet* 1927 drawing, Castor's isometric, constructed from a tri-fold 120-degree angle of projection, is distinct in its balanced bias towards the X, Y and Z axes all at once.

The architectural application of this technique resides in the latent alignment between the conventional bird's eye and worm's eye views, the latter often attributed to Auguste Choisy. If the bird's eye view exposes the world of the roof, the worm's eye reveals the inner workings of the dome, effectively two different symbolic realms. Donato Bramante conceived of both the Tempietto and St. Peter's Basilica a few years apart, making their conceptual connection somehow inevitable. The Tempietto, a martyrium dedicated to St. Peter, is a folly of sorts—at once a model, a mock-up and a miniature building in its own right with the gravitas of spatial, formal and linguistic tropes that advance the discourse of its time. In its crypt, a pit on center with the oculus, is purported to be the receptacle within which St. Peter's cross would have been planted upside down, looking up at the dome in his last living moments. In light of the eventual dual-shell construction technique adopted for St. Peter's dome, one can understand the absolute necessity of looking up and down simultaneously, because the domes are not only symbolically divided but structurally semi-autonomous. By extension, even though the Tempietto is a single-shell structure, the flip-flop technique in this drawing demonstrates the instrumentality of also looking inside and outside simultaneously.

Within the vicissitudes of representational techniques through the centuries, we are beneficiaries of many conceptual advances in the arts that, when seen in tandem, help build a rich repertoire for an analysis of this kind. For instance, Charles de Wailly's sectional perspectives show the connection between buildings and their urban context in full splendor, in effect bringing the city into the building. The graphic work of M.C. Escher also demonstrates how the latent connections between geometry, space and the construction of perception contribute to their hypnotizing architectural effect. We witness in Picasso's cubism the desire to overcome the impossibility of seeing many facets at the same time—the front, the back and the sides. In this tradition, as an extension of Castor's own work, this composite drawing looks up and down, inside and out, toggling back and forth, taking advantage of the isometric's unique visual sleight of hand to reveal the anomalous alignments, correspondences and reciprocities that would otherwise remain lost in the seemingly pure and idealized form of the Tempietto.

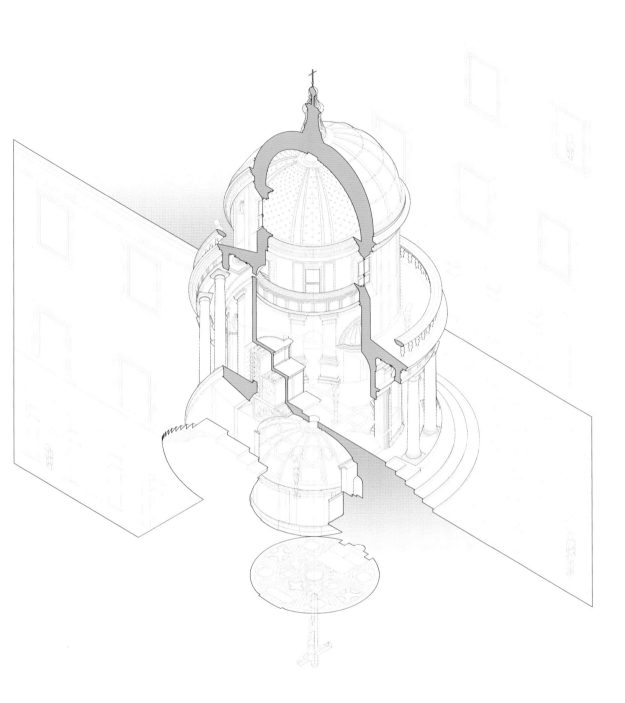

Credits: Nader Tehrani, NADAAA: Katherine Faulkner,
Lisa LaCharité, Mitch Mackowiak

[1] The complex relationship between the building's oculus, connecting the chapel and crypt, as well as the crypt's clerestory, diagonally drawing in light from the exterior, is lovingly depicted in Paolo Sorrentino's 2013 *La Grande Bellezza*, effectively linking the multiple centers in one shot (https://www.youtube.com/watch?v=OYwloxnUWjg).

[2] The Yves Alain Bois essay, 'Metamorphosis of Axonometry' makes reference to the Josef Albers painting *Structural Constellation*, wherein the visual symmetry of the drawing produces simultaneous depth and flatness. Accordingly, as the eye toggles back and forth between the two sides of the drawing, it can be seen to pop in or out, an optical illusion cited in 1832 by Louis Albert Necker in a similar reference to the Necker Cube.

Chapter 3

Resilience, Technology and Sustainability

What - if anything - are contemporary classicists doing about climate change, not just for Miami but also for other important heritage cities throughout the world where a discernible classical, and or vernacular, past exists, places such as Venice, Amsterdam, New Orleans, or Havana?[1] Critics of contemporary classicism might ask, "Are classicists really concerned with issues of resiliency, technology or sustainability?" Fortunately, classicists have always had the advantage of being able to "leap back" through history (what the Latin term *resilire* literally means) to situate such problems in a cultural and political - rather than technical - context. And, while it remains debatable as to whether or not history can teach us, we can indeed learn from the past. By studying precedents, we can develop a better understanding of the correlation between socio-economic identity, attitude towards defensive action, and the type of organization needed for concerted action.

Resilience

Miami-Dade County features on the list of the world's most vulnerable regions to the effects of sea level rise. Despite variations to the type and origin of the forecast model, over the next 45 years the southern tip of the Floridian peninsula will have to cope with up to three feet of higher water levels than the present. Without human intervention, this trend would transform the lowest laying landmasses, with Miami Beach as the most prominent example, into almost fully covered watersheds. The complexity of planning for such a predicament is compounded by the fact that the region is also prone to hurricane disasters. Depending on the strength of the coming storms, the combined effect and impact on city life can hence vary considerably.

While these conditions might be typical for the majority of flood-endangered places throughout the world, the Florida Peninsula has in addition the geological particularity of porous ground. It rests on a vast plateau of karst limestone with significant areas of dissolved rock, underground drainage, and numerous abrupt ridges, fissures, sinkholes, and caverns. Consequently, traditional flood control methods such as structural levees, floodways, channel improvement, and reservoirs may not be suitable solutions as water can still travel through the bedrock and rise wherever necessary. For this

Victor Deupi & Eric Firley

reason, and its consequences for flora, fauna, building foundations, drink water provision and the highly vulnerable ecosystem of the neighboring Everglades, Miami and the greater South Florida region, has been described as the ground-zero for sea level rise inquiry and discourse.

It is important to note that the alleged uniqueness of the contemporary version of sea level rise in the form of a continuously worsening trend is somewhat debatable. Earlier phenomena might not have been based on a global event such as the melting of ice caps, but subjectively must have appeared in a similar light. Just like us today, many cities in the past witnessed recurring and often-intensifying inundations, and their residents tried to agree on measures of how to prevent or limit their undesirable effects.

Consider the case of ancient Rome, which from the very beginning was mythically associated with flooding.[2] The well-known legend of Romulus and Remus rescued by the she-wolf sidesteps the key point that King Amulius had ordered the twins to be placed in a basket and thrown into the Tiber River. The basket washed ashore as the man charged with the drowning could not get far enough into the river to release the boys into the torrent. The Tiber had flooded due to winter rains, and standing pools of water prevented the basket from catching a current and floating down river, if not out to sea. The legend of Romulus and Remus underlines the complicated relationship Rome has always had with the flood-prone Tiber. The river that ironically saved the founders' lives would also frequently savage the city through relentless floods and other water-related destruction. Clearly, Rome's location was poorly chosen, a problem that continues to plague cities throughout the world. A large part of it was situated on land that was inherently marshy and on a point of the Tiber that was prone to severe flooding, a fact that goes against any common-sense planning. Not even Vitruvius, whose treatise *De architectura* appeared in the second half of the 1st Century BCE, mentioned flooding or the associated flood-related damages to buildings, though he warned of building in swampy, marsh-like places and the associated health risks that come from living in such environments. He also warned of poorly made masonry walls and improperly mixed Roman

Fig. 1 Orongo Station Conservation Masterplan, Poverty Bay, New Zealand, Thomas Woltz of Nelson Byrd Woltz (2002- 2012). Photograph by Nelson Byrd Woltz Landscape Architects

mortar, careless constructional techniques that when exposed to water and continuous moisture, could result in the loss of structural integrity or collapse. But, these are hardly comforting solutions to the problems of climate change and the associated sea level rise that will come with it.

Vitruvius' example is symptomatic of the challenges that face contemporary classicists today. The fact that the ancient author never explicitly mentioned the flooding issue suggests that he took it for granted or fatalistically accepted is as a *force majeure*. His omission also suggests that the consequences may have rarely been disastrous, leading one to believe that for Vitruvius, these kinds of random acts of nature may have been beyond one's ability to resist, let alone foresee. That is perhaps why contemporary classicists tend to rely on the belief that "tried and trusted" precedent (be it classical or vernacular), or "enduring" typologies are reliable instruments of green building, despite the fact that there is no scientific evidence to confirm such a position. Clearly there is much work to be done here, as can be seen in the case of Orongo Station (2012) in New Zealand by Thomas Woltz of Nelson Byrd Woltz (fig. 1). The sooner classicists start addressing these issues, the sooner they will be given greater credit.

Technology

What does it mean for the relationship between classicism and technology, if the latter is defined as "the practical use of scientific discoveries" (Cambridge Dictionary)? Such wording suggests that the topic can be treated from two major angles, one that dwells into the usual stereotypes, playing with the assumption that classical architects share a limited interest in technological advances, and a second one that focuses on

the complementarity and compatibility, or not, of classical architecture and new technological features. It certainly would be tempting to quickly dismiss the first angle as an impasse, claiming that we shall not reproduce prejudices of alleged technophobia that have grown out of a decades-old antagonism with questionable merit. Who would seriously doubt that the history of classical architecture has been shaped by technological progress as much as has been the history of modern architecture, from the pyramids over the Pont du Gard to Brunelleschi's dome? However, we argue that in the current context there still is something to be said about this alleged conservative argument, the tendency to value the culturally based semiotics of architectural language over sheer technological expression. Our point is certainly not to claim that both directions are mutually exclusive, but to scrutinize, if the general insistence on style in the understanding of a semiotic interplay can still be a timely reflection in the contemporary discussion about place-creation? The authors think that it is. The architectural profession finds itself increasingly in a role in which it has to prove performance, and give quantitative evidence of it. In addition, its work has been, more than ever, identified as a valuable marketing tool in the growing competition between cities to attract talent. Often, as can be seen for example in the proposals submitted as part of the "Réinventer Paris" competition, projects are prized whose exterior appearance symbolizes these ambitions, usually in the form of literally green features. This however, the attempt to situate buildings in the world of nature, or rather techno-nature, signifies a new deal, one that has no precedent in architectural history. Both phenomena together, the green symbolism and the focus on performance and data, project the style discussion far into the background.

Why is this considered a sign of awakened relevance for the classicist cause? Because the radical nature of this change underlines, once again, the question of the architect's role in place-making. Nobody asks today, if a façade is modern or traditional, but at the end of the day it has to be something, something that provides contentment and societal relevance. David Chipperfield, often presented as a neo-classicist, speaks in this context of the importance of "Gestalt and silhouette", also in regards to the confrontation with a building's spatial and cultural context. Theoretically, these positions are fully compatible with the growing role of technology, but they are threatened to be considered outdated, if not irrelevant. The modernist refusal to carry on with the historical canon of architectural expression has been substituted by outright disinterest in the topic. Classicism, for good reasons or not, is accustomed to these accusations of irrelevance, and

Fig. 2 Torre Velasca seen from the Duomo, Milan. Photograph by Eric Firley

might be able to play, once again, the role of the conservative short-sighted among the fashionable blind. Pure modernists, due to their philistine commitment to non-style, will struggle to express this "call for order". They are trapped in an argumentation of alleged functionality. As a matter of fact, for both streams it is an opportunity to jointly distance themselves from a legacy of universal values that threatens to propagate a culture of generic form-making, may it be green or not. On both sides, the initial fascination for global building culture, in the form of the "International Style" or the one of geographically spread imperial grandeur, has utterly been decimated by the contemporary recognition of this globalization trend as a promoter of fairly profane mass culture. Among architects and urban designers, rare are those who still consider globalization as a trump, even questioning the low-cost aspect of it for reasons of sustainability and human rights.

Regarding the second angle to the question, the "real-life" compatibility of classical architecture with technological progress - arguably the main and less polemical theme -, not a lot can be said, other than to refer as mentioned above to the necessity of further testing. Far and recent history is full of examples of classically designed buildings that are using new technologies. Interestingly, this is also the case for a building type that classicism always had difficulties to adopt, the high-rise (figs. 2-3). From the early New York and Chicago skyscrapers over Turin's Mole Antonelliana and Milan's Torre Velazca to Philipp Johnson's AT&T Tower, the adaptation of classical design to structural advances in the form of vertical extrusion appears surprisingly unproblematic. In view of this, another type of technology discussion reveals as the theoretically more interesting one. It is the one that applies to the design process itself, rather than the built outcome. While computer aided design (CAD) did not yet question the principles of classical design, parametrics represent a more profound challenge (see chapter 5). Substituting a codified language that is based in human history and civilization by computer algorithms seems at the first glance difficult to digest. At a second glance, realizing the diversity of parametric production, things become more complex, and reveal the dependence of the formal outcome from the specificities of human input and selection. The larger the scale, preferably up to the urban one, the easier it is to imagine a combination of parametric computation and classical architectural language.

It appears that classical architecture is not defined by a distinction in its relationship to technology compared to other architectural approaches. The questioning however has its merit, because it indirectly scrutinizes classical architecture's openness to experimentation. This in turn raises another point, the one of the commission. Architecture needs a client, and classical architecture will have to convince contemporary clients of its ability to deliver progress in the form of technological adaptation. What would classical architects have to embrace in order to build the new Google headquarters? Norman Foster might know.

Sustainability

Within the last several decades, a great deal of attention has been given to the issue of green architecture and design.[3] From the development of high performance building materials and methods of construction to new programs that support good neighborhood design, sustainability remains a white-hot issue that tends to be supported on social, environmental and economic grounds (the Triple-Bottom-Line). The United States Environmental Protection Agency (EPA) defines sustainability as creating and maintaining "conditions under which humans and nature can exist in productive harmony, that permit fulfilling the social, economic and other requirements of present and future generations." Yet classicists continue to argue for a form of "cultural sustainability" over any other approach, insisting that common sense, natural systems, memory, and appropriateness shape the quality and character of buildings, particularly in relation to the larger built environment.

Culture provides a framework in which memory and foresight are integrated into a continually shifting present, positioning the concept of "sense of place" as a mean between the past and the future. More specifically, "sense of place" is intimately linked with notions of well-being (*benessere*), rootedness, and belonging, ideas that are routinely used in current debates on planning without any significant method for their application. Additionally, culture is the principle vehicle through which creativity in the arts and humanities both renews and sets forth the artistic legacies of the future, and here the concept of continuity is essential for the predominant position today among historians and preservationists is that heritage is something that needs to be preserved whereas artistic culture is constantly shifting. Continuity, on the other hand, implies that artistic culture is the intellectual struggle that every generation faces in light of an increasingly distant past and an indeterminate future.

Opposite page Fig. 3 Miami-Dade County Courthouse. Photograph by Eric Firley | **Above Fig. 4** Francisco de Goya y Lucientes, The sleep of reason produces monsters *(El sueño de la razon produce monstruos)*, Etching, 1799, Metropolitan Museum of Art, NY

It may very well hold true that the search for a healthy middle way is in fact the main challenge of sustainability today, but until classical, traditional, and vernacular forms are scientifically tested to demonstrate their environmental performance, the argument for cultural sustainability will always remain a matter of personal preference. But of course, such a recommendation comes with a historical caveat, as Goya noted in one of his most influential *Capricho* prints, *El sueño de la razon produce monstrous* (Fig. 4) – 'the dream of reason produces monsters.' Cultural sustainability will always have to find a balance between the cultural and the sustainable, if classical architecture can contribute to this, then so be it.

[1] Extracts from this essay are taken from E. Firley and V. Deupi, "Miami Rising: Historical Perspectives on Sea-Level-Rise as a View into the Future," The Plan Journal, Vol. 2, no. 2 (2017), 187-206.
[2] See Gregory S. Aldrete, Floods of the Tiber in Ancient Rome (Baltimore: Johns Hopkins University Press, 2006), 10 ff.
[3] Selected passages are taken from V. Deupi, "Cultural Sustainability and the Renewal of Tradition," in Green Living: Architecture and Planning, edited by B. Kenda, and S. Parissien (New York: Rizzoli, 2010), 148-69.
[4] https://www.epa.gov/sustainability.

SELECTED WORKS

Orongo Station Conservation Masterplan
Poverty Bay, New Zealand | 2002-2012
Thomas Woltz of Neloson Byrd Woltz
142

Climate Refugee Camp
Arcadia, FL | ongoing
Jaime Correa
148

The Mexican Enclave, Upper Level Design Studio
University of Miami School of Architecture | 2017
Jaime Correa
156

Town Green
FL | 2014
Merrill, Pastor & Colgan Architects
160

Neighborhood Pool
FL | 2014
Merrill, Pastor & Colgan Architects
164

Escuelita Buganvilia
Guatemala | 2015
Cure Penabad
168

Brillhart Cabin
Bahamas | ongoing
Melissa and Jacob Brillhart
174

Orongo Station Conservation Masterplan
Poverty Bay, New Zealand | 2002-2012

Thomas Woltz of Nelson Byrd Woltz

Orongo Station is a 3,000-acre sheep station on the east coast of the North Island of New Zealand. The Station was the landing point for the Great Migration of Maori people in 1100, and again for Captain Cook's crew when they discovered New Zealand in 1769. Subsequent colonization subjected the site to ongoing resource depletion as a result of unregulated sheep farming. With approval from New Zealand Parliament and in collaboration with local environmental officials and Maori tribal leaders, NBW designed and implemented multiple productive farming operations, a restoration regime to repair ecological damage of the past 100 years, a series of gar-

dens inspired by vernacular cultural and environmental influences that have helped shape the New Zealand landscape. An important aspect of the project was the inclusion of native tribes people in the design process. NBW collaborated with the indigenous Maori tribe to restore a historic cemetery on the property that is still in use. Maori earthwork constructions - defense structures, food storage pits, and others - were preserved and revealed through various design strategies.

Over 500,000 trees have been planted to start reforesting the sheep-grazed land while still maintaining a farm that is even more economically viable than before forestation. Over 75 acres of fresh and saltwater wetlands have been restored and constructed. These projects have contributed to the local economy by providing opportunities for the local people to establish nurseries that supply trees and plants for ecological restoration. By integrating cultural and ecological landscape restoration with active, profitable agricultural operations, Orongo Station serves as a national model for sustainable land management.

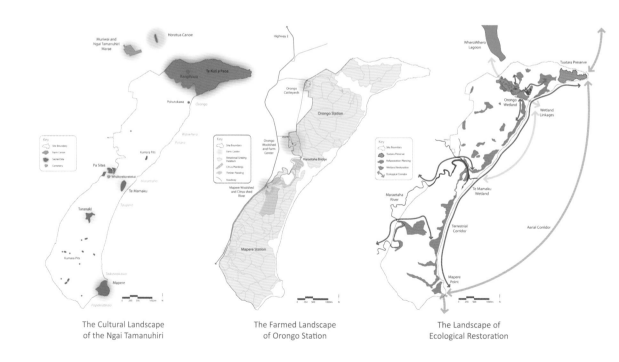

The Cultural Landscape
of the Ngai Tamanuhiri

The Farmed Landscape
of Orongo Station

The Landscape of
Ecological Restoration

This spread Photography by Nelson Byrd Woltz Landscape Architects | Following spread Photograph by Marion Brenner

Above, below right and opposite page above Photography by Marion Brenner | Below left and opposite page below Photography by Nelson Byrd Woltz Landscape Architects

Climate Refugee Camp
Arcadia, Florida | ongoing

Jaime Correa

Climate Refugee Camp 01

In the absence of a recognizable crisis, the crude and frightening reality of sea-level-rise is still under the radar in most American coastal areas; nevertheless, parts of the City of Miami are already struggling with the realities of its geological coral limestone base - a porous material that, during storms and high tides, produces puddles miles away from the coastline. Our purpose is not to forecast gloom and doom but to provide a viable context in which informed discussions about a plausible sea-level-rise future and its consequences may take place. The architect's imagination should never be disengaged from the global future nor his vision should ever cease providing a multiplicity of controversial proposals before the next sea-level-rise crisis starts crawling upon us. Despite the fact that the commonly used urban tactics of retreat, abandonment, and/or re-building are not design options currently on the planning table, this project is precisely grounded upon that type of investigation. The Climate Refugee Camp Unit project proposes an alternative City of Miami, built on Florida's high ground, for the enjoyment of the thousands of citizens who will eventually be displaced by the climate crisis over the next 50 years.

Climate Refugee Camp 02

Due to sea-level rise, and in terms of infrastructure and supra-structure assets, the City of Miami is the most threatened urban area in the world. Miami-Dade County is just about four feet above the mean tide and its underground geological porous composition does not permit either the construction of a protective wall or the assembly of a system of dikes and levees; with more than six feet of forecasted sea-level-rise by the end of the century, the urban prognosis is not very optimistic. This project assumes that raising the existing infrastructure, changing the building codes, requiring greater setbacks along the coastline, or putting apartments on pilotis are nothing but interim solutions without any real consequences. Although the idea of rebuilding Miami might sound repugnant, this project proposes a radical relocation of the City of Miami to Florida high grounds. In our opinion, this is the most credible solution on the current planning table. Due to the emergency of means required for this type of project, its configuration is rather generic; it is composed of five identical urban units located along the exiting Florida railroad line and on the outskirts of the existing City of Arcadia, Florida. The five mile-square units symbolize each one of the five letters in the word M-I-A-M-I; a surrounding wall connects the rural areas of the new satellite refugee camps – food protection will be an issue of greater importance in the near future; a new Metrorail system will join them at the basement level.

Climate Refugee Camp, Arcadia, Florida (Eye level view)

Climate Refugee Camp, Arcadia, Florida (Location Map)

Climate Refugee Camp 03

The city is raised on a base containing additional infrastructure storage and non-compact parking; its generic plan is composed of rectangular blocks of 50 ft. X 360 ft. – a morphology that provides a means for longer buildings, narrower streets, shaded sidewalks, and an infinite combination of open public spaces in their various dimensions. This block morphology tactic has been successfully implemented in the fishermen's district of Barceloneta, Spain; nevertheless, the city plan is an allegory that resonates with the abstract appropriation of plans from other American cities, including: Philadelphia, Savannah, New York City, and many more. A limited amount of retail is found along its main east-west axis, around some of its proposed public spaces, or within the spaces provided at the northern and southern vehicular entrances; retail is generally located under continuous linear galleries providing another layer of public space under their roofs. A central park is defined by two sets of urban areas – the northern one more urban and the southern one more rural (the use and configuration of the central park shall be autonomously decided by its residents). Civic buildings provide landmarks within the context of large urban public spaces.

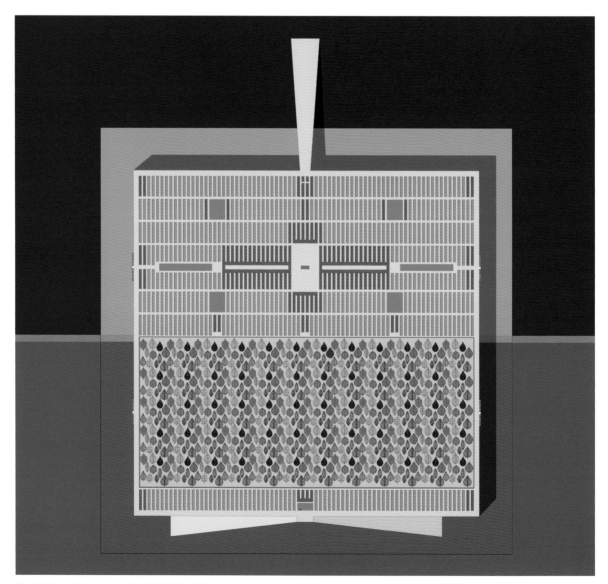

Climate Refugee Camp 03, Arcadia, Florida (Plan view)

Climate Refugee Camp 04

The generic plan is composed of building blocks of approximately 50 ft. X 360 ft. This type of building footprint provides opportunities for the development of a six-story structure composed of two-story townhouses on three levels (min. 24 townhouses per building).

Depending on the composition of the recipient family, the unit types range from micro-units to extra-large townhouses. Each mile-square urban unit will house no less than 135,000 residents (approx. 675,000 people within the five proposed units). Retail uses are tacked-in at the head and tail of the building units and along the main east-west axis of the plan – connected at the unit base by a small Metrorail system. A system of block passages, incorporating the main lobby of each building, is deliberately included to reduce the length of the block. If necessary, each housing unit could accommodate at least one parallel-parked car on the very narrow street surface (30 ft. ROW). Public spaces are designed to provide civic infrastructure as well as to protect the fragile natural landscapes of the State of Florida.

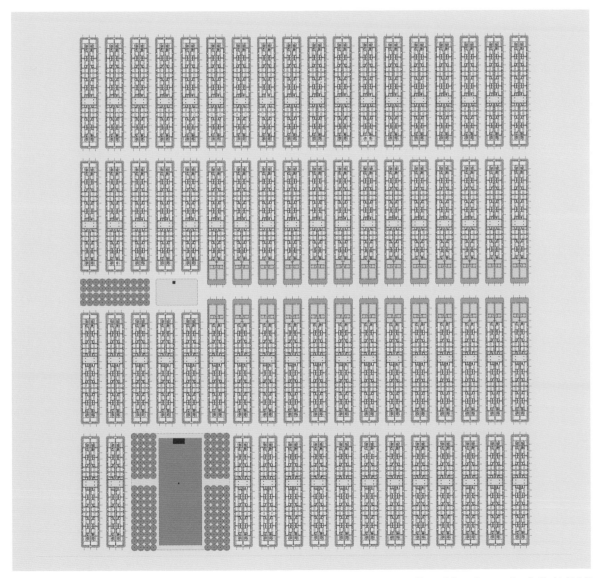

Climate Refugee Camp 04, Arcadia, Florida (Detail)

Climate Refugee Camp 05

Each building is composed of no less than 24 two-story townhouses distributed on six floors. The upper floor units count with small courtyards open to the Florida sky. The units at the bottom of each building have direct access from the street side. The generic, almost industrial, character of the building façade system is a symbol of the austerity necessary to accomplish the urban rebuilding task and its gargantuan dimensions. The diametric section shows the initial spatial arrangement of the townhouse units awaiting the autonomy of its residents and providing a frame for the adaptation of their interiors to individual circumstances. Each apartment unit would be equipped with, at least, a minimum amount of survival appliances and technical infrastructure.

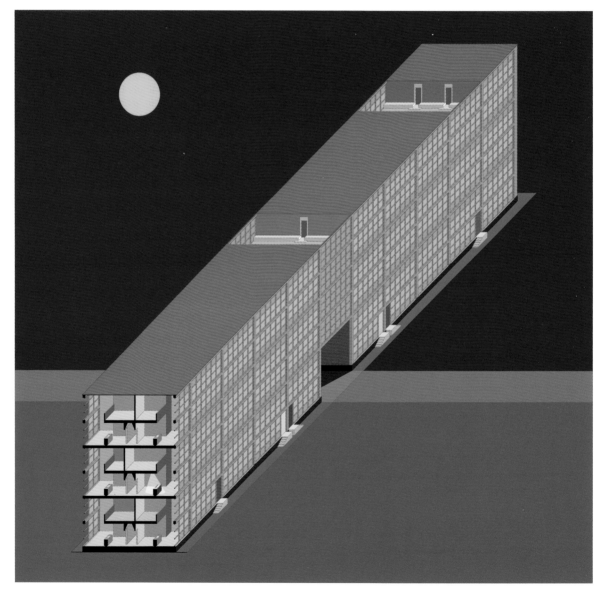

Climate Refugee Camp 05, Arcadia, Florida (Single Building – dimetric drawing)

Climate Refugee Camp 06

Retail areas occur along the main east-west axis or in the context of entrance gates and plazas. Every retail use is covered with a linear and continuous gallery providing the necessary sun protection as well as additional civic public spaces; the gallery space is also a favorite place for restaurants and informal pop-ups. Each urban unit will be branded with one of the letter in the word M-I-A-M-I. These letters appear at the entrance gates as monumental rental/sale offices and, eventually, will become important civic use buildings. In this case, the city is understood as a palimpsest of the marks left by the events of human history. The "M" is a biographical diagram signaling not just to a physical object but also to an intrinsic formal logic and to the existential experience of its users.

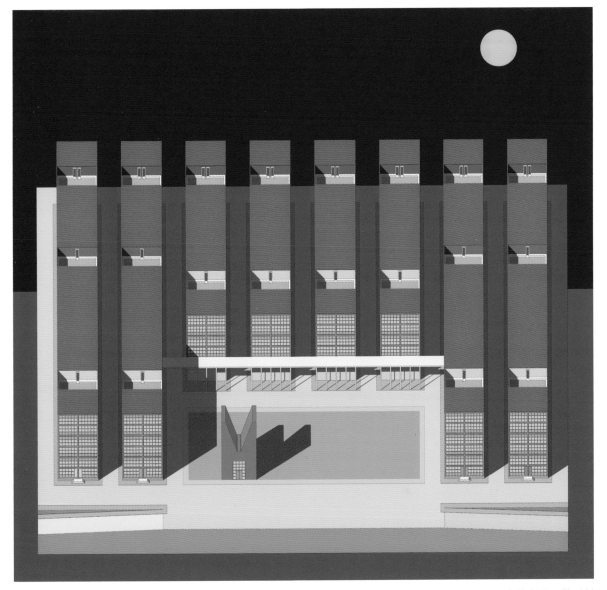

Climate Refugee Camp 06, Arcadia, Florida (M Plaza Dimetric)

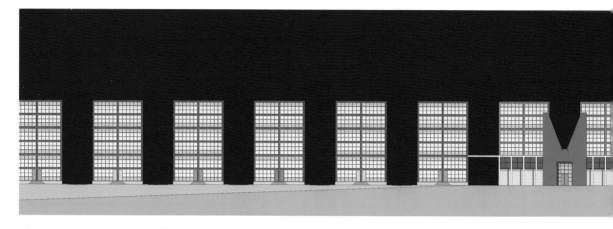

Climate Refugee Camp, Arcadia, Florida (Facades)

Climate Refugee Camp 07

There will be those who will see it coming and will take the necessary steps to leave before things really deteriorate or real estate values plummet. Others, particularly deniers or believers in adaptation, will hang around until city services will become unaffordable or until they realize the futility of battling against the wrath of nature. We still have an opportunity to make plans and lay foundations for structural changes that will have use-value for centuries to come. How will we do this? What type of government will insure the fair distribution of property at a time of real crisis? What will be the implications on our beloved mortgage system? Who will pay for this transition? Who will insure the whole process? What will be the consequences for the real estate market? These and more questions must be answered with full ethical commitment and moral responsibility before it is too late for us and for future generations of Americans.

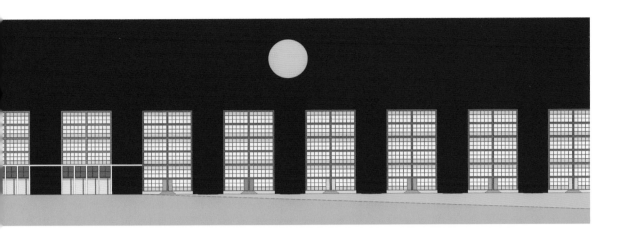

The Mexican Enclave
Upper Level Design Studio, University
of Miami School of Architecture | 2017

Jaime correa

The next four pages show some of the results of a research
studio at the School of Architecture of the University of Miami. The intent was to produce a master plan for a "Mexican
Enclave" in the City of Homestead, Florida – a city with one
of the largest temporary migrant agricultural populations in
the United States. Participants traveled to Queretaro, San
Miguel de Allende, and Guanajuato to understand the Mexican ethos and to develop contemporary design techniques
as referents to this building culture in the United States. The
studio did not focus on object-oriented proposals but on
permutations of courtyard archetypes and traditional public
spaces as a means for the production of cities.

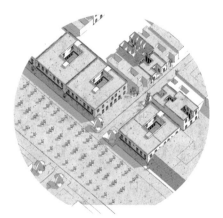

The projects adopted the relentless magic-realism that
characterizes Mexican urbanism and architecture. Combi-
natory transformations were applied to the "white and red"
project below where colored surfaces altered their meaning
to express degrees of publicness (white for buildings along a
perimeter wall and red for everything else except arcades);
amongst the many levels of reinterpretation are the abstraction of indigenous thatch roofs and Temaxcals as dissimilar
roof dispositions and circular saunas within the traditional
courtyard spaces. Public spaces became repositories for
urban agriculture and public buildings embodied tactics for
sustainable development. The last project shows a truncated
pyramid containing a hybrid space for water collection, solar
energy production, and vertical gardening.

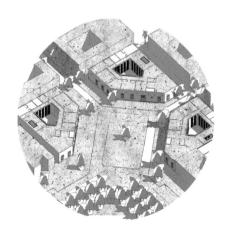

Opposite page The Four Pyramids (Urban Agriculture Project): a variety of public space configurations adapted to urban agriculture, water collection, and solar energy production (Robert Soldano, Nathan Morales, and Jessica Masangu with Jaime Correa) | **Above** The Redlands (White and Red Project): urban façade study showing the composition of abstracted thatch roofs (Bernardo Rieveling, Catalina Ruiz-Luzio, and Andrea Hernandez with Jaime Correa) | **Below** The Redlands (White and Red Project): public space detail showing arcaded buildings, bandstand, fountain, and clipped landscape (Bernardo Rieveling, Catalina Ruiz-Luzio, and Andrea Hernandez with Jaime Correa)

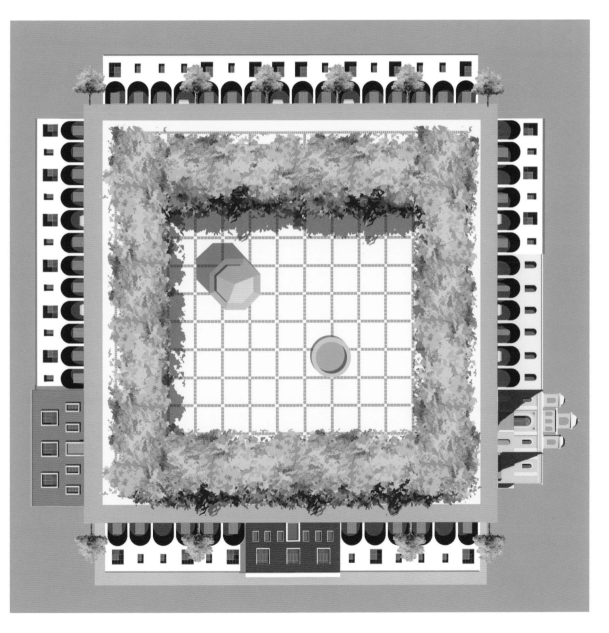

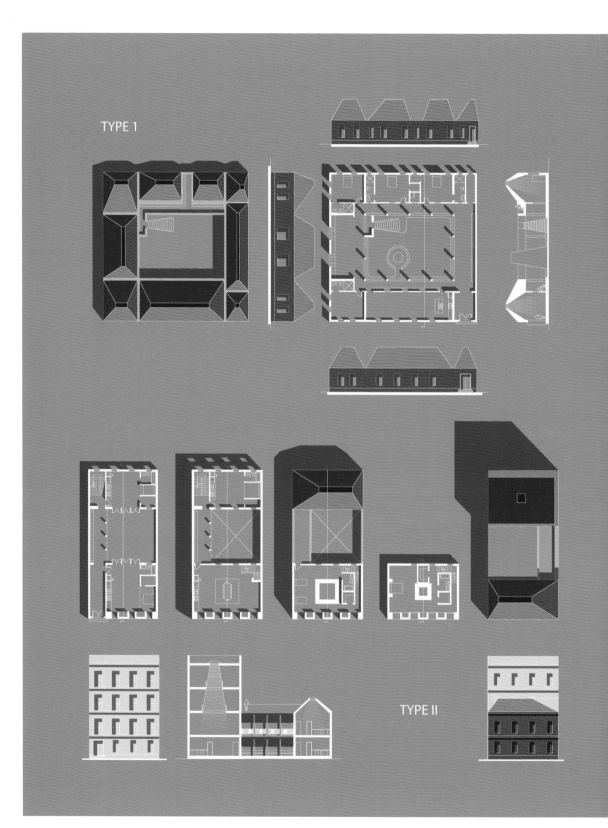

TYPE 1

TYPE II

THE REDLANDS

TYPE III

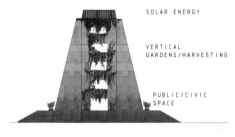

SOLAR ENERGY

VERTICAL
GARDENS/HARVESTING

PUBLIC/CIVIC
SPACE

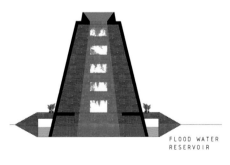

FLOOD WATER
RESERVOIR

Left The Redlands (White and Red Project): building types of various dimensions with a window detail (Bernardo Rieveling, Catalina Ruiz-Luzio, and Andrea Hernandez with Jaime Correa) | **Above** The Four Pyramids (Urban Agriculture Project): utilization of a truncated pyramid for urban resiliency (Robert Soldano, Nathan Morales, and Jessica Masangu with Jaime Correa)

Top The six gable building is flexible. In the image above, the two center bays can be vacated except for the porches that make an entry to the green from the park to the west. The long section in the lower right shows a version where the four interior bays accomodate a large double height space for the gym | **Above left** Perspective view from the Town Green | **Opposite page above** Axonometric drawings of Boathouse and Wellness Center Alternatives | **Opposite page below left** Axonometric section of Boathouse and Wellness Center Alternatives

Town Green
FL | unbuilt

Merrill, Pastor and Colgan Architects

Babcock Ranch was a 91,000-acre property sold to Kitson and Partners in 2006. The State of Florida bought 74,000 acres, the largest public purchase of land in the state's history, to help extend a wildlife corridor from Lake Okeechobee to the Caloosahatchee Estuary northeast of Fort Myers. Of the remaining 18,000 acres, another 9,000 will be set aside and so only ten percent of the former ranch will be developed. Much of the land that will be developed has to be restored after decades of timbering and gravel mining, and natural drainage corridors will have to be re-established.

These are studies for the center of the first phase of a much larger project. The site for this green is on the edge of old gravel mine. The lake's edge needs to be cleaned up but the water is remarkably clear. The green is about an acre and a half. The program around the green includes a gym, a boathouse, a café, small food retailers, an environmental learning center, and offices. The gym, central to the public program for the project has been given a piece of land with the prominence typically reserved for churches, town halls or important cultural institutions. It is a rare example of a gym as a civic building.

Building precedents proffered by the development team ranged from industrial hangers, to fieldhouses, to classical boathouses. The alternates described here afford a range of choices for the form that these civic buildings might take. They stress programmatic flexibility and a range of materials and languages.

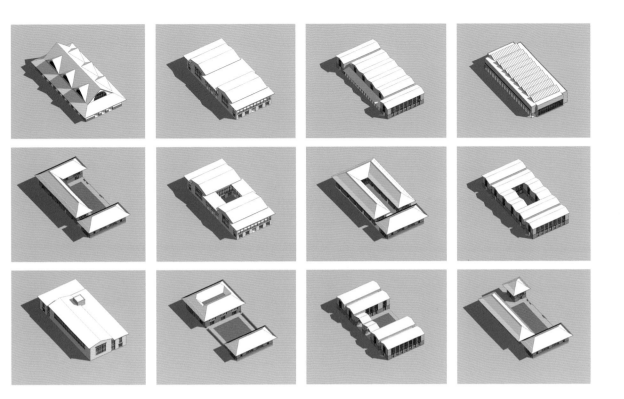

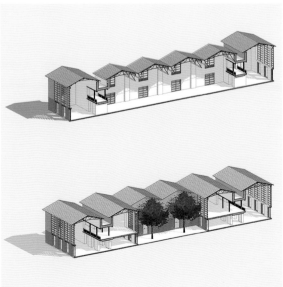

Above Perspective of boathouse courtyard | **Opposite page above** The drawing on this sheet describes a wellness center more like an old field house with larger, flexible central spaces surrounded by porches and top lit by large windows in the cross gables | **Opposite page below** Worm's eye axonometric of the Wellness Center Alternative

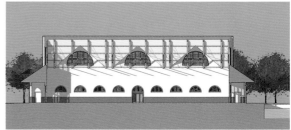

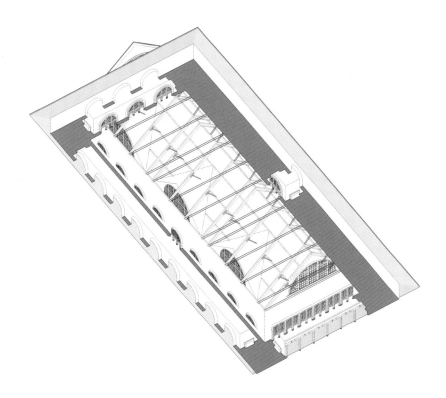

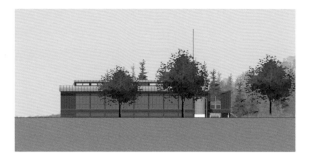

Neighborhood Pool
FL | unbuilt

Merrill, Pastor and Colgan Architects

This triangular site is between an old gravel pit and a pine and palmetto forest. The building sits at the edge of a new beach and within a new band of long grasses that is between the beach and the woods.

The program consists of three structures- an air conditioned building with a kitchen and a large room, a free standing porch that looks one way to the pool and the lake and in the other direction to the pine palmetto forest and a small structure with bathrooms and showers. The best views are straight out to the water and northeast up the beach and over the lake. The principal structure separates the pool from the road.

The three buildings form several entrances to the pool, which is elevated about five feet above the site. There is a ramp up from the neighborhood side of the site and steps up from the elevated trail along the entry road. The structures block views of the road and the neighborhood, and focus attention on the lake and the woods.

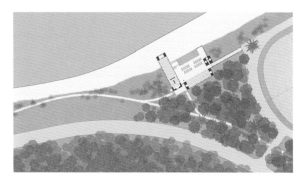

Escuelita Buganvilia
Guatemala | 2015

Cúre & Penabad

Situated on the remote and beautiful southwestern coast of Guatemala, the new classroom prototype serves a growing rural community, that up until recently had limited access to formal education. The design, is a collaboration between the architects, a local non for profit agency, the community and the School's director to address increased enrollment and an existing deteriorating physical facility. The project is intended to provide a comfortable and stimulating learning environment for the children, capable of being easily and affordably replicated throughout the site as the school continues to expand. Thus the project was developed with a selective kit of parts, capable of being assembled, edited and expanded as needed.

Built in concrete and steel, contemporary materials used in the vernacular constructions of the region today, the new building houses five classrooms and a set of bathrooms. Its overall form is a direct response to the particulars of the hot and humid tropical environment with a prominent metal roof that overhangs more than two and a half meters beyond the edges of the building. The overhang provides protection from the intense tropical heat and incessant rains and serves as a space of circulation and informal gatherings for the children. Its base is lined with concrete benches that transform this outdoor area into an impromptu classroom as well, nearly doubling the footprint of usable space.

Above Sketch of the Escuelita Buganvilia (drawn by Adib Cure), Guatemala, Cúre & Penabad (2015) | **Right** View of North Elevation. Photograph by Wasseem Syed

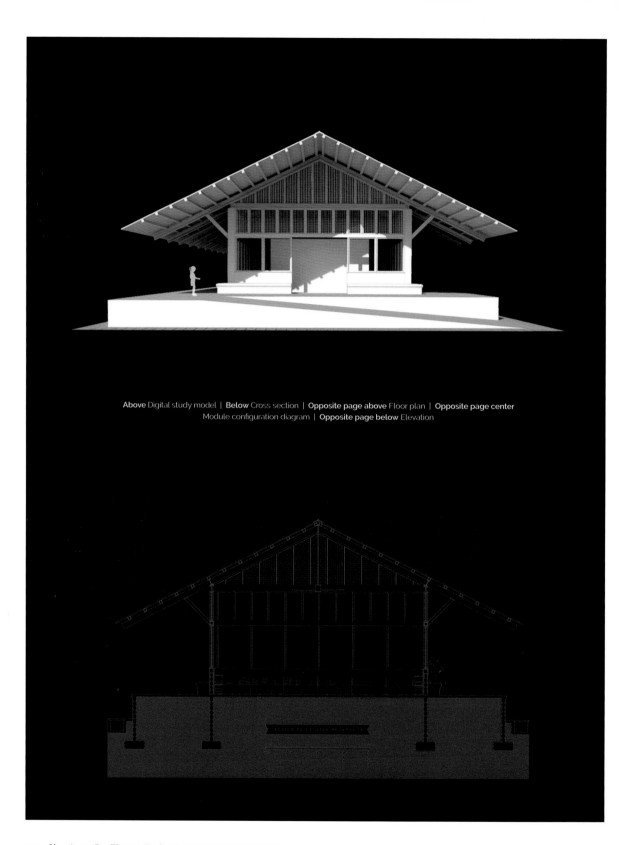

Above Digital study model | Below Cross section | Opposite page above Floor plan | Opposite page center Module configuration diagram | Opposite page below Elevation

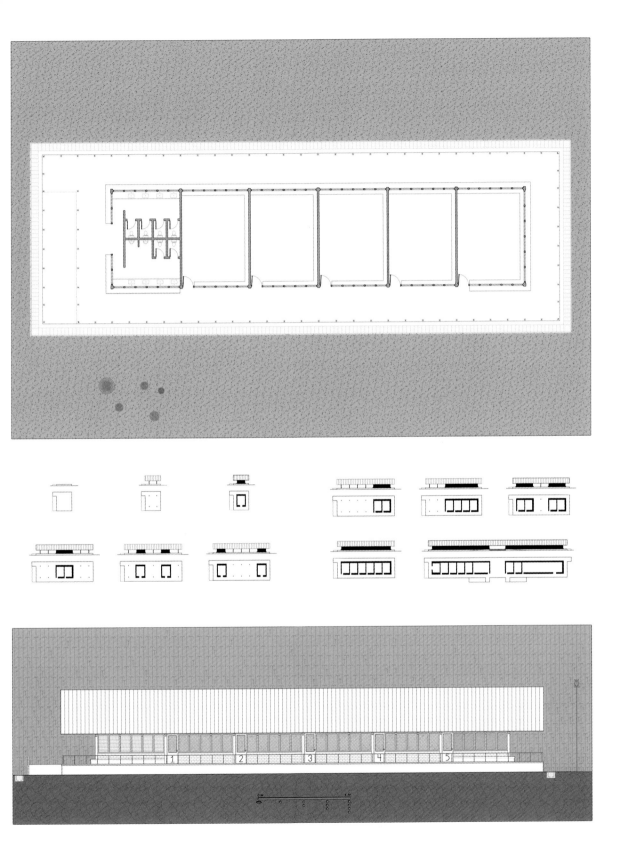

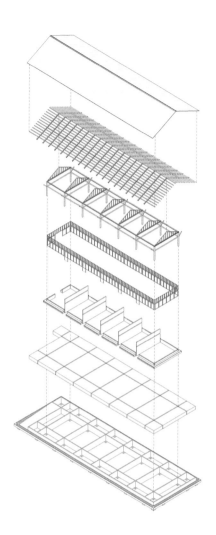

Above View of side porch. Photograph by Carlos Domenech | **Below** Rendering. Classroom interior | **Opposite page** Photograph by Carlos Domenech

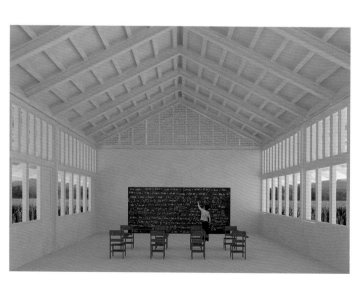

Brillhart Cabin
Bahamas | ongoing

Melissa and Jacob Brillhart

This 600 square foot cabin is a project for ourselves – an adventure into the out-islands of the Bahamas. Designed to be pre-fabricated, flat-packed, and shipped, the intent is to provide a "small house / big life" experience where one can trade in the ailments of modern life for the rewards of outdoor living. The 14' x 22' x 30' structure can stand alone, or be assembled in multiples to create a family compound as needs expand.

Our goal was also to create a place that is both contextual and somehow familiar, resuscitating the Ancient while celebrating the Modern. The building relies on the instinctual logic of the primitive hut; references the gabled cottages of nearby Harbour Island; and abstracts and reduces the Creole Cabinet-Loggia typology. The downstairs "loggia" offers flexible indoor/outdoor living, cooking and dining space, while the sleeping area and bathroom have been located in a secondary "cabinet" in the eaves. Meanwhile, the structural design strategy merges stick-frame and post and beam construction to not only reduce waste but also allow just two people to assemble it on site.

Because of its size and the need to be cost effective, a number of the elements and spaces serve multiple purposes. The overhangs, which can be manually operated with a pulley system, provide both covered outdoor space when they are raised, and security when battened down/closed. The stair not only gives access to the upstairs, while also adding structural integrity, preventing the building from racking. And the island functions as both working space and a table.

The all glass structure downstairs includes sliding glass doors and makes the surrounding landscape the focal point. The upstairs bedroom and bath feature two skylights, which orient your view towards the night sky, as well as windows that open to provide cross ventilation.

Lastly, the project seeks to create a unity between materials and landscape. Cedar shingles; structurally-insulated panels wrapped in western red cedar; and aluminum structural elements allow the building to blend seamlessly with the silvery bark of the palm trees.

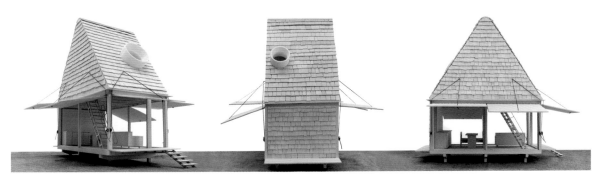

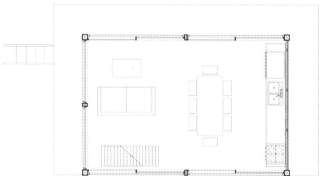

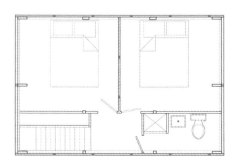

Chapter 4

Geography and Culture:
The Promise of Pluralism

The College of Charleston

One of modernism's greatest rhetorical successes is its claim to transcend the vagaries of geography and culture to achieve universal validity, clearly articulated by the name it acquired when it made its first transcontinental conquest: the "International Style." Central to this concept is the belief that modernism's program-centric design method and techno-materialist aesthetics are rooted not in any one particular culture but rather are the products of scientific rationalism, and are therefore as valid—and as irrefutable—to all peoples in all places as the hard sciences of physics and biology. This claim has always been problematic, but it was and remains motivated in part by a noble desire: making the most of globalization by creating an ecumenical, shared architectural language, literally gathering the nations together under one big (aluminum-framed) tent. The progressive transcultural ethos of modernism has proven politically useful to governments and corporations, and is of clear practical value in our polyglot architecture schools, where it is not uncommon to find representatives of every continent but Antarctica.

Contemporary classicists often fail to appreciate the cultural crises that a return to pre-modernist design traditions would present to our globalized societies. If every professor and student of architecture on the planet averted their gaze from global modernism and reverted to pre-modern traditional architectures, they would have to pick one or two from among many regional styles. Should Harvard teach only red-brick Georgian Palladianism and stop admitting Turkish students, because they need to go home to Istanbul to revive late Ottoman traditions? The problems with this are obvious, and would spill out of our classrooms to ignite the contested political and cultural sites of our cosmopolitan cities. It is a fact that scientific modernity has made our world smaller and complicated our old tribal affiliations. The old and enduring modernist aspiration to bring the planet's peoples together in a common world-building mission is therefore not merely a courteous gesture; it may prove central to our survival.

The many-headed hydra of postmodernism and a scattering of various revivalisms around the world have demonstrated that many societies find modernism's meanings and qualities

Nathaniel Robert Walker

unfulfilling on some level. For classicism to position itself as a viable global alternative, however, its practitioners will have to match the International Style's rhetorical power to transcend geography and culture. First and foremost, classicists will need to emphasize their humanism and demonstrably forsake historicism. In other words, they will need to take a scientific turn, behaving a little bit less like antiquarians and a lot more like anthropologists. The core classical value of beauty, for example, must be informed by a critical comparative study of many architectures from multiple cultural geographies, including modern ones, seeking out commonalities that are trans-historical and transcultural and thus speak to humanity's physiological and psychological needs as a single species on a shared planet. The good news is that cutting-edge genetic science has demonstrated that all human beings are intimate kin. Now we must rationally formulate an architecture that can support and delight all people, without privileging one particular heritage or tradition over the others.

Any attempt to locate the historical sources of classical architecture reveals that it was, from the very start, an intrinsically transcultural phenomenon. The Greeks did not invent the articulated column—with base, shaft, and sculpted capital—any more than they invented the door. They owed the germ of their architecture to the Egyptians and many of its refinements to the Persians, and this truth renders even the most conservative definition of classical architecture as the art of three continents. Europeans have intuitively emphasized the spread of classicism from the east to the west via Rome, but Asians and Africans also developed classical architectures in antiquity and the centuries that followed, from the canyon temples of Petra to the ascetic Corinthian capitals of Ai Khanoum, from the lacy stone piers of Leptis Magna to the stunning rock-hewn churches of Lalibela. These were places where great traditions mingled—where Nabateans traded with Greeks, where devout pilgrims chiseled statues of the Buddha in Hellenistic fashion, Berbers nursed Roman Emperors, and Ethiopian Christians prayed for the coming of the New Jerusalem. Their architectures share recurring formal devices that can only be described as classical: columns and capitals, of course, as well as proud cornices, windows and doorways sculpted as frames for human bodies, persistent

Fig. 1 Pavilion in the Nunnery Quadrangle, Late Classic Maya, Uxmal, Yucatan, Mexico, ca. 8th century AD. Photograph by the author

symmetry, arches that leap exuberantly from springers, and sinuous, rhythmic botanic ornamental motifs that reveal a reverence for nature. Some place-making concepts, such as the enclosed paradise garden or the ceremonial gateway, enjoyed consistent diffusion across thousands of miles, and consequently we see common forms and aesthetic themes among many of the great Old World traditions, from the symmetrical, colonnaded courts of Pompeii to the symmetrical, colonnaded courts of Angkor Wat.

This traceable transmission speaks, on the one hand, to the broad appeal and suitability of classical architecture, but on the other it complicates efforts to ascribe classical forms and aesthetics to human biological and cognitive conditions; one could argue that, in the end, classicism was just another Silk Road luxury trade ware. To make an anthropological argument for classicism that truly transcends geography and culture—and therefore transcends history—it is necessary to find a "control," which is to say an example of classical architecture that emerged in geographical and cultural isolation from the Old World. This is, fortuitously, quite possible. One example is the architecture

of the ancient Maya, which developed over many centuries in many polities and thus has a great deal of diversity, but which at a number of sites and in key moments displayed characteristics that are shockingly similar to Old World classicisms. Take, as one particularly potent example, a small Late Classic pavilion in the Nunnery Quadrangle (so named by a sixteenth-century Spaniard due to its visceral similarity to cloister gardens in Europe!), built starting in the eighth century AD at the city of Uxmal in the Puuc region of the Yucatan peninsula (Fig. 1). It is perfectly symmetrical, as many Mayan buildings are, and features a colonnade in its front façade, as many Mayan buildings do. The columns have horizontally articulated bases, vertically articulated shafts, and horizontally articulated capitals; they support an entablature not terribly unlike that of the Greco-Roman Ionic order, with an architrave consisting of four fasciae, a decorated frieze, and a flanged cornice. The frieze consists of a ground of latticework—perhaps a skeuomorphic echo of woven organic building materials, just as Greek triglyphs recall the ends of wooden beams—and figurative panels alternating with the columns below. At the corners are masks that are probably figure glyphs for the word *witz'*; these call the building out as a formation of living stone, and thus serve, as it were, as visual and spiritual *quoins*. There was zero contact between these builders and their European, African, or Asian colleagues. This pavilion rose and was adorned in this fashion because a social group of unusually intelligent organic beings contended with the physical realities of a site and local materials to make a structure that would serve and delight their bodies and minds. The aesthetic tools they deployed are strikingly similar to the tools that make up the architectures of other groups of this being, in other places and in other times. In Athens and at Uxmal one sees a single species at work—a species that still wanders this planet on the same two legs with the same two eyes feeding the same cognitive apparatus that has always appreciated and continues to appreciate a delicate turn.

The explosion of global international traffic in the eighteenth and nineteenth centuries brought about new architectural exchanges creating new strains of classicism; meanwhile, a proliferation of theories of progress and modernity prompted a number of people to envision ideal architectures of the future, many of them formulated along rational or even scientific lines. A globetrotting Scottish designer named Thomas Hope (1769-1831), for example, published a book in 1835 entitled *An Historical Essay on Architecture* in which he criticized the European fashion for reviving this or that particular style for specific associative meanings, whether nationalist or religious, or for pilfering Eastern architecture in search of "more striking novelty." He concluded by calling for a cosmopolitan architecture of aesthetic and functional openness:

> No one seems yet to have conceived the smallest wish or idea of only borrowing of every former style of architecture whatever it might present of useful or ornamental, of scientific or tasteful; of adding thereto whatever other new dispositions or forms might afford conveniences or elegancies not yet possessed; of making the new discoveries, the new conquests, of natural productions unknown to former ages, the models of new imitations more beautiful and more varied.

This vision of a transnational, transcultural architecture was shared by the English designer Owen Jones (1809-1874). As he travelled through Egypt, Istanbul, and Spain, he fell in love with the vibrant palettes and geometric intricacy of Islamic architecture. His gorgeously illustrated 1836-45 books documenting the Alhambra helped to popularize Islamic aesthetics in the West, and he began

Fig. 2 Chinese-European fusion in a shophouse in Melaka, Malaysia, late-nineteenth or early-twentieth century. Photograph by the author

to seek ways of incorporating Islamic lessons on color and fractal form into a new architecture that would serve the popular masses, not least by lending itself to machine production. In 1851, Owen Jones' color scheme for the interior of the Crystal Palace propelled him into international stardom, and five years later he published his hugely important book, *The Grammar of Ornament*. Featuring a visual encyclopedia of ornamental patterns from nearly every culture he could access, the book was emphatically not a catalog of foreign novelties to be selectively copied for exotic, Picturesque pleasure, but rather was designed to allow students of design to discover the underlying principles that unite all human traditions. Jones proposed nothing less than a science of beauty—a science that today is being carried forward by cognitive neuroscientists while most artists and architects sit by.

The impact of Owen Jones's work made waves across the Atlantic to America, where a number of important designers heeded the call. John Sweetman argued in *The Oriental Obsession* that American architects were less burdened

Previous spread **Fig. 3** Boult Residence, Khoury/Vogt Architects, Alys Beach, 2014. Photograph courtesy of Khoury/Vogt Architects. | **Fig. 4** Exterior of the Gaillard, David M. Schwarz Architectural Services, 2013-15. Photography by Steve Hall & Hedrich Blessing, courtesy of David M. Schwarz Architects | **Fig. 5** Gaillard column bases inspired by the woven forms of sweetgrass baskets, David M. Schwarz Architectural Services, 2013-15. Photograph by the author

by history than their European counterparts and therefore "more free to make use of whatever new stimulus would help them."[2] Whether or not this is the case, Louis Comfort Tiffany (1848-1933) certainly synthesized Eastern and Western forms into colorful hybrid designs such as at Laurelton Hall, rivaling European examples in both technological prowess and aesthetic exuberance. Louis Sullivan (1856-1924) incorporated so many different cultural resources into his architecture—from Moorish arabesques to Indian *chatri*—that it is nearly impossible to distinguish them. McKim, Mead and White blended European, American, and Asian design sources in the 1881-83 Isaac Bell House, arguably the high-water mark of the Shingle Style. On the opposite coast, Greene and Greene borrowed liberally from Japanese aesthetics in their Craftsman houses, while Julia Morgan (1872-1957) deployed her high-tech engineering know-now to design homes and civic buildings fusing Craftsman forms with the architectures of multiple Mediterranean cultures.

It is important to note that such cultural fusions were not the exclusive purview of enterprising Europeans and European-Americans. Ottoman architects, for example, combined Islamic and *Beaux-Arts* forms in a series of buildings that still grace Istanbul, and published a treatise of Ottoman columnar orders in French and German to expand the horizons of their European colleagues.[3] An entire hybrid design tradition developed in a cluster of Asian mercantile cities including, among others, Melaka, Singapore, and Guangzhou, where Chinese, Malay, and European classicisms were blended in hundreds of beautiful shophouses and *qilou* (Fig. 2), poetically revealing the innate mutual compatibility of ostensibly remote architecture traditions.[4]

The early-twentieth century *avant garde* famously attacked the "idiocies and impotence" of "neo-classicism," but they also derided the "stupid mixture" of "Egyptian, Indian, or Byzantine" design elements; their radical break with the past required the purging of all traditions, and certainly had no interest in their synthesis.[5] Over the subsequent decades, a number of different strains of modernism adopted more nuanced approaches to culture and history, the most famous among them probably being Critical Regionalism. But the rhetorical iconoclasm of modernism has nonetheless maintained its rejection of core classical values such as symmetry and naturalistic ornament, while the political and cultural needs of our globalized, pluralistic communities keep orthodox Western classicism at arm's length. Thankfully, a small number of contemporary classical de-

signers are picking up where Jones, Tiffany, and Morgan left off, working to produce a new classicism capable of serving our richly diverse modern communities. These architects are, unsurprisingly, found in some of our most cosmopolitan communities.

Marieanne Khoury-Vogt is of Egyptian, Spanish, Greek, Italian, and Lebanese extraction, and Erik Vogt is German; in 2001 they launched their design practice, Khoury/Vogt Architects, in the swirling melting pot of Miami. Perhaps their first project of civic import was Oak Plaza, a 2006 urban infill project designed in collaboration with Cúre and Penabad Architecture and Urban Design (see pages 184-187). It consisted of two adjacent buildings with shady loggias lining a narrow street and wrapping a tree-filled plaza. Simple but elegant floral sunburst column capitals crowned the piers, while one of the principle buildings was covered with an iridescent tile mosaic consisting of botanic and geometric forms reminiscent of Mediterranean and Islamic design. Sadly, much of the project was demolished in 2012, but Khoury/Vogt have since erected many more structures in the Florida Panhandle seaside resort town of Alys Beach, where they were installed by Duany Plater-Zyberk as town architects. Buildings such as the Boult Residence of 2014 (Fig. 3) creatively fuse Spanish, British, Guatemalan, Bermudan, and Islamic design sources, resulting in a harmonious and unified architecture that is more than the sum of its parts. The work of Khoury/Vogt is a visible expression of the dynamic openness and resourcefulness that characterize our modern global communities at their very best.

The city of Charleston, South Carolina has long been a cosmopolitan hotbed of intercontinental exchanges. It was the only British colony in North America to invent its own building type: the Charleston Single House, a European townhouse with a deep, full-length side porch drawn from Afro-Caribbean traditions.[6] The majority of local whites have been agonizingly slow to give credit to Africans and African-Americans for their contributions to the architecture of the city, but it is precisely the fusion of cultural influences that makes classicism culturally relevant to the pluralistic people of Charleston today. Recently, thoughtful designers have worked to rectify this problem. David M. Schwarz's 2013-15 Gaillard Center, a monumental performing arts venue (Fig. 4), features a new order of classical column with capitals featuring the South Carolina state icons of palmetto trees and crescents, and bases inspired by sweetgrass baskets (Fig. 5), a local craft tradition with West African roots. Not long after the Gaillard opened, it hosted a new production George Gershwin's 1935 opera *Porgy and Bess*. Local Gullah-Geechee artist Jonathan Green filled the role of production designer, and his sets celebrated the Charleston Single House while calling attention to its cosmopolitan pedigree by adding vibrant West African decorations. Several real houses throughout the city were subsequently covered in colorful diamond-shaped decals to reinforce the message (Fig. 6).

In Charleston, as in countless other cities, the past has many regrets, and the deep historical entanglements of classical architecture sometimes implicate it in these regrets, fairly or not. The trans-historical, transcultural, ecumenical inclusivity of modernism has long contributed to its popular appeal in our increasingly intimate and pluralistic world. Given the seemingly intractable human tendency towards tribal conflict, it is not hard to understand why. Classicism, however, has a comparable and perhaps greater power to serve the diverse array of humans that make up our global communities, not least due to its core humanist values of harmony and beauty. These values have been expressed in many manifestations of classicism all over the world, both in isolated triumphs and in glorious hybridities. Classicists can transcend geography and culture, and thus lift the burdens of history—indeed, they already have. It is time to recognize and celebrate this fact, and build beautifully for all.

Fig. 6 The porch-lined house at 91 Spring Street, Charleston, converted into a "Porgy House" by Jonathan Green, 2016. Photograph by the author

[1] Thomas Hope, *An Historical Essay on Architecture* (London: John Murray, 1835), 560-561; For other discussions of Hope in the context of nineteenth-century European explorations of global design traditions, see, for example, Mark Crinson, *Empire Building: Orientalism and Victorian Architecture* (London: Routledge, 1996), and Nathaniel Robert Walker, "Babylon Electrified: Oriental Hybridity as Futurism in Victorian Utopian Architecture" in Ayla Lepine, Matt Lodder, and Rosalind McKever, eds, *Revival: Memories, Identities, Utopias* (London: Courtauld Books Online, 2015), 226-227.
[2] John Sweetman, *The Oriental Obsession: Islamic Inspiration in British and American Art and Architecture, 1500-1920* (Cambridge University Press, 1988), 244.
[3] Alyson Wharton, "Armenian Architecture and 'Other' Revivalism," in Ayla Lepine, Matt Lodder, and Rosalind McKever, eds, *Revival: Memories, Identities, Utopias* (London: Courtauld Books Online, 2015), 150-167; Marie de Launay, et al, *L'architecture Ottomane* (Constantinople: Imprimerie et Lithographie Centrale, 1873).
[4] See, for example, Jun Zhang, "Rise and Fall of the *Qilou*: Metamorphosis of Forms and Meanings in the Built Environment of Guangzhou," *Traditional Dwellings and Settlements Review*, vol. 26, no. 2 (Spring 2015), 25- 40.
[5] Antonio Sant'Elia and Filippo Tommaso Marinetti, "Futurist Architecture" (1914), in Ulrich Conrad, ed., *Programs and Manifestoes on Twentieth-Century Architecture* (Cambridge, Massachusetts: MIT Press, 1971), 34.
[6] For more on the cosmopolitan classicism of Charleston, see the forthcoming essay Nathaniel Robert Walker, "'In a Light Oriental Style': Cosmopolitan Classicism in Charleston," *The Classicist*, vol. 13, no. 1 (2016).

SELECTED WORKS

Oak Plaza
Miami, FL | 2015
Cúre & Penabad
190

Cacique Housing
Costa Rica | 2016
Frank Martinez and Ana Alvarez
194

Various Projects
Miami, FL | 2002-2003
Trelles Cabarrocas Architects
198

Garden of the Rocca Sanvitale
Sala Baganza, Parma | 2008
Pier Carlo Bontempi
212

**William H. Harrison Design
Studio in Classical Architecture**
University of Miami School of Architecture | 2017
Peter Pennoyer, Richard John, and Timothy Kelly
214

Oak Plaza
Miami, FL | 2007

Cúre & Penabad
and Khoury & Vogt Architects
Collaborative project

The district in which the infill project takes place is a unique, 18 block community located just north of downtown Miami. This neighborhood, long forgotten during the periods when suburban sprawl became the standard pattern of growth in the city, is now experiencing a dramatic urban renewal. The Renaissance of the district can be largely attributed to an

enlightened developer and his dedication to creating a vibrant neighborhood for the city's design industry. His vision has included the commission of a masterplan, the development of a streetscape proposal, as well as the inclusion of public art projects. While the district has already attracted leading retailers it has yet to contain the elements necessary to create a vibrant neighborhood. Currently, the district is absent of public spaces which can serve to a sense of identity and a place of congregation for the community.

Thus the desire for the infill project was to define a true center for the district by creating the first public space in the neighborhood. Cure & Penabad transformed an existing parking lot with an existing stand of mature white oaks, was transformed into a paved plaza lined by a thin retail building and an adjacent loggia. The walls of the buildings were clad in an undulating pattern of green and blue glass mosaic tiles that transformed the ordinary masonry surfaces into a vibrant urban mural.

Beyond the new plaza, the project creates a new street which allows pedestrians to bisect the length of the existing block. The street provides an unprecedented moment for collaboration. At the onset of the project, the developer hired two independent firms to design new retail building on either side of the street. Rather than working in isolation the offices chose to establish a dialogue in the belief that structuring similarities within the urban realm would create a more memorable street section in striking contrast to the immediate environment which often lacks urban continuity.

Thus each of the buildings develop similar architectural elements which include:
-a repetitive bay system that organizes the covered colonnades at street level as well as the fenestration of the second floor
-open loggias on the upper storey of the primary façade
-a similar palette of materials including smooth white stucooed surfaces for the primary building elements and cement tiles in rich complementary hues for architectural details such as column capitals and inset panels
-a coherent lighting and streetscape design to enhance the visual unity of the street

While relatively small in scale, we hope that the project offers lessons for the future building of a young city. In a place often defined by disrespectful, non-descript structures that seldom strive to create memorable street or public space, the project offers a distinct and coherent urban architecture illustrating our fundamental belief that architecture is first and foremost a civic art.

Above View of plaza from proposed street. Photograph by Corey Weimer | **Below** Location map | **Opposite page** Loggia. Photograph by (c) Steven Brooke Studios

Opposite page Detail Photograph by (c) Steven Brooke Studios | **Above** View of plaza. Photograph by (c) Steven Brooke Studios

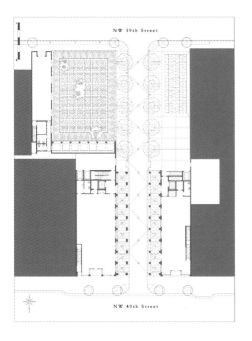

NW 39th Street

NW 40th Street

Oak Plaza Perspective From Loggia

NE. W™ Perspective

★ LOT 20 ★   CACIQUE · COSTA RICA ~ Martinez & Alvarez Architects   To Las Playas Beach Club 2007

Cacique Housing
Costa Rica | 2016

Frank Martinez and Ana Alvarez
Design Team: Frank Martinez, Ana Alvarez,
Marcela Gamarra, Victor Santana

The submission for the Cacique Design Competition features the approaches to beach-front a private villa and a larger resort villa for a 650-acre private development in Bahia Hermosa, Costa Rica. The seismic activity-prone site proved challenging due to the steep, irregular ground composed of rich organic loose material combined with intense rainfall resulting in maximum potential for erosion. This landscape was an important component of the project, and as such the design intent incorporated

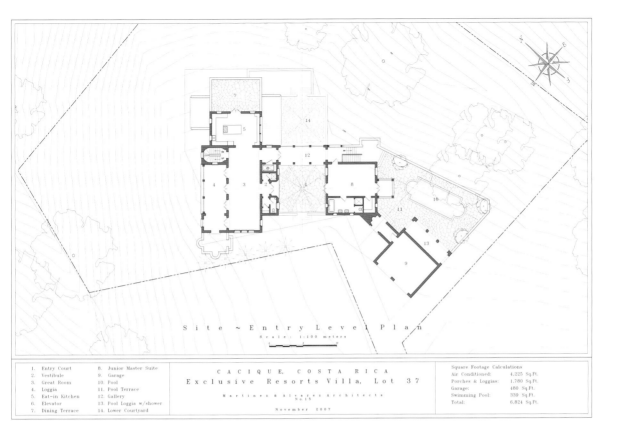

1.	Entry Court	8.	Junior Master Suite
2.	Vestibule	9.	Garage
3.	Great Room	10.	Pool
4.	Loggia	11.	Pool Terrace
5.	Eat-in Kitchen	12.	Gallery
6.	Elevator	13.	Pool Loggia w/shower
7.	Dining Terrace	14.	Lower Courtyard

C A C I Q U E,   C O S T A   R I C A
E x c l u s i v e   R e s o r t s   V i l l a,   L o t   3 7

M a r t i n e z   &   A l v a r e z   A r c h i t e c t s
No.15

N o v e m b e r   2 0 0 7

Square Footage Calculations
Air Conditioned: 4,225 Sq.Ft.
Porches & Loggias: 1,780 Sq.Ft.
Garage: 480 Sq.Ft.
Swimming Pool: 339 Sq.Ft.
Total: 6,824 Sq.Ft.

a number of sustainability strategies to ensure it was minimally disturbed. Arched openings, loggias and trellises dot the stucco facades of the villas, reminiscent of the Spanish classic colonial architecture of the historic Costa Rica and Nicaragua. Local building materials implemented include clay barrel tile roof, stucco, wood rafters, timber beams and decorative tile. The Villas designed were so positioned to take advantage of the surrounding views: the beach, the bay, the Atlantic Ocean, the adjacent and untouched tropical forest. The program for these villas was arranged to ensure privacy for the occupants, reinforcing a connectedness with nature and distance from every-day life. In coordination with the other structures within the development, these villas respect and build upon the existing site characteristics and heritage. The buildings are subordinate to the land but are adapted to modern resort typologies while celebrating the rich tradition of Costa Rica.

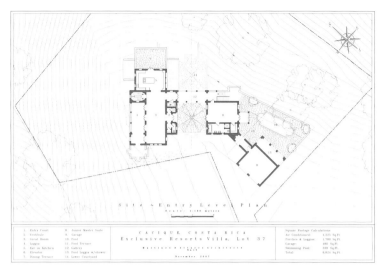

Site ~ Entry Level Plan
Scale 1:100 meters

1. Entry Court	8. Junior Master Suite
2. Vestibule	9. Garage
3. Great Room	10. Pool
4. Loggia	11. Pool Terrace
5. Eat in Kitchen	12. Gallery
6. Elevator	13. Pool Loggia w/showers
7. Dining Terrace	14. Lower Courtyard

CACIQUE, COSTA RICA
Exclusive Resorts Villa, Lot 37
Maitland & Llorens Architects
Inc.
November 2007

Square Footage Calculations
Air Conditioned: 4,325 Sq.Ft.
Porches & Loggias: 3,780 Sq.Ft.
Garage: 480 Sq.Ft.
Swimming Pool: 838 Sq.Ft.
Total: 8,024 Sq.Ft.

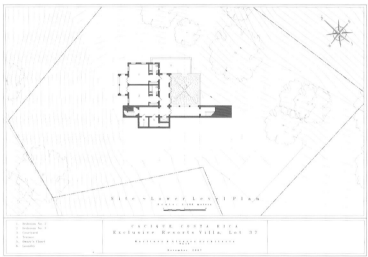

Site ~ Lower Level Plan
Scale 1:100 meters

| 1. Bedroom No. 2 |
| 2. Bedroom No. 3 |
| 3. Courtyard |
| 4. Terrace |
| 5. Owner's Closet |
| 6. Laundry |

CACIQUE, COSTA RICA
Exclusive Resorts Villa, Lot 37
Maitland & Llorens Architects
Inc.
November 2007

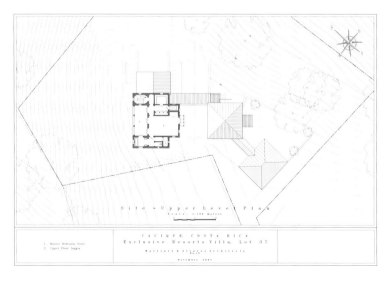

Site ~ Upper Level Plan
Scale 1:100 meters

| 1. Master Bedroom Suite |
| 2. Upper Floor Loggia |

CACIQUE, COSTA RICA
Exclusive Resorts Villa, Lot 37
Maitland & Llorens Architects
Inc.
November 2007

★ LOT 37 ★   CACIQUE · COSTA RICA ~ Martinez & Alvarez Architects

Various projects
Miami, FL | 2002-2003

Trelles Cabarrocas Architects

Trelles Cabarrocas Architects is a long-standing office in Miami, with my wife MariTere Cabarrocas and my brother Luis Trelles. Our interest in Classical Architecture dates to our education at Cornell University and with Professor Colin Rowe in the early eighties. His humanist curriculum inspired our knowledge of Art, Architecture and the Culture of Cities. The pictures we display reveal a method of design that originates with the ancient principles and built by the local Modern technique.

Our practice is 30 years old and we have had the pleasure of producing these projects alongside wonderful Interior Designer's, Landscape Architects, and Builder's. The projects are commissioned by private clients who bring an autobiographic provocation and desire to the Architecture.

Nya Ngyangu, 2002-2006. Photography by Raul Pedroso

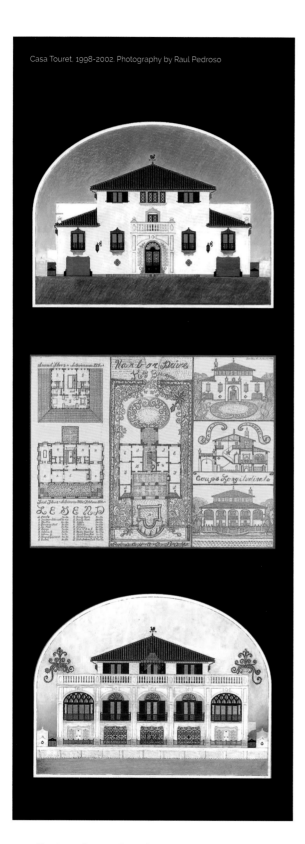

Ca' Rosa, 2006-2008. Photography by Carlos Morales

The City is seen and known by its collected memorable buildings, the built living Architecture. The placements of buildings on the idealized sites. The tropical sunlight, floral and aquatic colors and shapes compose the architecture

Miami is a garden with skyscrapers on a beautiful bay, The Floridian hammock
meets the blue water and the sky with its dark shaded green and brilliant rose |
Structural Architectural Durability. Constructed primarily in reinforced concrete and
Masonry and expressive of the spanning arch

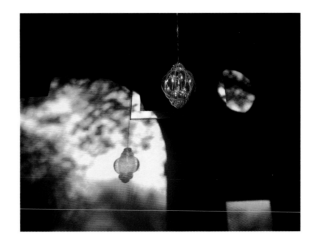

Fine House, 2003-2008. Photography by Carlos Morales

Vernacular and contemporary construction techniques persuade the style

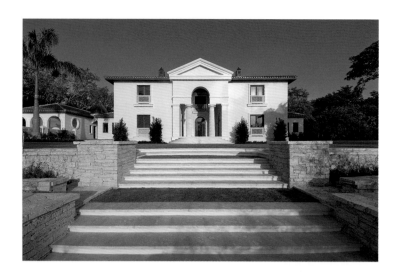

Modern novelty and timeless reference unite and remove the linearity of past, present, and future

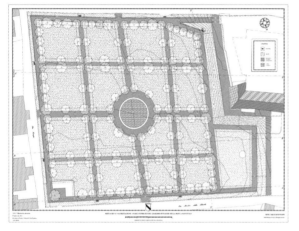

Garden of the Rocca Sanvitale
Sala Baganza, Parma | 2008

Pier Carlo Bontempi

On the East side of the Rocca Sanvitale in the small Parmesan town of Sala Baganza, there was an unusually large field (three hectares) that was undeveloped despite its position in the town centre. The field was enclosed on three sides by a long stone wall that was dilapidated and covered in ivy and brambles. The fourth side was completed by the imposing mass of the Rocca and by the retaining wall of the market square. This field was what remained of the old castle garden which was completely neglected and unkempt. Research carried out, with the students of a course of the Institute of Architecture of the Prince of Wales's Foundation, uncovered the original plans of the layout of the 18th century garden, that formed the basis of the reconstruction. Together with the horticultural advice of Paolo Pejrone, an expert and enthusiastic garden designer, four simple elements were identified to complete the entire intervention. The overall renewed structure consists of the perimeter frame of holm oaks, the chess-board pattern of the beds, the apples of apple trees that delineate the paths between the beds and the ring of quince pear trees around the large central pond. The garden wall was rebuilt in a second phase of work, with its three monumental portals that frame the scenic axes of the main avenues that lead to the central pond. Now the gradual process of nature will restore the garden to its maturity and elegance.

Opposite page top left View of the Garden of the Rocca Sanvitale, Sala Baganza (Parma), Pier Carlo Bontempi. Photograph by Pietro Bianchi | **Opposite page right and this page above** Photography by Pietro Bianchi | **Below** Photograph by Luigi Bussolati

William H. Harrison Design Studio in Classical Architecture
University of Miami School of
Architecture | Spring 2017

Peter Pennoyer, Richard John,
and Timothy Kelly

This studio departs from the usual format of a single design problem in order to study both the vocabulary (the orders) and the syntax (composition) of classical architecture through a number of smaller pedagogical exercises and esquisse problems. The role of classicism in civic architecture is particularly emphasized. Students follow a traditional course of instruction beginning with the principles of architectural composition as outlined in the books of Nathaniel Cortlandt Curtis and John Beverley Robinson. They then proceed to the Beaux Arts method of program analysis and parti development as taught by Paul Cret for designing rapidly "en loge". The first esquisse project, for a Three Teacher Village Schoolhouse, commences at this stage. The rules outlined by Palladio and others for the proportioning of rooms are studied, and students then apply these proportioning systems to refine the plan of their Schoolhouse project.

The final third of the semester focuses on a capstone design project - an exercise in campus planning using techniques of traditional urbanism and classical principles: A Y.M.C.A. for a Naval base in Manila. Students work in teams to develop a master plan in the tradition of either orthogonal or organic planning, and then work on their own to design individual buildings within their team's master plan.

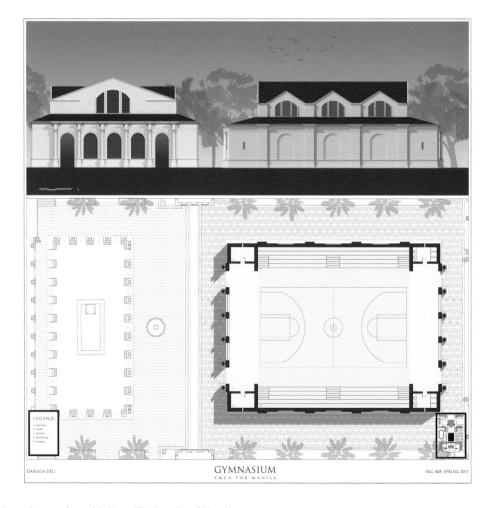

LEGEND:
1 VESTIBULE
2 COURT
3 SEATING
4 RESTROOMS
5 STORAGE

DANIELA DEU

GYMNASIUM
YMCA FOR MANILA

ARC 408. SPRING 2017

DANIELA DEU

LOCKER ROOMS
YMCA FOR MANILA

ARC 408, SPRING 2017

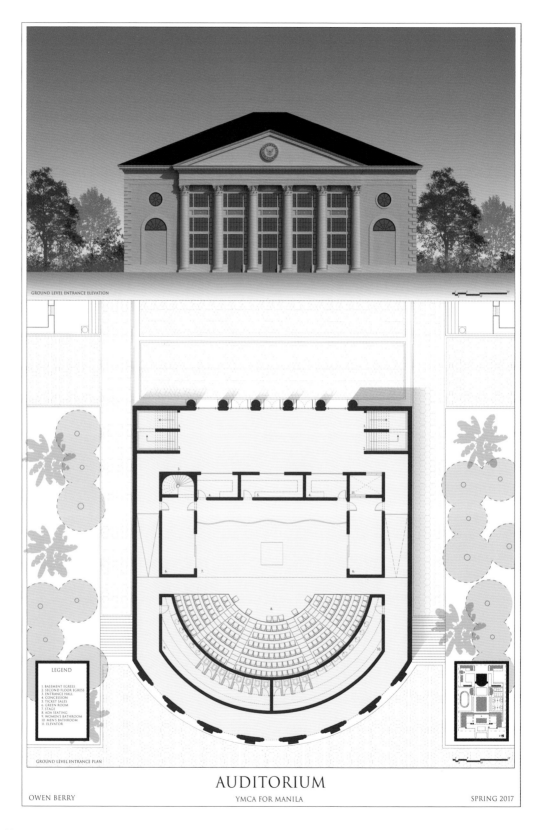

GROUND LEVEL ENTRANCE ELEVATION

LEGEND

1. BASEMENT EGRESS
2. SECOND FLOOR EGRESS
3. ENTRANCE HALL
4. CONCESSION
5. TICKET SALES
6. GREEN ROOM
7. STAGE
8. ADA SEATING
9. WOMEN'S BATHROOM
10. MEN'S BATHROOM
11. ELEVATOR

GROUND LEVEL ENTRANCE PLAN

AUDITORIUM

OWEN BERRY · YMCA FOR MANILA · SPRING 2017

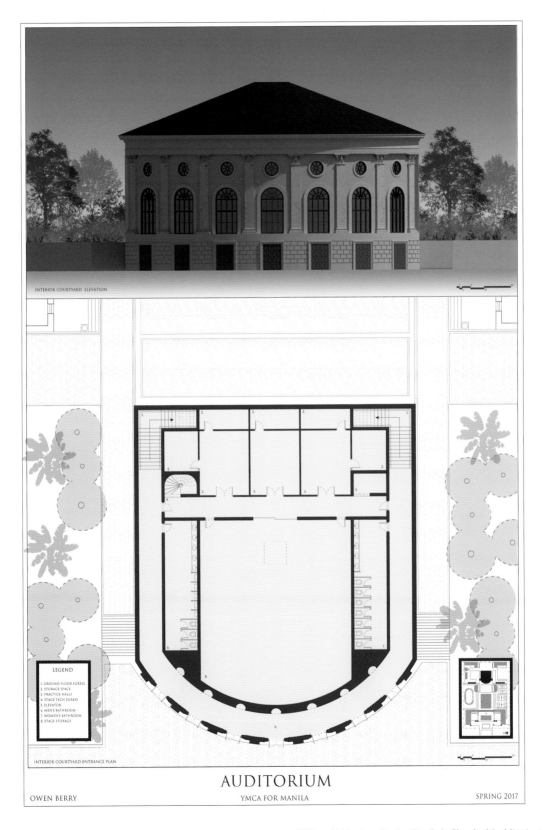

INTERIOR COURTYARD ELEVATION

LEGEND
1. GROUND FLOOR EGRESS
2. STORAGE SPACE
3. PRACTICE HALLS
4. STAGE TECH EGRESS
5. ELEVATOR
6. MEN'S BATHROOM
7. WOMEN'S BATHROOM
8. STAGE STORAGE

INTERIOR COURTYARD ENTRANCE PLAN

AUDITORIUM

OWEN BERRY

YMCA FOR MANILA

SPRING 2017

Chapter 5

Digital Technologies

We live in a time that praises progress. A time characterized by adaptability and ephemerality. One that challenges our traditional understanding of buildings as permanent and complete, to objects that are constantly in transition. It is no longer a question of designing with a certain style, or alluding to the past or to the future, but it is rather about designing for change.

Today's globalized and eclectic culture, fast-growing cities, developments in virtual reality, social media, and computerized manufacturing are but several testaments to a society that prioritizes progress. The architectural practice, serving this culture of progress, is inevitably forced to reinvent itself and adapt to changing demands. Some of which include the need for smarter buildings, faster construction, environmentally conscious designs, and adaptable spaces. This rapidly evolving culture continues to push the boundaries of architecture as an isolated practice while demanding buildings to anticipate perpetual cycles of transformations in program and spaces. This poses a new challenge in the way buildings and cities are designed, and relies on technology as means of advancing the practice.

Cultural Perception of Digital Technology

There is a tendency to correlate the use of digital tools to the experimental geometries and exuberant styles of the 21st century. A clear example is the false notion that digital parametric geometries fall within a style called "Parametricism", a term coined by Patrik Schumacher, principal of Zaha Hadid Architects. According to Schumacher, this is a style that reflects today's complex, contemporary society and a style only possible to achieve through digital, parametric tools.[1] The outcome of this style is often recognized by organic, soft and fluid geometries that are defined through variables in parametric equations.

While this example clearly illustrates how digital tools are expanding the design language, a key question is not how digital tools are generating new styles, but rather how they are allowing the architect to operate more intelligently and effectively.

In principle, digital processing gives the architect the ability to quantify and calibrate design inputs with increased efficiency; an efficiency that is particularly vital in a society driven by information, where data gathering technology is embedded in our

Juan Manuel Yactayo

everyday lives, and where an abundance of information requires tools for complex data management. Digital computation, which works through a binary, algorithmic logic, becomes an important aid in collecting, quantifying, and translating large data into architectural outputs.

The urban research done by the MIT Senseable City Lab, led by director Carlo Ratti, showcases a more productive implementation of parametric computation in the field. (Figs. 1-2) These projects focus on collecting data across cities to reveal social patterns, which in turn inform design decisions and adaptations that best meet the citizens' demand. This particular use highlights essential opportunities for digital applications to reshape the practice beyond a stylistic approach, but rather by providing architects and designers further understanding of their end user.

Parametric tools have also influenced the way architects analyze and understand the natural environment. In general, architects rely on weather patterns at the scale of the city to inform design decisions for a building. Through the use of parametric software, architects are now able to simulate the nuances of site-specific climate by processing vast amount of weather data collected in a given location. This is complemented with the ability to simulate shadows casted by nearby structures and natural obstacles. Along with simulations using CFD (Computational Fluid Dynamics), architects are further able to understand ventilation and air flow both inside and outside of buildings with relation to their surroundings. Parametric applications are thus expanding our understanding by enabling the fast and precise processing of large quantities of data that would otherwise be difficult to manage and translate into design outputs.

The use of parametric software has long been part of the architecture profession through CAD (Computer Aided Design) and BIM (Building Information Modeling) software. The growing obsolescence of hand-drafting tools is partly a reaction to BIM technologies developed in relation to a new economy that demands faster production and interdisciplinary, collaborative digital communication. As a result, through the use of BIM software, architects today can collaborate digitally, generate a construction drawing set from one digital 3D

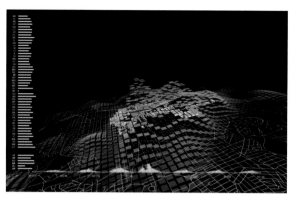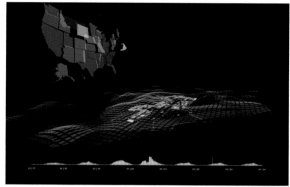

Figs. 1-2 Obama I One People - MIT Senseable City Lab. Cambridge, Massachusetts, US. Credit: Carlo Ratti

Figs. 3 -4 Bridge Project – Joris Laarman and MX3D, MX3D Test Lab, Amsterdam, Netherlands. Credit: Adriaan de Groot

model, and transfer it wirelessly to a contractor. In addition, with "cloud" storage systems, remote users can manipulate the 3D model simultaneously.

Nonetheless, while the efficiency of the architecture practice has changed, the fundamental principles have remained the same. Neither the principles of passive design strategies nor the basis of drafting have been altered through the digital. Digital architecture, although often misconstrued, is mostly an evolution as opposed to a revolution in the profession.

New Materials and Fabrication Methods

In a context of increasing awareness of diminishing resources, digital technology is also expanding the scope of what we consider to be building materials as well as their assembly. Numerical processing in architecture has brought about a more scientific understanding of the behavior and structural composition of materials at micro and nano scales. Together with a more precise knowledge of solar radiation, for example, material coating and insulation systems have improved radically. The windows of today are able to filter specific solar radiation through chemical coating while resisting high-speed impacts of projectiles from hurricane winds. Even further, in combination with wireless technologies, the windows of today can instantly change shades of color to maintain a desirable lighting quality programmed inside a room. Through a new understanding of materials, digital technology has expanded the scope of how they function.

In parallel, new fabrication techniques are being introduced to the architectural practice. From the transition of ancient Neolithic construction to the mechanical cranes of the 18th century, to the robotic arm of our digital era, there is a clear shift from the mechanical to the automated. The "Bridge Project" being produced by Joris Laarman and MX3D, which uses the robotic arm in combination with 3d printing technology, is allowing for the automated construction of structural pedestrian bridges. This project highlights the potential of the multi-axis robotic arm as an autonomous builder. (Figs. 3-4)

Similarly, developments in drone technology are beginning to resonate in the architecture profession. Besides providing an analytical perspective of buildings and sites through its aerial lens, or "bird's eye view", drones are opening doors to new assembling and construction techniques. The installation named "Flight Assembled Architecture" by Gramazio & Kohler and Raffaello D'Andrea showcases the ability of 'flying machines' to be programmed for the precise assembly of brick-like units at high altitudes. (Figs. 5-6)

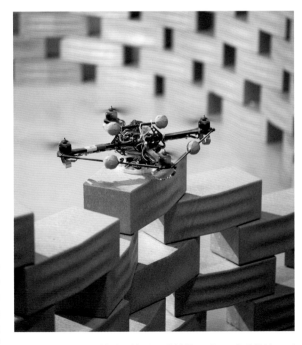

Figs. 5-6 Flight Assembled Architecture Exhibition – Gramazio & Kohler and Raffaello D'Andrea, FRAC Centre, Orleans, France. Credit: François Lauginie

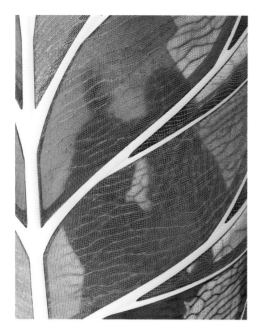

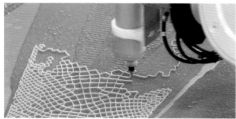

Figs. 7-11 The Aguahoja Pavilion - MIT Media Lab, Cambridge, Massachusetts, US. (2018) Credit: Mediated Matter Group, Neri Oxman

Both the "Bridge Project" and "Flight Assembled Architecture" display how fabrication technologies of today are expanding the manufacturing and installation of non-traditional forms using traditional materials. Conversely, there are those experiments with non-traditional materials being used to replace conventional building components. The project by Neri Oxman and MIT called "Aguahoja", introduces the use of biocomposite mixtures as 3d printing material through robotic fabrication. (Figs. 7-11) Such organic mixture provides an alternative to non-recyclable plastic waste traditionally produced with 3d printing.[2] Altogether, these innovations in construction and fabrication techniques are increasing the scope of tectonic possibilities for designers.

The Digital Craftsman

While the industrial revolution and Modernism brought a decline in traditional craftsmanship and ornaments, we are ironically seeing their return through the use of digital fabrication technologies. The "Arabesque wall" by Benjamin Dillenburger and Michael Hansmeyer, shown in page 236, is an art installation whose geometry is reminiscent of traditional Islamic arabesque decorations. Whereas arabesque ornaments are traditionally made out of flat ceramic tiles, Dillenburger and Hansmeyer's design breaks from the two-dimensional plane and brings the geometrical patterns into space through the use of parametric tools and 3d printing.

At a larger scale, the texture created by Herzog and De Meuron's use of convex and concave curved glass on the facade of the Elbphilharmonie in Hamburg, or the porous fiberglass shell of Diller Scofidio + Renfro's Broad Museum in Los Angeles, both introduce new contemporary, ornamental idioms achieved through modular prefabrication technology. (Figs. 16-17)

Just as artificial intelligence attempts to mimic the human learning process, advancement in fabrication methods are moving closer to resembling human sensibilities in making. One example is the multi-axis robotic arm, which can go as far as to mimic the nuances in the rotation of the human wrist to generate natural yet precise movements in space. In this sense, fabrication methods are becoming a contemporary extension of the traditional craftsman.

A Digital Ecosystem

When Le Corbusier described the "House as a Machine for Living" in his 1927 manifesto, he envisioned the building as an efficient, highly functional object that could be stan-

environment. The installation, using movement sensors, became an active cultural component rather than a static form. In this case, Foster Gage's installation challenged the traditional role of the ornament to become an action. (Figs. 12-15)

The benefit of embedded technology is by no means limited to an individual installation or a building. Being wirelessly connected means the ability to share real-time data. The information which is recorded by buildings, whether external environmental conditions or internal operational energy consumption, becomes data that can be collected throughout its lifecycle with the potential to generate feedback to future generations of buildings. The ability of buildings to evaluate performance, create a database, and generate feedback assures a smarter generation of buildings to follow. The building of our time is no longer a singular organism that can sense and respond, but one that can be calibrated to learn and grow as part of a larger network.

Perpetual Growth

If we analyze the journey of the Sagrada Familia by Antoni Gaudi, a highly regarded architectural landmark undergoing construction since 1882, there is a history of setbacks and delays caused by the complexity of the design, financial limitations, as well as socio political constraints such as the Spanish Civil War. Throughout this process, numerous methods of construction have been implemented. Ultimately, it is the adaptation of 3d printing and scanning technology that has played a crucial role in accelerating the construction and thus allowing for the expected completion date in 2026.[3] It is the digital tools of today that are allowing the ambitious design and vision of Gaudi, from more than a century ago, to come to life.

Technology is ever evolving, ever changing, and undefined. The one thing that is certain is that digital and fabrication innovations are expanding our capabilities while allowing us to understand aspects of our surroundings that were previously unattainable. If the profession is to become more efficient, more intelligent, and remain relevant, then it must embrace the past while adapting to the technological innovations of our day.

dardized yet customizable. In our information era, rather than the modernist vision of a machine, a building can be more adequately described as an organism - one that can sense and respond intelligently to its environment, and one that is no longer limited to a programmed function but capable of adaptation.

Similar to the trends of technology with smartphones and personal devices, there is a clear tendency towards embedded technology in architecture. Buildings are becoming sophisticated, smarter, and better connected. They are becoming part of an interactive network that can send, receive, and store information. Buildings can communicate with users, receive inputs, and produce outputs. Technology in architecture is thus enabling a break from the static by giving buildings the ability to sense and respond intelligently.

The interactive heart installation in Times Square by Mark Foster Gage in 2009, which changed brightness based on occupancy, gave a glimpse of architecture's role as a medium which communicates and reacts through the built

[1] University of Westminster. "Platform for Architectural Projects, Essays & Research." P.A.P.E.R, Issue no. 4, 2012.
[2] MIT Media Lab. "Mediated Matter." Water-Based Digital Fabrication Platform, 2018, matter.media.mit.edu/environments/details/water-based-digital-fabrication-platform.
[3] "3D Printing Helps Build the Sagrada Familia." BBC News, BBC, 20 Mar. 2015, www.bbc.com/news/av/technology-31923259/3d-printing-helps-build-the-sagrada-familia.

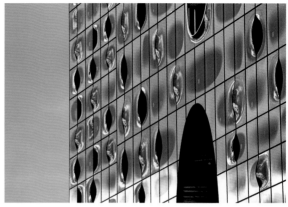

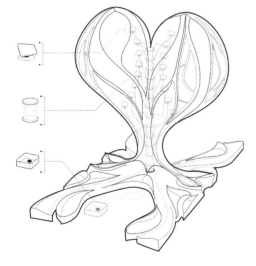

Figs. 12-15 Times Square Valentine Installation – Mark Foster Gage, Times Square, New York, US. (2009) Credit: Gage / Clemenceau
Fig. 16 (Top right) Elbphilharmonie Hamburg - Herzog & de Meuron. Hamburg, Germany. Credit: Jean-Francois St-Onge, https://eau123go.wordpress.com
Fig. 17 (Bottom right) The Broad Museum - Diller Scofidio + Renfro. Los Angeles, CA,USA. (2015) Credit: Iwan Baan

SELECTED WORKS

Baroque Topologies
University of Pennsylvania | ongoing
Andrew Saunders
228

Arabesque Wall
University of Toronto | 2015
Benjamin Dillenburger & Micheal Hansmeyer
242

Plaited Stereotomy (various projects)
Polytechnic University of Bari | ongoing
Giuseppe Fallacara
250

Cinema Center Matadero
Madrid | 2007
Josemaria de Churtichaga + Cayetana de la Quadra-Salcedo
262

**The Territory Between Ornament and Structure -
William H. Harrison Design Studio in Classical Architecture**
University of Miami School of Architecture | 2016
Robert Levit, Juan Manuel Yactayo & Victor Deupi
274

Baroque Topologies
University of Pennsylvania | ongoing

Andrew Saunders

Baroque Topologies: Novel Approaches to Analysis and Representation of the Baroque Interior in the Era of Big Data

"No generation is privileged to grasp a work of art from all sides; each actively living generation discovers new aspects of it. But these new aspects will not be discovered unless the historian shows in his field the courage and energy which artists have displayed in their use of methods developed in their own epoch." Sigfried Giedion, *Space, time and architecture: the growth of a new tradition*, 1994.

Introduction

Since its inception, the Baroque has presented challenges to any systematic approach of analysis. It wasn't until the late 19th century that historians adopted methodologies from the sciences to form an empirically based assessment of the Baroque. Since that time, architects have continually revisited and probed the enigmatic qualities of the Baroque through analytical approaches as different and biased as the ethos that fostered them.

The current era of "big data" has cultivated the need for new approaches to analysis and representation in all fields of design. Current surveying tools including LIDAR, photogrammetry and digital imaging allow the capture of high-resolution and precisely measured three-dimensional data sets previously unobtainable. The research presented here marks the first use of LIDAR surveying technology deployed systematically in the spatial analysis and representation of key works of baroque architecture. Non-reductive modes of analysis and representation reveal the blossoming evolution of the Baroque interior from the early and high baroque in Rome extending to the late baroque in the Piedmont Region in Northern Italy.

As a novel approach to spatial analysis and representation, *Baroque Topologies* redefines spatial understanding and perception of the of the most well-known baroque churches and their unique spatial consequences in the following ways:

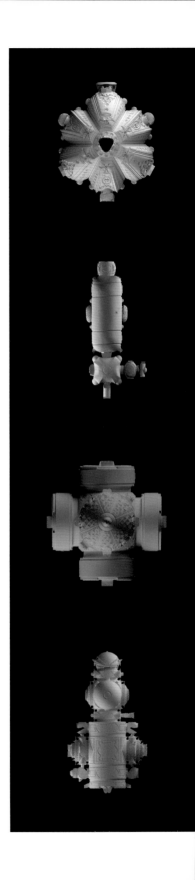

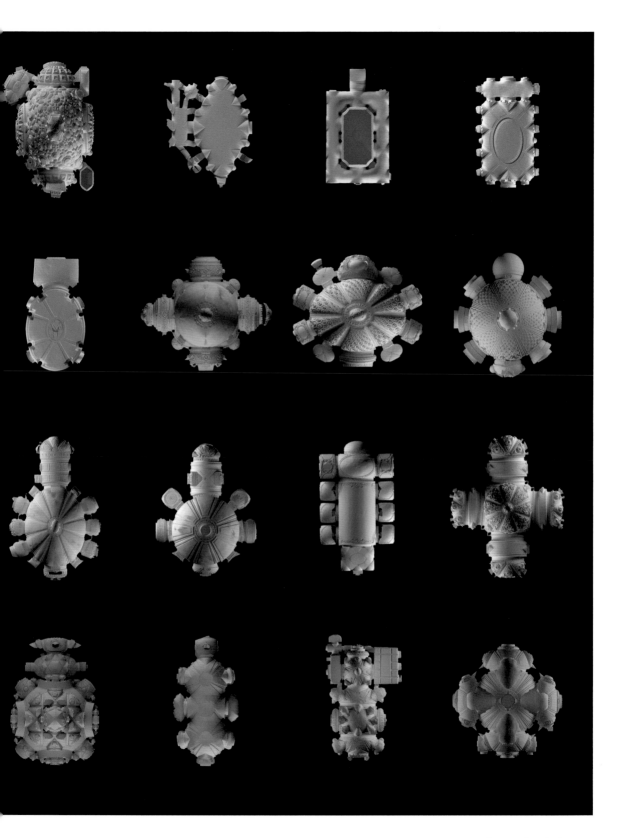

Geometric Polycentricism

Detached from the physical constraints of gravity and anthropocentric viewpoint, *Baroque Topologies* explores the geometric polycentricism of the baroque interior through privileged panoramic visions never examined. The perspectival viewpoint transcends the role of grounded participant becoming privileged spectator of the complete geometric symphony. Concurrent polar manipulation of plan, cornice and dome are exposed, revealing an integral participation in the pushing and pulling of space from inside and outside. The space of the baroque interior is a maelstrom of pressure and forces with a paradoxical desire of purely mathematical speculations and religious mysticism bound in a taut envelope.[1]

[1] Giedion, S. (2008). *Space, time and architecture: the growth of a new tradition.* Cambridge, MA: Harvard University Press. 108.

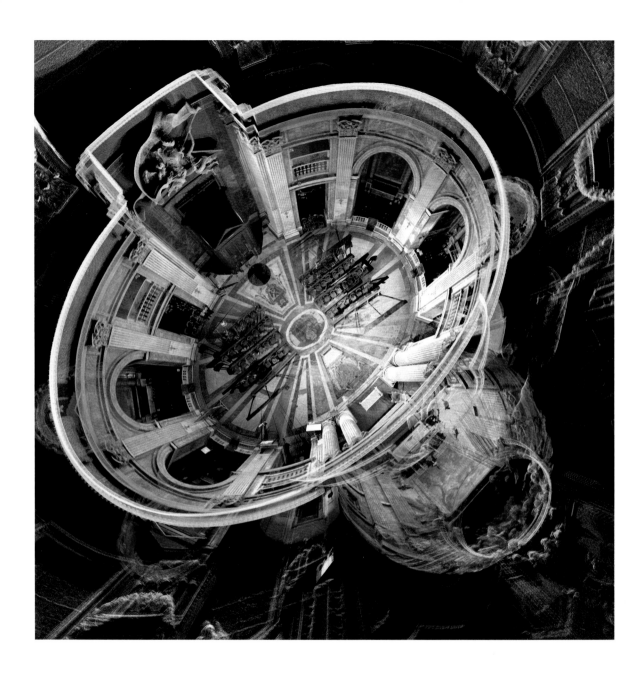

Compositional Synthesis

Domenico Bernini declares his father as the "first to attempt to unify architecture with sculpture and painting in such a way to as to make of them a beautiful whole [un bel composto], and that he achieved this by occasionally departing from the rule, without actually violating them."[2] *Bel composto* is an essential spatial trope played out to lesser degrees in all baroque architecture. It is near impossible to reconstruct and analyze the complete environment of painting, sculpture and architecture through traditional representation and modeling techniques. Complex figuration is often erased from reconstructive analysis, undermining its intentionality as an active architectural device. *Baroque Topologies* maintains the full synthesis of painting and sculpture and architecture revealing how inaccessible regions of architecture become animated arenas of varied space-filling activity.

[2] Lavin, I. (1980). Bernini and the unity of the visual arts. New York: Pierpont Morgan Library Oxford University Press. 6-13.

Figural Ambience

Formal and spatial analysis of baroque architecture rarely includes material or light, two critical elements of painterly. Previous approaches favor the linear, relying on vector reconstruction and clear articulation of the profiles of architectural elements - the complete antithesis of the painterly. *Baroque Topologies* represents form, light and material simultaneously through either surface or points (not lines). Millions of points record exact RGB values tracking subtle gradient shifts in color, light and shadow recording the thin polychromatic veil of the molting interior.

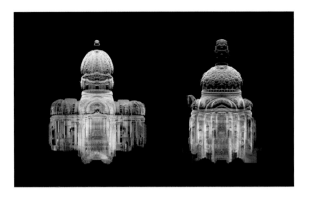

Inside from the outside

Beginning with sketches in Leonardo DiVinci's sketch book, the centrally planned church has been primarily an interior oriented spatial construct.[3] The figural presence of the internal volume is rarely fully expresses on the exterior of baroque churches. *Baroque Topologies* provides a novel method for analyzing the fully articulated depth of the interior volume through a dense transparency generated by proximity of scan points. The resulting representation offers both a view inside to the interior and outside of the interior simultaneously. Furthermore, as a topological construct, the single-sided nature of interior surface exposes the same information on the exterior of the manifold. Ungrounded from the familiar subjective view of interior space via perspective or parallax photography, the mind is free to grasp the baroque interior as a complex whole. *Baroque Topologies* presents concurrently an immersive and withdrawn experience of the infinite and contained worlds of the baroque interior.

[3] Frankl, P., & O'Gorman, J. F. (1982). Principles of architectural history: the four phases of architectural style, 1420-1900. Cambridge (Mass.): The MIT press.

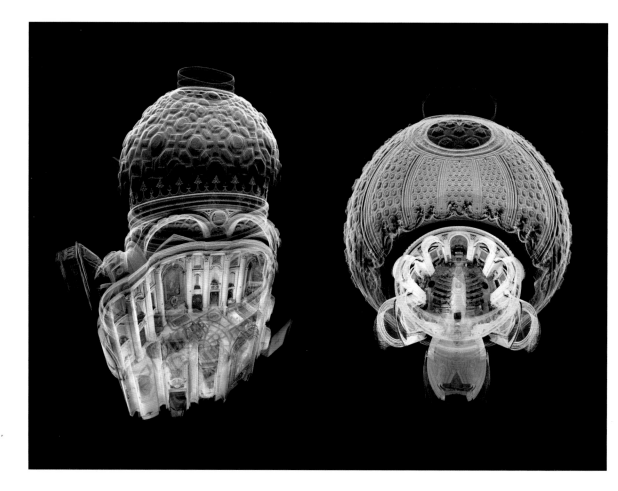

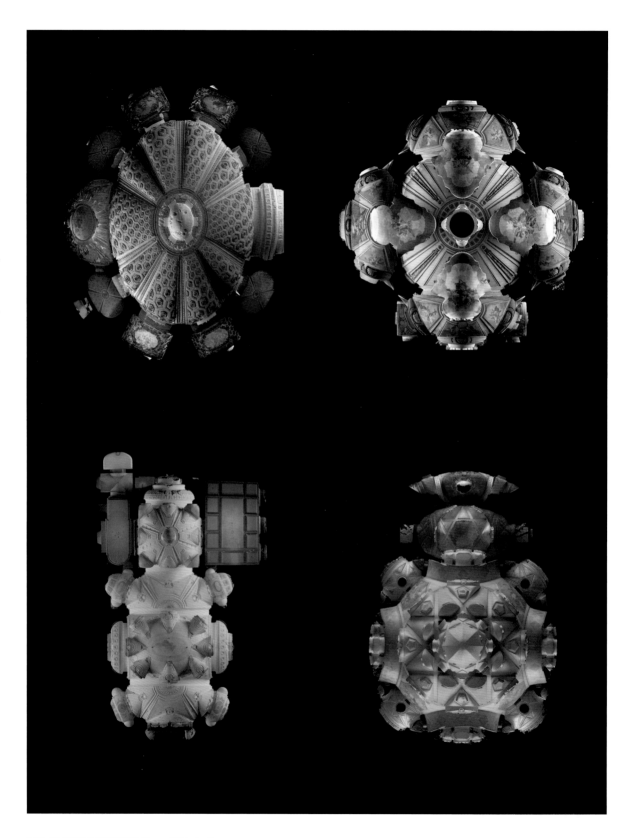

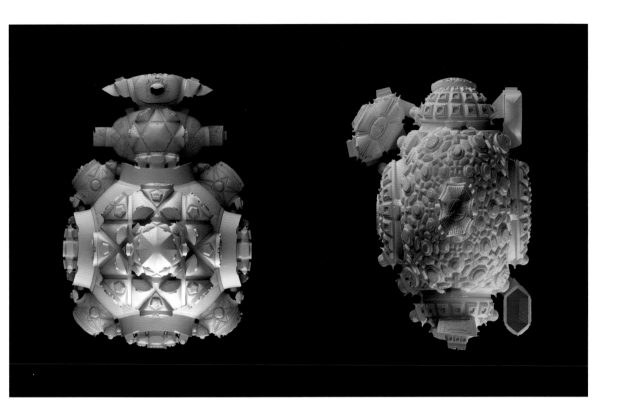

Explicit Resolution

The modernist approach of abstraction is both at odds with the very nature of the baroque and the contemporary paradigm of big data. *Baroque Topologies* is unencumbered by conventional representational biases governed by economies of reconstruction. The representation borders on realism. Digital renderings of are mistaken for photographs of physical models due to their unsettling nuances and explicit detail - artifacts that conventional digital modeling would disregard or be too cumbersome to reproduce. In *Baroque Topologies*, nothing is idealized and everything exists in equally high resolution and precise reconstruction (accurate up to .2mm).

Conclusion

As big data is increasingly coming into our habits, the days are gone when architects only knew how to analyze plan, section and elevation. With an ability to gather up to 976,000 points/second, LIDAR technology capturers and reconstructs nuanced detail with unprecedented speed and accuracy. Baroque Topologies marks a new reawaking from modernist tendencies of abstraction to the critical role of complete figural, chromatic and material articulation in baroque architecture and the formation of space.

Arabesque Wall

University of Toronto | 2015

Benjamin Dillenburger
& Michael Hansmeyer

Team: Farzaneh Victoria Fard, John Natanek, Timothy Boll, Paul Kozak, Andrew Lee

Architecture should surprise, excite, and irritate. As both an intellectual and a phenomenological endeavor, it should address not only the mind, but all the senses - viscerally. It must be judged by the experiences it generates.

From Sand to Stone

The Arabesque Wall is a massive 3D printed wall with ornamental details down to scale of millimeters. It plays with the aniconic, geometric tradition of arabesque ornaments by creating intricate constellations that are at once figurative and abstract. The Arabesque Wall's rhythmic, interwoven curve elicit viewers' individual interpretations and engage viewers to approach it, touch it and to explore. Each perspective offers new impressions.

Algorithm

Just as arabesque ornaments, the compositional principles of the Arabesque Wall are both geometric and mathematical. They are based on an iterative tiling and division of a surface. With custom software, these tiles can become microscopic and they can all be completely unique. An algorithm folds a single surface over and over again until a structure composed of millions of individual surfaces emerge. Shifting the design process to this abstract level has a dramatic impact, creating a complexity and richness of detail that would otherwise be almost impossible for a designer to specify or conceive of.

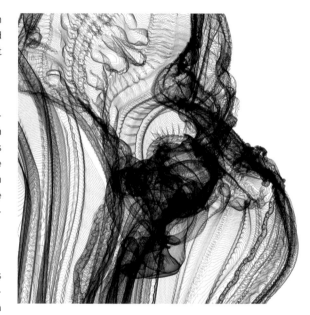

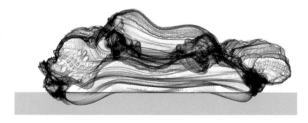

This page Design Development. Sketches Benjamin Dillenburger & Micheal Hansmeyer | Opposite page Design development. Credit: Hansmeyer/ Dillenburger | Following spread Exhibition, Hansmeyer, Dillenburger. Credit: Hansmeyer/Dillenburger

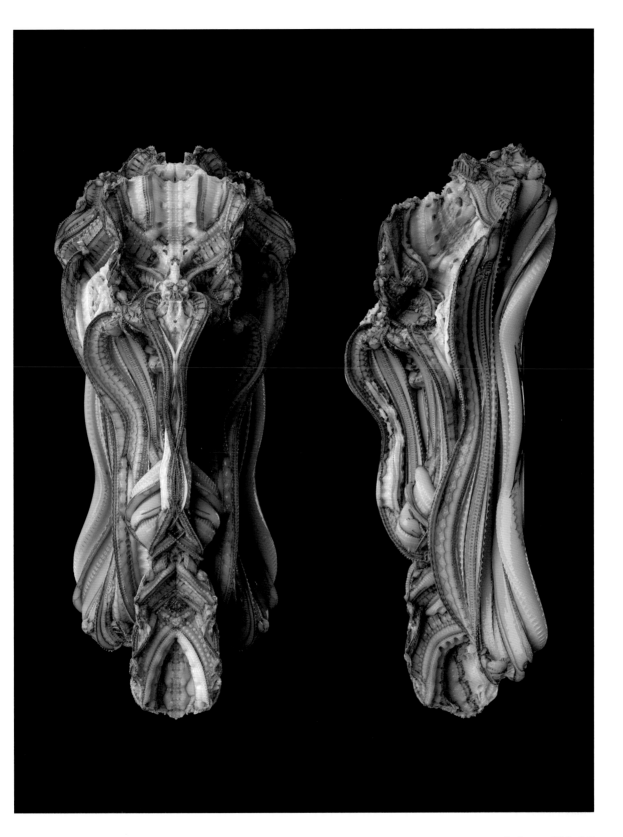

Above and opposite page left Production | **Opposite page right** Exhibition, Hansmeyer, Dillenburger. Credit: Hansmeyer/Dillenburger | **Following spread** Exhibition, Hansmeyer, Dillenburger and Details of Design development. Credit: Hansmeyer/Dillenburger

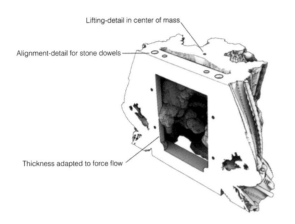

Lifting-detail in center of mass

Alignment-detail for stone dowels

Thickness adapted to force flow

Fabrication

New materials and fabrication methods have historically led to radical changes in architectural design. Today, additive manufacturing promises a design and manufacturing revolution. There is no longer a cost for complexity, nor is there a cost for mass customization. The Arabesque Wall exploits these newfound freedoms to the fullest.

Beyond Rationalization

In uniquely employing 3D printing for its fabrication, the Arabesque Wall heralds a highly differentiated and spatially complex architecture in which ornament and formal expression cease to be a luxury. It forecasts a one-of-a-kind architecture full of discovery and exuberance. Using computational design and digital fabrication, even the most lavish and complex architecture can now be materialized with relative ease. Freed from fabrication constraints, we can now return to design – we now have the opportunity to redefine what it is we want. The Arabesque Wall thus escapes the paradigms of rationalization and standardization and celebrates architecture as a precious cultural component of our environment.

Arabesque Wall in Figures:
Virtual
• Algorithmically generated geometry • 200 million surfaces
• 20 billion voxels • 50 GB production data
Physical
• 12 sand-printed elements (silicate and binder) • 3 meters
(~10 feet) height • 0.8 tons total weight
• 0.2 mm layer resolution
• 1.7 x 1.0 x 0.7 meter maximum print space

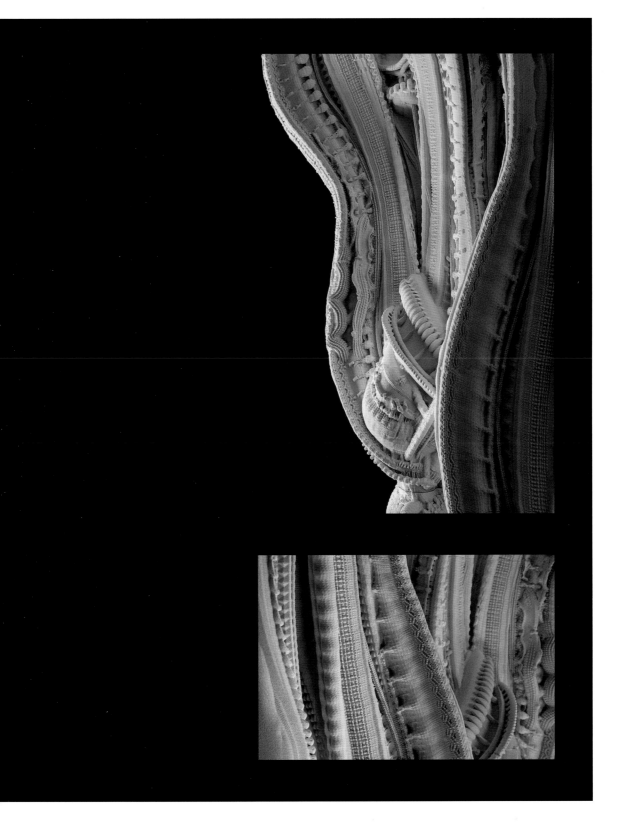

Plaited Stereotomy (various projects)
Polytechnic University of Bari

1. Modular Stone Wall
2015

Giuseppe Fallacara

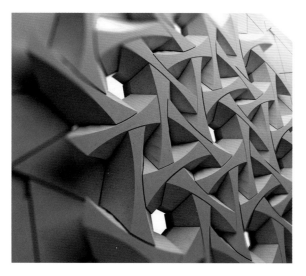

Design: Giuseppe Fallacara and Marco Stigliano, with Maurizio Barberio and Micaela Colella Company: Pimar and Xilux

Modular Stone Wall is a decorative wall made out of stone from Lecce (Apulia, Italy). It has an innovative design that establishes a building system studied specifically for the construction of vertical self-supporting diaphragms, assembled through the use of few quoins. The assembly of the single blocks allows for the stability of the structure to be understood, thanks to the interlacing textile morphology of the entire structural system. The system can be used for semi-transparent partition walls characterized by modern design and a typically Mediterranean materiality, thanks to the use of stone. The wall was presented at the Salone Internazionale del Mobile di Milano 2015, in the hAbitapulia 2020 space.

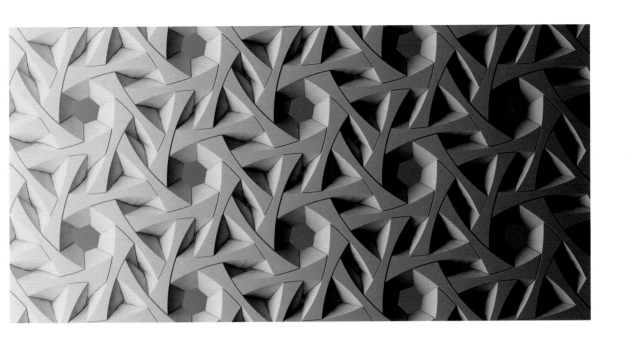

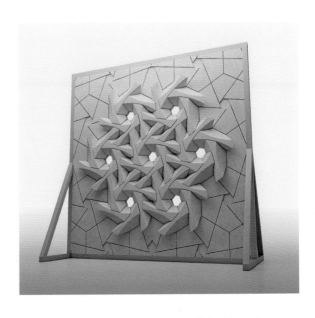

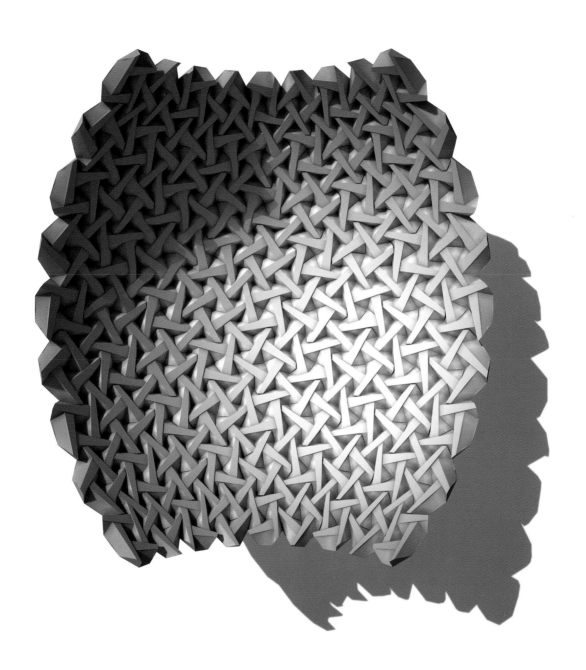

2. HyparWall
2016

Design: Giuseppe Fallacara with Marco Stigliano
Company: Tarricone Prefabbricati and Pimar

HyparWall is a modular perforated stone wall used for interiors or exteriors. One of the most relevant aspects is the multiplicity of configurations it can achieve: linear, curvilinear or cylindrical, thanks to two easily made and assembled specimens of quoins. Each quoin has a "saddle" shape (hyperbolic paraboloid) that takes advantage of the properties of streaked surfaces which optimize the production of the quoins through serial production by cutting them with diamond wire set on a robotic arm. The two types of quoins are specular. The production of these elements begins with a block of limestone that is cut and perfected, according to the necessary dimensions, using a circular water jet cutter with a linear laser projector that indicates the direction of the cut. Subsequently, the block is placed on the surface of the long edge with the smallest width, contoured with a five axes robotic arm, controlled by a software on which a diamond wire has been mounted, proceeding from top to bottom and at the same time rotating almost 90° on the horizontal plane. Depending on the direction of the rotation, the type of quoin produced is distinguishable. The use of the diamond wire is possible thanks to the very nature of the quoin which, being a corrugated surface, is characterized by the succession of straight lines and lends itself perfectly to robotic processing. The final passage before the assembly of the quoins is an ulterior cut with the circular water jet cutter, where the corners of the quoins are cut to generate supports. The assembly phase is followed by the classification of the quoins themselves, according to where their curvature is.

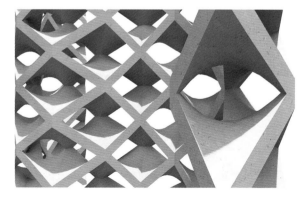

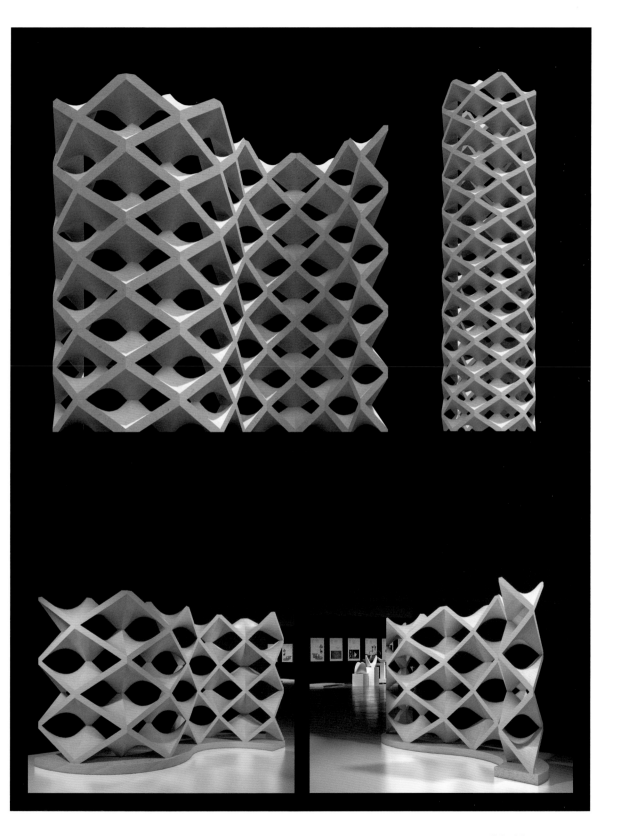

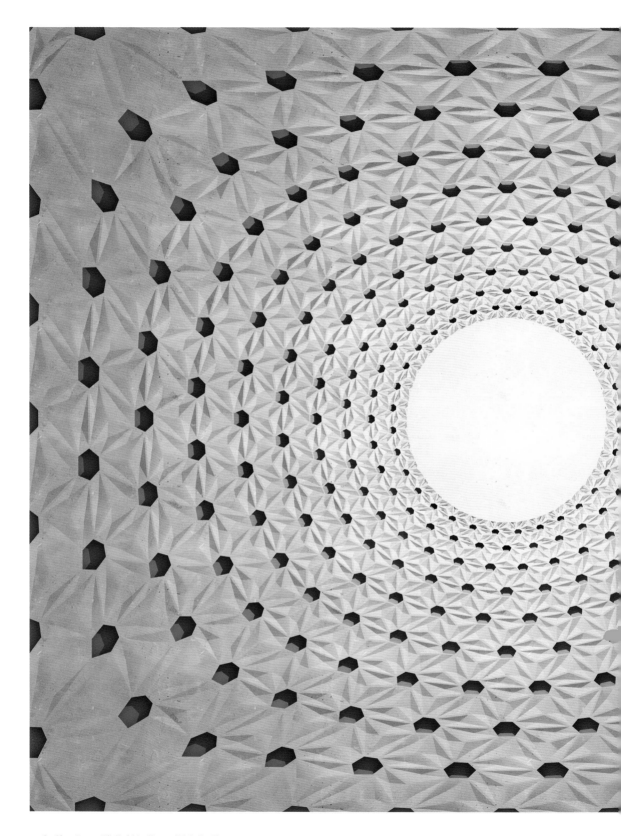

3. Stone Sky
2015

Design: Giuseppe Fallacara and Maurizio Barberio
Company: Pimar

Stone Sky is an installation that presents the use of leccese stone as pavement of the terraces above the typical rooms covered with leccese star vaults. Leccese stone is limestone known for its easy modeling properties which, regardless of its porousness, becomes impermeable thanks to the capable hands of the stonecutters who used to immerse the stone in milk (in Greek Galaxy galaxias). This is the basis of the idea behind Stone Sky, clearly an allusion to the Milky Way, the galaxy by antonomasia, of which our solar system is part. The designed pavement/mantle has a three-dimensional star-shaped geometry that recalls the theme of space and stars and collocates itself above the typical salentinian- vaulted structure. Stone Sky is a starry carpet above a star vault. The theme is ideally reconciled with the ampler theme of the extrados domes with geometric decorations which, in the Mediterranean, find their most interesting expression in Mamluk domes.

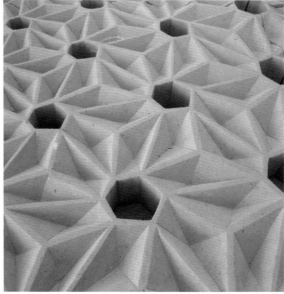

4. Ghibli
2016

Design: Giuseppe Fallacara and Micaela Colella

Ghibli was thought of as a minimal living unit, combinable into villages and realized according to a semi-spherical estradossal stereotomic geometry, optimized for its construction with planar intradosal faces, thanks to the use of a truncated icosahedron which allows geometric subdivision only with two types of quoins, one hexagonal and one pentagonal. The quoins are made out of sand contained in lightweight transparent plastic elements (which could be 3D printed, or rotationally printed recycled polymers), and therefore easily transportable and assembled without the help of construction site means or qualified personnel. Sand has excellent isolating properties, due to its elevated thermal inertia, and is therefore capable of guaranteeing good interior comfort conditions.

Moreover, reopening a study awarded at the Dutch Postcode Lottery Green Challenge of 2013, led by the American Architect Ginger Krieg Dosier, we know that it is possible to solidify the sand through a process which uses a solution containing urea, calcium chloride and non-pathogenic bacteria, bacillus pasteurii, for the realization of construction bricks without the use of ovens. This causes the sand to become solid sandstone in a short amount of time. With the necessity of living in a space comes the necessity of potable water: for this reason, we thought of conforming the extrados surface of the dome with spirals which, in addition to recalling the movement of sand dunes in the desert, convey the condensed water that forms on the plasticized surface of the quoins due to the strong nocturnal thermal excursion. At the center of the pentagonal quoins, the presence of a micro-helical system is foreseen, to use the energy generated by the wind of the desert and transform it into electrical energy for the main necessities of mankind. The spherical conformation of the dome and its spiral accent also make the aerodynamics of the construction better, allowing for a greater uptake of air currents and a better energetic performance for the whole installation.

5. Stone Poly Sphere
2016

Design: Giuseppe Fallacara and Maurizio Barberio
Company: Thibaut SAS

Stone Poly Sphere essentially is a 1.4 m-diameter lytic sphere, constituted by a massive lower side (obtained through the milling of a stone block with sides measuring 1.4 m a height of 0.8 m) and an upper stereotomic part made out of 120 perforated blocks, united in 13 groups of shapes. The quoins are inscribable in square blocks with 21 cm sides and 9 cm thickness. For production optimization, the quoins are grouped into 4 stone panels with average dimensions of 1.60 m on the side, containing 30 quoins each. The innovative aspect regarding the production of these quoins for this prototype is that it uses two layers of stone glued to one another, obtaining a bi-chromatic effect which can vary according to the morphology of the quoin itself (like a lamellar stone). For practical realization reasons, only two layers of stone have been used: Pierre Bleue de Savoie for the dark part, 7 cm thick, and Blanc d'Angola for the light part, 2 cm thick. From a geometric standpoint, Stone Poly Sphere is generated by the geodetic projection of a polyhedron, the icosidodecahedron, tasselated in the following fashion:

• All of the pentagonal faces are divided into triangles;
• All of the triangles are then divided into rhomboidal shapes, conjoining the midpoint of each side of the triangle with the center of gravity being the triangle itself;
• All of the vertexes of the rhomboidal meshes are projected onto the surface of the sphere, moving along the direction of the vector that each vertex forms, conjoining the centroid of the sphere.

The geometric construction that has just been illustrated is identical for the whole sphere, but is arranged in different ways depending if it is the inferior part (massive) or the upper part (stereotomic). From a computational standpoint, the parametrization necessary for the definition of the three-dimensional model is conceptually identical, using the "box morph" component of the plug-in Grasshopper. This component is used to transfer the basic geometric pattern – usually three-dimensional – onto a tasseled surface. The interest in this modeling procedure is justifiable in the measure in which the geometry (the quoin) that has to be transferred on the tessellated surface is complex, as in this case.

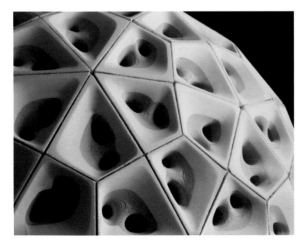
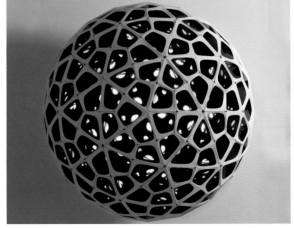

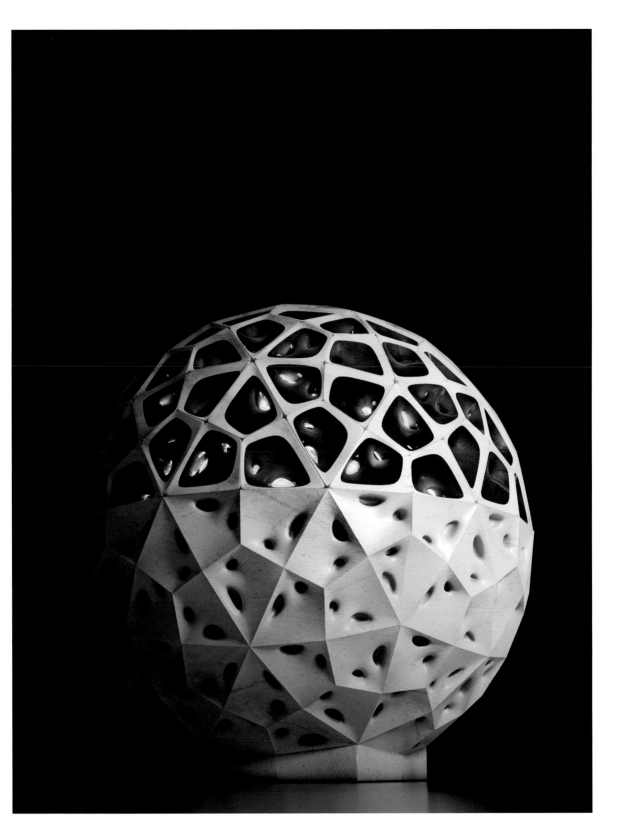

Photography credits Fernando Guerra | FG+SG

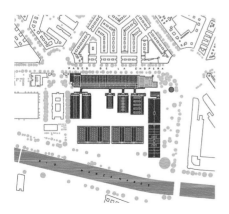

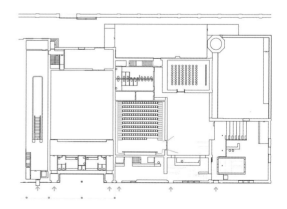

Cinema Center Matadero
Madrid | 2010

Josemaría de Churtichaga +
Cayetana de la Quadra- Salcedo

Memory, memories, even bad memory always twist and fly when we work on an architectural past, ... yes, make a story, choose the tone, cadence, rhythm, accents, a story that naturally coexists with the collective memory of the old slaughterhouse of Madrid, with another early report of new application dedicated to the movies, while curled up with the forgetfulness of their own recurrent obsessions...

The magical backlight and contrast of the films and the childhood fascination of basketry and technical human infinite geometries are the sensory triangle ... the rest is to surround in a spiral this atmosphere, this feeling, and define it constructively.

The tectonic history of "brick land" and the powerful rhetoric of the old slaughterhouse are the background, and figure at the scenes of the story, a story in which a continuous low background, a wooden mono-material painted in dark grey defines the new program deployed on walls, floors and ceilings, allowing a clear separation between story and History. Against this dark carpet background, our own memory puts out a floating figure, some huge vibrant baskets that define the main spaces.

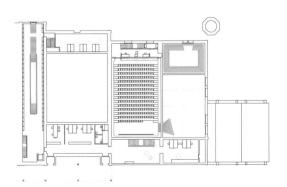

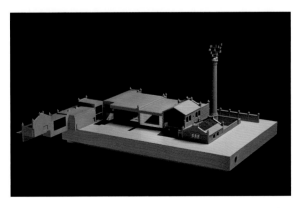

The Film Archive area is covered by a permeable basket, huge, walkable, that filters light and works as a lamp, a huge figure of a modest orange hose knitted infinitely. The Baskets that define Film rooms are shades of black. In the main room, the illuminated orange background makes the basket float until the movie begins, the background disappears and only a vibrant black surface stays. In the small projection room, a basket-banked trough - very black on black - dazzles the eye when you open a window, because the eye and limits of perception are ultimately the real protagonists of this history of cinema.

Silent Structure

There is a constructive and structural battle, a battle to defend the silent and hidden history. And to defend it is to disobey the pathological reports that distrust the history of the factory building, to not understand that factories of brick and masonry love to be charged... are happier and more cohesive... and that their logic is always a problem of stability and strength.

Relying on these unrepeatable walls of solid brick and lime mortar, the intervention has solved the great spam required by the program. The horizontal structure has been solved with reinforced concrete slabs, whose two-way working with the existing brick walls make a complete set of vertical load-bearing walls, distributing efforts through generous cloth walls.

The foundations of these walls were reinforced overloading batteries slightly inclined of micro-piles penetrating under the vertical projection of stepped masonry foundations.

Background and Baskets

Upon resolution of the structure, a continuous carpet of grey painted pine flooring covers walls, floors and ceilings defining the new architecture of space. Against this dark wood background are the mono-material woven baskets, frames made of bent steel tubing as the guarantors of geometry, woven with conventional industrial irrigation hoses.

Facilities

The spaces are defined by the tectonics of the pre-existing, the dark background of wood and the protagonists of the basket figures required a deliberate silence on the introduction of the facilities. The enormous demand of fresh air needed required huge conducts that were buried under ground. The areas without such large ventilation requirements, such as lobbies, offices and circulation areas were resolved with underfloor heating/cooling systems. The lighting is deliberately disordered, avoiding the perverse and sad homogeneity to which we are pushed by regulations. Clusters of bulbs create dances in the walls... stripes of woven LEDs lighten the baskets and the space underneath.

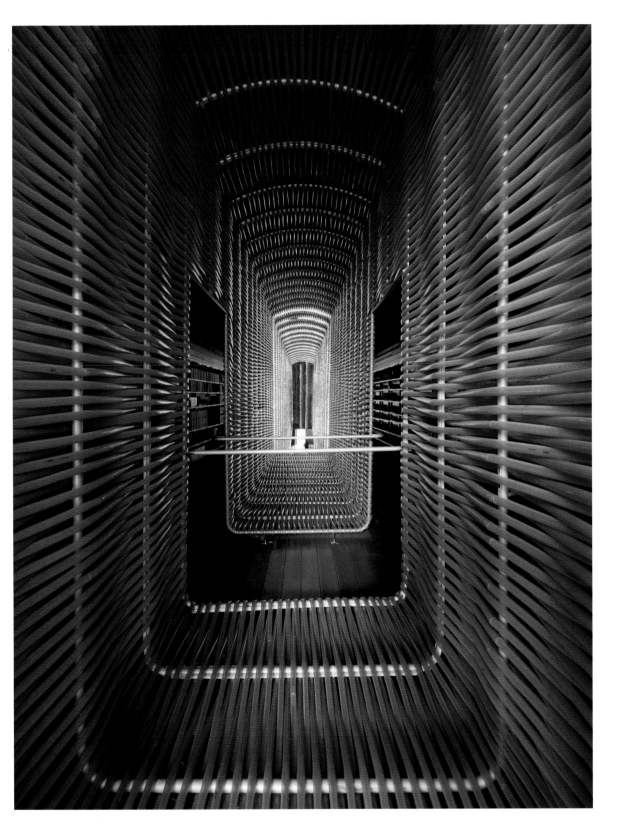

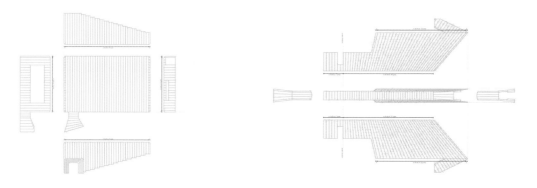

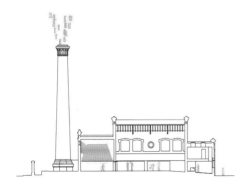

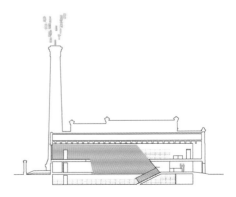

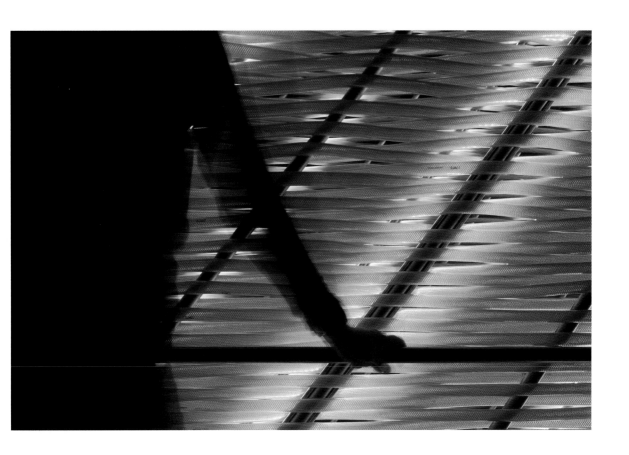

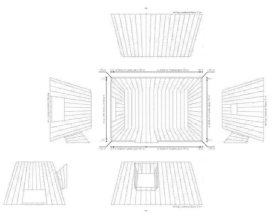

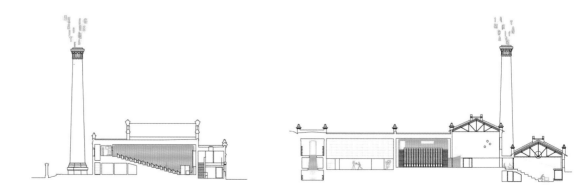

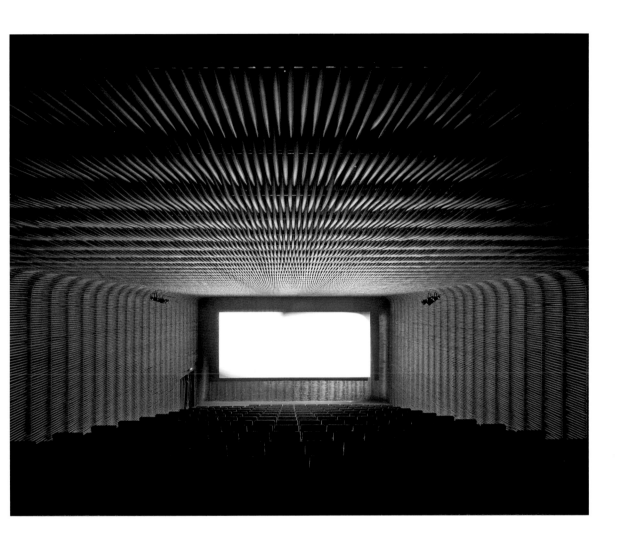

The Territory Between Ornament and Structure - William H. Harrison Design Studio in Classical Architecture
University of Miami School
of Architecture, Miami, FL | 2016

Robert Levit, Juan Manuel Yactayo
& Victor Deupi

The digital techniques available to architects since the 1990s have unleashed a wave of new formal idioms alongside renewed access to dormant but difficult geometrical formations of the past. Now, the discipline of material fabrication, of structural logic and, perhaps, an interest in rooting the forms in some manner in recognizable if innovative convention has recast the terms of digital form in architecture. This studio examined the links between gothic and classical languages of architecture and their generative capabilities for a contemporary idiom. Students explored the territory between ornament and structure that these two traditions offer, while recognizing that their categorical distinction is not watertight.

The studio analyzed through two and three-dimensional drawings gothic and classical works of architecture, and treated these as a spring board for a contemporary proposition of design set within the collegiate gothic architecture of the University of Toronto's historic campus. Students were asked to design a vaulted enclosure and/or arcade within one of the existing college courtyards. The work required the development of skills in digital craft and geometrical construction so that students could explore the interplay between ornamental articulations of vaulted forms.

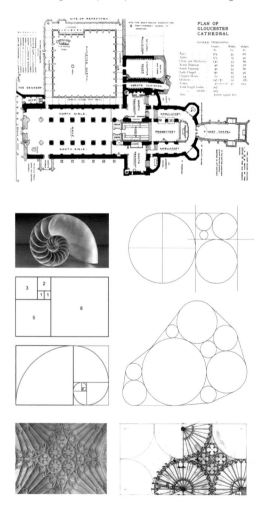

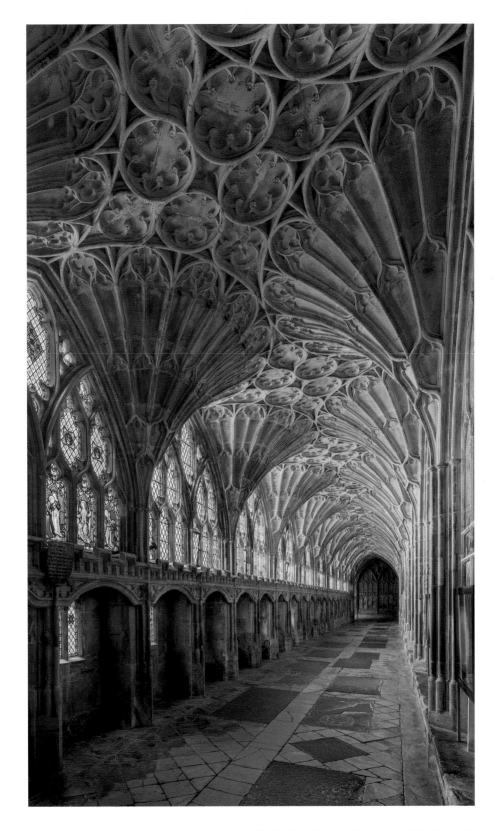

Jiayi Li, Gloucester Cathedral,
vaulting analysis

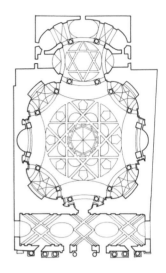

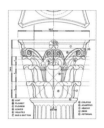

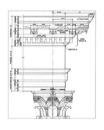

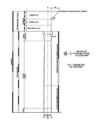

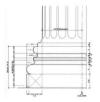

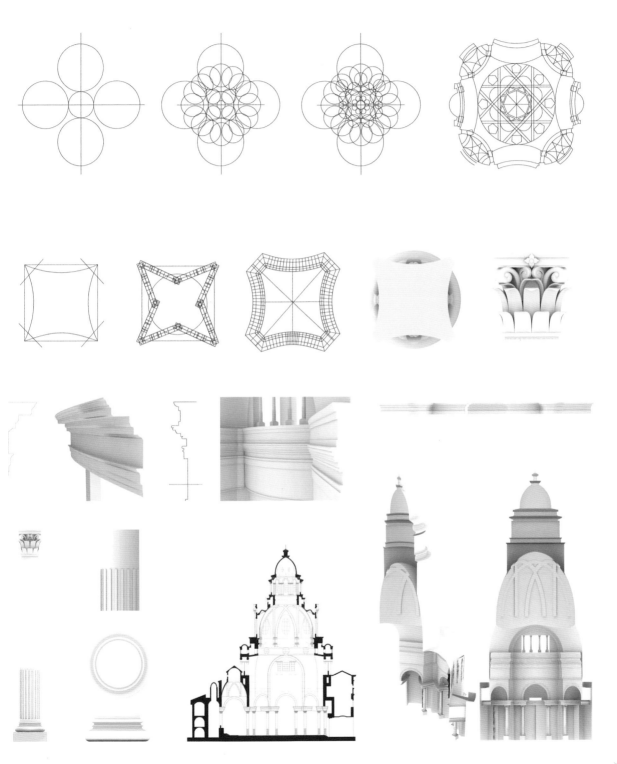

CLASSICAL ANALYSIS
BORROMINI'S ORATORIO DEI FILIPPINI
ROME, ITALY

JOSHUA DURKEE

UNIVERSITY OF MIAMI SCHOOL OF ARCHITECTURE
ARC 408 – SPRING 2016

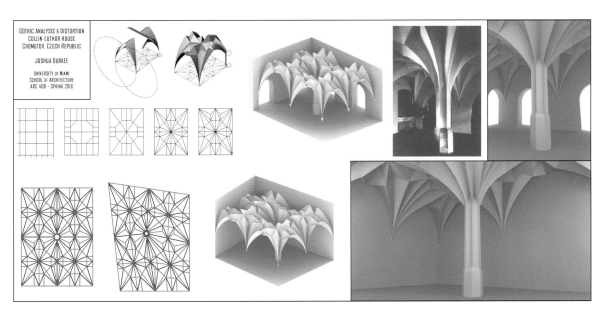

Opposite page above Joshua Durkee, Oratorio dei Filippini, Rome | **Above** Joshua Durkee, Collin-Luthor House, Czech Republic, vaulting analysis | **Below and opposite page below** Junjie Bu, San Carlo alle Quattro Fontane, vaulting analysis

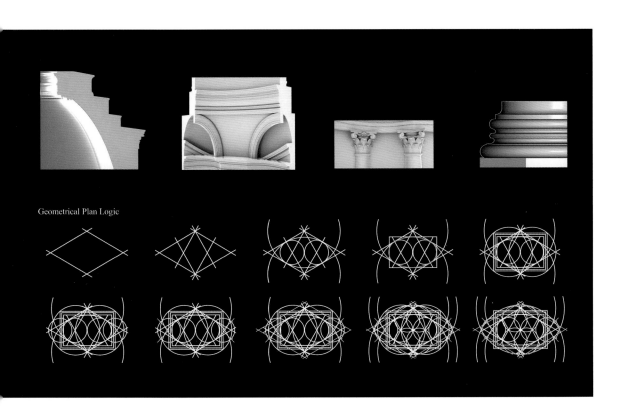

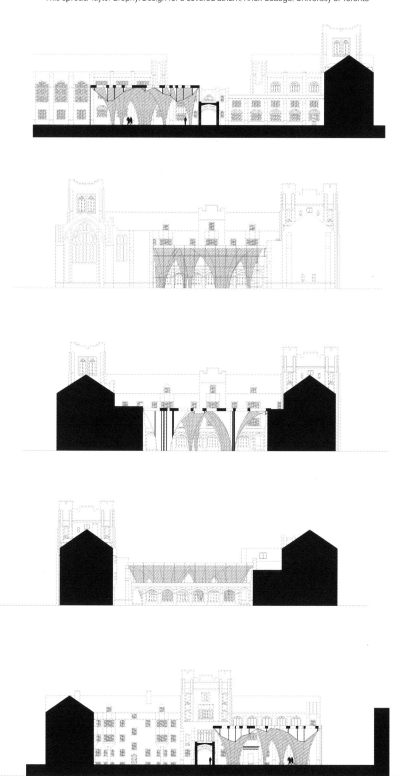

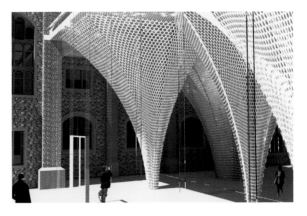

ROOF WITH SKYLIGHTS

COLUMN GRID

CONCRETE SLABS

METAL MESH

GLASS FACADE

TILE FLOOR

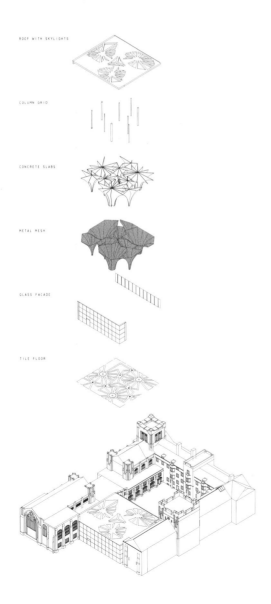

Chapter 6

Towards a Populist Classical Language

It may seem strange to suggest that a populist language of classicism can emerge from outside of the canon of classical architecture - or even from within it - but that is precisely what the book *Heterodoxia Architectonica* by Andres Duany, Javier Cenicalelaya, Katherine Pasternack and Iñigo Salona seeks to promote. Based on the study of unorthodox classical examples taken from the last 250 years of global architectural history, the *Heterodoxia* opens the door to a future of unpredictable classicism as a living tradition. The following are excerpts from the text of the forthcoming book, selected and edited by architect and scholar Steven Semes for publication with permission of the authors.

[Excerpts from this essay were previously published in *The Classicist*, Vol 12, edited by Steven Semes (New York: The Institute of Classical Architecture & Art, 2015), pp. 12-26.]

Heterodoxia architectonica

By Andres Duany, Javier Cenicacelaya, Katherine Pasternack, and Iñigo Salona.

On the conception of this treatise

Emerging from Greco-Roman Antiquity, Classicism has been the most persistent of cultural endeavors. But survival is not equivalent to success. If it were, Classicism would today be recalling to order an architecture in crisis—as it has repeatedly done in the past. The failure of the response to the current crisis calls for an inquiry.

The present crisis may be attributed to the failure of the Classical Discourse to have fully evolved to reflect the circumstances of the present. The available treatises have proven incapable of fully accepting, explaining, or otherwise intellectually engaging the past two centuries of Classical practice. Hundreds of superb Classicists have thereby been rendered invisible, or consigned to an amiable limbo.

The present Treatise dares to investigate the Classical Discourse in its entirety. This is made possible by a defining trait of Classicism: that its operating system is fractal. The part implies the whole; particularly so with the Orders. This approach is enabled by means of a platform specific to Clas-

Andres Duany, Javier Cenicacelaya, Katherine Pasternack, and Iñigo Salona

Edited by Steven Semes

sicism: the Treatise. The present Treatise participates in that peculiar, symbiotic construct of documentation, analysis, and theory. Treatises have time and again been extremely effective at deflecting the course of architectural practice.

If the conception of the present Treatise seems extravagant, hands-on reference to most of the originals discloses that the Treatises are human artifacts after all. They set an attainable standard. The authors have studied them in the original editions. Had they proven to be the preternatural artifacts of their reputation, there would not have arisen confidence necessary to participate so heedlessly in the Classical Discourse.

Heterodoxia Architectonica is a proposal to brace Classical Architecture to the circumstances of yet another century. It should be made clear from the outset that the intention of this Treatise is to strengthen Classicism. It finds that all modes of architecture are not equal. Classicism continues to display marked advantages over other architectural discourses. It confirms that the Orders and the concept of a Canon cannot be dismissed as a fiction no longer useful. It proves the Parallel to be a brilliant technical device even today. Properly understood, a Canon of the Orders analyzed by means of a Parallel establishes a base, while not precluding a very superior performance. Yet, this superiority is provisional. It falters as the Classical Discourse fails to complete its millennial evolution from doctrine imposed on practice to theory derived from practice. Concluding (provisionally) the long evolution of the Classical Discourse, the present Treatise is the first to present theory entirely based on evidence. In doing so, it must exclude the uses of doctrine—in spite of being within the protean range of Classicism. As such, more than for its chronological position, the present may be considered the first modern Treatise and, bracketed to the foundational Vitruvius, as the first and the last that restores the standing of empirical observation.

The present Treatise surveys respected Masters that have chosen to diverge from the doctrine of the Renaissance Treatises' standard. As Masters, their work is resistant to easy dismissal as mere ignorance or even kitsch. One must conclude that their work was intended not to undermine

Fig. 1 Giacomo Barozzi da Vignola, "Parallel of the Orders of Architecture," from the *Regola delli cinque ordini d'architettura*, Rome: Henricus van Schoel, [between 1602 and 1622] | Fig. 2 Claude Perrault, "Parallel of the Orders of Architecture," from the *Ordonnance des cinq especes de colonnes*, Paris: Jean Baptiste Coignard, 1683

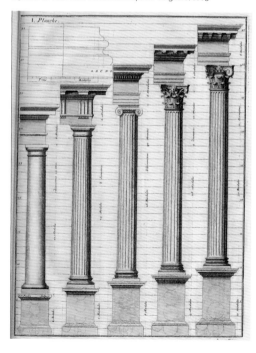

Classicism, but to expand it. The process of their assimilation to the Discourse necessitated a modern theory. Failing to evolve, Classicism will continue to wither as a Practice, becoming only History.

On the intentions of this treatise

· To demonstrate that the current persistence of Classicism is not an aberration in the hegemony of Modernism, but the opposite: that Modernism is a drift from a permanent Classical Discourse.

· To challenge the presumption that the Canon of the Five Orders is a determinant of Practice rather than evidence determined by Practice.

· To propose that the Renaissance has become a default standard because the Classical Discourse has failed to evolve a theory capable of explaining present Practice.

· To adjust the range of the Classical Discourse, reducing its conceptual distance to Modernism—and undermining the notion that Classicism has been transcended.

· To clarify the tension between Classicism's role as discipline designed to recover architecture from dissipation, and its potential for supple response to unprecedented situations.

· To inscribe into the discourse the plentiful evidence of the Classical language's formal agility to meet evolving circumstances.

· To correct the historiography that frames Postmodernism as a minor and dispensable episode.

· To demonstrate the expressive range of the Orders—and especially their legibility to popular culture. No other element of architecture is less dependent on histrionic or esoteric semantics.

· To explore Classicism as a living language subject to evolutionary process by which it is fortified by contamination with the vernacular—a process that can be both a means for survival and a buffer against wanton kitsch.

· To repatriate the so-called "Pioneers of the Modern Movement" by making the case—*pace* Pevsner—that they belong in the roster with Palladio.

· To challenge those modernist architects who maintain a hermetic personal manner, thereby avoiding critical comparison, and to honor those courageous architects who, by engaging in "the high game," dare to venture among the greats.

On the recalls to order

Classicism's *mission civilisatrice* is manifested as *rappels a l'ordre*: periods of Recalls to Order. Terms, even overarching ones, like "Renaissance," "Neo-Classicism" and "Beaux Arts" obscure their mutual affinity as the Recalls to Order from those periods of Drift when the Classical language dissipates. This Treatise proposes five periods of Classical ascendancy: the original Greco-Roman Antiquity, and four subsequent Recalls to Order.

The Treatises of this First Recall marshalled Vitruvius's authority to impose discipline on what was perceived to be a millennium of dissipation following the Fall of Rome. The First Recall was much later to be named the Renaissance. The discipline was based on a doctrine of proportional precision, and a severely limited Canon of Five Orders. That this was the appropriate instrument is confirmed by the categorical success of its mission. Not until the Modernist Drift of the twentieth century has architectural culture been so thoroughly deflected from its course. (Fig. 1: Parallel of the Orders by Giacomo Barozzi da Vignola).

This Classical ascendancy gradually dissipated in the sequence of Mannerism-Baroque-Rococo. The consequent Second Recall then deployed two platforms to restore discipline to that Drift. This Second Recall polemicized two instruments of austerity: The gravitas of Tyrrhenian Greece—recently discovered, of equal authority to the Ancient Roman and prompting an archaeological empiricism—conspired with the militant French rationalism of Perrault to achieve its mission. (Fig. 2: Parallel of the Orders by Claude Perrault.)

This Second Recall dissipated to an eclecticism consequent to archaeological discoveries further afield, and more exotic than those of Greece. The free-wheeling eclecticism was curtailed by the Third Recall, which imposed the professionalism of the French Beaux-Arts and the Anglo-American distance-learning. This eventually evolved world-wide to a machined, stripped Classicism. As the discipline of the professional Academies became rigid and desiccated, it was subsequently out-maneuvered in its own pragmatic territory by the great Modernist Drift.

With modernism's desiccation from functionalism into commercialized rationalization (pragmatism) came the groping transition of Postmodernism, from which the current Fourth Recall emerged—the faltering viability of which is the concern of the present Treatise.

On the present situation

At the turn of the twenty-first century, Classicism is in the midst of one of its periodic Recalls to Order—the fourth since the one that is now called the Renaissance. The present Fourth Recall had its origins when a generation of audacious Postmodernists risked opprobrium to attack an ex-hausted Modernist Drift that had been so protracted, so effectively dedicated to dismissing Classicism, that few could have then foreseen that a Classical practice could recover.

Evidence of the achievement is that Classicism can again be taught. But a certain weakness persists. Scholarship dominates theory; theory defaults to doctrine; doctrine thrives on esoterica. Treatises centuries old are assumed still capable of projecting a future. Technological evolution is very reluctantly engaged, if at all. Practice fails to evolve and the discourse is presented in publication as a collection of buildings.

Classicism, which was able to absorb worldwide influence while participating at the front lines of the evolution of technology is presently dominated by Italian Renaissance Treatises based on the lithic performance of stone in compression! Wholly absent is the polemical élan marking the prior Recalls—and presently displayed by a resurgent Parametric Modernism. While the first phase of the Fourth Recall based on Renaissance doctrine did effectively recover the practice from the dissipation of Post-Modernism, persistent retrenchment is a strategic blunder. Creativity is confined by an orthodoxy set four centuries ago. Heterodox instances of Classicism are conceded to Modernism—without which illustrious genealogy the Modern Movement would be a cultural orphan.

The present Treatise recovers this territory, disengaging modernity from Modernism. Classicists cannot long thrive on tales of glories past. Each generation finds its mission. The present challenge is to project an architecture capable of engaging the lean, populist buildings required by civilization in the twenty-first century.

On columns and orders

An Order entails a column, but a column does not always indicate the presence of an Order. An Order may be defined as a column dedicated to three purposes: First, to the visual resolution of spanning and bearing; second, to the indication of the organizational discipline of the associated building; and third, to the conveyance of meaning condensed in its form. For the purposes of the present Treatise the presence of these first and last parameters determine if a column is an Order—to be inducted into the Classical Discourse by means of a Parallel—and excluding those columns not intended by their designers to engage in the Classical Discourse. The first purpose—the resolution of spanning and bearing—excludes instances where the Modernist polemic intends an expression of weightlessness. The second purpose is extremely rare in any but the most elevated of Classical buildings. It is too onerous to subject civic buildings to such a demanding formal discipline. The third purpose is the most common and useful: to append a portico to a building not otherwise disciplined (by the second role) bestowing meaning at frugal expense—what Venturi would call the "decorated shed."

On the canon of the orders

It has always been possible to posit a Canon but not to fix it permanently. A Canon of the Classical Orders, beginning with Vitruvius' inaugural proposition, has consisted of an unstable set, as Serlio roughly and surreptitiously adjusted it, confirming the tentative Tuscan and adding the Composite. Diversity, despite the strictures of the First Recall, is intrinsic to Classicism. The Canon has reflected the evolution of the Classical language over each of the subsequent Recalls. The present Treatise will discern three hierarchies of the Classical Orders: A persistent Primary Canon of three syntactically necessary Orders, as introduced by Vitruvius; Secondary Canons adjusted to the evidence of each Recall; and then the Master's Orders themselves—which are derived from the Canons but also inform its composition.

The persistence of the Primary Canon is not due to its primogeniture, but because it addresses the irreducible syntactic problems of "joining column to beam." This Canon has expanded:
1. To address unprecedented tectonic problems;
2. Reflect archaeological discoveries; and
3. To increase the semantic range.

The Parallel thus survives as an instrument to integrate evolutionary diversity to the Canon in a systematic manner analogous to language in the *Oxford English Dictionary* or the protocols of the French, Italian and Spanish Academies. (Fig. 3: The Doric Order, plate from HA.)

On the evolution of the canon

This Treatise proposes that a Canon of Orders must continue to brace Practice, and that an evolving Practice must continue to inform the composition of the Canon. The study of the Practice subsequent to the First Recall, forces reconsideration of the Classical Canon, not only for the present, but to retroactively determine what indeed were the Canons at the other Recalls.

This Parallel does not replace the Five Orders as stabilized by Serlio, and confirmed by Palladio, Vignola, and Scamozzi. They are referenced by the 250 plates of this Treatise. It does restore a preliminary thirteen. Empirical evidence of practice confers on them a stature in the modern Canon. This ex-

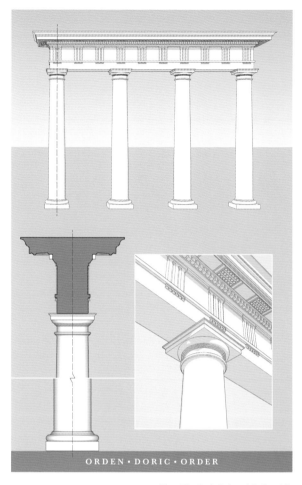

ORDEN · DORIC · ORDER

Fig. 3 The Doric Order, plate from HA

panded Canon is not to be established by scholarship, nor imposed by an institution. As with all prior Treatises, its authority will be confirmed by its logic, its ability to explain practice, and its palpable influence on the practice of architecture.

On the selection of the orders

In considering candidates for the present Parallel, the authors' judgment on the virtues of an Order is not considered sufficient for its inclusion. The present Parallel therefore establishes that an Order must be the design of an acknowledged master. Mastery is to be established by the scholarly convention of publication of an architect or a building; quality (or perhaps credibility) is confirmed by incidence of citation. Thus the Orders included meet the only objective standards in the subjective subject of art. This method is flawed, but it does represent the hurdle of the substantial investment of time and treasure that all books require. It is not usually by whim that an architect or a building appears repeatedly in publication. Ar-

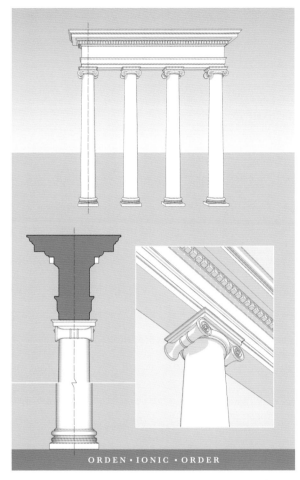

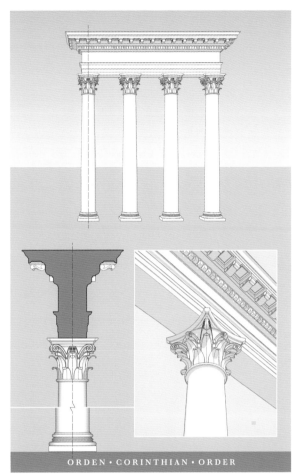

ORDEN · IONIC · ORDER

ORDEN · CORINTHIAN · ORDER

Fig. 4 Ionic Order, plate from HA

Fig. 5 Corinthian Order, plate from HA

chitecture is usually published when it is designed by the high rank of architects at their peak of accomplishment.

This Parallel does not exhaust the sources. Despite diminishing returns, there are yet more Orders to be analyzed. If the standard were adjusted to trust the authors' discretion, more excellent but anonymous work could substantially increase the roster of the Plates. This Parallel must therefore be considered provisional, as when there were ruins of Antiquity still to be discovered. (Fig. 4: Ionic Order, plate from HA)

On the composition of the plates

The five Orders of the First Recall are easily presented in the graphic of a Parallel because of the very narrow range of proportional deviation between them. However, the Orders in the present Parallel manifest a tremendous dimensional and proportional range. Their heterogeneity precludes the conventional layout of identical scale.

The present Parallel nevertheless follows a strict protocol in the graphic presentation of the plates:

1. The column on the left of the colonnade is always shown frontally, while the others are displayed in perspective—progressively rotating from the frontal viewpoint. This shows an important aspect of their formal performance.

2. The disparity in the size of the Orders undermines conventional scalar discipline. Scale is therefore provided by a human figure with the eye level at 1.6 meters above nominal ground. This figure is uniformly located in plan at the center of an intercolumniation (or bay).

3. The inscribed upward view is taken from the viewpoint of the human figure. Upon arrival at the threshold defined by the colonnade, the capital is seen from this angle.

The Plates extract the Orders from their building of origin so that the model may be adapted to other buildings. This process of abstraction proceeds as far as the Orders' par-

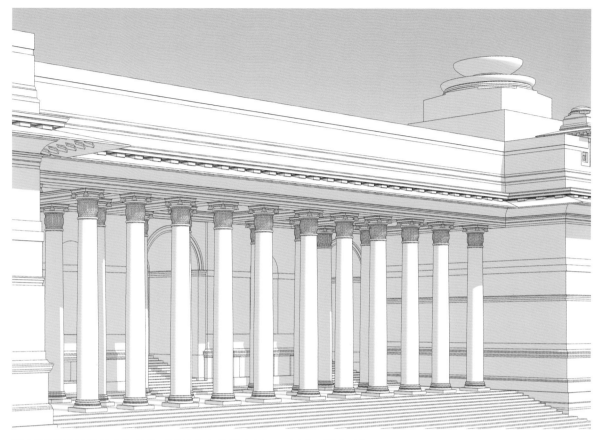

Fig. 6 Order from the Viceroy's House, New Delhi, India, by Sir Edwin Lutyens, plate from HA, Book II, p. 231

ticulars will allow with proportion, intercolumniation, and formal detail retained, because these are always integral to an individual Order.

Some relatively extraneous elements may selectively be diluted, eliminated, or generalized in the process of abstraction. Thus, the curve of a portico is straightened, since it is considered incidental to the Order. Extensions of the ornamental system beyond the capital and entablature are cauterized. Where possible, arches and vaults are transformed into a more generic trabeated system. A dipteral exemplar will be extended to a standard tetra-style. Texture and color may be diluted. The materiality of brick, stucco, iron, wood, and stone is sometimes eliminated, but when the material's identity is essential to the Order it is retained. (Fig. 5: Corinthian Order, plate from HA.)

On trends discerned from the plates

The most general trend is towards simplified detail. This is to be expected as the rise of Modernist architecture since the Third Recall accustoms the eye to abhor clutter. This has been abetted by the general decline in craftwork, resulting in an evolution toward forms which are easy to craft, primarily by turning on a lathe. Orders derived from the Doric predominate—but not quite as much as one might expect. The Ionic and the Corinthian, too, can be radically simplified.

This trend may be reversed with the advent of three-dimensional printing technology in which manufacturing the complex form is as cost-effective as the simple. The emergence of fine detail in cast metal, and terracotta is easily repeated. A resurgence of fully executed Ionic and Corinthian ornament may again emerge—permitted by the economics of computer-controlled robotic carving—technologically-driven like the cast iron of the Third Recall.

Freedom of proportion is the essential difference between the Academic Orders and the Idiomatic ones. The Academic Orders were once bearers of meaning. They provided the mystique of technique which supported the fundamental doctrine of the First Recall. Ever since, when the prescribed narrow range is applied unquestioningly in Classicism, it becomes mute or prudish. When imposed by authority, it is an unwarranted despotism which catalyzes rebellion, as occurred in the robust Modernist Drift. Masters, as demonstrated by the Plates of the Present Treatise, more fully understood the semantic essence of the Classical language than the Renaissance Treatises, with their simplistic allusions to a lost world of antiquity. Following the recommendation of Vitruvius to incorporate observation as well as doctrine, they were referential but not reverential toward the Conventional Orders.

Above all, Idiomatic language provides voluble architects a way to communicate with the public and not just their fellow professionals. From the political right to the left, from the nationalist to the druidic (in current parlance, the "green"), there is motivation for particular architects to embrace the heterodox, so long as deviation from Classical semantics can be understood as a function of eloquence, not just ignorance, which results in kitsch. (Fig. 6: Order from the Viceroy's House, New Delhi, India, by Sir Edwin Lutyens, plate from HA, Book II, p. 231.)

On The Linguistic Analogy

While Classicism has at times been conceptualized by typological and biological anal- ogies, a more common trope is that of language. Linguistic Theory proposes Academic, Idiomatic, Vernacular, and Vulgar forms. The present Treatise explores these forms towards a theory for the evolution of the Classical language. It attempts to do so without diminishing the authority of Academic Classicism—or countenancing the Vulgar—as well as providing theory to explain the Orders of the recent masters. The analogy of language also happens to explain the present crisis of the Classical Discourse. The translation to architecture is relatively direct.

Language consists of semantics (meaning) and syntax (grammar). The syntax of the Orders has been exhaustively explored. The systems of proportioning have been brought to levels of sophistication approaching theological disquisition—but all this activity has been refinement within the limits of the First Recall. It does not explain the explosive divergence of proportions which define the subsequent Recalls.

On the other hand, the semantic aspect has not evolved. The attribution of columns' proportions to the relative body-types of men, women, and maidens is absurd today, and not only because the gendered ideal has changed. The ideal woman today may approach the physique of a Spartan hop-

Fig. 7 The three theatrical scenes in plates from Serlio's treatise

lite, while the ideal male is arguably that of a waif. There is no meaning remaining in the Corinthian's implausible derivation from a basket overgrown in a graveyard. That the Doric is associated with Athena and her warrior attributes, however elegant, is as obtusely antiquarian as the ancient Greek language. The Orders cannot enter the twenty-first century with a semantic system confined by the myths of ancient tribes. The present Treatise proposes to revitalize the language of Classicism based primarily on the direct, visceral semantic dimension of form.

This concern with meaning is, like so much else, originated by the Vitruvius, which introduced syntax by means of proportion and semantics by means of the "theatrical" scenes. Vitruvius' culture knew nothing of linguistics, but it was equipped with highly developed notions of rhetoric. He was reduced to the trope of theater back-drops in lieu of a theory of language. Serlio memorably illustrates three backdrops for stage scenes, illustrating Vitruvius's verbal descriptions. They are a matched set. An identical perspectival armature depicts three architectural ensembles of differing character; translated as the Tragic Scene, the Comic Scene and the Satirical Scene. Within the severe limits of Serlio's compositional skills, woodcutting technique, and the dismally under-edited original text of Vitruvius, it is evident that the Tragic Scene is intended to be as correctly Classical as possible. Orders and arches are arrayed in symmetrically composed façades. The buildings in the Comic Scene are not strictly Classical in detail, nor do they deploy the Canonical Orders. The composition of the façades is accretive and quirky. The third, the Satirical Scene is frankly rustic. The columns are timber or almost-raw logs. There is no urbanism—other than a woodland road. (Fig. 7: The three theatrical scenes in plates from Serlio's treatise.)

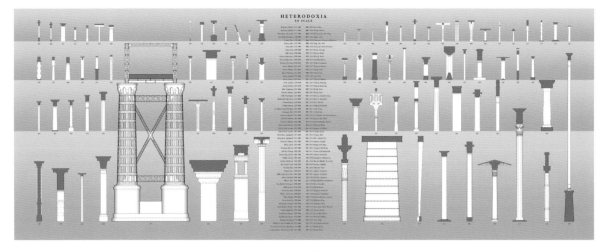

Above and opposite page above Heterodoxia Ex Scale | **Below** Cranbrook School Plate | **Opposite page below** Cranbrook School View

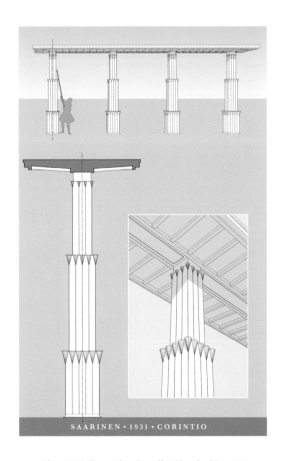

SAARINEN • 1931 • CORINTIO

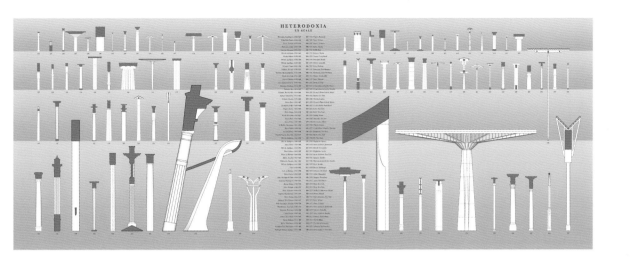

Andres Duany, Javier Cenicacelaya, Katherine Pasternack, and Iñigo Salona **291**

For three centuries the Classical discourse has assumed that these scenes are stage sets for Tragedies, Satires, and Comedies, but a more likely proposition is that these scenes are illustrations of architectural character in general. Vitruvius was attempting to elucidate levels of architectural language in the absence of linguistic theory. There was in their time no theory of linguistics and the proximate trope was rhetoric—the medium of theater. Assuming that theatrical character is a surrogate for an absent linguistics, the three Scenes take on a didactic purpose that is more universally applicable to architecture.

On the levels of the language

The four levels of architectural language may be described as follows, in declension of authority:

1. Like language, the Academic Orders are said to be "conventional," "standard," "correct," or "proper." They constitute an orthodoxy certified, protected, and taught by the Academy. These are usages that have been confirmed by a) the appropriation by acknowledged masters, b) the authority of their cultural persistence, or c) inclusion in architectural masterpieces.

2. Idiomatic Orders belong to individual artists. They are personal and authorial. They intentionally deviate from the Academic for the sake of enhanced expression. Unless they are accepted by the academy they can be admired, but they cannot be copied without fear of being considered derivative and unoriginal.

3. The Vernacular Orders aspire to the Academic language from memory. They are improvised anonymously, a) adapting to circumstances, b) limited by craft or budget, and c) by an organic culture. The Vernacular is usually conceived and built personally by anonymous craftsmen. They evolve as an open system by cooperative adaptation.

4. Vulgar Orders aspire to the Academic culture in ignorance of its rules. As with all kitsch they lack either sincerity or irony. They are concocted by the unlearned and unrefined, often through mechanical repetition. The Vulgar is characterized by weak or erroneous semantic correspondences. They undermine rather than participate in the Classical Discourse.

On the canons

What is the Canon? Its purpose is variable. In the First Recall, the Canon was cultural literacy. It was an ideal to uphold and to approach. For the Second Recall, it is a source of clarity after the Baroque excess. Its cultural authority corresponded to archaeological authority. For the Third Recall, the Canon became a point of professionalism. Today, for the Fourth Recall, the Canon aspires to communicate by consensus. It must be populist, to recover territory from the prevalent kitsch.

The derivation of authority

Vitruvius' description of the Orders was derived from observation of the great buildings and texts that he studied: on them he explicitly based the authority of his Treatise. Palladio and Vignola and the other Treatises of the First Recall, in turn, claimed that their Canonical Orders were derived from Vitruvius and from their study of those buildings of antiquity that had survived. This bestowed authority to theirs. Desgodetz introduced the Ancient Orders derived from measurement of the surviving buildings and that is what gave them their authority. At what point did this combination fail? Why did Canon cease to reflect a consensus derived from the built works, and become dedicated to imposition on the built work? Is that not the point upon which the Classical Discourse begins to lose its authority?

Rather than prolong this misunderstanding, would it not be true to its time if the Present Treatise were to derive a Canon from critical assessment by means of a Parallel and explanation of the built masterworks—rather than attempt yet another filter that excludes them? This has not been attempted since Normand—for two centuries there has not been a Treatise that reflects Classicism as practiced, or that accounts for the cognitive dissonance of the Classical Discourse today: That is, the simultaneous assertion that the Canon of the Five Conventional Orders must be followed while many buildings that do not follow it are considered excellent Classicism. The Fourth Recall will continue to falter until an applicable theory has been formulated.

What has been issued as Treatises in the course of the current Recall to Order—the Fourth since Antiquity—have been the commentaries and explications of the ancient Treatises that accompany their reprinting (by Ingrid Rowland, Thomas Gordon Smith, Donald Rattner, Steven Semes and Richard Sammons, among others). The one exception is Leon Krier's *The Language of Town and Cities*, which has the polemical vigor and the aspect of persuasion that undergirds all proper Treatises. There are also original instruction manuals—updates of the "Carpenter's Companions"—by Robert Adam, Marianne Cusato, Steven Mouzon and the *Architectural Graphic Standards* of Ramsey and Sleeper. But they assimilate only orthodox Canonical Orders. They do not attempt a theory that might propose the past two centuries of Heterodox Practice. While flawless, none of these is a modernized Treatise.

Does the weakness of the current Recall to Order call for the robust theoretical underpinning of its own, modern Treatise? There is an accretion of problems that undermine the intellectual integrity of Classicism. It is evident from the internal and external arguments and counter arguments deployed that there has been a devolution to the assertion of doctrine. There is constant recourse to validation by sacred texts and graven images, whose principal authority is their age. There is no assault at the unresolved contradictions within and between those texts and images. The observable deviations in the built work from the prescriptions of the graven images are not engaged. If today's Academy will not initiate the research to resolve these matters, then it devolves to the less well-prepared to clarify these issues by Treatises adequate to the task. In the absence of a constituted authority, this Treatise endeavors to be authoritative—by fulfilling this purpose: to thrive, not by imposition, but by its ability to explain fully a past in such a way that it can project a future for Classical Architecture.

An attempt at a summary

The following conclusions are drawn from the present Parallel of the Orders. They are presented as the most succinct propositions that explain the phenomena observed.

• That Classical Discourse is most useful to Practice when understood as cyclical.

• That the Classical Discourse alternates between periods of Drift and Recalls to Order. The present is the fourth such Recall.

• That the various interludes of dissipation were in fact attempts to recover what was unwarranted to exclude by the prior Recall, modernism being the most extreme example.

• That the Present Recall is, after 30 years, still fragile, for want of the kind of theoretical underpinning that initiated or sustained the others. Filling the void is the role of the present Treatise.

• That since the First Recall of the fifteenth century, the Classical Discourse has gradually evolved from an operating system based on doctrine to one based on theory.

• That the present Treatise discards the last of the doctrines and completes the evolution to theory.

• That most of the masters of the 20th century have, at least once, practiced within the Classical language.

• That the persistent inability of the Classical Discourse to assimilate them results from the absence of a theory that would allow it.

• The alienation of much of the most creative Classical practice of the past two centuries has granted modernism an illustrious paternity. This has been the greatest strategic blunder of the Classical Discourse.

• That the most convincing metaphor for Classicism is language, which when presented exclusively in terms of Academic language cannot account for current practice. However, a linguistic theory that has Academic, Idiomatic and Vernacular variants does, in fact, provide a very adequate explanation.

• This notion was originally proposed by Vitruvius in the theatrical scenes but, misinterpreted, it has remained sterile.

• That the Classical Language of the Fourth Recall has emphasized syntax and allowed semantics to whither. The apparatus must be restored to balance.

• There is also the aspect of tectonics, the role of modern materials, which must be re- integrated to the discourse.

• That the Classical Discourse has evolved by addition and elaboration, without discarding. The genetic material was complete in antiquity.

• That the only possible Classical education must include the evolution of the discourse is to instruct by *ontogenesis*—for the student to experience sequentially the evolution of the Classical Discourse from the First to the Fourth Recall.

• That the polemic of Serlio, Palladio, Vignola, and Scamozzi was a necessary strategy for the First Recall, but this doctrinal basis required for post-medieval circumstance is no longer necessary, nor is it adequate for present post-modern circumstances.

• That a present problem is not with "Palladio" but with "Palladians" who continue to administer an archaic regime. Too much of classicism that is excellent has been excluded by the application of the doctrines of the First Recall.

• That the nomenclature pertaining to the Orders is unsystematic. The Vitruvian System was distorted by Cesariano's addition of the Composite Order. This prevents a proper identification and growth of the Classical language.

• The Treatises of the First Recall present rules for the Orders as normative. The Treatises of the Second Recall proved that these dimensions did not coincide with the revered models of antiquity. They did not even coincide with the built work of the authors of the rules. These inconsistencies were exposed by the Treatises of Fréart and Desgodetz, but this outing of the discrepancies within the received texts and graven images somehow had no negative effect on the prestige of the original Treatises. This must again be considered by the present Fourth Recall to undermine the false authority of texts which were relevant to their times, and to free the contemporary architect for circumstances that were not envisioned by those ancient Treatises.

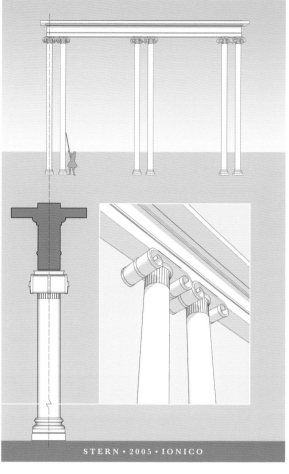

STERN · 2005 · IONICO

This spread Jacksonville Public Library, Robert A.M. Stern Architects, Jacksonville FL (2005). Photography by Peter Aaron/Otto for Robert A.M. Stern Architects | **Opposite page top left** Courtyard looking west | **Opposite page above left** Grand Reading Room looking toward Al Held mural | **Opposite page below left** Courtyard looking north

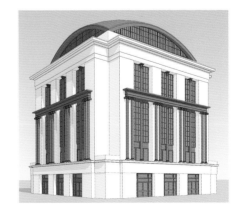

SELECTED WORKS

The Vistana Apartment Building
San Antonio, TX | 2006
Michael G. Imber Architects
298

Various Projects
ongoing
Harrison Design
302

Santorini's Market, Cafe & Restaurant
Alys Beach, FL | ongoing
Khoury & Vogt Architects
308

Iglesia de Nuestra Señora de la Merced
Miami, FL | ongoing
various artisans
310

**Heterodoxia Studies - William H. Harrison
Design Studio in Classical Architecture**
University of Miami School of Architecture| ongoing
Andres Duany, Victor Deupi, Richard John, et al.
312

The Vistana Apartment Building
San Antonio, Texas | 2008

Michael G. Imber Architects

Historically San Antonio's downtown has been defined by its vertical masonry architecture. Defining the Eastern side of San Antonio's historic Milam Park, Vistana reflects the city's unique character as its Western edge.

An awning shelters the street level sidewalk and shops. Levels 2 to 5 express solidity while accommodating parking. Brick patterns and an offset at the 4th level are designed to scale and articulate the building to the street. The body of the building, made up of 247 loft-like units, is simple and expressively vertical. Above parking, the 6th level accommodates a pool and spa with a pavilion for social and business functions.

The building is articulated to reduce its scale; folding its mass into the city landscape. The building is crowned by double high "Z" type penthouse units, providing views West over Milam Park. A tower anchoring the southwest corner of the building realizes a 3 level penthouse suite.

Various Projects
ongoing

Harrison Design

Since 1991, Harrison Design has been dedicated to creating custom residences, townhomes and specialty commercial projects that are inspired by the best of classical and modern architecture. With offices on the East and West Coasts, the company shares a singular belief that a well-designed building is a work of art, and an enduring investment and place to express the client's individuality. With a team of more than 65 architects, designers, landscape architects and interior designers, the firm creates an array of distinctive homes and public structures through the thoughtful study and application of traditional hierarchies, proportions, materials and detailing. The firm has offices in Atlanta and St. Simons, Georgia; Los Angeles and Santa Barbara, California; Long Island, New York; Naples, Florida; Washington, D.C., and Shanghai, and works throughout the U.S. and internationally.

1. Shingle-Style Cottage

Georgia

This traditional, American shingle-style home has a relaxed and inviting exterior. Inside, classical design proportions and details add a sense of formality to the residence without detracting from its accessible look. The programmatic flow connects the living room with an open kitchen and dining room. On a cross-axis, this hallway features a barrel-vaulted ceiling with archways, wood mouldings and paneling painted in a lustrous white to contrast the stained oak floor. The hall opens to the foyer and dining room and leads to an enclosed porch with captivating perspectives of the river and sound.

Photography by Richard Leo Johnson

2. Modern Villa Renovation

California

In renovating this 1980s home, Harrison Design wanted to honor its ornamental Chinese design but update it to suit the new owners. The architects eliminated heavy doors, interior walls and entire rooms to open the interior and accentuate the home's architectural character, such as the arched, 30-foot ceiling in the foyer and a dramatic series of pagoda-shaped portals leading to the living room. A black-and-white color palette acts as a striking backdrop to the couple's modern art collection. The exterior preserves the residence's original fretwork windows, clay-tile roof and Chinese statuary.

Photography by Roger Davies

3. Sunridge Estate

California

This vernacular modern residence utilizes simple shapes and geometry to create bold lines, a traditional characteristic of the style. Omitting ornamentation from the design brings focus to the simple geometry of the building. Details like eaves, sills and all instances of overlap are deliberately omitted, creating a simple and straightforward look with windows and doors appearing as punched-out openings. This causes the building to read simply as glass, stucco, and slate. The powerful aesthetic symmetry is reflected in the landscaping, creating a strong continuity throughout the design.

Photography by Peter Vitale

Anglo-Caribbean Estate - Florida. Photograph by Nick Shirghio

Santorini's Market, Café and Restaurant
Alys Beach, FL, | ongoing

Khoury & Vogt Architects

Anchoring the southeast corner of Alys Beach's town center, Santorini's is modeled on the al-fresco dining and market cafés found along the Mediterranean coast. A tall single-story building encloses an open-air courtyard, with a broad stairway leading to a roof terrace on its eastern and southern flanks.

Interior dining is contained in its southern wing and the market operates as a free-standing hall, connected by a wooden bridge at the terrace level. A loggia with built-in banquette seating provides for outdoor dining within the courtyard, while a rooftop bar and awning-topped lounges along the terrace afford views of the Gulf of Mexico by day and dining under the stars by night. In keeping with the architectural character of Alys Beach, the masonry volumes are clad in white stucco, with timber posts, beams, and awnings, all weathered grey under the Florida sun.

Iglesia de Nuestra Señora de la Merced
Miami, FL | ongoing

VARIOUS ARTISANS

Text by Carol Damian

Inspired by 17th-century churches in Peru and Bolivia, a version of a colonial Baroque chapel has been constructed on the grounds of Corpus Christi Church in Allapattah, a neighborhood in downtown Miami. The vision of parish priest Father José Luis Menendez, La Iglesia Museo Perú de Nuestra Señora de la Merced (the Virgin of Mercy) is the focal piece of the proposed Colonial Heritage Cultural and Convention Center. Built by local craftsmen in the style of the 17th and 18th centuries in what was the Viceroyalty of Peru, with gilded ceilings and columns, intricately carved altars and statuary, and exquisite details, the Chapel is home to a treasure of paintings and sculpture from Colonial Peru,

Bolivia, Ecuador, Mexico, Guatemala and Colombia. The Chapel broke ground in 2005 and is in the final two years of finish work. It has been a labor of love for the community, with skilled laborers, carpenters, plasterers, painters, and artisans who have been trained by visiting experts from Peru and Bolivia to carve, gild, paint, and supply the workmanship for this unique replica of an Andean church.

The collection of over 170 Colonial paintings and sculptures in the Chapel is among the largest in the United States. The works represent Spanish Catholic religious and artistic influence on the people, and demonstrate the extraordinary artistry of the local craftsmen, many of them indigenous artists with a long tradition of metallurgy and carving that adapted easily to the dictates of their new rulers. The result was often a unique form of artwork that became distinctive in the Americas for its attention to detail. The most famous, and beautiful, works are from the Cuzco School, considered the first school of painting in the Americas. Distinguished by its extraordinary gold stenciling, Cuzco paintings maintain their significance to the present day. The collection also features polychrome statuary, complete with silver ornaments and glass eyes, life-size archangels made of repoussé silver and encrusted with jewels, and other religious objects.

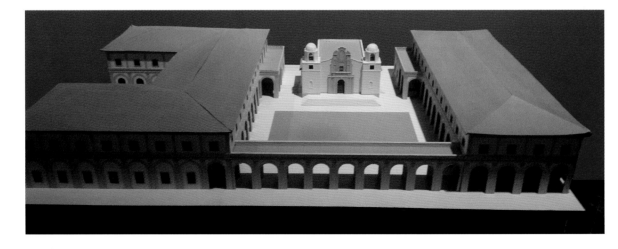

Above Main Altar with image of patroness Virgin of Mercy and the Lord of the Earthquakes | **Opposite page** Proposed conference center for Colonial Heritage project | **Below left** Examples of gilding | **Below center** Carved wood for ceiling | **Below right** Detail

Heterodoxia Studies, William H. Harrison
Design Studio in Classical Architecture
University of Miami School of
Architecture | ongoing

Andres Duany, Victor Deupi,
Richard John, et al.

Studio Manifesto:
Heterodoxia completes the millennial evolution of the Classical discourse from dogma to theory. As have all previous
ones, it is intended to be the final Treatise on Architecture.
Heterodoxia concludes that two theories emerge from the
comparative study of some sixty previous parallels of the
Orders, and from the three hundred newly drawn parallels
of orders that do not coincide with the Renaissance Canon,
but that are nevertheless designed by Masters.

Of the theories, one is syntactic and the other semantic.
The syntactic theory is based on the Vitruvian construct
of a canon, but rather than one of three or five Orders, to
nine. This is based on the evidence of the practice of the
last 250 years. These nine orders recur as necessary to
visually resolve the requisites for bearing and spanning
of modern, rational building types. The semantic theory is
based on the Vitruvian theory of the three theater scenes,
which is classical rhetoric's equivalent of modern linguistic
theory. In its modern form it conveys meaning integrally
and with extraordinary economy.

Both theories involve (or allow) declensions based on
local and cultural techniques of construction and/or the
rural-urban transect. While the individual interpretation is
ever more central, the discipline of the Orders continues to
be the essence of all else Classical. Heterodoxia confirms
the superiority of the Classical Discourse over all other
architectonic systems--albeit diminishing the protago-
nism of the Renaissance. The purpose of the Heterodoxia
is to enable an architecture that is operational within to
the severe material limits of the 21st century, while also
being responsive to the popular culture in whose power
architecture now rightfully belongs. It is very conservative.

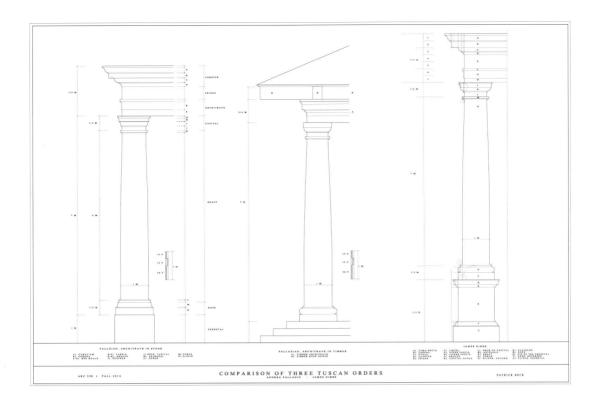

COMPARISON OF THREE TUSCAN ORDERS
ANDREA PALLADIO · JAMES GIBBS

PALLADIAN, ARCHITRAVE IN STONE

PALLADIAN, ARCHITRAVE IN TIMBER

JAMES GIBBS

ARC 508 – FALL 2014

PATRICK BECK

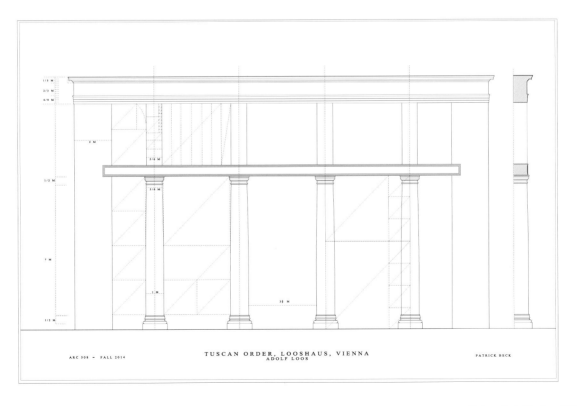

TUSCAN ORDER, LOOSHAUS, VIENNA
ADOLF LOOS

ARC 508 – FALL 2014

PATRICK BECK

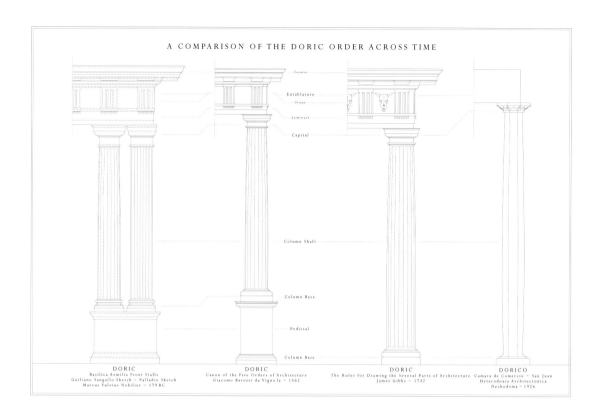

A COMPARISON OF THE DORIC ORDER ACROSS TIME

Cornice

Entablature

Frieze

Architrave

Capital

Column Shaft

Column Base

Pedistal

Column Base

DORIC
Basilica Aemilia Front Stalls
Guiliano Sangallo Sketch ~ Palladio Sketch
Marcus Fulvius Nobilior ~ 179 BC

DORIC
Canon of the Five Orders of Architecture
Giacomo Barozzi da Vignola ~ 1562

DORIC
The Rules for Drawing the Several Parts of Architecture
James Gibbs ~ 1732

DORICO
Camara de Comercio ~ San Juan
Heterodoxia Architectonica
Nechodoma ~ 1926

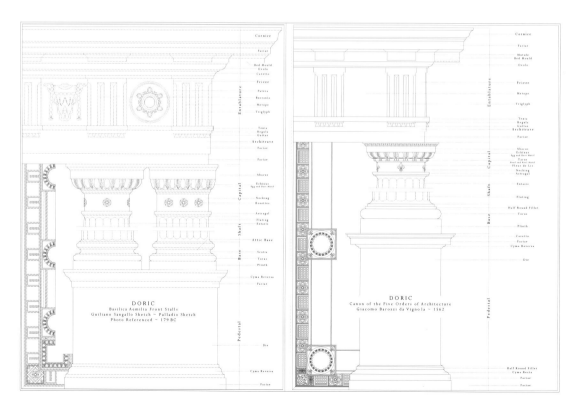

DORIC
Basilica Aemilia Front Stalls
Guiliano Sangallo Sketch ~ Palladio Sketch
Photo Referenced ~ 179 BC

DORIC
Canon of the Five Orders of Architecture
Giacomo Barozzi da Vignola ~ 1562

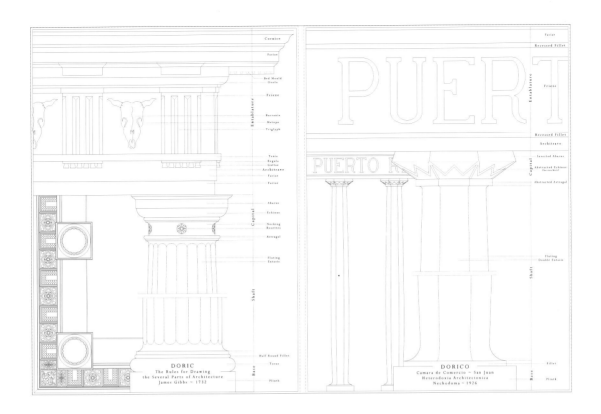

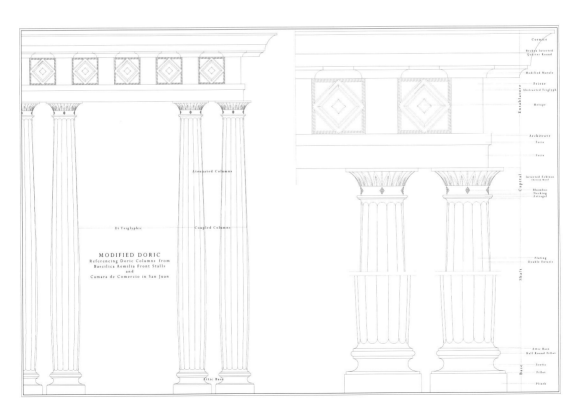

Chapter 7

Towards a
Utilitarian Classicism

Resorting to the classical tradition in architecture is a real source of ideas in every field, and for all kind of purposes, especially for the practice of architecture. In this respect, it is a fact that architecture has its feedback in the making of architecture itself. To say this is as much as accepting the existence of a discourse in the history of architecture, with no real interruption. I will briefly refer to three examples in which resorting to the classical tradition does not mean literally replicating pre-existing cases.

The Mosque of Cordoba. Spain (780 AD – 1002 AD)
The first case is the Mosque of Cordoba begun in 780 and finished, after a few extensions, by Almanzor (976 AD -1002 AD). The successive extensions formed a real "forest" of columns, a hypostyle hall (Fig. 1). The Mosque of Cordoba became a huge building covering a surface of almost six acres. The columns were set in parallel rows of the same length. They were all re-used, coming from different pre-existing Roman or Visigoth sites. All of the rows were perpendicular to the wall of the *qibla*, (the wall where there is a niche or the *mihrab*) which indicates the direction of Mecca that all Muslims have to face when

praying. The columns are surmounted by two superimposed arches. The lower arch springs from the capital and the upper arch from a pillar that also stands on the capital, but projects slightly from it (Figs. 2-3). The upper arch is therefore wider. Given the fact that the columns were re-used and not particularly high, the builders introduced the upper arch for attaining a proper height in the interior. The lower arch acts as buttressing while the upper one supports the roof. The first impression for the visitor to the Mosque of Cordoba is the amazing vision of a forest of columns. It really is impressive. And after that first impression comes a second one when the visitor discovers the upper level of arches. Why all this? Why introduce so many columns? There are clear reasons that I will briefly try to explain.

This vast space needed to be roofed. But how could the rainwater be driven out of the roof? The Arabs knew the Roman aqueducts, and from that knowledge they built on every row of columns the canal of an aqueduct. The roofing has therefore as many aqueducts as row of columns (Figs. 4-5). In order to make room for the canal, the upper arches were built wider. This is the reason of placing those arches springing from the pillars which

Javier Cenicacelaya

project out of the capital of the column. This explains why there are two arches, and why the upper one was wider.

Borromini and his obsession for a central plan

Borromini is undoubtedly a very fascinating figure, I will not go through many details of his life, but I will just focus on his obsessive fight for getting as close as possible to a central plan in his religious architecture in Rome.

Beginning with the Church of *San Carlino* (1638 - 41), Borromini deals with the entablature running on top of the columns in a rather flexible manner. It is a first step in the way he deals with this element. At the *Oratorio dei Filippini* (1637- 40) the rectangular plan has its four corners at forty-five degree angles to the main sides of the rectangle. Here Borromini repeats the same approach as in the courtyard of *San Carlino*. He tries to give continuity to the wall avoiding the rupture (or intersection of plans) produced by having the corners at right angles.

To emphasize that idea of continuity he proposes a ceiling where a set of bands (as the "nerves" in vaults) spring from the corners in a diagonal direction. They are apparently unrelated to the plans of the walls. With this approach he suggests a precinct where an axis does not exist, though there is obviously one from the entrance to the altar. Those bands encounter an oval, marking in a sense the centre of the room in the ceiling. I would dare to say that there is a subtle element of gothic in Borromini, as proponents of the Gothic were at that time often associated with Protestantism. In fact, we have to observe the interest of Borromini in avoiding any horizontal interruption in the ascension of the pilasters up to the bands of the ceiling, therefore pretending to create with the pilasters and those bands a kind of net; a kind of continuity of walls in both senses horizontally and vertically. We can see how the entablature disappears at certain parts (the entrance) and it is only the cornice of the entablature that remains, though as the banister of the upper floor.

Sant'Ivo alla Sapienza (1642 - 1660) is undoubtedly the most original of all churches built in the 17th century. Here it is quite obvious that Borromini has achieved the centrality he was looking for, though it is not strictly speaking a central plan.

Fig. 1 , Mosque of Cordoba. Interior. Photograph by Timor Espallarga

But the most common plan for the churches by Borromini is a rectangular plan hall. Therefore, it is interesting to continue the exploration with the *Cappella dei Re Magi* (1662 – 64) at the Palace of Propaganda Fide. Features described before are expressed here probably with the greatest emphasis (Fig. 6). For example, there is a clear verticality to the pilasters, with the complete disappearance of the architrave and the frieze, just the cornice remains. But above the cornice and in the vertical line with every pilaster, Borromini placed a short pilaster with a narrow impost operating as a capital. Between those short pilasters, and within the lunettes of the vault, there are round arches with a window. From the short pilasters spring bands that cover the vault, and are arranged diagonally creating a kind of basket, or net, that encloses in its centre an image of the Holy Spirit.

In this chapel Borromini shows in a clearer way than in any previous example the verticality of the flat pilasters that

continue in the ceiling, intertwining the flatness of the pilasters with the flatness of the ceiling bands until they create a basket. On top of this, such verticality is underlined by the fact that there are spaces behind the pilasters, producing a contrast against the darkness of those spaces. In a sense the pilasters operate as a skeleton separated from the wall of those spaces. It is what the Germans call *Zweischaligkeit* (Double spatial delimitation).

I will make a brief reference to the unfinished Church of *Santa Maria dei Sette Dolori* (1643 – 1655), a project Borromini had to abandon due to a lack of resources. The plan is rectangular with rounded corners in order to obtain a continuous wall. In this case the church has a continuous entablature that appears very malleable, since the architrave, frieze and cornice run continuously, even when arriving at an arch. The ceiling is the least Borrominian element, most probably due to economic constraints.

Detalle de la arquería en una de las naves de la Mezquita de Córdoba.

1.- VIGA
2.- TABLERO DE TECHO.
3.- CANAL DE EVACUACION DE LA CUBIERTA.
4.- BOVEDA DE ARISTAS FALSAS. DE ESCAYOLA.
5.- ARCO DE MEDIO PUNTO.
6.- PILAR RECTANGULAR.
7.- ARCO CODAL DE HERRADURA.
8.- MODILLÓN DE ROLLOS.

Fig. 2 , Mosque of Cordoba. Section detail.

Fig. 3 Photograph by Michal Osmenda

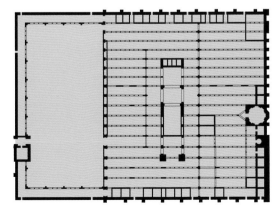

Fig. 4, Mosque of Cordoba. Plan

Fig. 5, Mosque of Cordoba. Aerial view. Photograph by Toni Castillo Quero

Fig. 6 Chapel of the Re Magi

Fig. 7 Bank Stock Office. Interior

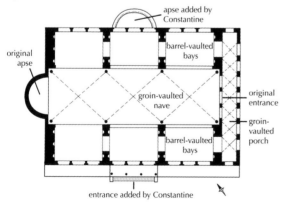

Fig. 8 Basilica of Maxentius. Plan

Summing up, I consider that the *Cappella dei Re Magi* summarizes this attempt of creating a "container" where there is a continuity of all the plans, walls and ceiling. Intending an impossible centrality[1].

Sir John Soane´s rooms in the Bank of England

The next example that I would like to refer to is the work that Sir John Soane made at the Bank of England, London, a project that was largely demolished between 1925 and 1939[2]. In particular, I will comment on the ground floor rooms at the Southeast corner of the bank. It is a group of six rooms and a vestibule for access from the street. Five out of the six follow the same scheme in plan: a tetrastyle room. The sixth one is a rotunda. The group of rooms are perfectly enclosed units, as they do not have windows or practical connections with each other. The vestibule and four of the rooms have continuous windowless walls separating them from Bartholomew Lane and Threadneedle Street. Obviously, just the vestibule has the opening of the entrance door that allows access.

One can understand the idea of banks being completely walled and blind to the streets, as real fortresses. But such an approach means that the issue of natural lighting and ventilation has to be solved in a different way from what is ordinary. Normally using lanterns or some sort of clearstory light.

What I find of interest is the way in which Sir John Soane has solved this problem of introducing light to all of these rooms[3]. And for that purpose he just plays with the heights and roofing of the nine parts in which a tetrastyle room is divided. If we take for example the Bank Stock Office (Fig. 7), we see a central square and four spaces on each of its four sides. Each one of these four spaces is covered with a barrel vault of segmental section. The ceiling in the central space consists of a spherical vault, which being cut off in the four sides of the square produces a pendentive dome, also known as saucer vault.

The pendentive dome is the result of intersecting a spherical vault with a square side prism. Soane opens a large oculus in the dome and places a quite large cylindrical lantern on top of it. This may be seen as a process of inverting what is more conventional, the vault on top of a drum (or cylinder). This lantern lightens generously the whole room. On top of this important entrance of light, the large room provides four more windows. Two of the spaces that make up the arches of the pendentive dome on opposite sides of that central space, have their barrel vaults crossed by other barrel vaults, thus generating a groin vault. It is this fact that allows openings on the two groin vaults. In the end, the space is lit in a very ample manner.

The scheme of this space, a tetrastyle room, appears in many other buildings in history. But the way this type of room is roofed differs so substantially that the character of the building changes completely. We have the same scheme in the Basilica of Maxentius (308-312 AD), in Rome (Fig. 8). Though a much larger space, it is probable that Soane took it as reference, since the dimensions of length and width keep the same relation in both cases (80 x 59 metres at the Basilica and 20 x 14 metres at the Bank). Though this plan relation is the same, the nine parts of the tetrastyle space do not keep a similar relationship in the two buildings.

The Basilica has a longitudinal nave covered by a barrel vault crossed by three perpendicular barrels, the result being three groin vaults. The lateral spaces, lower as they are, act as buttresses to the central and higher nave. They too have barrel vaults. Thermal windows lighten the central nave, while the lateral spaces present few openings in their exterior wall.

Soane did not have the option of opening windows in the perimeter of the Bank Stock Office, and treated the space in an ingenious manner: one that had not been seen before.

Conclusion

This case by Soane, and the two previous ones that I have included, demonstrate how classicism continues to be present in the history of architecture. We could say that it is an asset for architectural practice, serving all kinds of utilitarian works, and expressing different character. The designers of the Mosque of Cordoba, Francesco Borromini, and John Soane granted great value resorting to precedent experiences, or to memory. The same attitude is obviously valid today. Therefore, the knowledge of history becomes an important and fundamental tool for architecture and urbanism.

[1] Other works of Borromini can highlight his interest in the gothic universe of forms. Though in this text I will just refer to the most known churches fully made by him.
[2] Growth and need of space prompted the Bank to demolish all of Soane's rooms between 1925 and 1939. Sir Nikolaus Pevsner commented on the demolition of the old Bank as "the worst individual loss suffered by London architecture in the first half of the 20th century". The Bank Stock Office has been rebuilt to be used as the place for the museum of the Bank of England. Keyworth, John. 1989. The Bank Stock Office Revived, in in *Composición Arquitectónica, Art & Architecture*, p.106. Bilbao. Fundación F. Orbegozo.
[3] Soane was perfectly conscious of the difficulties of his work. There is a comment by Soane, that I quote below where it seems that he acknowledges the originality of his own work. "Architecture is an Art purely of invention (as opposed to imitation in painting and sculpture), and invention is the most painful and the most difficult exercise of the human mind". John Soane, Lectures on Architecture, ed. A.T. Bolton, 1929. P. 119. John Soane Museum.

SELECTED WORKS

Jeddah Superblock
Saudi Arabia | 2013
Merrill, Pastor & Colgan Architects
324

Mecca Housing Prototypes
Saudi Arabia | 2013
Merrill, Pastor & Colgan Architects
328

Mecca Housing
New Town of Dhahait Sumou' in Mecca, Saudi Arabia | 2016
Frank Martinez and Ana Alvarez
336

Sego Homes Townhouses at Daybreak
South Jordan, Utah | ongoing
Urban Design Associates
340

The Lucian
Alys Beach, FL | 2017
Khoury & Vogt Architects
342

**Transect Studies, William H. Harrison
Design Studio in Classical Architecture**
University of Miami School of Architecture | 2015
Andres Duany & Victor Deupi
350

Jeddah Superblock
Al Malik Road, Kingdom of Saudi Arabia | 2013

Merrill, Pastor & Colgan Architects

This was a collaborative competition with the master planners, DPZ. The architecture was designed and documented over a period of two weeks. Roads and streets in Saudi Arabia are typically very wide so the most interesting prospect of designing the architecture for DPZ's plan was the further development of a relatively narrow pedestrian retail street in a zone of the parcel that required seven story buildings that meet allowable densities. This street extended approximately 500 meters in length. The retail street had to rise over sub-grade parking from two directions, but this rise and fall in the street was combined with a narrowing of the street toward the plaza, and the combination had the effect of enhancing the approach to the central space in the project.

The central plaza is about 50 by 100 meters. It is entered diagonally on the corners. It is distinguished in part by a colonnade called for in the master plan, and in part by one of the hotel sites that sits on the long closed side of the plaza. The hotel has a semi-public forecourt separated from the plaza by a loggia.

Blocks throughout the master plan are 75 meters on a side. Buildings are typically 17 or 18 meters wide and suitable for any of the uses contemplated. The site coverage limit is 60%, and with narrower streets this allows for large semi-public mid-block spaces. There is a system of walks and passages that connects these courtyards in a continuous circulation system.

Opposite page Al Malik Road, Jeddah, Saudi Arabia, 2013 | **Above left and right** View of arcade and main plaza | **Below left** Plaza Hotel elevation. The hotel facade is 30 by 60 meters, the size of the Palazzo Farnese. It faces the main plaza which is the size of the Piazza Farnese | **Bottom left** Aerial view | **Bottom right** Arcade

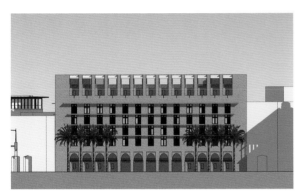

Above Elevation at traffic circle | **Opposite page top** Section facing hotel with key | **Opposite page above** Section facing court with key

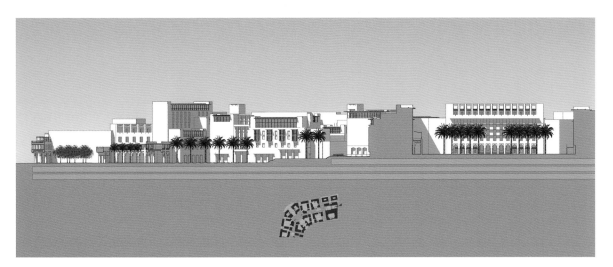

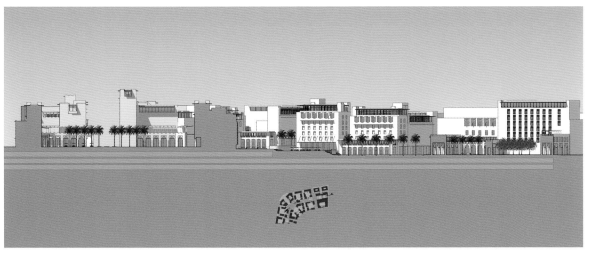

Mecca Housing Prototypes
Kingdom of Saudi Arabia | 2013

Merrill, Pastor & Colgan Architects

These housing prototypes are for a large master plan by DPZ either side of the highway from Jeddah to Mecca. House types ranged from freestanding villas to large rowhouses, small apartment buildings and large 6-8 story apartment buildings with one level of sub-grade parking and ground floor commercial program.

Each large apartment building had a different geometry. Deep mid-block lots were a little more difficult to plan as they had the same FAR as corner lots with more street frontage. Lots with obtuse angles were also a little more difficult to plan as the most rational and efficient structural bays had to be abandoned to a degree. Elevations employed a 4.25-meter module and for the most part repeated the same windows, so any variety had to come from the aggregated patterns of the windows and a modest amount of variety in the massing of the buildings.

Where any apartment's primary exposure was to a common property line with a small setback, we tried to provide another exposure to a larger courtyard. In buildings this reduced envelop efficiency a little. On lots 1 and 8 we could form courtyards out of more efficient double loaded buildings.

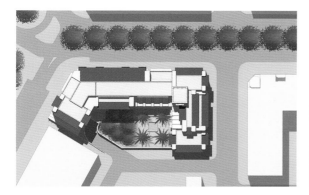

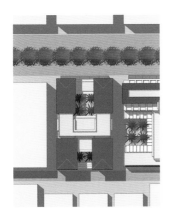

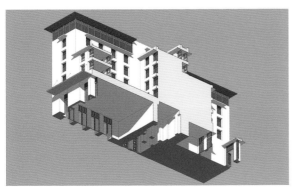

This spread Mixed use 3

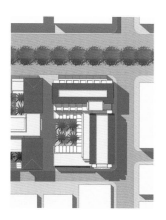

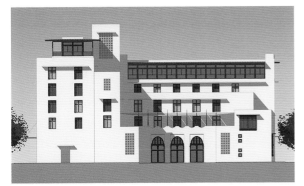

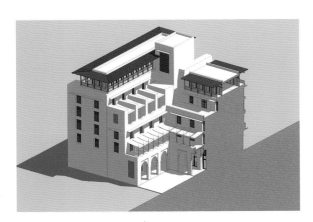

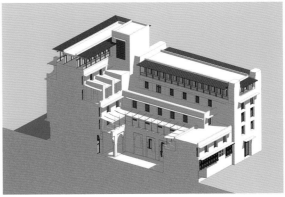

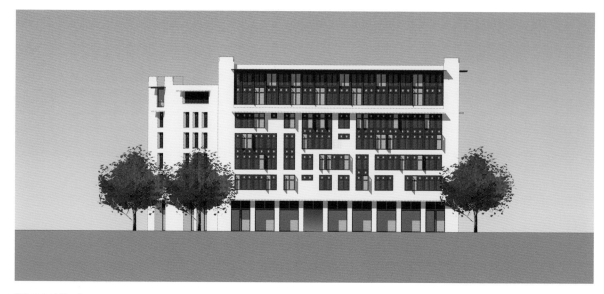

This spread Mixed use 4

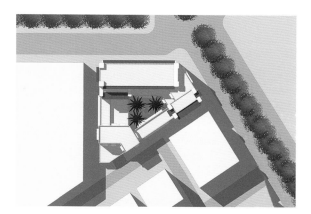

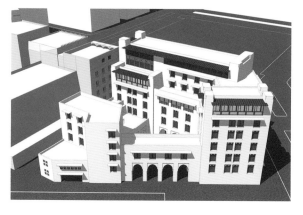

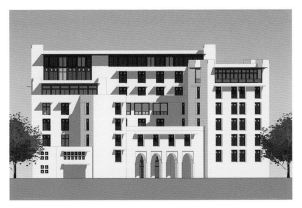

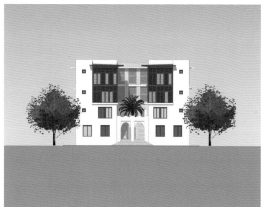

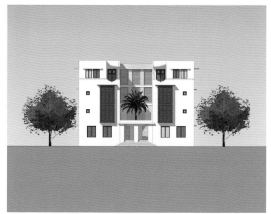

This spread Apartment

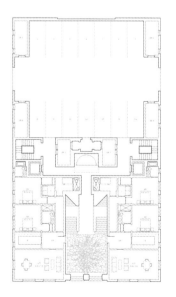
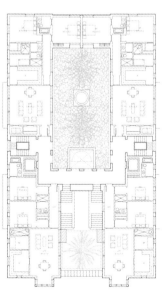
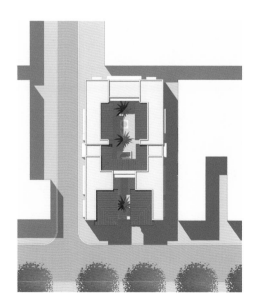

Mecca Housing
New Town of Dhahait Sumou' in Mecca, Saudi Arabia | 2016

Frank Martinez and Ana Alvarez

Designers: Frank Martinez & Ana Alvarez with Ricardo Lopez
Project Team: Marcela Gamarra, Alice Cimring, Marianna Yerak, Simi Varghese & Ram Krishnan

The housing studies and design work done for the new town of Dhahiat Sumou' in Mecca, Saudi Arabia were the result of a Town Design & Charrette by firm Duany Plater Zyberk & Company in 2013. The project encouraged architects to develop a range of building types of varying densities for a new planned neighborhood, to set tone and standards for the development of the region over the next few decades. The designs encompass the project objectives to provide a high quality of life, accommodating new development while preserving the region's natural resources, and its rich heritage.

The architects various residential building types, as defined by the architectural code, including a townhouse and a small multi-family building that blend traditional, compact urban patterns with contemporary building forms adapted to Makkah's culture and climate. The designs employ climate-responsive techniques and features such as loggias, covered terraces, and screened openings. These sustainable design objectives were combined with the careful arrangement of program to adapt to cultural requirements, such as separate "public" and "family" entrances, the "dirty" and "regular" kitchens. The separate typologies were flexible enough to accommodate various spatial/ecologic/cultural requirements, and to be repeated throughout a vibrant, mixed-use neighborhood woven together with pedestrian-friendly public realm within appropriately-scaled streets and a rich open-space system.

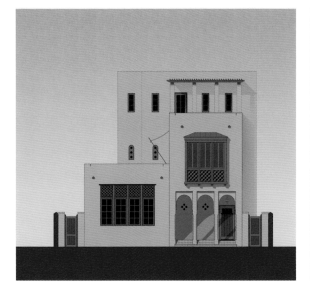

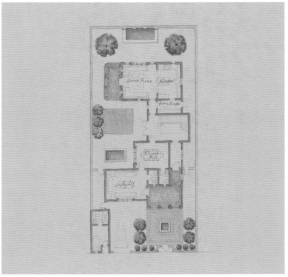

This page Housing Studies: Townhouse and Small Apartment Building Design for the New Town of Dhahiat Su-mou' in Makkah, Saudi Arabia (Town Design & Charrette by Duany Plater Zyberk & Company), 2013

First floor plan   Second floor plan   Third floor plan

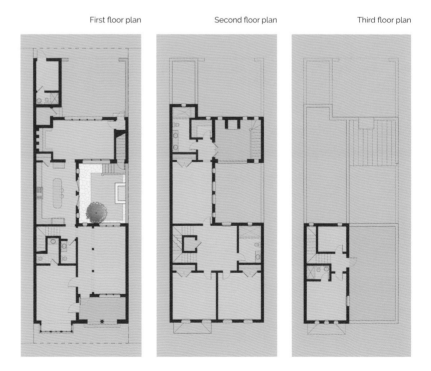

Groundfloor plan

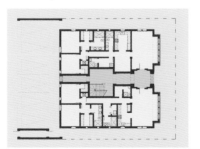

First floor plan

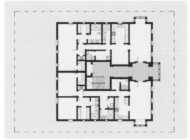

Second floor plan

This spread Housing Studies: Townhouse and Small Apartment Building Design for the New Town of Dhahiat Sumou' in Makkah, Saudi Arabia (Town Design & Charrette by Duany Plater Zyberk & Company), 2013

Sego Homes Townhouses
Daybreak South Jordan, Utah | ongoing

Urban Design Associates

Text by Eric Osth

Having broad choices in the new housing market remains a significant challenge for architects, developers and builders alike. For decades, many American cities have grown without new housing that addresses the diverse interests of buyers, and without any regard to place-making and local tradition. Although there are many great examples in the custom housing market, few homebuilders have been able to deliver the "hand of the architect" at the affordable and middle scales.

The production homebuilding market is in desperate need of rigorous design. Today, homebuilders develop the largest percentage of the residential market, and thus remain responsible for major transformations in the built environment. This is not only critical from a place-making point of view, but also from a social one, improving the sense of social mobility by distributing good design to all.

Historically, the attached townhouse typology has been a cornerstone in the development of some of the most delightful cities in America. Townhouses have an urban tradition in most American cities that were developed before 1940. Today, townhouses are not only part of the past, but a bridge to the future. Twenty-first century multi-family financing is complex and fought with challenges. Fee-simple townhouses are an effective and easy way to deliver high density urban living. And because of the townhouse's human scale and great flexibility, a designer can easily construct a sophisticated urbanism of streets, squares, and passages at a reasonable cost.

The work of Urban Design Associates (UDA) at Daybreak Utah achieves these goals. It is inspired by a broad series of influences. The first, and most obvious, is the use of the basic townhouse prototype. The design introduces three typical plans, but by using three elevations per plan, highly unique street compositions can be achieved. This creative and inventive place-making strategy has deep roots in urban city-building, most notably in the Garden City Movement. The elevations are unmistakably inspired by classical precedent and traditional building languages. However, in this case, UDA's designs have deepened the reach and broadened the classical tradition beyond current boundaries of practice and pedagogy. The Sego Homes Townhouses include affordable modern materials used in modern ways, as well as a modern sensibility of a seamless connection from the interior to exterior. Through large openings and corner windows, UDA has developed a very livable, affordable language of architecture that is appropriate to the context.

Above North Elevation of Building 1 along South Daybreak Rim Way | **Below left and right** The work included a master plan and the architecture. These axonometric drawings of the master plan highlight the new key public spaces

that are framed by the new architecture | **Opposite page** Internal spaces were planned to have the intimacy and character of great pedestrian medieval cities in today's development context. Photograph by Eric Schramm Photography

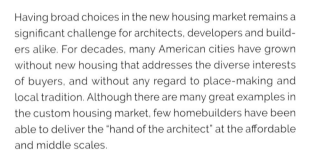

The Lucian
Alys Beach, FL | 2017

Khoury & Vogt Architects

Situated along Route 30A on the southwest corner of Alys Beach's Amphitheater, the Lucian is its first mixed-use Town Center Building. Eight residences of various sizes rise above a full-floor restaurant, accessed by open-air lobbies and galleries. Each unit spans a bay along its southern frontage, divided by white stuccoed masonry piers. Between these, recessed wood porches and projected timber balconies extend from the living spaces, providing broad views of the Gulf of Mexico beyond. The building corner is marked by a chimney pier of civic stature, reflecting its place of importance in the overall townscape.

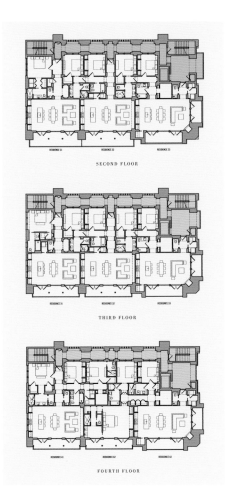

SECOND FLOOR

THIRD FLOOR

FOURTH FLOOR

Transect Studies, William H. Harrison Design Studio in Classical Architecture

University of Miami School
of Architecture | 2015

Andres Duany & Victor Deupi

The studio is conceived to explore an architectural design responsive to the exigencies of the 21st Century. The coming practice has at least two unprecedented requirements. The first is that of efficiency; what Sigfried Gideon called "the problem of large numbers" or as Rem Koolhaas brutally put it: "The typical Chinese architect is 200 times as efficient as the typical American architect." The limits that are upon us--economic and environmental--require of the future architect a design process that is very, very quick and that dependably results in buildings that succeed in their construction and their use. To this end, the classical language is, indeed the only available open-shelf prefabrication system in the United States. It is the default setting of the building material depots and catalogs. There is an emerging movement which is conscious of the need to respond to this challenge of efficiency. It is called Lean Urbanism.The second requirement of the coming practice is that the buildings have to be popular: There is today a "customer" for architecture--very few buildings are any longer commissioned by patrons. It is only recently that the middle class has the economic clout to substantially affect the built environment. This is quite different from a past where an impoverished laboring class led to building with

Nikita Chabra

the dignity of simplicity--while a ruling class concentrated wealth in coincidence with a high level of culture. These were the patrons who are today scarce indeed. The architecture of today has an enormous, culturally deficient middle class with a surplus wealth that leads to the production of kitsch. If authenticity is to be restored to the formal language of architecture it will be by communicating to the common culture in a transparent, non-academic language. Classicism of a certain kind has been able to achieve this connection like no other architectural proposal. This is part of another emerging movement; this one called Heterodoxia.

To both of these challenges: the efficiency forced upon architects by the limits; and the populism required of a market-empowered consumer of architecture, the language of Classicism offers potential solutions that will be studied in this course.

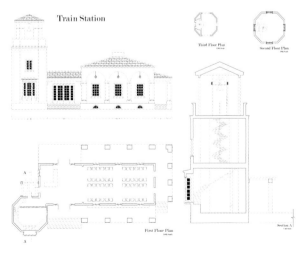

Train Station

Third Floor Plan

Second Floor Plan

First Floor Plan

Section A

Top Nikita Chabra, Transect Study | **Above** Nikkita Chabra, Design for a local train station

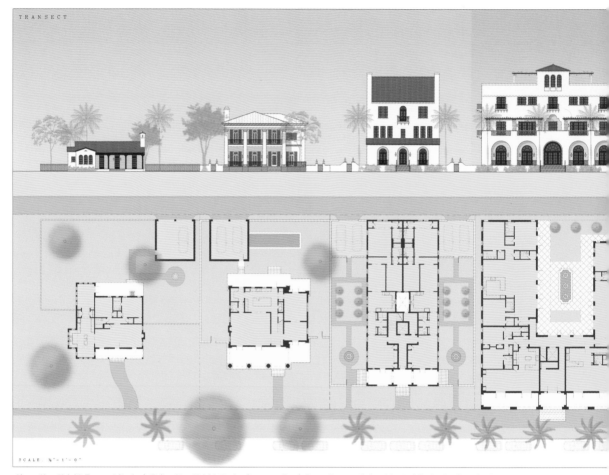

SCALE ¼"=1'-0"

Above Kara Knight, Transect Study | **Below** Kara Knight, Design for a mansion | **Opposite page below** Kara Knight, Design for a duplex

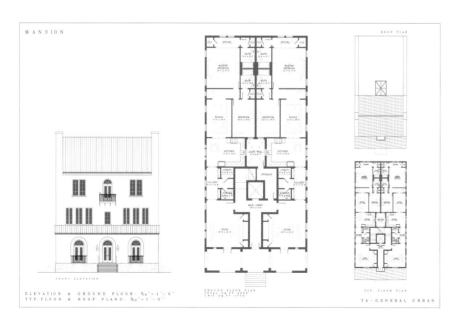

MANSION

ROOF PLAN

ELEVATION & GROUND FLOOR · ⅜"=1'-0"
TYP FLOOR & ROOF PLANS · ³⁄₃₂"=1'-0"

GROUND FLOOR PLAN
TOTAL SQ FT 4000
UNIT SQ FT 1770

TYP FLOOR PLAN

T4 · GENERAL URBAN

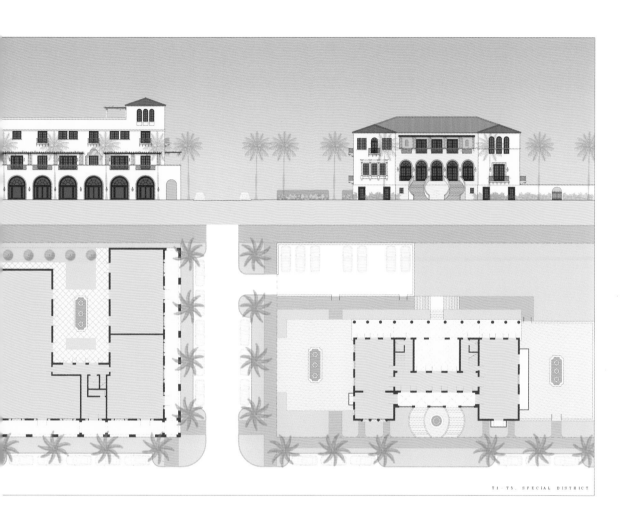

T1 - T5, SPECIAL DISTRICT

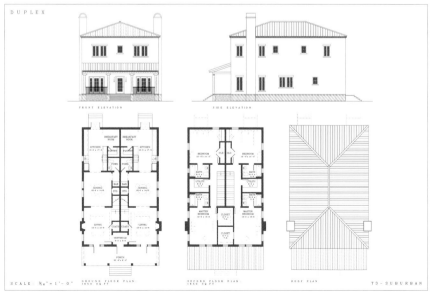

DUPLEX

FRONT ELEVATION   SIDE ELEVATION

SCALE: ¾" = 1'-0"   GROUND FLOOR PLAN   SECOND FLOOR PLAN   ROOF PLAN   T3 - SUBURBAN
                     1850 SQ FT   1850 SQ FT

Chapter 8

The Scientific Method

Classical Architecture and The Scientific Method: In Praise of Experimentation

The world in which we live has been and continues to be transformed by the results of ever more rapid scientific discovery. Transportation, communication and healthcare are just some of the areas in which technological progress has accelerated to such an extent that it is readily perceptible to individuals not just over the course of a lifetime, but now from one decade to the next. A vital factor in the growing speed at which science advances is the shared methodological basis for the creation of new knowledge known as the Scientific Method[1]. In its simplest form this involves making observations of an unexplained or problematic phenomenon, developing a hypothesis to explain what has been observed, and then testing the hypothesis, preferably through experimentation. This last step is important, because it is only through an experiment that an investigator is able to interrogate nature rather than merely observing it. Experiments can be designed - and their conditions can be controlled - so that a very precise question can be posed and answered.

When this idea of experimentation is applied in other fields of human endeavor, for instance in the arts, a much less precise role is usually envisaged. The word "experimental" is often used rather vaguely to mean something innovative or out of the ordinary rather than part of a rigorous process of testing a specific hypothesis or theory. But, whether one is referring to the precise methodological meaning or the more nebulous definition, without experimentation progress in any field cannot occur. This is as true of architecture as any other field. The practice of classical architecture today is essentially static because it is lacking in this vital component of experimentation. Most classical and traditional buildings which are designed and built at present are so conservative, either by closely following precedent or carefully following the canonic rules, that little progress is being made. Without mistakes, wisdom cannot accrue. Trial and error are an essential part of the learning process. Let us consider an example of how an architect used experimentation to solve a very particular problem in the Renaissance.

During the 1460s and 70s the palace of Federico da Mon-

Richard John

tefeltro, Duke of Urbino, was being rebuilt and extended, initially by Luciano Laurana and then later by Francesco di Giorgio[2]. One of the most visually striking parts of the project is a new courtyard designed in a refined *all'antica* idiom with an open arcuated colonnade on all four sides on the ground floor. The story above the loggia is enclosed, with a regular system of fenestrated bays articulated by pilasters. The proportions and regularity of the arches of the loggia and the upper pilaster bays give the four elevations facing the courtyard a measured air of confidence. Where these elevations meet at the corners of the courtyard, however, this confidence evaporates and the sequence of arches is abruptly terminated by a giant pilaster just before one wall meets the other at the re-entrant corner, interrupting the regular metrical beat of the bays with a dramatic caesura. The designer was clearly unsure how to turn the corner using the order of the arcuated colonnade, and therefore decided it was best to bring the sequence to an end, leave a small gap at the corner, and then start afresh with a new system on the adjacent wall. The two colossal pilasters standing just a short distance apart at the corners read very clumsily and the resulting awkwardness betrays the limit of the designer's ability to handle the classical language.

While this courtyard in Urbino was being planned and built, Donato Bramante was training as a painter at Federico's court. When Bramante came to practice architecture a little later in life, we can see him experimenting with how to solve exactly this challenge of the re-entrant corner in a classical courtyard. His earliest attempt is in 1492 at Sant'Ambrogio in Milan where he designed the Canonica, a residence for the canons arranged around a cloister[3]. Here there is no change in the spacing of the bays as they transition from one side of the courtyard to the next, and the same column is used at the re-entrant corner as between the regular bays in the adjacent ranges. The result is a very smooth transition at the corner - the measured beat of the colonnade is not interrupted at all - but visually it appears weak because the corner column looks insufficiently substantial for its tectonically important location. It seems that in reaction to his memory of the heavy-handed corner treatment at the Urbino courtyard, Bramante had here experimented by taking the solution to the other extreme.

Above left Courtyard, Ducal Palace, Urbino. Photograph by Gengish Skan | **Above right** Donato Bramante, Canonica, Sant'Ambrogio, Milan. Photograph by Giovanni Dall'Orto | **Below** Donato Bramante, Cloister, S. Maria della Pace, Rome. Photograph by Marie-Lan Nguyen

Five years later, Bramante was commissioned by Cardinal Ascanio Sforza to design a monastic complex for the Cistercians adjacent to Sant'Ambrogio, on the opposite side of the church from the Canonica. Though four cloisters were originally planned, only two were ever completed and only one was begun during Bramante's lifetime. In this cloister the arches are carried by Ionic columns except at the corner position where one finds a square pillar instead of a round column. Bramante was deliberately experimenting with a different solution from the one he had used at the nearby Canonica, which he must have judged as not completely successful.

With the fall of the Duke of Milan, Ludovico Sforza, in 1499 Bramante moved to Rome where his first major project again posed the challenge of a re-entrant corner in a classical courtyard. Cardinal Oliviero Caraffa commissioned him to add a small cloister to the new church of S. Maria Della Pace[4]. Inspired, no doubt, by the ancient remains littering Rome, Bramante here adopted a more authentically antique treatment for the ground floor arcade and employed the fornix or theater motif of arches framed between pilasters rather than the arches carried by columns he had used in Milan. Even though he was dealing with piers rather than columns in this cloister, the question of how to treat the corners was crucial to the success of the project, particularly because of the small scale of the space being enclosed by the arcades. If the piers were positioned to show a full pilaster on each side at the corner, the combination of the two piers together at right angles would produce a large L-shaped mass of masonry which would look very heavy-handed. Another option would be to show only a half pilaster on each side of the corner, which would reduce the size of the corner pier but with the result that it would look as though a pilaster had been folded down the middle at 90 degrees. The solution that Bramante chose was to allow the two piers to overlap or interpenetrate to such an extent that the pilasters on each side disappear almost completely into the wall - only a sliver of shaft and two fragments of volutes are left peeking out to indicate that the pilasters are now immured within the corner pier. This technique of showing fragments of immured orders at corners had a clear precedent in Brunelleschi's Barbadori chapel and Sagrestia Vecchia in Florence.

Bramante had an opportunity to think about the challenge of the classical cloister yet again just a couple of years later when he received the commission for a monument to be erected to the memory of St Peter at the presumed site of his martyrdom in a small courtyard adjacent to the church of

Above Donato Bramante, Proposed cloister for the Tempietto from Sebastiano Serlio, *Il terzo libro...nel quale si figurano, e descrivono le antiquità di Roma*, Venice 1560, p. XLI

S Pietro in Montorio. Bramante modeled the memorial itself, the Tempietto, after circular peripteral temples, antique examples of which could be seen in Rome and Tivoli. To complement this unusual form, he proposed that the courtyard should be refashioned as a circular colonnaded cloister[5]. This proposal was never executed but is known to us from a woodcut published by Sebastiano Serlio. The idea was perhaps inspired by the surviving circular colonnade of the Teatro Marittimo at Hadrian's Villa at Tivoli but its primary appeal was surely that it would give a powerful radial emphasis to the round form of the Tempietto, each column of the cloister concentrically reinforcing the corresponding one in the peristyle of the rotunda. In the context of the current discussion, however, there is the intriguing possibility that another factor might have helped recommend it as a solution to Bramante. He might have found the idea of a circular cloister particularly appealing because of his awareness of the problem inherent in the re-entrant corner - it didn't solve the problem but rather did away with it altogether because now there were no corners to deal with.

Let us turn now to an example of the second kind of experimentation - the more generalized type which is not necessarily addressing a specific problem, but is simply trying out new ideas in the hope that it might yield results. An interesting example which occurred at a key moment of the modern classical revival is the Howard Building at Downing College, Cambridge, by Quinlan Terry[6].

During the 1970s a research scientist at Cambridge University, Dr. Alan Howard, developed a very low calorie diet initially for use in obesity clinics and then later made available to the general public under the name "The Cambridge Diet." Its success was such that Howard was able to generously fund a major new building for his college which would provide a hall with a stage that could be used for lectures, performances and the summer conference trade. The architect, Quinlan Terry, had been deeply disillusioned with modernism during his training at the Architectural Association and so in 1962 had joined the practice of Raymond Erith, one of the very few classical architects working in Britain through the 1950s and 60s. Terry, now in his mid-forties and in sole charge of the practice following Erith's death, had not previously been given the opportunity to tackle a public building and so he leapt at the challenge with gusto. The nature of the commission, with an ample budget and an institutional client, gave him the chance to work in a much richer idiom than the restrained Palladian style favored by his residential patrons. Eschewing the austere Grecian neoclassicism of the earlier buildings of the college designed by William Wilkins and his successors, Terry instead attempted a deliberately experimental essay in the Italian Baroque.

The main façade of the Howard building consists of seven bays of varying width, gradually enlarging towards the middle: The end bays are three column diameters wide, the next two bays on either side are four diameters each, and the middle bay is five diameters wide. The hall is placed on the upper floor with correspondingly large windows high up on the façade; below these, on the ground floor where a reception room and cloakrooms are located, there are small windows of the sort one usually expects to find not below but above large windows to indicate the presence of a mezzanine floor. The front and side façades are articulated by a colossal order of fluted Corinthian pilasters rising from a continuous pedestal. In the central bay the order changes to unfluted Composite columns which are engaged in the wall but they are set rather too deeply so that as they taper upwards they seem to be sinking into the wall surface. This projecting central bay frames an elaborate door derived from Baldassare Longhena's staircase at San Giorgio Maggiore, Venice, and carries a pediment which dramatically thrusts three bold urns into the sky. The continuous pedestal wraps around the front and sides of the building but on the rear façade immediately after turning the corner it drops out, to be replaced instead by a single-story Doric porch sitting directly on the ground. The dramatic change of scale from the colossal Corinthian pilasters at the corners to the widely-spaced short Doric colums

in the middle disconcertingly suggests the collision of two completely different buildings, one monumental, the other domestic. The elements of the orders - pilasters, columns, entablature and pediment - are all in a whitish-grey Portland stone, while the wall is in the same warm honey-colored Ketton stone traditionally used for Cambridge colleges. The drama of this polychromy is heightened by the deep rustication of the walls in the end bays and on the side facades.

Terry's strange and mannered experiment was not well received by critics who derided its restlessness, over-elaboration and self-importance, but despite the criticism, much of it fair, it is a curiously informative building[7]. In the same way that a failed experiment can enlarge our scientific understanding, so too the aesthetic failure of this building yielded important knowledge for the nascent classical revival. After the classically impoverished decades of the 1960s and 70s, Terry's desire to cram as much architecture as he could into the building was as understandable as a starved man stuffing food into his mouth. The Howard Building showed how easy it was to overegg the pudding when drawing on such a long and rich tradition as classicism and demonstrated the value of restraint. Today, thirty years later, it is apparent that restraint has become the default setting for most classical architects and this conservatism is stifling progress in the field. It is time now for the restraining hand of good taste to loosen its vice-like grip on classical architecture. Experimentation, either precisely targeted as in the case of Bramante, or more general as seen with Terry, is vital if we are to enrich classicism for the future.

[1] For a useful introduction to this topic see Peter Kosso, *A Summary of Scientific Method*, Dordrecht 2011.
[2] See Janez Höfler, *Der Palazzo ducale in Urbino unter den Montefeltro (1376-1508): neue Forschungen zur Bau- und Ausstattungsgeschichte*, Regensburg 2004.
[3] For Bramante's projects at Sant'Ambrogio see Luciano Patetta, "Bramante e la trasformazione della Basilica di Sant' Ambrogio a Milano", *Bollettino d'arte*, Ser. 6, vol. 21 (1983) pp. 49-76; Luciano Patetta, *Bramante e la sua cerchia: a Milano e in Lombardia 1480-1500*, Milan 2009; and Anna Elisabeth Werdehausen, *Bramante und das Kloster S. Ambrogio in Mailand*, Worms 1990.
[4] Marconi, Paolo, "Il chiostro di Santa Maria della Pace in Roma." *Studi Bramanteschi*, Rome 1974, pp. 427-436.
[5] On the proposed courtyard see H. Günther, "Bramantes Hofprojekt um den Tempietto und seine Darstellung in Serlios dritten Buch." *Studi Bramanteschi*, Rome 1974, pp. 483-501.
[6] Clive Aslet, *Quinlan Terry: The Revival of Architecture*, London 1986, p. 200-06; David Watkin, *Radical Classicism: The Architecture of Quinlan Terry*, New York 2006, p. 220 ff; and Richard John, *Robert Adam: The Search for a Modern Classicism*, Mulgrave, Victoria 2010, p. 44.
[7] For instance see Gavin Stamp *et al.*, "Classics Debate", *The Architects Journal*, 11 March 1988, pp. 34-51; and Giles Worsley, "Architecture: How to be Classical without being crude", *The Independent*, 1 September 1992.

Above Quinlan Terry, Howard Building, Downing College, Cambridge. Photograph by The wub

SELECTED WORKS

Labirinto di Franco Maria Ricci
Fontanellato Parma | 2015
Pier Carlo Bontempi
362

Casa de las Lomas (Horton Residence)
Austin, TX | 2015
Michael G. Imber Architects
374

Bertolet Residence
Alys Beach, FL | 2015
Michael G. Imber Architects
388

Santigua House
Alys Beach, FL | nd
Gary Justiss,
398

House in Ohio
Ohio | ongoing
Peter Pennoyer Architects
404

Labirinto di Franco Maria Ricci
Fontanellato, Parma | 2015

Pier Carlo Bontempi

The Masone Labyrinth is the largest landscape maze in the world. Conceived by the great publisher, designer and collector, Franco Maria Ricci, it is located near the small town of Fontanellato, in the countryside of Parma, the place of his origins. Together with the Castello di Fontanellato, already rich with enigmatic frescoes by Parmigianino, this astonishing wonder forms an impressive pair.

Always having been fascinated by labyrinths as places of meditation and imagination, Franco Maria Ricci created a nine-hectare maze from various species of bamboo. Since he was a boy, Franco Maria Ricci dreamt of realizing a labyrinth. When he met Jorge Luis Borges he shared with him the idea and Borges said: "the largest maze in world already exists: it is the desert." Franco Maria Ricci then answered: "well, I will create the largest green labyrinth in the world."

The labyrinth complex also contains buildings constructed entirely of hand-made brick, a construction material typical of the Po River valley. These buildings house cultural spaces for Franco Maria Ricci's art collection, and a library with the foremost examples of graphic art and typography, including many works by Bodoni. Of course the collection also includes all the books edited by the publisher during his fifty years of activity. At the center of the maze there is a large courtyard surrounded by porticos and large rooms suitable for concerts, exhibitions and other cultural events.

The courtyard is closed at the end by a pyramidal chapel that reminds us that the maze is a metaphor for life guided by faith. Visitors will encounter a cafeteria, a restaurant, a Parmesan delicatessen and a bookshop. Architect Davide Dutto collaborated in the design of the seven-pointed star-shaped plan of the maze's greenery.

Photography credits Mauro Davoli and Massimo Listri | **Above** Watercolor rendering by Giuseppe Greci

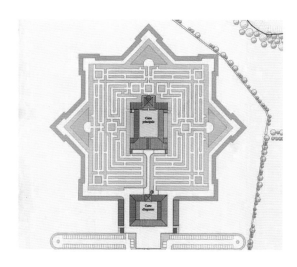

Below Watercolor rendering by Giuseppe Greci

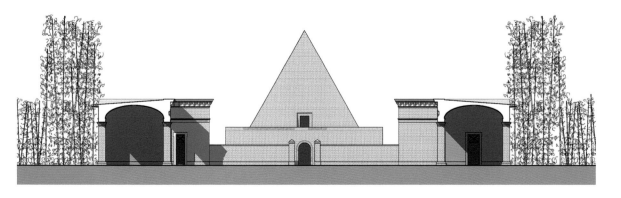

Photography credits Casey Dunn

Casa de las Lomas (Horton Residence)
Austin, Texas | 2015

Michael G. Imber Architects

This residential project brought together the great potential of architecture in Texas – a rugged hilly landscape with appeal-ing natural views, masons who can achieve desired effects, and stone, tile and terra cotta that settle the building into its complementary natural terrain. With a site overlooking the hills topped by distant views of Austin, Texas, Imber chose to place this residence at the edge of the hillside thus providing an arrival space, plus dramatic views of the building as it layers down the hillside. The house is entered from the second level to take advantage of the views and to tuck its mass into the hillside. The expressive aesthetic of variously toned rough-hewn stone, Moorish motifs, and tiled concrete dome reminiscent of southern Spain, feels at home in the Texas landscape.

Arrival in the forecourt accented with native cedar and the twisting trunks of live oak, and natural exposed stone, hints at the building beyond the walled garden. The main façade is accented with a parapet in front of the tiled dome and creates a dramatic silhouette against the Texas sky. Built in Guatemala, the Spanish cedar entry door opens within a decorative wood panel reminiscent of Spanish zaguans with the front door cut into a larger scaled door, and is surrounded by a Cordova Cream limestone tympanum carved in the Mudejar manner.

The foyer is accented with arched stained glass windows and a lightly dripping tiled fountain that softly reverberates in the space floored in a marble Cosmatesque pattern. From here an axis connects the public spaces with the cubic music room contained beneath a vault to the right, and the living room, kitchen and library are interconnected to the left. Dining and outdoor living spaces open out to capture the breezes and views down to the terrace and swimming pool. The second floor dining loggia has a heavy timber framed ceiling and a fireplace for warmth in the cooler months. This loggia angles away from the primary mass of the house to capture distant views of downtown Austin, as well as the cooling southeast breezes.

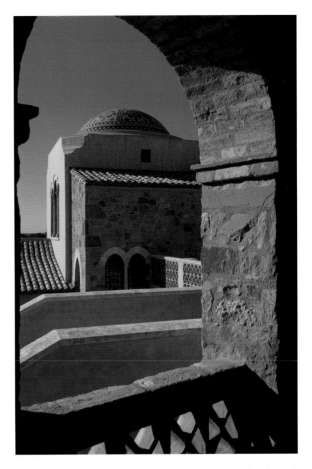

Decorative tile surmounts the double height Mudejar domed library, connecting the upper level to the master suite below. The shallow dome springs from squinch arches – a most unusual feature that further connects the design to exotic roots. Private rooms occur on the lower level surrounding the primary courtyard focused on the pool pavilion. Looking from the pavilion across the pool, the full height of the house, its terraces, external stairs, tiled dome, and varied building masses can be fully enjoyed.

Watercolor by Michael G. Imber

HORTON

AUST

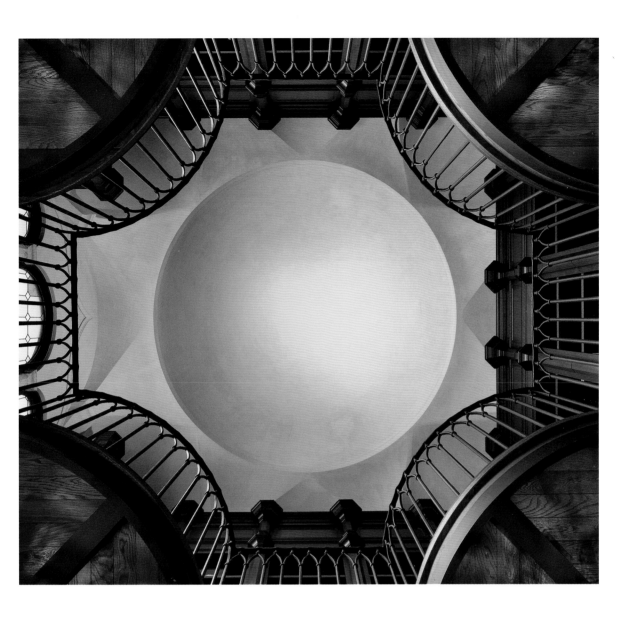

Bertolet Residence
Alys Beach, FL | 2015

Michael G. Imber Architects

Our first involvement with the new resort community of Alys Beach was in developing the architectural syntax of the town. Dictated by our client, the developer of Seaside, interests lay in the dense courtyard archetypes of Antigua, Guatemala and the pure white-washed aesthetics of Bermuda braced against the cobalt sea of the Florida Coast. The solid masonry construction of the town would make it the first "Hurricane Hardened Community." The residence was designed to the highest level of coastal fortification in order to insure sustainability of structure in an extreme hazard zone. The site not only offered an architecturally prominent location on Gulf Green, but was critical to the effect of the urban plan. The form-based code required building to the street on two sides and dictated a 4-story element on the corner lot, creating a "Gateway" from the sea to the town. The massing along with the all-white aesthetic, left us with a block from which we were to derive the articulation- a deductive process of design, similar to that of a sculptor carving from a block of white marble.

Photography credits Richard Powers

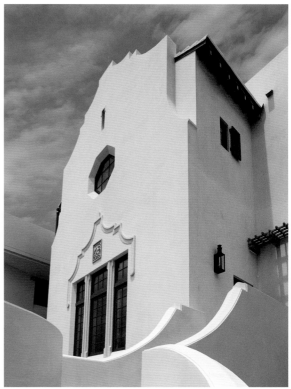

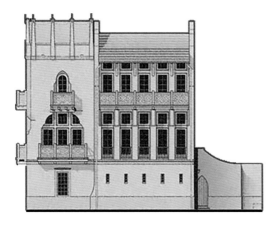

Masonry construction was expressed purely as white mass, while elements such as railing, windows and doors contrast as simple wood elements inserted into the mass. The 4,029 sf. residence was carved out to be as experiential as possible, drawing one up, around and through the light-filled block- always to a view and eventually the open tower overlooking the town and sea. Elements such as the buttresses of the piano noble, not only block the intense Florida sun, but radiate light back into the space illuminating the materials within.

Photography credits Jack Gardner, except page 403 upper right by Tommy Crow

Santigua House
Alys Beach, FL

Gary Justiss

The Santigua House was designed during the first Alys Beach housing charrette. Eight architects were charged with defining the look of Alys Beach, a hybrid of the aesthetic DNA of Bermuda and the courtyard house type of Antigua. The Bermuda "Style" was chosen due to it's simplicity and durability and the Antigua courtyard type due to it's privacy and comfort in a temperate climate.

The nearby New Urbanist villages of Seaside and Rosemary Beach were largely coded for freestanding homes with minimal side setbacks. The planner of all three villages, DPZ, observed the need for true privacy and elected to

code Alys Beach to eliminate side setbacks in favor of common walls and interior courtyards. It was a rather counter-intuitive move that has resulted in a truly private realm. Rather than a 5' dribble of land along each side of the home, the result is a romantic and useful outdoor room to be used for lounging, swimming, dining and private views. This space can also be used for exterior circulation opening up opportunities for greater plan efficiency and detached suites.

Chosen to be the first model home for Alys Beach, the Santgua House was tasked with further defining the "Alys Beach" interior style. Working with Sandy Frazer on décor, the team decided to hybridize further by incorporating elements of design from the Greek Cyclades Island. Interior finishes we chosen and detailed to blend as seamlessly as possible with the exterior finishes. Dominican shell stone floors flow from outside to in. Venetian plaster wall finishes echo the exterior stucco. Trimless door and widow openings retain the simplicity of the exterior detail. Wood accents provide interest.

Above Rendering of the east elevation | **Opposite page above** Rendering of the south elevation | **Opposite page center** Rendering of the east elevation from garden | **Opposite page below** Rendering of the north elevation

House in Ohio
2018

Peter Pennoyer Architects

Set on a high plateau, the site for this house for a collector of 20th century and contemporary art and furniture, sits above a ravine that wraps dramatically down to a valley of horse farms below. The massing draws on the American Arts & Crafts tradition with stucco walls, stone details, and a slate roof. The design uses strong symmetries on all four sides and each facade has a particular variation of the forms of the house, with each slightly different but still relating to the others. Parking is kept below one of the terraces enabling the house and landscape to have an uninterrupted relationship for 360 degrees.

While the house is symmetrical in plan and symmetry rules the rooms, from the massing to the smallest details, the design embraces the crystalline esthetic of the briefly lived style Czech Cubism. Within a language of angles and angular forms, the house is made into one coherent essay in form-making by the consistent application of principals of geometric composition. Hence what is in its parts a house of tremendous complexity is made to feel simple and calm by the mastery of the language of this style. Art Deco motifs are eschewed in favor of explorations in geometry that resolve themselves into completed forms.

The program includes a double-height library with a sculpted cubist ceiling with one wall dimensioned to accommodate the painting "The Horse" by Michaël Borremans. In other spaces, including the basement gallery, rooms and walls are shaped to welcome the display of an ever-evolving art collection.

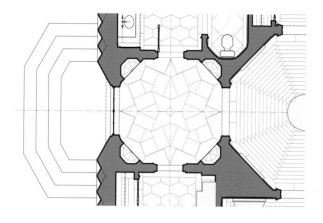

ENTRY FLOOR PLAN

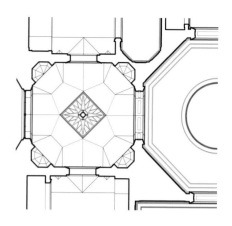

ENTRY REFLECTED CEILING PLAN

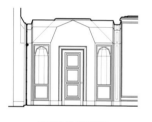

NORTH ELEVATION

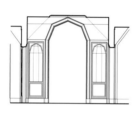

EAST ELEVATION

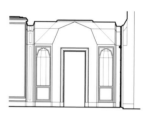

SOUTH ELEVATION

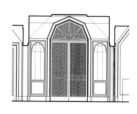

WEST ELEVATION

FIRST FLOOR PLAN

SECOND FLOOR PLAN

Above Digital rendering of the entrance gallery where the faceted walls will be covered in red and orange mosaics inspired by the Red Room at One Wall Street

EAST - WEST BUILDING CROSS SECTION

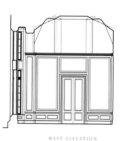

SOUTH ELEVATION

WEST ELEVATION

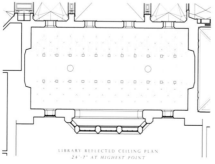

LIBRARY REFLECTED CEILING PLAN
24'-7" AT HIGHEST POINT

LIBRARY

Opposite page above and above Digital renderings of the double-height library with sculpted cubist ceiling | Below left and right Digital renderings of the living room

List of contributors

Victor Deupi is a Lecturer at the University of Miami School of Architecture where he teaches history and theory, design, and representation. He has taught previously at Fairfield University, the New York Institute of Technology, the University of Notre Dame, and has been a "Visiting Critic" at the College of Architecture at Georgia Tech. The principal focus of his research is on the art and architecture of the Early Modern Ibero-American world, and mid-20th-century Cuba. His book Architectural Temperance: Spain and Rome, 1700-1759 was published by Routledge in 2015, and he is currently co-writing a book on Cuban Modernism: Mid-Century Architecture 1940-1980, with Jean-Francois Lejeune (Birkhäuser Verlag, 2018). Dr. Deupi is also the President of the CINTAS Foundation dedicated to promoting Cuban art and culture.

Rodolphe el-Khoury is Dean of the University of Miami School of Architecture. Before coming to UMSoA in July, 2014, he was Canada Research Chair and Director of Urban Design at the University of Toronto, Head of Architecture at California College of the Arts, and Associate Professor at Harvard Graduate School of Design. His current research focuses on applications of digtal technology that aims for enhanced responsiveness and resilience in buildings and cities. Articles on his projects and research have appeared in the Wall Street Journal, The Globe and Mail, The Toronto Star and WIRED Magazine. He was also featured online (Gizmodo, DeZeen, Fast Company, Domus, Reuters) and on television and radio shows (CBC, Space Channel, NBC, TFO, BBC World). el-Khoury is a partner at Khoury Levit Fong, an award winning professional practice based in Toronto.

Jean-François Lejeune is Professor at the U-SoA, where he teaches architectural design, urban design, and history-theory. From June 2009 to December 2014 he was the Director of Graduate Studies. He taught at the Oregon School of Design (1985-87) and was Visiting Professor at the Universidade do Rio Grande du Sul (Brazil), the Università La Sapienza Roma, and the Universidad de Alcalá in Alcalá de Henares in Spain. In 2007 he was an Affiliated Fellow at the American Academy in Rome. Born in Belgium, he graduated from the University of Liège (Belgium) with the Diploma of Engineer-Architect. He is now a Ph.D. candidate and researcher at TU Delft, Netherlands, where he is completing his dissertation on Reciprocal Influences: Rural Utopia, Metropolis and Modernity in Franco's Spain. He is currently at work on two monographs: Loos and Schinkel: The Metropolis between the Individual and the Collective (Routledge) and The Modern Village: Rural Utopia and Modernity in Franco's Spain (DOM, Berlin).

Rocco Ceo is a professor of architecture at the University of Miami, School of Architecture where he teaches design, drawing, design/build and advanced drawing research courses. He was educated at the Rhode Island School of Design where he received his B.F.A. in painting in1983 and B.Arch. in 1984 and at Harvard University Graduate School of Design where he received his M.Arch.II degree in 1986. He has produced drawings of the elements of Florida's landscapes as well as the documentation of seminal sites in the history of South Florida such as Vizcaya, the Marjory Stonemen Douglas Home and the Orchid Jungle. His most recent work includes Drawing from Casts: The Plaster Casts Collection at the University of Miami School of Architecture, co-authored with Jose Peralta, and three essays in Miami Modern Metropolis, edited by Allan Shulman. His architecture practice focuses on the symbiotic relationship between architecture and landscape found in the American tropics. His work has received awards from the Florida Trust for Historic Preservation, Progressive Architecture, and I.D. Magazine. Recently his professional work is primarily in stone and includes monument and tomb projects for figures important to Florida's history.

Eric Firley is of French-German nationality and was born in Düsseldorf, Germany. He studied economics, architecture and city design in Fribourg, Lausanne, Weimar and London, and started his professional career in the real estate sector in Paris. Afterwards he worked for several years in design practices in Paris and London, before dedicating himself full-time to research and writing between 2007 and 2010. In 2011 he became assistant professor at the University of Miami School of Architecture. Firley is the initiator and co-author of Wiley's Urban Handbook Series that consists of three reference works in the field of housing, high-rise urbanism and masterplanning. He has lectured in institutions around the world, including the Skyscraper Museum and Cooper Union in NYC, the Architectural Association and Bartlett School in London, UC Berkeley, the National University of Singapore, the Parisian Planning Office (APUR), Queensland University of Technology and McGill University in Montreal. Firley's research has been funded by various public and private sector entities, including Grosvenor, Stanhope, the Arts Council and Design for London. His current research focuses on urban design practice, alternative models of housing production and the impact of immigration on urban form.

Nathaniel Robert Walker took up his position as Assistant Professor of Architectural History at the College of Charleston after earning his PhD at Brown University. He specializes in the history of public space such as squares and streets, particularly in the United States and Europe, but he has also worked with the urban forms of the Classic Maya and with Chinese Daoist architectural representations. Many of his studies are focused on the relationships between architecture, urban planning, and the utopian dreams of progress and futurity that proliferated in nineteenth- and twentieth-century literature, film, advertising, and other media. His research has been published in the Journal of the Society of Architectural Historians, Buildings & Landscapes, Traditional Dwellings and Settlements Review, Utopian Studies, and a number of edited volumes, including Revival: Memories, Identities, Utopias and Function and Fantasy: Iron Architecture in the Long Nineteenth Century.

Juan Manuel Yactayo is an designer, a researcher, and a maker. He has diverse work experience in renowned architecture offices including Diller Scofidio + Renfro, UNStudio, Preston Scott Cohen Inc, SOM, and Arquitectonica. He received his Master of Architecture degree from Harvard University and holds a Bachelors in Architecture from the University of Florida. At Harvard, he worked closely with Patrik Schumacher from Zaha Hadid Architects, with the former architecture chair, Preston Scott Cohen, as well as dean Rodolphe El-Khoury. Throughout his professional and academic experience, he has used various types of digital media and fabrication technologies as an integral part of the design process. One of his main interest involves the intersection of technology with architecture, and how these function in society as an interrelated cultural artifact. This interest is best highlighted during his professional experience in projects such as the Zaryadye Park in Moscow, the Highline in New York, and the Broad Museum in Los Angeles. Currently, he is a practicing architect at Perkins + Will and a lecturer at the University of Miami School of Architecture, where he has taught upper level and graduate studios, digital workshops, and visualization courses."

Andres Duany has admired Classicism ever since befriending the pioneering colleagues of the 1970s--Stern, Greenberg, Krier, Beebe, and Porphyrios. His town planning has subsequently been associated with some brilliant traditionalists such as Charles Barrett, Scott Merrill, Lew Oliver, Chris Ritter, Michael Imber, Bobby McAlpin, Khoury-Vogt and many others. But, he was not a serious student of Classicism until, with his partner Elizabeth Plater-Zyberk, he received the Driehaus Prize in 2011. He has, since that time, undertaken an in-depth study of the Treatises in the original editions found in the library of Katherine Pasternack. This has resulted in a revisionist treatise called Heterodoxia Architectonica, which the Canon of the Orders of the 21st century. His essay is an extract from that treatise, which should be published in 2017.

Javier Cenicacelaya is a Spanish architect, historian and educator with a consistent practice, publishing record and many academic distinctions. He edited *Composicion Arquitectonica*, and published and edited many books internationally, was the Dean of the University of Miami and has been teaching history and architectural composition for many years at the Basque University of San Sebastian. Javier Cenicacelaya is on the honorary board of INTBAU and is a founding member of CEU (Council of European Urbanism).

Richard John is an Associate Professor at the University of Miami School of Architecture. He was a scholar at Peterhouse, Cambridge, and studied architectural history and classical archaeology at Columbia University, before completing an MPhil and a PhD at the Warburg Institute. He taught mediaeval and Renaissance Italian history for three years at Oxford University as a fellow and lecturer at Merton College, and in 1995 was appointed Director of The Prince of Wales's Institute of Architecture in London. He has written extensively on contemporary architects, including books on Thomas Gordon Smith, John Simpson, and Robert Adam. In 2007-8 he served as the Harrison Design Associates Visiting Scholar at Georgia Tech. From 2008-2013 he was the editor of The Classicist, the peer-reviewed academic journal of The Institute of Classical Architecture & Art.

Book credits

Art Director: Oscar Riera Ojeda
Graphic Design: Lucía Bauzá

Additional Photographic Credits
Cover Photograph: Arabesque Wall, University of Toronto, 2015, Benjamin Dillenburger & Micheal Hansmeyer
End Paper: Labirinto di Franco Maria Ricci, Fontanellato Parma, 2015, Pier Carlo Bontempi
Page 2-3: Giuseppe Fallacara, HyparGate, collaborators: N. Rizzi with V. Varano and D. Malomo (structural analysis), M. Barberio and N. Martielli (Archviz), 2014-2016
Page 4: Andrew Saunders, S. Carlo alle Quattro Fontane, Rome, from the "Inside from the Outside" series, 2017
Page 6-7: Arabesque Wall, University of Toronto, 2015, Benjamin Dillenburger & Micheal Hansmeyer
Page 8: Giuseppe Fallacara and Micaela Colella, Ghibli, 2016
End paper: Giuseppe Fallacara with Marco Stigliano, Hyperwall, 2016
Back cover: Digital study model, Escuelita Buganvilia, Cúre & Penabad, 2015

OSCAR RIERA OJEDA
PUBLISHERS

Copyright © 2018 by Oscar Riera Ojeda Publishers Limited
ISBN 978-1-946226-22-8
Published by Oscar Riera Ojeda Publishers Limited
Printed in China

Oscar Riera Ojeda Publishers Limited
Unit 4-6, 7/F.,
Far East Consortium Building,
121 Des Voeux Road Central, Hong Kong
T: +852-3920-9312

Production Offices | China
Suit 19, Shenyun Road,
Nanshan District, Shenzhen 518055
T:+86-135-5479-2350

www.oropublishers.com | www.oscarrieraojeda.com
oscar@oscarrieraojeda.com